50% OFF
Online aPHR Prep Course!

By Mometrix

Dear Customer,

We consider it an honor and a privilege that you chose our aPHR Study Guide. As a way of showing our appreciation and to help us better serve you, we are offering **50% off our online aPHR Prep Course**. Many aPHR courses are needlessly expensive and don't deliver enough value. With our course, you get access to the best aPHR prep material, and **you only pay half price**.

We have structured our online course to perfectly complement your printed study guide. The aPHR Prep Course contains **in-depth lessons** that cover all the most important topics, over **1,050 practice questions** to ensure you feel prepared, and more than **400 digital flashcards**, so you can study while you're on the go.

Online aPHR Prep Course

Topics Included:

- Talent Acquisition
  - Identify Staffing Needs and Guide Talent Acquisition Efforts
- Learning and Development
  - Employee Orientation
- Compensation and Benefits
  - Benefits and Insurance Programs
- Employee Relations
  - Supporting Organizational Goals and Objectives
- Compliance and Risk Management
  - Laws and Regulations

Course Features:

- aPHR Study Guide
  - Get content that complements our best-selling study guide.
- Full-Length Practice Tests
  - With over 1,050 practice questions, you can test yourself again and again.
- Mobile Friendly
  - If you need to study on the go, the course is easily accessible from your mobile device.
- aPHR Flashcards
  - Our course includes a flashcard mode with over 400 content cards to help you study.

To receive this discount, visit us at mometrix.com/university/aphr or simply scan this QR code with your smartphone. At the checkout page, enter the discount code: **aphr50off**

If you have any questions or concerns, please contact us at support@mometrix.com.

FREE Study Skills Videos/DVD Offer

Dear Customer,

Thank you for your purchase from Mometrix! We consider it an honor and a privilege that you have purchased our product and we want to ensure your satisfaction.

As part of our ongoing effort to meet the needs of test takers, we have developed a set of Study Skills Videos that we would like to give you for <u>FREE</u>. These videos cover our *best practices* for getting ready for your exam, from how to use our study materials to how to best prepare for the day of the test.

All that we ask is that you email us with feedback that would describe your experience so far with our product. Good, bad, or indifferent, we want to know what you think!

To get your FREE Study Skills Videos, you can use the **QR code** below, or send us an **email** at <u>studyvideos@mometrix.com</u> with *FREE VIDEOS* in the subject line and the following information in the body of the email:

- The name of the product you purchased.
- Your product rating on a scale of 1-5, with 5 being the highest rating.
- Your feedback. It can be long, short, or anything in between. We just want to know your impressions and experience so far with our product. (Good feedback might include how our study material met your needs and ways we might be able to make it even better. You could highlight features that you found helpful or features that you think we should add.)

If you have any questions or concerns, please don't hesitate to contact me directly.

Thanks again!

Sincerely,

Jay Willis
Vice President
<u>jay.willis@mometrix.com</u>
1-800-673-8175

aPHR

Study Guide 2024-2025

4 Full-Length Practice Tests

Exam Prep Book Secrets for the Associate Professional in Human Resources Certification

2nd Edition

Written and edited by the Mometrix Test Prep

Printed in the United States of America

This paper meets the requirements of ANSI/NISO Z39.48-1992 (Permanence of Paper).

Mometrix offers volume discount pricing to institutions. For more information or a price quote, please contact our sales department at sales@mometrix.com or 888-248-1219.

Mometrix Media LLC is not affiliated with or endorsed by any official testing organization. All organizational and test names are trademarks of their respective owners.

Paperback
ISBN 13: 978-1-5167-2522-9
ISBN 10: 1-5167-2522-0

DEAR FUTURE EXAM SUCCESS STORY

First of all, **THANK YOU** for purchasing Mometrix study materials!

Second, congratulations! You are one of the few determined test-takers who are committed to doing whatever it takes to excel on your exam. **You have come to the right place.** We developed these study materials with one goal in mind: to deliver you the information you need in a format that's concise and easy to use.

In addition to optimizing your guide for the content of the test, we've outlined our recommended steps for breaking down the preparation process into small, attainable goals so you can make sure you stay on track.

We've also analyzed the entire test-taking process, identifying the most common pitfalls and showing how you can overcome them and be ready for any curveball the test throws you.

Standardized testing is one of the biggest obstacles on your road to success, which only increases the importance of doing well in the high-pressure, high-stakes environment of test day. Your results on this test could have a significant impact on your future, and this guide provides the information and practical advice to help you achieve your full potential on test day.

Your success is our success

We would love to hear from you! If you would like to share the story of your exam success or if you have any questions or comments in regard to our products, please contact us at **800-673-8175** or **support@mometrix.com**.

Thanks again for your business and we wish you continued success!

Sincerely,
The Mometrix Test Preparation Team

Need more help? Check out our flashcards at:
http://mometrixflashcards.com/aPHR

TABLE OF CONTENTS

Introduction

Thank you for purchasing this resource! You have made the choice to prepare yourself for a test that could have a huge impact on your future, and this guide is designed to help you be fully ready for test day. Obviously, it's important to have a solid understanding of the test material, but you also need to be prepared for the unique environment and stressors of the test, so that you can perform to the best of your abilities.

For this purpose, the first section that appears in this guide is the **Secret Keys**. We've devoted countless hours to meticulously researching what works and what doesn't, and we've boiled down our findings to the five most impactful steps you can take to improve your performance on the test. We start at the beginning with study planning and move through the preparation process, all the way to the testing strategies that will help you get the most out of what you know when you're finally sitting in front of the test.

We recommend that you start preparing for your test as far in advance as possible. However, if you've bought this guide as a last-minute study resource and only have a few days before your test, we recommend that you skip over the first two Secret Keys since they address a long-term study plan.

If you struggle with **test anxiety**, we strongly encourage you to check out our recommendations for how you can overcome it. Test anxiety is a formidable foe, but it can be beaten, and we want to make sure you have the tools you need to defeat it.

1

Secret Key #1 – Plan Big, Study Small

There's a lot riding on your performance. If you want to ace this test, you're going to need to keep your skills sharp and the material fresh in your mind. You need a plan that lets you review everything you need to know while still fitting in your schedule. We'll break this strategy down into three categories.

Information Organization

Start with the information you already have: the official test outline. From this, you can make a complete list of all the concepts you need to cover before the test. Organize these concepts into groups that can be studied together, and create a list of any related vocabulary you need to learn so you can brush up on any difficult terms. You'll want to keep this vocabulary list handy once you actually start studying since you may need to add to it along the way.

Time Management

Once you have your set of study concepts, decide how to spread them out over the time you have left before the test. Break your study plan into small, clear goals so you have a manageable task for each day and know exactly what you're doing. Then just focus on one small step at a time. When you manage your time this way, you don't need to spend hours at a time studying. Studying a small block of content for a short period each day helps you retain information better and avoid stressing over how much you have left to do. You can relax knowing that you have a plan to cover everything in time. In order for this strategy to be effective though, you have to start studying early and stick to your schedule. Avoid the exhaustion and futility that comes from last-minute cramming!

Study Environment

The environment you study in has a big impact on your learning. Studying in a coffee shop, while probably more enjoyable, is not likely to be as fruitful as studying in a quiet room. It's important to keep distractions to a minimum. You're only planning to study for a short block of time, so make the most of it. Don't pause to check your phone or get up to find a snack. It's also important to **avoid multitasking**. Research has consistently shown that multitasking will make your studying dramatically less effective. Your study area should also be comfortable and well-lit so you don't have the distraction of straining your eyes or sitting on an uncomfortable chair.

 The time of day you study is also important. You want to be rested and alert. Don't wait until just before bedtime. Study when you'll be most likely to comprehend and remember. Even better, if you know what time of day your test will be, set that time aside for study. That way your brain will be used to working on that subject at that specific time and you'll have a better chance of recalling information.

Finally, it can be helpful to team up with others who are studying for the same test. Your actual studying should be done in as isolated an environment as possible, but the work of organizing the information and setting up the study plan can be divided up. In between study sessions, you can discuss with your teammates the concepts that you're all studying and quiz each other on the details. Just be sure that your teammates are as serious about the test as you are. If you find that your study time is being replaced with social time, you might need to find a new team.

Secret Key #2 – Make Your Studying Count

You're devoting a lot of time and effort to preparing for this test, so you want to be absolutely certain it will pay off. This means doing more than just reading the content and hoping you can remember it on test day. It's important to make every minute of study count. There are two main areas you can focus on to make your studying count.

Retention

It doesn't matter how much time you study if you can't remember the material. You need to make sure you are retaining the concepts. To check your retention of the information you're learning, try recalling it at later times with minimal prompting. Try carrying around flashcards and glance at one or two from time to time or ask a friend who's also studying for the test to quiz you.

To enhance your retention, look for ways to put the information into practice so that you can apply it rather than simply recalling it. If you're using the information in practical ways, it will be much easier to remember. Similarly, it helps to solidify a concept in your mind if you're not only reading it to yourself but also explaining it to someone else. Ask a friend to let you teach them about a concept you're a little shaky on (or speak aloud to an imaginary audience if necessary). As you try to summarize, define, give examples, and answer your friend's questions, you'll understand the concepts better and they will stay with you longer. Finally, step back for a big picture view and ask yourself how each piece of information fits with the whole subject. When you link the different concepts together and see them working together as a whole, it's easier to remember the individual components.

Finally, practice showing your work on any multi-step problems, even if you're just studying. Writing out each step you take to solve a problem will help solidify the process in your mind, and you'll be more likely to remember it during the test.

Modality

Modality simply refers to the means or method by which you study. Choosing a study modality that fits your own individual learning style is crucial. No two people learn best in exactly the same way, so it's important to know your strengths and use them to your advantage.

For example, if you learn best by visualization, focus on visualizing a concept in your mind and draw an image or a diagram. Try color-coding your notes, illustrating them, or creating symbols that will trigger your mind to recall a learned concept. If you learn best by hearing or discussing information, find a study partner who learns the same way or read aloud to yourself. Think about how to put the information in your own words. Imagine that you are giving a lecture on the topic and record yourself so you can listen to it later.

For any learning style, flashcards can be helpful. Organize the information so you can take advantage of spare moments to review. Underline key words or phrases. Use different colors for different categories. Mnemonic devices (such as creating a short list in which every item starts with the same letter) can also help with retention. Find what works best for you and use it to store the information in your mind most effectively and easily.

3

Secret Key #3 – Practice the Right Way

Your success on test day depends not only on how many hours you put into preparing, but also on whether you prepared the right way. It's good to check along the way to see if your studying is paying off. One of the most effective ways to do this is by taking practice tests to evaluate your progress. Practice tests are useful because they show exactly where you need to improve. Every time you take a practice test, pay special attention to these three groups of questions:

- The questions you got wrong
- The questions you had to guess on, even if you guessed right
- The questions you found difficult or slow to work through

This will show you exactly what your weak areas are, and where you need to devote more study time. Ask yourself why each of these questions gave you trouble. Was it because you didn't understand the material? Was it because you didn't remember the vocabulary? Do you need more repetitions on this type of question to build speed and confidence? Dig into those questions and figure out how you can strengthen your weak areas as you go back to review the material.

 Additionally, many practice tests have a section explaining the answer choices. It can be tempting to read the explanation and think that you now have a good understanding of the concept. However, an explanation likely only covers part of the question's broader context. Even if the explanation makes perfect sense, **go back and investigate** every concept related to the question until you're positive you have a thorough understanding.

As you go along, keep in mind that the practice test is just that: practice. Memorizing these questions and answers will not be very helpful on the actual test because it is unlikely to have any of the same exact questions. If you only know the right answers to the sample questions, you won't be prepared for the real thing. **Study the concepts** until you understand them fully, and then you'll be able to answer any question that shows up on the test.

It's important to wait on the practice tests until you're ready. If you take a test on your first day of study, you may be overwhelmed by the amount of material covered and how much you need to learn. Work up to it gradually.

On test day, you'll need to be prepared for answering questions, managing your time, and using the test-taking strategies you've learned. It's a lot to balance, like a mental marathon that will have a big impact on your future. Like training for a marathon, you'll need to start slowly and work your way up. When test day arrives, you'll be ready.

Start with the strategies you've read in the first two Secret Keys—plan your course and study in the way that works best for you. If you have time, consider using multiple study resources to get different approaches to the same concepts. It can be helpful to see difficult concepts from more than one angle. Then find a good source for practice tests. Many times, the test website will suggest potential study resources or provide sample tests.

Practice Test Strategy

If you're able to find at least three practice tests, we recommend this strategy:

UNTIMED AND OPEN-BOOK PRACTICE

Take the first test with no time constraints and with your notes and study guide handy. Take your time and focus on applying the strategies you've learned.

TIMED AND OPEN-BOOK PRACTICE

Take the second practice test open-book as well, but set a timer and practice pacing yourself to finish in time.

TIMED AND CLOSED-BOOK PRACTICE

Take any other practice tests as if it were test day. Set a timer and put away your study materials. Sit at a table or desk in a quiet room, imagine yourself at the testing center, and answer questions as quickly and accurately as possible.

Keep repeating timed and closed-book tests on a regular basis until you run out of practice tests or it's time for the actual test. Your mind will be ready for the schedule and stress of test day, and you'll be able to focus on recalling the material you've learned.

Secret Key #4 – Pace Yourself

Once you're fully prepared for the material on the test, your biggest challenge on test day will be managing your time. Just knowing that the clock is ticking can make you panic even if you have plenty of time left. Work on pacing yourself so you can build confidence against the time constraints of the exam. Pacing is a difficult skill to master, especially in a high-pressure environment, so **practice is vital**.

Set time expectations for your pace based on how much time is available. For example, if a section has 60 questions and the time limit is 30 minutes, you know you have to average 30 seconds or less per question in order to answer them all. Although 30 seconds is the hard limit, set 25 seconds per question as your goal, so you reserve extra time to spend on harder questions. When you budget extra time for the harder questions, you no longer have any reason to stress when those questions take longer to answer.

Don't let this time expectation distract you from working through the test at a calm, steady pace, but keep it in mind so you don't spend too much time on any one question. Recognize that taking extra time on one question you don't understand may keep you from answering two that you do understand later in the test. If your time limit for a question is up and you're still not sure of the answer, mark it and move on, and come back to it later if the time and the test format allow. If the testing format doesn't allow you to return to earlier questions, just make an educated guess; then put it out of your mind and move on.

On the easier questions, be careful not to rush. It may seem wise to hurry through them so you have more time for the challenging ones, but it's not worth missing one if you know the concept and just didn't take the time to read the question fully. Work efficiently but make sure you understand the question and have looked at all of the answer choices, since more than one may seem right at first.

Even if you're paying attention to the time, you may find yourself a little behind at some point. You should speed up to get back on track, but do so wisely. Don't panic; just take a few seconds less on each question until you're caught up. Don't guess without thinking, but do look through the answer choices and eliminate any you know are wrong. If you can get down to two choices, it is often worthwhile to guess from those. Once you've chosen an answer, move on and don't dwell on any that you skipped or had to hurry through. If a question was taking too long, chances are it was one of the harder ones, so you weren't as likely to get it right anyway.

On the other hand, if you find yourself getting ahead of schedule, it may be beneficial to slow down a little. The more quickly you work, the more likely you are to make a careless mistake that will affect your score. You've budgeted time for each question, so don't be afraid to spend that time. Practice an efficient but careful pace to get the most out of the time you have.

6

Copyright © Mometrix Media. You have been licensed one copy of this document for personal use only. Any other reproduction or redistribution is strictly prohibited. All rights reserved.
This content is provided for test preparation purposes only and does not imply an endorsement by Mometrix of any particular political, scientific, or religious point of view.

Secret Key #5 – Have a Plan for Guessing

When you're taking the test, you may find yourself stuck on a question. Some of the answer choices seem better than others, but you don't see the one answer choice that is obviously correct. What do you do?

The scenario described above is very common, yet most test takers have not effectively prepared for it. Developing and practicing a plan for guessing may be one of the single most effective uses of your time as you get ready for the exam.

In developing your plan for guessing, there are three questions to address:

- When should you start the guessing process?
- How should you narrow down the choices?
- Which answer should you choose?

When to Start the Guessing Process

Unless your plan for guessing is to select C every time (which, despite its merits, is not what we recommend), you need to leave yourself enough time to apply your answer elimination strategies. Since you have a limited amount of time for each question, that means that if you're going to give yourself the best shot at guessing correctly, you have to decide quickly whether or not you will guess.

Of course, the best-case scenario is that you don't have to guess at all, so first, see if you can answer the question based on your knowledge of the subject and basic reasoning skills. Focus on the key words in the question and try to jog your memory of related topics. Give yourself a chance to bring the knowledge to mind, but once you realize that you don't have (or you can't access) the knowledge you need to answer the question, it's time to start the guessing process.

It's almost always better to start the guessing process too early than too late. It only takes a few seconds to remember something and answer the question from knowledge. Carefully eliminating wrong answer choices takes longer. Plus, going through the process of eliminating answer choices can actually help jog your memory.

Summary: Start the guessing process as soon as you decide that you can't answer the question based on your knowledge.

How to Narrow Down the Choices

The next chapter in this book (**Test-Taking Strategies**) includes a wide range of strategies for how to approach questions and how to look for answer choices to eliminate. You will definitely want to read those carefully, practice them, and figure out which ones work best for you. Here though, we're going to address a mindset rather than a particular strategy.

Your odds of guessing an answer correctly depend on how many options you are choosing from.

Number of options left	5	4	3	2	1
Odds of guessing correctly	20%	25%	33%	50%	100%

You can see from this chart just how valuable it is to be able to eliminate incorrect answers and make an educated guess, but there are two things that many test takers do that cause them to miss out on the benefits of guessing:

- Accidentally eliminating the correct answer
- Selecting an answer based on an impression

We'll look at the first one here, and the second one in the next section.

To avoid accidentally eliminating the correct answer, we recommend a thought exercise called **the $5 challenge**. In this challenge, you only eliminate an answer choice from contention if you are willing to bet $5 on it being wrong. Why $5? Five dollars is a small but not insignificant amount of money. It's an amount you could afford to lose but wouldn't want to throw away. And while losing

$5 once might not hurt too much, doing it twenty times will set you back $100. In the same way, each small decision you make—eliminating a choice here, guessing on a question there—won't by itself impact your score very much, but when you put them all together, they can make a big difference. By holding each answer choice elimination decision to a higher standard, you can reduce the risk of accidentally eliminating the correct answer.

The $5 challenge can also be applied in a positive sense: If you are willing to bet $5 that an answer choice *is* correct, go ahead and mark it as correct.

Summary: Only eliminate an answer choice if you are willing to bet $5 that it is wrong.

Which Answer to Choose

You're taking the test. You've run into a hard question and decided you'll have to guess. You've eliminated all the answer choices you're willing to bet $5 on. Now you have to pick an answer. Why do we even need to talk about this? Why can't you just pick whichever one you feel like when the time comes?

The answer to these questions is that if you don't come into the test with a plan, you'll rely on your impression to select an answer choice, and if you do that, you risk falling into a trap. The test writers know that everyone who takes their test will be guessing on some of the questions, so they intentionally write wrong answer choices to seem plausible. You still have to pick an answer though, and if the wrong answer choices are designed to look right, how can you ever be sure that you're not falling for their trap? The best solution we've found to this dilemma is to take the decision out of your hands entirely. Here is the process we recommend:

Once you've eliminated any choices that you are confident (willing to bet $5) are wrong, select the first remaining choice as your answer.

Whether you choose to select the first remaining choice, the second, or the last, the important thing is that you use some preselected standard. Using this approach guarantees that you will not be enticed into selecting an answer choice that looks right, because you are not basing your decision on how the answer choices look.

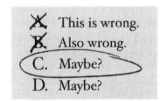

This is not meant to make you question your knowledge. Instead, it is to help you recognize the difference between your knowledge and your impressions. There's a huge difference between thinking an answer is right because of what you know, and thinking an answer is right because it looks or sounds like it should be right.

Summary: To ensure that your selection is appropriately random, make a predetermined selection from among all answer choices you have not eliminated.

Test-Taking Strategies

This section contains a list of test-taking strategies that you may find helpful as you work through the test. By taking what you know and applying logical thought, you can maximize your chances of answering any question correctly!

It is very important to realize that every question is different and every person is different: no single strategy will work on every question, and no single strategy will work for every person. That's why we've included all of them here, so you can try them out and determine which ones work best for different types of questions and which ones work best for you.

Question Strategies

☑ READ CAREFULLY

Read the question and the answer choices carefully. Don't miss the question because you misread the terms. You have plenty of time to read each question thoroughly and make sure you understand what is being asked. Yet a happy medium must be attained, so don't waste too much time. You must read carefully and efficiently.

☑ CONTEXTUAL CLUES

Look for contextual clues. If the question includes a word you are not familiar with, look at the immediate context for some indication of what the word might mean. Contextual clues can often give you all the information you need to decipher the meaning of an unfamiliar word. Even if you can't determine the meaning, you may be able to narrow down the possibilities enough to make a solid guess at the answer to the question.

☑ PREFIXES

If you're having trouble with a word in the question or answer choices, try dissecting it. Take advantage of every clue that the word might include. Prefixes can be a huge help. Usually, they allow you to determine a basic meaning. *Pre-* means before, *post-* means after, *pro-* is positive, *de-* is negative. From prefixes, you can get an idea of the general meaning of the word and try to put it into context.

☑ HEDGE WORDS

Watch out for critical hedge words, such as *likely, may, can, sometimes, often, almost, mostly, usually, generally, rarely,* and *sometimes*. Question writers insert these hedge phrases to cover every possibility. Often an answer choice will be wrong simply because it leaves no room for exception. Be on guard for answer choices that have definitive words such as *exactly* and *always*.

☑ SWITCHBACK WORDS

Stay alert for *switchbacks*. These are the words and phrases frequently used to alert you to shifts in thought. The most common switchback words are *but, although,* and *however*. Others include *nevertheless, on the other hand, even though, while, in spite of, despite,* and *regardless of*. Switchback words are important to catch because they can change the direction of the question or an answer choice.

10

⊘ FACE VALUE

When in doubt, use common sense. Accept the situation in the problem at face value. Don't read too much into it. These problems will not require you to make wild assumptions. If you have to go beyond creativity and warp time or space in order to have an answer choice fit the question, then you should move on and consider the other answer choices. These are normal problems rooted in reality. The applicable relationship or explanation may not be readily apparent, but it is there for you to figure out. Use your common sense to interpret anything that isn't clear.

Answer Choice Strategies

⊘ ANSWER SELECTION

The most thorough way to pick an answer choice is to identify and eliminate wrong answers until only one is left, then confirm it is the correct answer. Sometimes an answer choice may immediately seem right, but be careful. The test writers will usually put more than one reasonable answer choice on each question, so take a second to read all of them and make sure that the other choices are not equally obvious. As long as you have time left, it is better to read every answer choice than to pick the first one that looks right without checking the others.

⊘ ANSWER CHOICE FAMILIES

An answer choice family consists of two (in rare cases, three) answer choices that are very similar in construction and cannot all be true at the same time. If you see two answer choices that are direct opposites or parallels, one of them is usually the correct answer. For instance, if one answer choice says that quantity x increases and another either says that quantity x decreases (opposite) or says that quantity y increases (parallel), then those answer choices would fall into the same family. An answer choice that doesn't match the construction of the answer choice family is more likely to be incorrect. Most questions will not have answer choice families, but when they do appear, you should be prepared to recognize them.

⊘ ELIMINATE ANSWERS

Eliminate answer choices as soon as you realize they are wrong, but make sure you consider all possibilities. If you are eliminating answer choices and realize that the last one you are left with is also wrong, don't panic. Start over and consider each choice again. There may be something you missed the first time that you will realize on the second pass.

⊘ AVOID FACT TRAPS

Don't be distracted by an answer choice that is factually true but doesn't answer the question. You are looking for the choice that answers the question. Stay focused on what the question is asking for so you don't accidentally pick an answer that is true but incorrect. Always go back to the question and make sure the answer choice you've selected actually answers the question and is not merely a true statement.

⊘ EXTREME STATEMENTS

In general, you should avoid answers that put forth extreme actions as standard practice or proclaim controversial ideas as established fact. An answer choice that states the "process should be used in certain situations, if…" is much more likely to be correct than one that states the "process should be discontinued completely." The first is a calm rational statement and doesn't even make a definitive, uncompromising stance, using a hedge word *if* to provide wiggle room, whereas the second choice is far more extreme.

✅ BENCHMARK

As you read through the answer choices and you come across one that seems to answer the question well, mentally select that answer choice. This is not your final answer, but it's the one that will help you evaluate the other answer choices. The one that you selected is your benchmark or standard for judging each of the other answer choices. Every other answer choice must be compared to your benchmark. That choice is correct until proven otherwise by another answer choice beating it. If you find a better answer, then that one becomes your new benchmark. Once you've decided that no other choice answers the question as well as your benchmark, you have your final answer.

✅ PREDICT THE ANSWER

Before you even start looking at the answer choices, it is often best to try to predict the answer. When you come up with the answer on your own, it is easier to avoid distractions and traps because you will know exactly what to look for. The right answer choice is unlikely to be word-for-word what you came up with, but it should be a close match. Even if you are confident that you have the right answer, you should still take the time to read each option before moving on.

General Strategies

✅ TOUGH QUESTIONS

If you are stumped on a problem or it appears too hard or too difficult, don't waste time. Move on! Remember though, if you can quickly check for obviously incorrect answer choices, your chances of guessing correctly are greatly improved. Before you completely give up, at least try to knock out a couple of possible answers. Eliminate what you can and then guess at the remaining answer choices before moving on.

✅ CHECK YOUR WORK

Since you will probably not know every term listed and the answer to every question, it is important that you get credit for the ones that you do know. Don't miss any questions through careless mistakes. If at all possible, try to take a second to look back over your answer selection and make sure you've selected the correct answer choice and haven't made a costly careless mistake (such as marking an answer choice that you didn't mean to mark). This quick double check should more than pay for itself in caught mistakes for the time it costs.

✅ PACE YOURSELF

It's easy to be overwhelmed when you're looking at a page full of questions; your mind is confused and full of random thoughts, and the clock is ticking down faster than you would like. Calm down and maintain the pace that you have set for yourself. Especially as you get down to the last few minutes of the test, don't let the small numbers on the clock make you panic. As long as you are on track by monitoring your pace, you are guaranteed to have time for each question.

✅ DON'T RUSH

It is very easy to make errors when you are in a hurry. Maintaining a fast pace in answering questions is pointless if it makes you miss questions that you would have gotten right otherwise. Test writers like to include distracting information and wrong answers that seem right. Taking a little extra time to avoid careless mistakes can make all the difference in your test score. Find a pace that allows you to be confident in the answers that you select.

⊘ KEEP MOVING

Panicking will not help you pass the test, so do your best to stay calm and keep moving. Taking deep breaths and going through the answer elimination steps you practiced can help to break through a stress barrier and keep your pace.

Final Notes

The combination of a solid foundation of content knowledge and the confidence that comes from practicing your plan for applying that knowledge is the key to maximizing your performance on test day. As your foundation of content knowledge is built up and strengthened, you'll find that the strategies included in this chapter become more and more effective in helping you quickly sift through the distractions and traps of the test to isolate the correct answer.

Now that you're preparing to move forward into the test content chapters of this book, be sure to keep your goal in mind. As you read, think about how you will be able to apply this information on the test. If you've already seen sample questions for the test and you have an idea of the question format and style, try to come up with questions of your own that you can answer based on what you're reading. This will give you valuable practice applying your knowledge in the same ways you can expect to on test day.

Good luck and good studying!

Talent Acquisition

Identify Staffing Needs and Guide Talent Acquisition Efforts

FORECASTING

Forecasting in business is the ability to predict or estimate, based on past data, the likelihood of a particular event becoming a reality. In HR, forecasting is used to predict the staffing needs of an organization as well as the financial impact of all costs related to labor (benefits, training, etc.). HR forecasting can be short- or long-term and is dependent on many factors in an organization, such as revenue, growth, and attrition. Forecasting assists the HR plan for the number and types of employees the organization will need and related costs. Forecasting enables the organization to plan for growth based on educated, quantitative information and also permits the organization to make decisions in the event of downsizing. In addition to using forecasting for direct staffing needs, an organization also uses it for budgeting. For example, forecasting may reveal that an organization needs more employees in the months of November and December. HR must examine its budget and determine if it makes more sense to pay overtime to existing workers, hire temporary workers, or have a small staff of part-time employees.

JOB ANALYSIS METHODS AND JOB DESCRIPTIONS

Job analysis involves the systematic evaluation of activities and responsibilities in a specific job. The three main products of a job analysis are job competencies, job specifications, and job descriptions. **Job competencies** are a detailed list of all broad skills and traits needed for a particular position. **Job specifications** are detailed descriptions of all specific qualifications an individual must have to perform the role. A **job description** is a detailed, written breakdown of all tasks that a worker in that role must complete, as well as the job competencies and job specifications required to be qualified for that role. Some of the major uses of job analysis include the following:

- HR planning to develop job categories
- Recruiting to describe and advertise job openings
- Selection to identify skills and criteria for choosing candidates
- Orientation to describe activities and expectations to employees
- Evaluation to identify standards and performance objectives
- Compensation to evaluate job worth and develop pay structures
- Training to conduct needs assessments
- Discipline to correct subpar performance
- Safety to identify working procedures and ensure workers can safely perform duties
- Job redesign to analyze job characteristics that periodically need updating
- Legal protection to identify essential functions that must be performed and safeguard the organization against claims

CONDUCTING JOB ANALYSIS

A job analysis is an essential part of any workforce planning process because it identifies specific skills and knowledge required to meet staffing goals and objectives. It also identifies the specific skills and qualifications required to meet the strategic goals and objectives set for the organization as a whole. A job analysis not only allows the organization to identify which tasks need to be performed, but also breaks those tasks into specific skills, traits, and knowledge that would qualify an individual to perform each task appropriately.

15

INFORMATION COLLECTION FOR USE IN JOB ANALYSIS

Job analysis begins with the collection of pertinent information about a particular job. This information can best be described as job characteristics that differentiate a specific job from other jobs. These characteristics may include the following:

- Level of supervision, whether provided or received
- Computer, machine, or other technical equipment used
- External and/or internal interaction
- Specific work activities and behaviors needed
- Knowledge or education needed, sometimes referred to as "knowledge, skills, and abilities" (KSAs)
- Performance standards
- Working conditions

Grouping jobs by similar function is usually advantageous during the job analysis process. This is frequently accomplished by defining the overall job family and drilling down to job responsibilities, then specific details about work performed. For example:

- Job family: HR service center
  - Job: HR call center representative
    - ❖ Task: Provides support by phone and/or email for customer inquires

COMMON JOB ANALYSIS METHODS

Collecting information for job analysis can be tricky, and there is no specific formula because it depends on the job and information available. As a general rule, direct observation of the job and work performed, in conjunction with information obtained from previous job holders, is the most useful. However, this information might not always be available, there may be circumstances that make it impossible to collect the data, or the data might not be reliable. The following are some of the most common job analysis methods that can be deployed, depending on a variety of circumstances:

- **Observation**—After someone literally observes the job, a record of job tasks is documented and categorized into the knowledge, skills, and abilities (KSAs) needed to perform the job. This method is best suited for production jobs or short-cycle processes.
- **Interview**—The interviewer asks pre-scripted questions to qualified people in the job or job incumbents with the goal of obtaining KSAs for the job. This method works well with most professional jobs.
- **Behavioral event interview**—This method is called a "competency-based" form of job analysis because it is designed to get behavioral descriptions about how a person performs a given job instead of KSAs. The goal is for the interviewer to get the interviewee to talk about specific stories or occurrences that happened on the job and gather information about their behaviors, thoughts, and actions in real-life situations. This method is used in jobs that may be considered high-stress.
- **Structured questionnaire**—These questionnaires only permit very specific responses to obtain information about the frequency of particular tasks and the importance of the skills required to perform those tasks. This finite data set helps clarify jobs that are challenging to understand, and the data generated from this type of questionnaire lends itself to being easily used for computer modeling analysis.

- **Open-ended questionnaire**—This type of questionnaire is completed by job incumbents and/or manager(s) to determine the KSAs needed for a particular job. This information is then compiled into a summary document of job requirements. This method is useful for most jobs where the information is available.
- **Work diary**—This method involves an employee keeping a record, typically over a period of weeks or months, of the frequency and timing of tasks. The information recorded is analyzed and compiled for the purpose of identifying duties, responsibilities, and trends. This method involves sifting through a tremendous amount of data that may or may not be useful and may be difficult to interpret and keep current.

JOB DESCRIPTIONS

A **job description** documents the duties, tasks, and responsibilities for a particular position based on information obtained in a job analysis. More specifically, it provides detailed information about who does a particular job and how the work is to be performed and completed, and it links the work performed to the organization's mission and goals. There are many explanations for why an organization should have job descriptions for all of their positions, including calculating salary levels, performance reviews, initially setting job titles and grades of pay, measure for reasonable accommodations, and recruiting purposes. Job descriptions are also needed for operational purposes such as training and legal compliance obligations, and possibly in the situation when an employee's performance is in question and may need improvement.

ESSENTIAL FUNCTIONS IN A JOB DESCRIPTION

Essential functions are documented within a **job description**, detailing what a job applicant unquestionably must be able to do because it is essential to the job. Capturing all essential functions in a job description is important because they are used to determine the legal rights of an employee with a disability under the American with Disabilities Act (ADA). If an employee cannot perform the essential function, even with reasonable accommodations, then that employee is not qualified for the job and cannot be safeguarded from discrimination as outlined in the ADA. In other words, a person cannot bring a disability lawsuit against an employer if the person, due to a disability, could not perform the essential functions as documented in the job description. A job analysis is significant in determining essential functions because if an essential function is not truly an essential function, then the employer cannot exclude a person with a disability from the given position because they cannot perform the function. The following are some guidelines to consider when documenting essential functions for every task:

- Ensure the task is truly a requirement to perform the job.
- Evaluate and determine the frequency and time spent performing a task.
- Evaluate whether not performing the task would be detrimental to the employer.
- Determine whether the task could be redesigned, conducted in a different manner, or altered in a way that doesn't severely compromise the end product or service.
- Decide whether the task could be accomplished by a similar employee.

After drafting a job's essential functions, the employer should carefully consider whether the functions are truly essential or marginal. The words "essential function" are part of a typical job description and should clearly state that those functions are essential to perform the job.

COMPONENTS OF JOB DESCRIPTIONS

There is not a specific template for any job description because it is dependent on the particulars of the job and the organization. However, a job description is usually standardized in appearance in most organizations. The following are some of the most important elements that should be included in a job description:

- Job title.
- Classification (exempt, nonexempt, contractor).
- Date when the job description was written.
- Summary of the job and key objectives.
- Listing of all essential functions, knowledge, skills, and abilities (KSAs). KSAs may or may not be included in essential functions. If not, there should be a separate section for competencies.
- Level of supervision—Whether the role has direct reports (and, if so, how many) or is an individual contributor with no supervisory responsibilities.
- Work environment conditions such as temperature and noise, and physical demands such as bending, sitting, and lifting.
- Hours—The hours to be spent working on-site and remotely; and/or the percentage of travel required, if applicable.
- Education and/or experience required, including college, certifications, and/or number of years of experience in a specific industry or environment.
- Salary range for the position.
- Affirmative action plan and/or equal employment opportunity statement. These are especially necessary if the position is a federal contractor, but are usually common practice.

ALTERNATIVE STAFFING PRACTICES

OUTSOURCING

Outsourcing is the practice of hiring a separate third-party business to perform services that were previously performed internally by employees within the organization. The rationale for outsourcing is almost always cost-cutting, but it can also be an avenue to hire expertise that is not within the company or not financially feasible to hire. Additionally, the decision to outsource allows the company to focus on more critical aspects of the business, thereby improving their competitive advantage. There are three different types of outsourcing:

- **Onshore**—The outsourcing vendor is located in the same country as the parent business.
- **Nearshore**—The outsourcing vendor is in a neighboring country to the parent business.
- **Offshore**—The outsourcing vendor is in a country that is usually not near the parent company.

While outsourcing in general has many advantages as a staffing alternative, it also has some disadvantages, such as difficulty managing the third-party vendor and their employees, loss of control and confidentiality, and negative impact on morale (existing employees may worry about job security).

JOB SHARING

Job sharing is when two or more employees share the job responsibilities of one full-time job, meaning each employee works part-time, with specific work hours differing slightly between those sharing the single job. Most often there are two types of job-sharing scenarios: (1) the twins model, in which two or more employees work seamlessly together on the same project or service; and (2) the island model, in which two or more employees share a job but work independently from one another. Job sharing is an arrangement designed by the employer and employee, and therefore not specifically addressed under the Fair Labor Standards Act (FLSA). Usually, an organization will enter into this type of arrangement with employees to assist in the retention of good employees who need flexibility in their work schedule, and to attract job candidates for other positions by maintaining a workplace that supports a work-life balance. This may help an organization become an employer of choice or achieve a competitive advantage in the marketplace. Job sharing requires excellent communication between those in a twin model scenario because they must be able to function as one. Depending on an employer's benefits policy and federal, state, and local laws, job sharing could decrease benefits costs because neither employee is full-time.

Phased Retirement

Phased retirement is a process that enables an employee to incrementally decrease their full-time working hours and at the same time draw upon retirement benefits like Social Security or a pension. Depending on the situations and applicable laws, this could mean an employee near retirement could possibly work part-time, job share, or use some other method to reduce their working hours. There are several benefits to phased retirement: it helps slowly transition full-time older workers into retirement, provides adequate time to transfer knowledge to remaining employees, and gives HR time to recruit new talent or strategize new talent acquisition.

However, there are also several disadvantages. An employee switching from full-time to part-time can negatively impact the benefits they will receive in the future. For example, if an employee chooses phased retirement and their salary is significantly reduced for a few years before retirement, it could reduce the Social Security benefits the retiree could receive once fully retired. Additionally, many federal, state, and local laws, and also legal compliance issues that vary substantially from state to state, must be considered before an employer can devise a plan for phased retirement.

Gig Economy and Gig Workers

A **gig economy** is based on the premise that independent freelancers, contractors, or short-term workers can provide services that are less expensive and more efficient for businesses in a free market system. This is a drastic contrast to more traditional employees in a business, who work standard hours with benefits. The term "gig" is often used by musicians or others in the field of performing arts to describe a short-term job. Hence, a **gig worker** is an independent contractor that provides specific services to businesses, performing a specialized service efficiently and thereby reducing cost for the business. A variety of gig workers, such as food deliverers, drivers, shoppers, musicians, IT service technicians, digital sales personnel, and tutors are utilized to perform assignments.

The propagation of gig workers has been driven by several forces, including technology decoupling work from a physical location, businesses reacting more quickly to market forces without the financial burden of traditional employment, and workers desiring work flexibility and independence. However, gig workers must also contend with modest pay (forcing them to perhaps seek multiple jobs); having no benefits; and not being legally classified as employees, meaning income and Social Security taxes are not withheld. Gig workers must buy and maintain whatever is necessary to sustain their particular area of expertise, and must manage the stress of constantly looking for their next gig. Businesses utilizing gig workers should adhere to any federal, state, or local laws regarding compensation and work classification.

Talent Sourcing Tools and Techniques

RECRUITING BASICS

Recruiting refers to the strategies and procedures used to identify qualified people for potential employment by an organization, including analyzing job responsibilities, sourcing or finding applicants, and finding the most qualified candidates. In short, recruiting adds new qualified people to an organization in order to fill vacancies for open positions. There are generally three types of recruiting:

- **Internal**—Identifying qualified candidates within an organization for a lateral position, transfer, or promotion to fill a job vacancy. Some of the benefits of internal recruiting include the fact that the person is already familiar with the organization's culture and procedures, the motivation for employees to work harder for a promotion, and reduced organization cost and recruiting efforts.
- **External**—Identifying and locating qualified job applicants outside an organization. There are many benefits to external hiring, including a large applicant pool to select from, new talent with different perspectives or ideas, and the possibility of increasing diversity within an organization.
- **Alternative or other**—This type of recruiting is primarily derived from volunteers, internships, or temporary workers. Sometimes a temporary worker can be promoted to a full-time employee in an organization.

RECRUITMENT SOURCING OF ACTIVE, SEMI-ACTIVE, AND PASSIVE CANDIDATES

Recruiting candidates can be categorized into three primary groupings, depending on the level of candidate interest:

- **Active**—Candidates that are fully engaged in the search for a new job. This type of individual could be employed or unemployed, but is energetically seeking new employment.
- **Semi-active**—While not fully engaged in the process of obtaining new employment, a semi-active candidate is open to the idea of a new job if it presents itself and is a better fit than their current position.
- **Passive**—This type of candidate is not looking for new employment. However, a passive candidate might have a particular skill set or experience that is sought by an employer. If a recruiter identifies such an individual, the burden is on the recruiter to convince the individual of the benefits of a new employment opportunity.

CANDIDATE PIPELINES

The work of a recruiter doesn't start when a manager opens a job requisition. Just like sales professionals should always be selling, recruiters should always be recruiting. That's how a talent acquisition professional can build a strong **candidate pipeline**.

A candidate pipeline is made up of individuals who may be interested in joining a company when a suitable role becomes available. For example, a recruiter who works for a call center may continuously accept applications and conduct screening interviews for call center representatives, even when there are no jobs available.

Because this talent pipeline is in place, the recruiter will have a head start when the company needs to staff up for a new project or fill vacancies due to turnover. Rather than having to quickly post a job and filter through a lot of applications, the recruiter can reach out to people already in the talent pipeline. They're already prequalified, so they can immediately be scheduled to interview with the hiring manager.

SOCIAL NETWORKING

Social networking means connecting with individuals by using social media sites. Social media lets people more efficiently increase their network of contacts. LinkedIn, Facebook, and Twitter/X are very popular for recruiting because they are cost effective, efficient, and quick to reach a large audience of potential job candidates. This is especially important if candidates are needed in different or remote areas of the world. Recruiting over social media also allows the recruiter to examine the potential job candidate in further depth by viewing the candidate's social media presence and learning about the candidate's interests, goals, and personal preferences. Additionally, social media is an excellent way for recruiters to identify candidates not actively looking for new employment, based on search criteria and matches.

Social media is also a powerful communication tool for HR. An organization's presence on numerous platforms helps capture and communicate their culture, which is another means to attract top job applicants. HR should consider an organization's presence on social media and how it influences a prospective job candidate's impression of the organization's values and cultural fit.

EMPLOYER BRANDING

Employer branding is a very important aspect of talent acquisition. A company's **employer brand** is the perception that employees and potential applicants have regarding what it's like to work for the company. In other words, it's an organization's reputation as an employer.

Employer brand is based on a variety of factors, including:

- What current and former employees say about their experience
- The ease of finding openings and applying for employment
- How candidates are treated during the screening process
- Pay and benefits, in relation to what other similar employers offer
- The company's reputation and standing in the community and industry

A company looking to successfully recruit and retain top talent should strive to be perceived as an **employer of choice** in its industry or geographic area.

RECRUITMENT METHODS

EMPLOYEE REFERRALS

An **employee referral** is a recruiting method within an organization whereby existing employees identify and recommend friends or colleagues in their network for job openings. This is usually a documented program that encourages employees to recommend qualified people they know for job openings. These formal programs usually specify how long the referred person needs to remain employed and who is eligible to participate in a referral program. Additionally, the employee who made the referral is frequently monetarily rewarded or recognized for placing a qualified person within the organization. There are many benefits for an organization to have an employee referral program:

- Employees know their organization and who would or would not be a good cultural fit.
- It is a win-win for the applicant because sourcing through an employee referral program could enable a job applicant to stand out more, placing the applicant in a better position for an interview or other type of screening.

21

- It costs significantly less than most other forms of recruiting and saves time sourcing a candidate.
- It is one of the ways recruiters can reach qualified passive candidates, especially for hard-to-find jobs.

JOB FAIR RECRUITING

Job fairs are used as a recruitment tool to reach a large audience of job seekers in one location. Job fairs can be narrow in scope and size, such as on a college campus; or broader and larger, like in a large convention center. Larger job fairs can be expected to attract a larger variety of potential job candidates. Some job fairs can also be industry-specific. Generally, job fairs tend to be excellent recruiting opportunities for entry-level positions, college graduates, and veterans. They can also be a great opportunity to showcase an organization to different audiences and other professionals in attendance. Before deciding to attend and recruit at a job fair, an organization should make sure it is an appropriate job fair for their hiring needs. For example, it would not make sense for a company to attend a college job fair if the hiring needs were for professionals with five years of management experience. Similarly, the costs, time, and effort needed to prepare for a job fair should be taken into consideration. There needs to be a good return on this recruiting method for the organization. In other words, a significant amount of potential job applicants should be identified as a result of the job fair.

RECRUITMENT ADVERTISING

Recruitment advertising is a method used by organizations to attract candidates for the purpose of talent acquisition, both for the present and the future. Recruitment advertising can help an organization of any size reach potential candidates across almost all industries and levels of experience. This method of advertising can reach active job seekers as well as passive candidates whose interest in an organization may have been piqued by an advertisement. Traditional advertising for recruitment on TV, radio, and newspapers is still used, but is severely limited in its ability to reach a larger audience when compared with web-based recruitment advertising. Online web-based advertising on general job boards, niche job boards, social networks, and more, is usually the preferred method for organizations to recruit candidates for immediate job openings, and it motivates candidates to learn more about the company, thereby developing a potential talent pipeline. Remember, while recruitment advertising is a method most organizations deploy to attract talent, it is rarely the only tool an organization will utilize for talent acquisition.

ONLINE RECRUITMENT ADVERTISING

Online recruitment advertising is a method used by organizations to attract potential job candidates via various forms of web-based media outlets. It is available in many different formats and for different strategic hiring objectives. However, it is not a one-size-fits-all recruitment method because the choice depends on an organization's desired audience, timing, related costs, and marketing plan. The following is an overview of several formats for recruitment advertising:

- **Job boards**—These are websites used by employers to advertise their job openings and where job seekers search for open positions. There are many job boards for employment, such as Indeed and Glassdoor. Deciding upon which job board(s) to use to advertise the job openings depends on the position, size of potential audience, cost of advertising, and possibly integration with an organization's applicant tracking system. Additionally, job boards are considered to be user-friendly, making it easy for a candidate to apply.

22

- **Niche job sites**—These sites specialize in posting jobs specific to a certain industry or position, or for a specified job seeker. These could be sponsored by clubs; professional organizations; or really any grouping, such as groups of accountants, medical assistants, or those who have virtual employment.
- **Social networks**—Most social networks such as Facebook and LinkedIn provide job-posting capabilities. Also, technologies like artificial intelligence and machine learning used by these networks have the potential to display targeted job ads for a specific audience.

WORD OF MOUTH

Word of mouth is a tried-and-true method of recruitment. Basically, it means that current employees, or those familiar with the hiring needs of an organization, talk with their friends, their associates, and people in their network about job openings. This type of advertising is usually a reliable supplement to more traditional recruiting methods and can also be quite effective and cost-efficient. Word of mouth is particularly useful with employers of choice—usually large, well-known brands or multinational companies—because they are frequently approached by job seekers for employment in their company. These jobs are viewed as coveted positions. Also, very small companies or businesses that are the main employer in a given location can benefit by communicating to as many people as possible that there are open positions in their organization.

INTERNAL PROMOTIONS, TRANSFERS, AND FORMER EMPLOYEES

Internal recruiting, defined as identifying and selecting a candidate within an organization, is sometimes used when it is not optimal or possible to find the desired requirements from external candidates. There may be open positions that require certain knowledge or skills that can be easily obtained from an individual already within an organization. Organizations may prefer internal hires for many reasons, including a motivational incentive for employees to work harder, an increase in company morale, or knowledge of an employee's pre-existing skill set and past performance evaluations. Internal hiring is an efficient recruiting methodology for large and small organizations across a wide variety of industries.

One of the common methods for internal recruiting is **promotions,** whereby an individual is selected for a hierarchically higher position that usually includes an increase in compensation and responsibilities. A promotion is sometimes seen as a reward for previously displaying talent in a particular area.

Similar to a promotion, a **transfer** involves moving an employee from one job to another job that is comparable in some way. A transfer can be referred to as a lateral movement within an organization because it is a shift that is usually without substantial changes in responsibilities or compensation. A transfer may occur for a variety of reasons: it gives an employee a wider experience within the organization, it may improve any conflicts that arise in the current situation, or a slight change in position may relieve employee boredom.

A different method for internal recruiting is through **former employees**, those who left the organization on good terms for any number of different reasons. Former employees understand the company, and the organization is familiar with the former employees. This method could also reduce cost per hire.

RESUME MINING

Resume mining can be a beneficial tool to use when sourcing candidates. Resume mining involves using search terms to scour the resume database on a job board (such as Indeed or ZipRecruiter) or applicant tracking system (ATS) a way to identify candidates who have qualifications that match an open position.

- The searchable resumes in a job board belong to people who have applied for a job via the site, or who have uploaded their resume in hopes of being discovered and contacted by employers looking to hire people with their credentials.
- The resumes in a company's ATS belong to people who have applied to work with the company.

Resume mining makes it possible to use technology to quickly identify applicants in the pool who have required skills or experience. It reduces the time it would take for a human to review resumes in search of specific qualifications. However, it's important to avoid using search terms that are too specific or too limited. Without using a variety of descriptive search terms, it would be easy to overlook the resumes of some strong candidates.

Recruiting Procedures and Strategies

STAFFING AGENCIES

A **staffing agency** is an external vendor that offers employees for an organization to hire, usually for temporary assignments. Staffing agencies can be industry-focused, specialized, or broader-based across industries and specialties. The most important distinction is that the staffing agency hires the worker. Therefore, the agency is the employer of record, not the organization. Hence, it is the staffing agency and not the organization that payrolls the worker and offers benefits. Typically, staffing agencies work with candidates that might be considered more entry- to mid-level management. Frequently, staffing agencies are utilized during a company's busiest season, during special projects, or possibly to replace someone on leave. Additionally, most staffing agencies interview, test, and prepare workers for placement instead of the organization.

RECRUITMENT FIRMS

A **recruitment firm** is an external vendor that supplements an organization's internal recruiting effort, primarily helping an organization hire full-time, permanent employees. A recruiting firm usually has a network of potential candidates with whom they have fostered a relationship. Other times, a recruitment firm may be utilized for a specialized role that internal recruiters may not have experience hiring. This type of specialized recruiting is sometimes referred to as "niche recruiting." Similarly, a recruitment firm could also specialize in executive recruiting through their network of pre-identified, qualified candidates; these firms are sometimes called "headhunters." In many cases, regardless of the position, the recruiter will handle the initial screenings by sifting through resumes and conducting phone screenings and first interviews so that they can present qualified candidates to the organization. Some organizations—especially startups, smaller companies, and those with infrequent staffing needs—may not have an internal recruiter and may find it more efficient to use a recruitment firm.

Recruitment firms can be an advantageous external partner to an organization, but there are a few drawbacks. For example, they are not fully immersed in an organization's culture, and thus are not always able to represent the organization completely. They also may not be totally aware of the exact skills an organization is seeking in a candidate, and may be a bit slower to understand small nuances to changing candidate requirements. Overall, external recruitment firms that are measurably recruiting good hires are beneficial to partner with, as long as there is open communication.

INTERVIEWING TECHNIQUES
STRUCTURED VS. UNSTRUCTURED INTERVIEWS

A **structured interview** is when the interviewer has a predetermined set of questions that are asked of each interviewee, so that their responses can be fairly compared to one another. An **unstructured interview** is when the interviewer may have a few questions beforehand, but the majority of the interview is more spontaneous or unplanned. Basically, each interviewee may be asked different questions depending on the direction of the question and follow-up questions.

A structured interview is measurable in the sense that the questions are the same and the responses could be judged against one another with a quantitative component. An unstructured interview is more qualitative in that the information gathered is not equally comparable, but more insight into the applicant may be obtained. A structured interview is frequently used when there is a large candidate pool that needs to be compared to one another in order to judge who may be a better fit. An unstructured interview might be more useful when there are fewer candidates with qualifications that are almost identical, but the hiring manager needs to have a better feel for their thoughts and personality.

BEHAVIORAL INTERVIEWS

A **behavioral interview** is a common interview technique designed to assess how an interviewee reacted to past job-related situations. The rationale is that future behavior can be predicted based on past behavior, especially behavior in the workplace. In a behavioral interview, the interviewer will not ask about certain desired skills; instead, they will ask the interviewee to speak about an occasion or circumstance where they displayed knowledge of a certain skill. An interviewer is trying to assess how an applicant behaved in the past versus how they will behave in the future. Common questions in a behavioral interview include, "Tell me about a time when you had to handle a difficult situation with a coworker," or "Can you think of an occasion when you had a hard deadline for a project and were constantly interrupted with unrelated matters?" The interviewer will often ask follow-up questions looking for details—asking specifically what was said or felt, or why the applicant said something or reacted the way they did. Throughout the interview, the interviewer is assessing the applicant's behavioral responses to workplace scenarios.

The best way for an interviewee to prepare for this type of interview is to try and remember stories they feel may be related to the job description. A useful method to accomplish this for the interviewee is the STAR technique: recall a **specific** situation, identify the **tasks** needed to be accomplished, the **actions** taken, and the end **result**.

SITUATIONAL INTERVIEWS

During a **situational interview**, the interviewee is usually provided a scenario and then asked how he or she would respond. The objective of a situational interview is for the interviewer to gauge the interviewee's reaction to any number of conditions, including their behavior and how a problem is solved. These responses are then used to evaluate how the interviewee would perform when faced with similar situations on the job. It could be said that behavioral interviews look at the past and situational interviews look at the future. The questions in a situational interview are frequently hypothetical, such as, "If you knew your boss was making a wrong decision, how would you handle it?" or "What would you do in the following situation?" The questions are usually related to actual problems encountered in the workplace. The interviewer is interested in hearing if the interviewee has the basic knowledge to answer the question and solve the problem, exhibiting expertise in their profession or job. The interviewer may also listen to his or her ability to quickly assess the situation, and to the logic behind decisions.

PANEL INTERVIEWS

A **panel interview** is when a group of people interview a prospective job candidate at the same time. The panel of interviewers are typically brought together in order to get different perspectives about whether or not a candidate is a good fit for a position. Panel members tend to be those who will interact with the hired individual and have a good understanding of the organization and its culture. However, an effective panel interview should have a diverse assortment of personalities and viewpoints to accurately assess candidates. Everyone on the panel should also be allowed to freely offer their honest opinion. The goal of a panel interview is for the panelists to offer their insights and collectively reduce the risk in hiring a candidate that will not be a good fit. Usually, the hiring manager leads the panel, but individuals on the panel often have opening questions, and possibly follow-up questions that can be asked by anyone on the panel. Typically, this type of interview is longer than a traditional interview—about 90 minutes to 2 hours. Panel interviews can be conducted in many industries and for a variety of positions, but are most often used in senior executive positions, public-sector government organizations or agencies, academic institutions, and large not-for-profit organizations.

GROUP INTERVIEWS

A **group interview** consists of one or more interviewers who interview several interviewees at the same time. Group interview situations are more likely to occur in the hospitality industry, meaning hotel employment, rental agents, food service, and retail. Interviewing many people at once is time-efficient. Additionally, group interviews give the interviewer an opportunity to see and hear how well the interviewees interact with one another and behave under stress. Social interaction and stress under pressure are the two key characteristics of those who work in the industries noted above. Typically, interviewees are informed of the group interview format ahead of time so they are not surprised. The person(s) doing the interview will usually prepare questions ahead of time, and also be able to pivot and change direction if follow-up or clarification is needed. Group interviews usually begin with the interviewer(s) making the candidates comfortable and asking each one to say a little about himself or herself. Ground rules for courtesy and respect are outlined, and then the interviewer(s) begin asking questions.

STRESS INTERVIEWS

A **stress interview** creates a scenario whereby the interviewee is placed under some form of psychological (not physical) pressure and then evaluated on how well the individual operates under stress. Most other types of interviews try to put the interviewee at ease and garner information by engaging in a respectful communication exchange. Stress interviews are usually only used by certain industries and for specific positions that will encounter a tremendous amount of stress on the job. For example, stress interviews are sometimes used by law enforcement, sales agencies, and airlines. These are positions that may encounter conflict and rudeness daily.

Stress interviews can be conducted any number of ways, but generally the interviewer could use words to deliberately intimidate the interviewee, make the interviewee wait a long period of time, interrupt frequently, ask the same questions multiple times, act aggressively, walk around while asking questions, raise their voice, speak very softly, etc. The goal for the interviewer is to evaluate how calm the interviewee remains or if the individual buckles under the pressure. It is extremely important to note that stress interviews are controversial and reserved only for special positions. Legal counsel should be consulted before designing and implementing a stress interview.

SKILLS ASSESSMENTS

Skills assessments can be an important part of the applicant screening process. For example, a job may require creating or troubleshooting spreadsheets using advanced functions like pivot tables or "if" statements. However, the fact that an applicant's resume lists Excel as a skill doesn't necessarily mean that they have the level of ability required for the position. Instead of just asking if they know how to work with pivot tables or "if" statements, a hiring manager could have them complete a skills assessment that requires them to apply their expertise. This is a more objective way of verifying their skill level.

The job description is a great tool for identifying what kinds of skills assessments could be beneficial in the hiring process. Hiring managers can use the list of essential job functions to make a list of skills that candidates must have, then decide the best way to determine if the candidate's abilities meet the requirements. This may involve working with management to create skills assessments specific to certain jobs or purchasing pre-employment assessments from a testing vendor.

Pre-employment skill assessment platforms like eSkill and TestGorilla offer many skill-specific tests, including skills with computer applications, quantitative skills, verbal skills, and customer service. Their tests can be used as is or customized based on job requirements. Skills assessments used in the hiring process must be free from bias and administered in a nondiscriminatory way.

BIASES

Every aspect of the recruiting and hiring process should be free from bias. This means that everyone involved in the process should take care to avoid prejudging applicants based on perceptions they may have regarding traits, characteristics, or individual differences.

Bias can be conscious or unconscious, so it's important to be aware of some of the ways that bias may find its way into the hiring process.

- **Stereotyping**—Making assumptions based on generalizations, such as assuming that someone who has been a manager won't want a non-supervisory job, or assuming that a female applicant won't want a job that requires extensive travel.
- **Halo effect**—Allowing something perceived as positive to overshadow other information, such as assuming that an applicant who attended a prestigious college must be an ideal candidate even if they don't have much (or any) experience.
- **Horns effect**—Allowing something perceived as negative to overshadow positive characteristics, such as dismissing a candidate from being considered because they were flustered at the beginning of an interview even though they have all required skills and are otherwise a good fit.
- **Confirmation bias**—Making up your mind about a candidate and then only paying attention to information that reinforces what you already believe (for example, deciding that a candidate has poor attention to detail and then looking for slip-ups that reinforce that belief while disregarding evidence to the contrary).
- **Contrast bias**—Comparing a candidate to a particular individual—such as the person who is leaving the job or a preferred candidate who turned down the position—instead of to the essential job functions and other job requirements.
- **Gender bias**—Assuming that a job is more suited to a person of a particular gender, such as presuming that men lack the listening skills to work in a call center, or that women aren't strong enough for production work.
- **Similar-to-me bias**—Presuming that candidates who share characteristics in common with the interviewer are best-suited for the job, such as showing preference to a candidate who is from the interviewer's hometown or attended the same college.

The Life Cycle of Hiring and Onboarding

REFERENCE CHECKS

Before offering a job to a candidate, it's a good idea to check the individual's references. This generally involves contacting an individual's previous employers to verify the information on their application and to ask about their work habits and behavior. It may also involve contacting personal or professional references provided by the candidate.

- Companies often have policies that restrict subjective references, so previous employers usually only provide fact-based information such as verifying dates of employment, job title, compensation, and whether the individual is eligible for rehire.
- Personal or other professional references may provide more subjective information, such as information about a candidate's character, work ethic, or communication style.

Reference checks may be conducted by phone, mail, or email. An employer may contact references directly or use the services of a background screening company.

OFFER LETTERS AND COUNTEROFFERS

It is best practice for job offers to be made in writing, in the form of an offer letter. An offer letter should include:

- Job title
- Salary or hourly rate of pay
- Job classification (exempt or nonexempt)
- Expected start date
- Work location
- Contingencies (such as background check, drug test, fit-for-duty physical)
- Usual work schedule or shift
- Benefits overview
- Relocation package (if applicable)
- Contact information for questions
- Deadline to accept or decline
- How to accept or decline

If a candidate declines an initial offer, the company may wish to make a counteroffer based on the reasons the candidate gave for declining. For example, a counteroffer may include:

- Higher rate of pay
- Sign-on bonus
- Retention bonus
- More paid time off (PTO)
- Revised or flexible schedule
- Other inducements

Counteroffers should be made in writing and include the same type of information as an initial job offer.

EMPLOYMENT CONTRACTS

When a company offers a job to a candidate and the candidate accepts, the job offer itself becomes a contract. This is true whether the offer is made verbally or in writing. It's best for offers to be made and accepted in writing so there is no question regarding the terms and conditions.

In some cases, an employer may also have a new hire sign an employment contract, also referred to as an employment agreement. This type of document has more detail than the offer letter and may include specific performance requirements such as sales quotas, revenue or profitability targets, or other performance metrics, along with the consequences if specified benchmarks are not achieved. An employment contract may also include a noncompete agreement, confidentiality requirements, or ownership of intellectual property.

Formal employment contracts are not required in the United States, but they are fairly common for executive-level positions and sales jobs, as well as other positions with specific production or performance requirements. Some employers use employment contracts for most or all positions. A company should consult with legal counsel to draw up employment contracts.

POST-OFFER ACTIVITIES

CAUTIONARY MEASURES WHEN DESIGNING DRUG TESTING PROGRAMS

Many employers utilize drug testing to screen applicants and, in some cases, current employees. Generally speaking, employers can legally require applicants to pass a **drug test** as a condition of employment or adopt programs that test active employees as long as the programs are not discriminatory. Due to the controversial nature of drug testing, employers must be meticulously cautious when designing these programs to ensure practices will be upheld if brought to court. In addition, employers should make sure their drug testing program and related policies are in compliance with all state and local laws. For example, employers in some states can document that they have a zero-tolerance policy for drug usage, such as repercussions including employee termination, while employers in other states need to promote assistance programs for drug use. It is important to remember that the drug test results received from the testing company are confidential and should be filed and secured separately from the hired employee's personnel file. *Wilkinson v. Times Mirror Corporation* established the following elements for testing programs:

- Samples are collected at a medical facility by persons unrelated to the employer.
- Applicants are unobserved by others when they furnish samples.
- Results are kept confidential.
- The medical lab only notifies employers of whether the applicant passed or failed.
- Applicants are notified by the medical lab of the portion they failed—some instances will provide applicants an opportunity to present medical documentation prior to the employer receiving results.
- There is a defined method for applicants to question or challenge test results.
- Applicants must be eligible to reapply after a reasonable time.

CONSIDERATIONS REGARDING PRE-EMPLOYMENT BACKGROUND CHECKS

Many employers will conduct pre-employment background checks on candidates to ensure that employees have sound judgment and are unlikely to engage in improper conduct and/or do not have a criminal record. HR departments often order credit checks or criminal record searches through online service providers and then review results. The Fair Credit Reporting Act, like many legal regulations, requires not only that employers notify applicants that they administer background checks, but also that applicants must sign a written release consenting that the employer may receive their personal information. Furthermore, when implementing a pre-

29

employment background check, employers must consider if doing so may be discriminatory, and therefore must validate the business necessity.

Many states have joined the Ban the Box movement, which prohibits employers from asking about an applicant's criminal history at the time of application. If an offense is found, employers are urged to consider the severity of the offense, the amount of time elapsed since the offense, and whether the offense is related to the nature of the job. Applicants must also have the opportunity to contest or explain adverse results before officially being turned down for employment. The prospective employer must furnish a copy of the report to the applicant. The Federal Trade Commission advises employers to give the applicant five days to respond before sending them an official letter of rejection.

Post-Offer Medical Exams

A post-offer medical exam is usually requested by an employer to evaluate if the selected person can safely perform the essential functions of the job in such a manner as to not risk injury to themselves or anyone else. The medical exam findings can also help determine if the individual will need accommodations in order to safely perform the job. The decision to institute a medical exam is based on detailed job requirements that clearly document which positions specifically require a medical exam. An employer usually has a written policy about which applicants need exams, procedures, and advance notification to the candidate of this requirement.

Employer planning is necessary to set up a cost-effective medical examination program with a third-party doctor performing the medical exam. The doctor must be completely familiar with the job requirements and necessary good health needed to perform those duties. The doctor's summary report back to the employer is only supposed to contain information that will impact the individual's ability to perform the job, and nothing else, in order to maintain the examinee's privacy. It is important to remember that the file received from the doctor is confidential and should be filed and secured separately from the hired employee's personnel file.

Distribution and Collection of Company-Mandated Documents

A company should distribute company-mandated documents to new hires on their first day of employment. Employees should be required to sign off indicating that they have received, read, and understood each document.

Employee Handbook and Policy Acknowledgements

A company should distribute an employee handbook or policy manual to new employees at the beginning of employee orientation so that new hires can become familiar with company policies and procedures right away.

The handbook can be printed, emailed, or posted to the company intranet in a manner that all employees can access. Employees should be provided with time to review each document and ask questions before signing an acknowledgement that will be stored in their personnel file.

Nondisclosure or Other Agreements

An employee handbook isn't a contract and doesn't extend to former employees. Any policy that needs to extend beyond an individual's employment and/or be legally binding should be presented to employees as a formal agreement that they're required to sign, separate from the employee handbook or policy manual.

A nondisclosure agreement (NDA) is an example of a document that companies often require employees to sign separate from the handbook or policy manual. The purpose of an NDA is to protect the confidentiality of important company information, such as client lists, marketing strategies, and product formulations. This type of document is particularly important for employees with access to proprietary information.

Other documents that employers often require employees to sign as standalone agreements may include, but are not limited to, a noncompete agreement, privacy policy, anti-harassment policy, or code of ethics. Signed agreements should be kept in each employee's personnel file.

BENEFITS PAPERWORK

New employees should be provided with benefits paperwork on the first day of orientation, including details about each plan. Depending on what the company offers, this may include information about the company's health insurance, retirement plan, life insurance, dental plan, vision coverage, cafeteria plan for health and dependent care expenses, and available supplemental group benefits.

Benefits paperwork may be distributed in print or digital form. It should include:

- Plan details
- Cost
- Eligibility
- Enrollment forms

New employees should be given a few days to review the information so they can make an informed decision on which benefits they want. They should also be informed of the company's open enrollment date, so they'll know how long they'll have to wait to opt in on any benefits that they decline at this time. The company should collect their benefits enrollment paperwork, along with documentation that specifies any benefits they are declining.

ORIENTATION AND ONBOARDING

ONBOARDING VS. ORIENTATION

The terms "onboarding" and "orientation" are sometimes used interchangeably, but there is a difference. **Onboarding** is the overall strategic process of acclimating a new hire into the business and its culture. This process can last anywhere from a month to a couple years. Meanwhile, **orientation** is a part of the onboarding process designed to introduce new employees to their specific job, including colleagues and others they may interact with on the job. Orientations are one-time events, but depending on the organization and the job, they can last anywhere from an hour to a few days. During an orientation, the new hire will be instructed about their specific job and the tools, methodologies, interactions, and instructions needed to perform the job. An orientation is critical in the onboarding process because it helps the new hire understand how their position contributes to overall organizational goals.

BASICS OF THE ONBOARDING PROCESS

Onboarding, sometimes called organizational socialization, is a strategically choreographed process that enables a new employee to holistically understand an organization, its culture, and how the individual fits into the business. Onboarding varies depending on the organization and the position. There is not one particular correct format because it is dependent on many factors. However, the overall goal is to assist the employee with being a productive contributor. The onboarding process can be a few months to a couple years, although one year is more common. Typically, the following is covered during the onboarding process, though not necessarily in this order, and delivery

31

methods could include virtual, in-person classroom, self-directed learning, one-on-one instruction, and meet-and-greets:

- An overview of **policies and benefits**—This may include paperwork that needs to be completed, such as benefit selection, payroll, proof of citizenship, emergency contact information, and an instructional overview of company policies and procedures, including the employee handbook and the organization's diversity policy. This portion of onboarding could also be called "orientation."
- Understanding how the **role fits into the organization**—This includes information about an employee's job expectations and related interactions with other areas of the organization.
- Customized **role-specific training**—Training can be conducted with the employee's supervisor or any other person knowledgeable about the position. Many organizations have a continuous learning environment to maintain a competitive advantage, making it an ongoing process.
- Organizational **culture training**—This can be a formal or more casual process whereby an employee learns company values and engages in activities related to vision and mission, such as team-building events, dinners, and classroom trainings.
- **Facilitated social connections**—This could be a simple meet-and-greet facilitated by the employee's manager, a formal "buddy system" whereby another more tenured employee is assigned to help facilitate social connections, or many other scenarios.

ASPECTS OF AN EMPLOYEE ORIENTATION

Orientation is the first step in the onboarding process and the beginning of the employer-employee relationship. Orientation tends to be more administrative in nature, as it is usually a series of tasks that need to be completed before an employee can proceed into their specific role. For example, it may include a tour of the work facilities, I-9 verification, benefit selection, payroll forms, and processing information. Orientation also covers company policies and where to go for various types of information. An overview of the organization and introductions may also take place. Orientation is a two-way process, in that an employee's questions and concerns are discussed and answered. The goal of orientation is not only to get the new employee paperwork processed logistics handled, and introductions made, but to help the new employee feel welcome and quickly transition into being a productive employee.

Use of Technology

TECHNOLOGY TOOLS TO COMPILE DATA

HR utilizes large volumes of data about the organization and the people it employs for the purpose of recruitment, performance management and evaluations, payroll, equal employment opportunity (EEO), etc. Tools to compile data make organizational functions more efficient and productive. Some tools are unique to HR management, such as a human resource information system (HRIS), and others are more commonplace, like Microsoft Office with Excel, Word, and PowerPoint. HR specifically compiles data to include types of employees, employee specifics, compensation, training, open jobs, etc. This type of data is vital to HR for many reasons, such as budgeting, succession planning, salary surveys and reviews, ensuring EEO compliance, and applicant presentations. It is important to remember that different tools or software are used for different purposes. Therefore, the key is to understand available HR tools and software and use those that best suit the functions needed for a specific project. Frequently, it is necessary to filter and

download data from one source or tool and bring it into another to optimize data manipulation or present information. An example of this would be using data from an HRIS to complete an Excel file.

APPLICANT DATABASES

APPLICANT TRACKING SYSTEMS

An **applicant tracking system** (ATS) is a computer database used by employers to automate and manage all or some aspects of the job application and hiring process. Other names used for ATS programs include talent acquisition software, recruitment software, hiring database, or hiring platform. The primary purpose of an ATS is to efficiently manage information in the job application process. An ATS captures everything an applicant submits for a job posting, including name, resume, education, experience, contact information, and cover letter. In response, the ATS can be programmed by a recruiter to filter resumes for keywords or experiences, give online tests, schedule interviews, mail rejection letters (if applicable), and much more. An ATS allows multiple people to view job candidate information, including interview notes and evaluations. After a candidate is selected, the information obtained in the ATS can often be seamlessly transitioned to other software, such as a payroll system. An ATS creates efficiencies that allow an employer to optimize the hiring process.

> **Review Video: Applicant Tracking System**
> Visit mometrix.com/academy and enter code: 532324

APPLICANT FLOW DATA REPORTING

Applicant flow tracking is required by the Equal Employment Opportunity Commission (EEOC) and necessary for any employer to complete if they have a federal contract. The information should detail the gender and race of every applicant that applies for an open position. The objective is to analyze source data and identify the selection rate among groupings by race and gender for a position to ensure that a fair grouping of people is being sourced for the open job. Organizations with a federal contract are supposed to make a reasonable effort to collect and maintain this information. Typically, this information is voluntarily self-reported by the job candidate or casually observed by an HR representative in an interview situation.

An ATS assists in the recordkeeping of this information as well as the ability to generate reports needed to analyze the data. It is extremely important to note this information cannot be used in hiring decisions. During the application process, the job applicant is also made aware, in writing, that the hiring decision will not be based on self-reported EEOC-related personal information. In fact, HR is to secure that information, either electronically or in paper format, and keep it separate from the employee's application. An ATS makes collecting and reporting this type of data more accurate and efficient.

ADVANTAGES

There are many specific benefits an employer can derive from utilizing an ATS:

- **Job posting**—Employers can post job requisitions across multiple third-party job boards as well as in a company job posting.
- **Easier application process for candidates**—Job candidates can more expediently apply for jobs via an ATS, allowing an employer to be seen as more favorable.
- **More efficient resume filtering**—Due to specialized keyword searches across resumes, recruiters can eliminate resumes more quickly.
- **Everything is in one spot**—Manage everything about a job applicant in one place, with no need for spreadsheets or computer folders.

- **Increases overall administrative efficiency**—More efficiently complete administrative tasks associated with recruiting and hiring job candidates, including resume filtering, phone screenings, evaluations, interview scheduling, and tests.
- **Captures and tracks job applicant data for reporting**—Efficiently and accurately capture job applicant information that may need to be tracked and reported to comply with Equal Employment Opportunity (EEO) and Office of Federal Contract Compliance Programs (OFCCP) regulations. Allows an employer to analyze the database of applicants for specific EEO categories and job classifications. Additionally, an employer can use the database for recruiting analytics.
- **Assists in the onboarding process**—An ATS streamlines the onboarding of a selected job candidate, as the information captured in the ATS can usually be transferred to other systems an employer might utilize, such as payroll or information technology. This may also eliminate a significant amount of paperwork.

SAFEGUARDS

Overall, an ATS makes the recruitment process more efficient, but there are some limitations an employer should consider and address. Frequently an ATS is used to filter out resumes if the candidate does not have a certain skill or experience. This filter is based on a pattern of keywords. If applicants have the desired skill or experience, and they use synonyms or words not close enough to the keyword filters, then they might be eliminated from consideration. Furthermore, an ATS sometimes has character-restricted fields, meaning that a candidate might be qualified, but the character restriction did not allow them to provide enough information. Occasionally, an ATS might scan a resume incorrectly; this could occur if there is something in the resume that the system is not programmed to recognize. Usually, an ATS can be modified, and recruiters usually make an effort to ensure that qualified candidates do not slip through the cracks.

ADVANTAGES AND DISADVANTAGES OF TECHNOLOGY SYSTEMS

A **human resource information system** (HRIS) enables employees to have greater and more expedient access to their personal HR-related data. Some advanced HRIS programs allow employees to immediately request time off, change their mailing address, adjust 401(k) contributions, etc. In this respect, HR technology has automated very labor-intensive paperwork, thereby creating more organizational efficiencies and possibly enabling HR professionals to expand into more strategic roles.

An **applicant tracking system** (ATS) automates the application process from the beginning through the hiring of an employee. This has many benefits for realizing efficiencies, but could also overwhelm recruiters with unqualified candidates they must weed through.

An HR **knowledge management system** (KMS) is a central repository for HR information that can be quickly accessed by employees, usually considered a 24/7 self-service portal. Frequently, it may provide access to onboarding information, benefit selection and policy information, requests for time off and historical attendance information, general HR policy information, etc. The main benefits of a KMS include the increased ability for an employee to quickly access information, that the information can be updated easily and thus reduce misinformation, and that it reduces the administrative workload for HR. However, the system needs to be maintained, and permissions must be managed so that employees have access only to information that is pertinent to them.

Integration of technology tools—HR now has many technological tools to manage employees. Access to too much data, and sometimes irrelevant data, can be a consideration in effective data usage. Also, the integration of various technology platforms can be challenging.

OTHER TOOLS TO COMPILE DATA
SPREADSHEETS

A **spreadsheet** is a computer application used to store, analyze, and organize data in a tabular format of horizontal rows and vertical columns. Data, both numeric and text, is entered into cells that can be used to calculate and display information. For example, a spreadsheet could contain information such as employee names, job titles, locations, and compensation, which could be used to calculate compensation information by title or location. This information can also be referred to as a database. One of the most popular spreadsheet programs is Microsoft Excel. The following are some key functions performed in Excel for HR analysis:

- Query—A request for data that filters and formats information from a spreadsheet or database.
- Sorting—The process of arranging data in a specific order, such as alphabetical or lowest to highest.
- Filter—A condition that qualifies data to be revealed or hidden, such as showing data from a certain location or department.
- Vlookup—a function that returns a specific piece of information by looking up a supplied entry name and finding data in a specified column.
- Pivot table—Permits data to be summarized using interactive fields and filter buttons. Enables easy retrieval of specific data from a large amount of data.

STATISTICAL TOOLS

Statistics usage in HR is a data-driven approach to managing people and other variables in an organization. Statistics can help people understand a situation, can forecast future possibilities based on previously obtained data, and can sometimes help an organization mitigate risk. For example, statistics might help an organization better gauge when people will leave, discover possible bias in the hiring process, and help guide benefit decisions. There are many tools and software applications available to organizations for statistical analysis. The following are some commonly used HR statistical tools:

- R—A programming language that is a powerful statistical tool for data analysis and visualization, designed to manipulate enormous datasets.
- Python—Similar to R, offers fewer visualization and statistical analysis features, but is easier to learn.
- Power BI (business intelligence)—Statistical software that can aggregate large amounts of data as well as perform analysis and offer visualization benefits. Useful when multiple data sources need to be combined.
- Tableau platform—Similar to Power BI, good for aggregation of data and considered to be outstanding at visualization.
- Excel—The most basic statistical software for smaller sets of data and the easiest-to-use statistical package.

IMPORTANT CALCULATIONS

ROI

Return on investment (ROI) is a ratio or percentage comparing the gains of an investment versus its initial price. In other words, ROI measures the return of an investment relative to the cost. The formula is:

$$\text{ROI} = \frac{\text{Value investment} - \text{Cost investment}}{\text{Cost investment}}$$

For example:

- A company invests in an applicant tracking system (ATS) that costs $15,000.
- The company has been paying a staffing agency $25,000 per year to screen entry-level applications. (This can be calculated manually from invoices, or more simply by using the company's tech-based accounting platform to pull a report.)
- The ATS allows the company to bring entry-level candidate screening in-house without incurring additional related expenses.

To calculate ROI, first determine the gain, which, in this case, is the amount of money the company saves because of investing in an ATS. The company eliminated a $25,000 staffing agency expense by spending $15,000 on an ATS, so the gain is $10,000. ROI is the gain realized by the investment, divided by the cost of the investment:

$$\text{ROI} = \frac{\$25,000 - \$15,000}{\$15,000} = \frac{\$10,000}{\$15,000} = 0.67, \text{or } 67\%$$

The example above shows the manual calculation, but a company can set up an ROI formula template using spreadsheet software. With that in place, calculating ROI would be as simple as plugging in data pulled from the IT system and the actual expenditure.

ROE

Return on equity (ROE) is a ratio or percentage measuring the earnings of the organization during a period of time as compared to the amount of money invested in shareholder equity. ROE reveals whether an organization is efficiently using investments to make profits by measuring the organization's rate of return on shareholder equity. In other words, it signals to shareholders whether their investment is being used wisely.

For example, suppose Company B has $1 million in net income and $10 million in shareholder equity. Dividing net income by shareholder equity reveals the ROE: $\frac{\$1 \text{ million}}{\$10 \text{ million}} = 10\%$. This is a 10% return on the shareholders' investment. Sometimes a company will compare their ROE with similar competitors in the field. The basic formula for ROE is:

$$\text{ROE} = \frac{\text{Net income}}{\text{Shareholder equity}}$$

COST PER HIRE

Cost per hire is an HR recruitment metric that measures the total money invested to hire someone divided by the number of hires in a given time period. Internal costs might include employee referral awards, recruiter salaries, or cost of internal recruiting systems. External costs might include advertising, events, job fairs, background checks, or assessments.

The formula is:

$$\text{Cost per hire} = \frac{\text{Total internal \& external recruiting costs}}{\text{Total number of hires in given time period}}$$

This is a strategic metric used to assess the efficiency and effectiveness in an organization's recruiting process, and is frequently benchmarked against similar organizations and industry peers.

Cost per hire is usually calculated annually but can also be considered on a quarterly basis. For example, a company that has a lot of seasonal college recruiting expenses may want to look at cost per hire for that specific time frame separate from the rest of the year.

The first step in calculating cost per hire is to determine total recruitment costs for the designated time period. Total recruiting costs may include (but are not limited to):

- Recruiter salaries
- Compensation for others involved in recruiting, selection, and onboarding
- Cost of operating the careers page on the company website
- Applicant tracking system costs
- Candidate assessments, including skill testing and/or behavioral assessments
- Screening fees, such as background checks, drug tests, or fit-for-duty physical exams
- Other expenses related to recruiting and onboarding new hires

Coding recruitment-based expenses as such in the company's information technology system or accounting platform can be helpful. This makes it possible to quickly and easily pull a report from the information technology system that shows recruitment-related expenses in a defined period before a solution was implemented, and for the same length of time after the solution was implemented. Meanwhile, the HR information system (HRIS) makes it easy to quickly determine the total number of employees hired during those time frames. This information can then be used to calculate cost per hire for those time periods.

If a company's total recruitment costs for a year are $150,000 and the firm hired 50 employees that year, the cost-per-hire calculation would be $\frac{\$150,000}{50} = \$3,000$. That means the company has a cost per hire of $3,000.

This can be calculated manually, but setting up a template in a spreadsheet application would make this calculation as easy as plugging in data accessed via the company's technology systems.

An HRIS may even automatically calculate cost per hire on an ongoing basis. This is very beneficial, as having access to this metric makes it easy to stay aware of cost per hire and the impact of adjustments to recruiting expenditures in real time.

TIME TO FILL

Time to fill is an indicator of how long it takes a company to staff open positions. It is the length of time between when a position becomes available and when a candidate accepts the job.

Time to fill for a specific job is calculated by subtracting the offer position vacancy date from the offer acceptance date. For example, if a company opens a job order on July 1 and a candidate accepts the position on July 25, then the time to fill for that specific job is 24 days ($25 - 1 = 24$).

A company usually discusses time to fill as an average for a certain type of position over a specific period of time, such as annually or quarterly.

An ATS or HRIS is likely to provide this metric in real time, but it can also be calculated manually. Calculating average time to fill requires two steps:

- Calculate the sum of time to fill for all job openings of a certain type during the defined period of time.
- Divide that number by the total number of people hired for that type of position during the time frame.

Average time to fill can help hiring managers know approximately how long they should expect a position to be open before it can realistically be filled, so it's important to evaluate this data point continually.

Time to fill can also help identify hiring difficulties or evaluate recruitment effectiveness. When time to fill starts to increase, that's a good time to evaluate whether the company needs to adjust its recruiting strategy or to reconsider job-related factors such as compensation, job design, or flexibility.

SELECTION RATIOS

Selection ratio is used in the HR recruiting process to assess and evaluate sourcing for job positions. It is a ratio obtained by taking the number of candidates that the business desires to hire and dividing it by the total number of candidates for the open jobs. A low ratio means the organization can be more selective, while a high ratio indicates the organization need not be as selective. The formula for selection ratio is:

$$\text{Selection ratio} = \frac{\text{Number of hired candidates}}{\text{Total number of candidates}}$$

Selection ratios can be applied in many ways. For example, they can be used to evaluate applicant acceptance of offers; divide the number of offers accepted by those that were extended. Additionally, the percentage of minority applicants can be determined; take the number of minority applicants divided by the total number of applicants for that same position in the same time period.

TURNOVER AND TURNOVER STATISTICS

Turnover refers to when an employee permanently leaves an organization. Turnover is typically captured as a rate or percentage on a monthly or yearly basis and is useful in predicting the number of new employees that must be hired to replace those that have permanently left the organization. More often, turnover statistics are analyzed on a monthly basis to also highlight at what point in the year employees tend to exit the organization. The formula to calculate monthly employee turnover is:

$$\text{Monthly turnover rate} = \frac{\text{Number of separations during month}}{\text{Average number of employees during month}} \times 100$$

For example, if 30 employees leave the organization in the month of January, and there was an average of 200 employees in the month of January, then the turnover rate is 15%. Turnover statistics are more than just a number or percentage. This rate gives an organization a starting point to analyze why employees are leaving and take corrective actions, if needed, to maintain a

healthy organization. Some of the reasons for turnover might include poor performance, better pay, personal reasons, or career advancement.

Learning and Development

Employee Orientation

Onboarding is a critical first step of employee development in any business. Many important processes occur during the first few days and weeks of employment. It is important to help employees understand overall business goals, strategy, and the way work is structured so they connect to the company mission.

NEW HIRES

New hires are employees recently added to an organization or team. They can be early in their career and just starting out, college graduates who are entering the workforce, or experienced hires who are switching roles or companies. New employees are expected to represent the organization in a responsible way in and out of work, partner collaboratively with stakeholders to achieve business results, and work with honesty and integrity. New hire expectations are frequently outlined in employee handbooks, which often include code of conduct policies that outline expectations for conduct and behavior.

Helping new hires establish themselves at work and understand the mission, goals, and ways of working can determine how quickly they adjust and start to add value. Onboarding is the process of socializing with new employees to share the knowledge, skills, behavior, and attitudes required to successfully function. Onboarding plans that provide visibility to leaders and decision makers and facilitate touchpoints with key partners help to provide structure and exposure at the right intervals for maximum impact. A successful onboarding plan should:

- Help new employees learn the company's mission, vision, values, and strategic goals.
- Help new employees understand performance expectations for their new role.
- Help new employees meet team members and internal stakeholders.
- Help new employees complete any compliance or regulatory requirements.
- Help new employees gain access to systems and tools necessary for the job.
- Help new employees complete personal tasks related to pay, benefits, and taxes.

A planned approach to setting expectations, building relationships, and acclimating new hires and employees is essential for a successful onboarding program.

OTHER TYPES OF HIRES

Not all new hires are "new" to an organization. **Internal transfers** are existing employees who move teams or business units and have unique onboarding needs. They often have experience with the company and don't need to complete the same administrative tasks as new hires but require assimilation to new projects, processes, and teams. **Rehires** are former employees who are hired again and rejoin an organization. These groups have unique needs to be considered when planning onboarding, such as bridging tenure, benefits, or other policies that may have been in place during their prior tenure. Understanding the different types of new hires—and their unique requirements—will help with the effectiveness of employee orientation programs.

SETTING EXPECTATIONS

Organizations must start early when setting expectations with new hires to increase their ability to add immediate value and to accelerate their performance. It is important to establish clear objectives to help employees understand the job duties and overall requirements for their role.

They must understand how their responsibilities align to the larger organizational goals to increase their sense of belonging and connectedness. Management should:

- Explain to new hires what "good" looks like and share performance expectations that address how and why work gets done.
- Spend time reviewing company goals, how resources are structured, how the organization makes money, and desired behaviors and expectations. This will ensure employees understand the professional standards around conduct in and out of work.
- Help new joiners build relationships and form the right networks, and equip them with tools to boost collaboration.

Knowing the needs of each new hire and notifying internal stakeholders will help accelerate the new hire's ability to hit the ground running. As employees become active and visible within an organization, they are positioned to start building relationships in a more meaningful way.

BUILDING RELATIONSHIPS

New hires can reset where a team is in the group development cycle. Onboarding employees is often a team activity—work gets restructured, and existing team members are tasked to support a new team member either directly or indirectly. Team members can offer support formally, by acting as a resource and knowledge partner. Informally, they can help clarify information, provide useful history and background, and guide employees on where to find support and resources. Creating the right connections early—with peers, team members, leadership, and the broader organization—enhances feelings of belongingness and shortens the time it takes for an employee to start adding value. Opportunities such as mentoring programs and employee resource groups help to foster a sense of connection and belonging at work while providing exposure to more of the business. A successful transition into the company can increase feelings of connection to the team and the broader company mission.

Relationships are key to helping employees acclimate and navigate a company's culture. HR leaders can support employees in building relationships within a department or on project teams. Below are some important ways HR can support relationship-building for new employees:

- Encourage organization announcements to introduce new employees.
- Structure relationship building with direct reports, line managers, and other stakeholders using onboarding calendars.
- Promote information relationship building using mentorship or buddy programs.
- Create onboarding templates to ensure a standardized experience for all new employees.
- Invite employees to connect with internal affinity groups or volunteer efforts.

HR professionals can help employees establish relationships that are essential for success. Developing onboarding plans and designing systems with the right one-on-one and team touchpoints can facilitate meaningful relationships and partnerships.

GETTING ACCLIMATED

Helping employees understand the goals, strategy, and structure of an organization helps them connect their individual contributions to the overall success of the company. Sharing information about leadership teams, department structures, and how they work together adds clarity and helps orient new employees in an organization. Employee training is a critical function of onboarding. Training requirements can vary by industry or role, and can be required before employees gain access to critical internal systems and documentation. Helping employees understand what they

41

need to do, by when, and why, is important in helping them understand how work is performed. This training becomes a platform to introduce important policies and processes, as well as provide contact information for follow-up questions.

Robust onboarding programs account for all resources that perform work on behalf of a company, not just new hires or employees. This can include:

- Internal transfers
- Temporary workers (interns, co-ops)
- Contingent workers (contractors, consultants, freelancers)
- Rehires

HR professionals play an important role in planning and structuring onboarding programs that satisfy individual, team, and business needs. Investing in employees through salary, benefits, and training and development is often a company's biggest expense. Supporting employees during this critical transition can affect an employee's tenure, satisfaction, and productivity, which all impact company profitability.

Instructional Design and Organizational Learning Strategy

Training and development is one of several critical functions within HR departments. The goal of training and development in the overall business context is to promote learning. Learning refers to the acquisition of the knowledge, skills, competence, and experience that result in lasting behavior change. A learning organization is one that promotes a culture of lifelong development, provides formal and informal learning opportunities, and enables employees to acquire job-related skills and experiences. Establishing an organizational learning strategy has many benefits:

- It provides a proven method of increasing the knowledge, skills, experience, and abilities of employees.
- It enhances the employer value proposition and brand in a competitive talent market.
- It appeals to employees interested in continuous learning and increases the human capital assets of an organization.
- It acts as an incentive and total rewards benefit to employees.
- It is a cost-effective approach to develop internal talent and promote skills development.
- It can be used as part of a performance improvement plan.

Developing a tailored learning strategy that incorporates the current and future needs of the business is an important way for HR leaders to add value to the company.

There are several ways for learning to occur within an organization. The main components of learning within a training and development strategy are formal training, informal learning, and knowledge management.

FORMAL TRAINING

Formal training refers to the planned teaching of a particular skill or behavior. The objective of training is to facilitate the mastery of knowledge, skills, and abilities in job-related competency areas. At work, training is often presented in the form of dedicated events, which can be hosted in-person or online. Formal training can be instructor-led, by internal or external experts, and is often accompanied by physical or digital supporting material that participants can reference during or after the presentation. Formal training events offer flexibility in scope and are suitable for individuals, teams, or entire organizations.

INFORMAL LEARNING

Informal learning is learner-led and unstructured, and involves actions and doing. Instead of featuring a dedicated training event, informal learning's breadth, depth, and duration are driven by the employee. Informal learning can be motivated by a desire to develop longer-term skills, and can take the form of on-the-job learning, unplanned and casual interactions, networking and mentoring, and feedback from customers, former employees, and social media channels.

KNOWLEDGE MANAGEMENT

Knowledge management is the ability to create, use, and share information within an organization. This information can take the form of explicit (documented), implicit (know-how), or tacit (personal and experiential) knowledge. The systems and processes an organization uses to manage and transfer information are important to develop human capital assets and improve business performance.

COMPONENTS OF COMMONLY USED MODELS AND METHODS

Change practitioners are responsible for creating a change-positive culture that engages employees at all levels. Important knowledge, skills, and abilities needed to be successful in these roles include understanding how to think creatively, communicate effectively, distill complex topics into simple and digestible formats, and coach leaders and employees through all the changes that lead to desired business outcomes and behaviors.

Organizational learning can be delivered using a variety of methods: in-person or online, cohort or instructor-led, e-learning, videos, workbooks, and more. The right approach will incorporate the learning needs of participants, overall business objectives, and desired learning outcomes. Thinking through how best to design and deliver training allows HR leaders to use design principles to optimize impact.

After training is completed, creating continued opportunities to recall, share, and apply knowledge helps enhance learning. Creating ongoing interactions between learners and content, between learners and instructors, and between learners and other learners, can successfully promote learning and knowledge development long after a training event is finished. In addition, creating communities of practice (CoPs)—groups of people who share a passion, skill, or interest for something and learn to do it better by working together regularly—is an effective way to reinforce training and increase engagement on a topic.

INSTRUCTIONAL DESIGN

Instructional design, also known as instructional system design, is the systematic approach to designing, developing, and delivering training programs and materials in a consistent and reliable manner. This process helps outline the activities that steer the development of learning and helps to communicate its purpose and reason. The goal of instructional design is to analyze learning needs and develop improved learning experiences. Four popular instructional design models are:

- The ADDIE model
- Merrill's principles of instruction
- Gagne's nine events of instruction
- Bloom's taxonomy

ADDIE MODEL

The **ADDIE model** is a set of instructional design guidelines commonly used by organizations to develop human resource development (HRD) programs. "ADDIE" stands for the model's five steps: **analyze**, **design**, **develop**, **implement**, and **evaluate**. This is a systematic approach where each step of the process has outcomes that feed into the next step. Some critical activities include conducting a needs assessment, determining participant readiness for training, creating a learning environment, ensuring effective knowledge transfer as part of the training, developing an evaluation approach, selecting and using a training method, and monitoring and evaluating the effectiveness of the training.

The ADDIE model is commonly used in HRD because it is a simple but effective way of creating a training program. It can also be applied to a variety of fields and is not limited to training programs.

MERRILL'S PRINCIPLES OF INSTRUCTION

This framework leverages five principles when it comes to solving problems and completing tasks:

- Learning starts when participants must solve real-world problems they can relate to.
- Activating existing knowledge is important to connect to new information.
- Encouraging learners to demonstrate knowledge using a mix of visuals and storytelling helps with retention.
- Learning is enhanced when participants apply the knowledge or skill in practice and solve problems.
- Learning should be integrated through discussion, application, and sharing of new knowledge.

GAGNE'S NINE EVENTS OF INSTRUCTION

This framework takes a behaviorist approach to learning using the following steps:

- Gain attention by asking thought-provoking questions to engage the learner.
- Inform the learner of objectives, desired outcomes, and methods of measuring success.
- Stimulate recall of prior learning to utilize existing knowledge as a foundation to build on.
- Present the content in easy-to-digest and consumable chunks of information.
- Provide learner guidance with discussions, case studies, and other instructional support materials.
- Elicit performance with activities that prompt recall, utilization, and analysis of information.
- Provide feedback immediately to reinforce knowledge.
- Assess performance to test the knowledge and understanding against established criteria.
- Enhance retention and transfer to job with job aids and other strategies.

BLOOM'S TAXONOMY

This framework includes six dimensions of cognitive learning, starting with the simplest at the bottom and moving to the most complex at the top. This model guides the learner past lower levels of knowledge and recall, to deeper areas of understanding, application, and evaluation of impact. This process can foster creative solutions, with new information generated by moving through the levels.

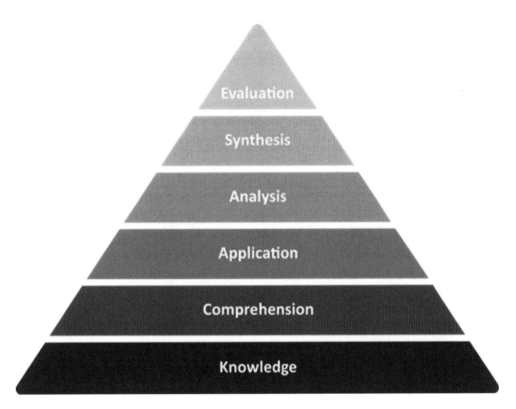

Each of these models has strengths, opportunities, flaws, and weaknesses. Depending on the learning objectives and desired outcomes, one or more elements of each model may be appropriate to use. HR professionals should be familiar with a range of instructional design methods to present the best solution based on business needs.

NEEDS ANALYSES

It is important for an organization to perform a needs analysis before designing a training program for several different reasons. First, an organization should accurately identify problems. Second, even if a particular problem is known prior to the analysis, it can be difficult to identify the cause of that problem. Third, and most importantly, it is impossible to design an effective training program without first identifying the specific knowledge, skills, and abilities required to achieve goals or to correct a problem. A **needs analysis** can be an essential part of the training development process because it helps to identify and detail problems so possible solutions can be found.

There are a variety of steps that might be taken during a needs analysis, but most analyses begin by collecting data related to the performance of each part of the organization. This information is usually gathered from surveys, interviews, observations, skill assessments, performance appraisals, and so on. Once this information is collected, problems are identified within specific areas of the organization, and solutions are proposed. Advantages and disadvantages of each solution are then identified, and the plan that seems to provide the greatest benefit for the lowest cost is chosen.

PERSON

A **person** needs analysis is a type of needs analysis that determines several key items. The person analysis will determine how an employee performs a task compared to the expectation. Not all individuals within the organization will require training, so the person analysis establishes which specific employees need training or development. Once individuals are identified for training, the type of training will be selected.

45

ORGANIZATION

The **organization** needs analysis is conducted to ensure that the training is aligned with the overall business strategy, and that there are adequate resources and support available for training.

TRAINING

A **training** needs analysis is completed to determine what gaps may exist in the actual knowledge, skills, and abilities in a role versus the desired levels. The difference between the actual competency and the standard will determine what training may be required.

Training Formats and Delivery Techniques

Training improves performance for employees and organizations. Understanding how to develop, organize, and deliver training promotes continuous learning and is a competitive advantage that contributes to business growth. HR professionals tasked with developing training programs and demonstrating value to business leaders should:

- Conduct a needs assessment.
- Understand the characteristics of the learners and the organization.
- Choose appropriate training methods and delivery techniques.

TRAINING GOALS

The need to deliver training can stem from a number of scenarios: hiring new employees, rolling out a new product, entering or exiting a new market, or changing policy. Conducting a thorough needs analysis ensures that the right program is designed by revealing what exists and what needs to change, and identifying any challenges that could impact successful implementation.

Understanding the type of learners in an organization and any unique needs helps to ensure that all training goals are appropriate and that the overall training programs are delivered successfully. Characteristics such as where employees work and are located, translation and accessibility needs, stakeholders' needs, and legal and regulatory requirements will impact the scope of the training plan.

TRAINING FORMATS

Choosing the appropriate training methods for an organization should start with a needs assessment. A needs assessment is a systematic assessment of the roles, individuals, and business to determine the characteristics and needs of the intended audience.

Technology has transformed training and development and provides new ways for organizations to help employees learn. Traditionally, in-house training programs were in high demand: content was created by internal teams with or without the help of external partners. Today, there are a number of development strategies that can be used to train, re-skill, and upskill existing teams. A few of these methods include the following.

TRADITIONAL CLASSROOM TRAINING

A traditional classroom training is conducted in a teaching space and allows for face-to-face instruction. This mode of training can take place internally at an employer's work site, externally at a training facility, or possibly at an industry conference. Classroom training offers many options to deploy multiple learning modalities. To begin, a classroom can be conducive to teaching new information to a small or large number of students. A classroom presentation can be made lecture-style, with or without visual aids; or it can include demonstrations of material, allowing for multiple

46

formats to teach information. If the group is small enough, classroom training can be an environment for interactive discussion, whereby the instructor gauges students understanding and immediately changes course if needed. Depending on the training, classroom training can permit employees to interact with one another, thereby enhancing the learning experience. Lastly, a classroom environment provides a human element that is challenging to capture in other training delivery formats.

ON-THE-JOB TRAINING (OJT)

On-the-job training (OJT) is usually provided by managers or supervisors utilizing real-time demonstration of the material or equipment the employee will be using to complete job tasks. This hands-on approach is sometimes more effective than lecturing or a theoretical approach. Seeing and being allowed to perform the desired function is a simple and cost-effective method for learning. This method also allows for immediate feedback and helps to ensure the employee is immediately productive.

However, there can be disadvantages to OJT. First, the person teaching may not be a certified trainer, but rather someone who knows how the work needs to be accomplished. Teaching requires clear communication and patience, and not everyone possesses necessary teaching skills. Second, another reason for OJT is to get the new employee up to speed quickly, but in doing so, there could be safety issues and the potential for accidents. This is especially true of high-risk jobs. Lastly, OJT could be distracting to coworkers, creating work disturbances and causing lack of concentration, especially in a space-constrained environment.

E-LEARNING OR VIRTUAL LEARNING

E-learning, also known as virtual learning, is a training delivery format that permits students to learn via a form that utilizes technology. E-learning can take a number of different formats, including web-based, mobile computer applications, and virtual classrooms. E-learning can be synchronous, in which the instructor and students are interacting in real time. Alternatively, e-learning can be asynchronous, enabling students to access the same training and related materials on demand at different days and times.

There are many benefits to using e-learning, such as delivering a large volume of information quickly, assisting globalization efforts through virtual learning, scheduling flexibility, and cost effectiveness. However, there are considerations that should be examined, including technology constraints and user access, concerns about intellectual property, lack of face-to-face interaction possibly causing uneasiness with students, and the potentially significant costs involved in training development.

BLENDED LEARNING OR HYBRID FORMAT

A blended learning or hybrid format combines multiple methods of delivering training material. Research suggests that a mix of learning strategies and formats might be more effective than one single method. Typically, blended or hybrid learning involves face-to-face, traditional classroom instruction combined with an online, technological component that might also give the student control over their pace of learning. The following are two examples of blended or hybrid learning:

- A course with synchronous learning in a virtual setting using video, as well as independent, web-based, self-paced learning modules that complement classroom instruction.
- A training program that involves a web-based book with case studies, as well as traditional face-to-face classroom instruction coupled with a mobile application for simulation exercises.

Blended learning or hybrid instruction has many advantages: it works well with different student learning styles, enables both independent and collective learning, supports learning in a global workforce, and provides scheduling flexibility. On the other hand, there are some concerns that must be addressed; for example, more advanced planning is necessary, students need to be organized in how they will attend, students potentially need more motivation with this format, there may be feelings of not being connected and needing more encouragement, and development costs can be higher. This integrated, blended learning environment is constantly evolving as technology affords the organization more options.

DELIVERY TECHNIQUES

How work gets done continues to change thanks to macro trends toward globalization, digitization, and changes brought on by the COVID-19 pandemic. With continued focus on collaboration and working across team and cultural boundaries, HR professionals should be well versed in multiple approaches to increase training effectiveness. Some popular styles include:

- **Role play**: This allows the learner to act and speak like the character they are trying to portray. Benefits include practice, which builds experience, and more chances for real-time feedback, which can be applied to enhance performance.
- **Facilitation**: This allows learners to be introduced to the content by a facilitator who guides learners through the content, asks questions, and steers the overall discussion. This style promotes real-time feedback.
- **Case studies**: This involves reviewing a real-life historical situation to learn from others' lived experiences. This can occur in person, online, or in a blended learning situation. This approach gives learners perspective and insights into unique challenges and allows for low-stakes learning opportunities.
- **Games and simulations**: These bring the strategies, rules, and social experiences of game play into a learning setting. This style incorporates digital and gamification tools into learning content and delivers training in a way that increases engagement with learners.

IN-HOUSE VS. EXTERNAL TRAINING SERVICES

A critical question that comes up when assessing the learning needs of an organization is whether the training should be developed and delivered in-house or through a third party. Deciding whether all elements or specific components of the instructional design will be outsourced will help to clarify the value proposition of the training program. Companies can choose to partner with external vendors on specific elements ranging from content creation to design, illustration, voice-over, translation, and accessibility services.

Some important considerations when deciding whether to insource or outsource learning content include:

- Type of training (e.g., legally required, role-specific, business-specific)
- Length and duration of training (how often learners will need to retest)
- Location of training audience (whether multiple languages are needed)
- Data privacy and accessibility (single sign-on or externally hosted site)
- Trademark and copyright considerations
- Feedback mechanisms needed to get input on the end users' experience

LEARNING MANAGEMENT SYSTEMS (LMSS)

The increased use of e-learning—training that is delivered through an online platform via computers and mobile devices—means organizations must invest in software that helps to create, manage, distribute, and track employee training. Learning management systems (LMSs) are often used in business settings to deliver online training and track employee progress. An LMS allows organizations to harness analytics to evaluate training offerings, enhance the learner experience, and increase effectiveness of training programs. A well-integrated LMS will complement career development efforts by delivering relevant learning content to strong performers, employees new to the company or new in their roles, or those looking to re-skill for the future.

A huge benefit of investing in an LMS is the ability to pull reporting and analytics that provide useful measurements around spending on learning, utilization, compliance, and engagement with enterprise learning systems.

Change Management Process

Learning is the acquisition of knowledge through experience, leading to lasting behavior change. Change refers to the adoption of a new idea or behavior. The consistent application of learning as knowledge creates change. Change management refers to the collective approach to initiating, organizing, implementing, and supporting organizational change for individuals, teams, and entire groups. A good way to think about change is to examine what happens when someone learns something new. When done consistently and repeatedly, this kind of change can be an accelerant for business transformation and a source of competitive advantage.

FORCES FOR CHANGE

An essential ingredient to successfully implement change is the ability of people leaders to distinguish between the external changes that occur and the concurrent intrinsic and psychological changes that affect individual employees, including change leaders. Understanding external factors that prompt change in organizations, along with individual approaches to behavior change, can equip HR teams with the knowledge they need to support leaders and businesses through change scenarios.

Change can result from businesses experiencing volatility, uncertainty, complexity, and ambiguity (VUCA) events. Most recently, COVID-19 and the pandemic ushered in a "new normal" and transformed many ways of working, including how HR teams develop and deliver business-critical training and learning in a remote manner. Many companies quickly adapted their operating models, supply chains, vendor relationships, and communication models to engage customers and consumers through years of uncertainty and ambiguity. Other global trends that have precipitated change recently include:

- Globalization and increasingly complex operating environments impacting approaches to risk management and compliance, talent pipelines, vendor relationships, and business models
- Digital transformation and technology enabling advanced solutions and tools for employees and customers
- Emphasis on diversity, equity, and inclusion initiatives including employee resource groups, employee well-being resources, and accessibility tools for the differently abled
- Shifts in attitudes on total rewards advocating for more pay transparency, increased parental leave, debt support, and mental wellness

APPROACHES TO CHANGE

Individual change is at the center of everything that is achieved within organizations. Many change scenarios require employees to learn new things on their own and come together in teams and networks to apply those learnings in new and innovative ways. Leaders play a crucial role in guiding individuals and teams through changes that facilitate business transformation. Managers play a dual role of creating urgency with individuals around a big opportunity, while managing themselves through the change as well. The more tools a leader has to influence behavior, the more successful they will be in leading teams through change. To understand how change impacts people, it is important to know these four schools of thought:

- The **behavioral approach** focuses on individuals influencing other individuals with reward and punishment mechanisms. If the desired results are not achieved, an analysis of the individual's behavior is conducted to better understand non-achievement. A downside of this approach is that it relies solely on observable behavior to measure progress.
- The **cognitive approach** focuses on individuals' capacity for problem-solving and asserts that emotions and reactions are a result of how things are perceived. This view maintains that attitudes and behavior are driven by how individuals view the world. This approach centers on the ability to change how people think. A drawback of this approach is underestimating the inner emotional world of individuals and the impact that it has on their outlook and ability to work through change.
- The **psychodynamic approach** explains that individuals go through a range of internal emotions in response to external circumstances. This approach is useful to understand reactions to a change and how to handle them. This approach is criticized for not accounting for an individual's ability to think, act, and control their own behavior.
- The **humanistic approach** takes a holistic view of individuals as more than their thoughts, emotions, and behaviors and focuses on the ability to choose. A drawback of this approach is that it requires an individual to have a minimum amount of verbal fluency, intellect, and confidence to express themselves.

There are a variety of models and frameworks used for each approach that offer insight to leaders on the impact of organizational change. Understanding the different approaches and the advantages and disadvantages associated with each style can help HR professionals provide solutions that meet the needs of many types of teams and businesses.

Anticipating resistance to change and understanding the roots of concerns is another powerful way that HR leaders can support change management efforts. Most individual struggles fall into one or more versions of "I don't understand it," "I don't like it," or "I don't need it."

ELEMENTS OF THE CHANGE MANAGEMENT PROCESS

Taking practical steps to assess the readiness of individuals for a planned change can help leaders prepare to manage across the organization. Any behavior changes or project plans that require employees to do something new or different will require a few steps:

1. Create a burning case for change with leaders, decision makers, and key stakeholders to collaborate and gain alignment, commitment, and support for the change.
2. Define the future state and identify the needs of the organization: list the desired behaviors, performance, processes, and initiatives that will help to realize the strategic opportunity.
3. Do a gap analysis to measure how often the desired behaviors are currently used across the organization.

4. Create short-term milestones and celebrate achievement in a public way to increase motivation and buy-in.
5. Develop robust communication plans for stakeholders, with key messages, job aids, checklists, and other tools. Communicate about the impact of the change and solicit feedback about employee sentiment on the change.
6. Leave room in future phases to incorporate stakeholder feedback to deepen buy-in and support.

Throughout each of these steps, leaders should offer ongoing support in the form of additional resources and training to provide information about the need for change and reinforce desired outcomes throughout the change journey. To be effective, training must align with and reinforce the strategic goals of the business. Using both quantitative measures (e.g., surveys) and qualitative measures (e.g., focus groups) will provide a more comprehensive view of how the change is being received. Offering resources to increase understanding around change, soliciting real-time and continuous feedback about change, and incorporating end-user feedback will boost support and limit any disruptive impacts.

CONTINUOUS IMPROVEMENT

Implementing change in an organization should trigger a continuous process that focuses on how to get change to stick. A desired outcome for most changes is implementing the new behavior as status quo, which involves an ongoing campaign of outreach, engagement, and communication. An important way to measure progress is to establish metrics and assess whether desired outcomes are occurring in the organization. By identifying forward-looking measures for how things will operate in the future, HR leaders can use data to confirm that the right changes are taking hold.

Change leaders must tune in to the environment to monitor how change is taking hold across the organization. It is important to build coalitions of passionate supporters—and detractors—to get feedback on how change is being communicated across teams. When possible, it is also helpful to reinforce key messages with this group, remove barriers, and empower them to go back to their teams with information and updates on the change. Many teams leverage these networks of change agents and change champions to build trust at the grassroots levels and drive implementation.

Change management plans are all about deconstructing change into small steps. Understanding what motivates individuals, and how they respond to change, can equip business and HR leaders with perspectives and tools that drive results that directly impact the bottom line.

Employee Development and Training Effectiveness

PURPOSE OF TRAINING EVALUATION

Evaluating and measuring the effectiveness of training programs has many benefits. It supports learning effectiveness, helps to align training investment to business strategy, and engages participants in the design and delivery process. Many leaders view training evaluation as the end of learning, but it actually serves as the beginning of the continuous improvement process. Successful measurement results in feedback that is incorporated into the future content and structure of training events and can boost training efficacy. Soliciting feedback from participants—and actively incorporating those inputs—builds trust and drives engagement, which are key drivers of retention.

Possibly the most common method of evaluation is Kirkpatrick's training effectiveness model, which has been successfully used across a range of businesses and industries. This framework can be used to evaluate formal and informal training events, which makes it ideal for numerous scenarios. The model consists of four levels of response to a training or learning event:

- Level 1: Reaction—How did participants respond to the training?
- Level 2: Learning—How much did participants learn from the training, and did their skills improve?
- Level 3: Behavior—How have participants applied the training in their work?
- Level 4: Results—What has improved or been impacted as a result of the training?

Over time, the original work has been expanded into what is called the New World Kirkpatrick model. This version turns the model upside down; it emphasizes identifying level 4 (results) up front and focusing on the collective efforts of interested parties to achieve a return on stakeholder expectations.

METHODS AND TOOLS

A variety of tools exist to help measure training efficacy, and certain measurement tools are more suitable for certain levels. Donald Kirkpatrick introduced a **four-level training evaluation model** for planning, evaluating, and preserving. The four levels of the Kirkpatrick evaluation model are as follows:

- Level 1 training evaluations are the most common, and they can be relatively easy and fast compared to other methods. Surveys that measure participants' knowledge, skills, attitudes, and reactions are common for this level.
- Level 2 training evaluations measure learning. These methods must be both reliable and valid to be useful. They can take the form of pre- and post-tests and include self-assessments on how knowledge has been applied. Providing job aids, quick reference guides, and other tools to use after training is another best practice to enhance learning.
- Level 3 training evaluations measure how information is applied. Data collection at this stage can take the form of self-reporting by the learner (often surveys and questionnaires), on-the-job observation to see if new skills are being applied, or obtaining 360-degree feedback from leaders, teammates, and business partners on changes in behavior. While it may be difficult to prove that behavior changes resulted directly from training, a variety of evaluation methods and feedback can home in on drivers of change.
- Level 4 training evaluations measure results and can be the most time-consuming and expensive to implement. These can look like focus groups, strategic interviews, and observations.

Other tools for evaluating training effectiveness include reports and participant feedback, which can be used at each level to obtain valuable insight into the success of any training offering.

A popular tool that supports all levels of training evaluation is a learning management system (LMS) software solution with built-in functionality to collect training feedback, aggregate evaluations, and offer reporting capability for deeper insights. A strong LMS can streamline how HR leaders approach training evaluation.

TECHNIQUES TO EVALUATE TRAINING PROGRAMS
PERFORMING A NEEDS ANALYSIS BEFORE DESIGNING A TRAINING PROGRAM

It is important for an organization to perform a needs analysis before designing a training program for several reasons. First, an organization can accurately identify problems. Second, even if a particular problem is known prior to the analysis, it can be difficult to identify the cause of that problem. Third, and most importantly, it is impossible to design an effective training program without first identifying the specific knowledge, skills, and abilities required to achieve goals or correct a problem. A needs analysis can be an essential part of the training development process because it helps to identify and inform about problems so that possible solutions can be found.

PRE- AND POST-TRAINING EVALUATION

The end goal of any training is to have the participants learn and apply the new knowledge or material in the most effective manner possible. Information obtained in a **pre-training survey** can help ensure the training meets expected learning outcomes, gauge student expectations, and provide information about the students' abilities and their learning preferences. The data gathered from the pre-training evaluation will help the instructor customize the training to improve learning. Pre-training survey questions need to be tailored for the intended audience—the right questions need to be asked in the right format. This can vary tremendously depending on the training and the participants. The objective is to have a clear assessment of the participant's skill-based knowledge before the training.

Meanwhile, the questions asked in a **post-training survey** should measure whether the content taught was learned and understood. Frequently, skills-based questions in the post-training survey will be similar to those asked in the pre-training survey. This is done intentionally to measure whether the information taught was truly learned, meaning there should be improved scores in the post-training evaluation. Organizations will typically do another survey anywhere from 30 days to 6 months after the training to gauge training effectiveness.

PARTICIPANT TRAINING SURVEYS

Training is an essential function for almost any organization. Sometimes, in cases of sexual harassment, corporate policy, discriminatory practice and legislation, etc., it can even be mandatory. In other cases, it is a necessity because information and technology are constantly advancing. Additionally, companies spend a considerable amount of money on training and should see a return on their investment. Therefore, organizations should always evaluate and assess training effectiveness.

One of the ways to assess training is through a training participant survey. This type of survey involves asking employees questions to better gauge how they view the effectiveness of the training. Individuals have different learning styles and learn in many different ways. Their input can help an organization improve future training programs. The survey is usually done electronically and can vary enormously depending on the training needs and makeup of the organization. Generally, questions will either be quantitative, meaning they are evaluated on a numeric scale, or qualitative, meaning they require verbiage and/or accurate responses. Possible questions might be:

- What was your overall impression of the training program?
- What particular part of the training did you feel was the most useful?
- On a scale of 1 to 5, with 1 being the worst and 5 the best, answer the following questions:
    - How would you rate this training program?
    - How would you rate the instructor?

53

o How would you rate the technology used?
o How would you rate your ability to immediately use the information learned?

AFTER-ACTION REVIEW

The term **"after-action review"** was originally used by the military after field operations as a structured approach to identify the group's strengths, weaknesses, and areas for improvement based on real-life events. Many companies, including GE, BP, and Motorola, use an after-action review to improve their operations. This approach is focused on three primary questions:

- What was supposed to happen, and what actually happened?
- What went well, and why?
- What can be improved, and how?

An after-action review is a structured debriefing that allows an organization to gain insights and knowledge that will enable it to learn from past missteps or mistakes so they are not repeated. Moreover, this reflective, knowledge-is-power method can correct situations that were not ideal and/or help replicate situations that were handled well. The following are the typical processes and objectives when conducting an after-action review:

- Conduct the after-action review as soon as possible after the event so it is fresh in everyone's memory.
- Include everyone involved and set ground rules so that honest opinions are offered with respect to all present.
- Ask all structured questions (listed above) and document responses for lessons learned.
- Document a report detailing all learned strengths, weaknesses, and areas for improvement or areas to be replicated.
- Implement needed changes immediately.

Compensation and Benefits

Compensation Strategy

PAY STRUCTURES AND PROGRAMS

IMPORTANCE OF PAY STRUCTURES

Pay structure is the way an organization groups jobs and defines the compensation associated with a collection of jobs. Pay structure is critical because every organization needs qualified and talented individuals to build and run a business. One of the best ways to obtain and retain good talent is through a fair and attractive pay structure. Additionally, as in most areas of HR, pay structure needs to demonstrate that an organization has fair and consistent policies surrounding all aspects of pay. This structure will help an organization meet necessary compliance requirements, as well as clearly demonstrate fair practices related to pay opportunities for all employees.

One of the most important considerations in pay structure is the balance between internal and external pay equity. Internal pay equity is how an employee's pay compares to the pay of others in similar positions within the organization. External pay equity is the comparison of pay to similar jobs outside the organization. A balance indicates the pay is fair, which will help attract new employees and also help retain existing employees in the organization.

CREATING A PAY STRUCTURE

Methods of creating a pay structure can vary greatly, but most organizations begin the process by conducting a job evaluation for each position. A **job evaluation** is the process whereby the value of a job to the organization is determined—it is how a job's worth is established. Once all positions are evaluated and assigned a value, they are categorized based on their importance to the organization. The organization will usually gather information from salary surveys to determine the market median for each category and the wages an individual would receive at the midpoint of a similar pay category for another organization. Finally, using all of this information as a guide, a **pay range** is developed for each category.

Pay ranges can be a challenge because this is a very fluid process. Occasionally, an employee is paid above the range maximum or below the range minimum. When an employee is paid above a range maximum, it is called a **"red-circle rate"** and could mean that an employer's pay range is below the market value and should be researched to remain competitive. If the pay rate is below the range minimum, it is called a **"green-circle rate"** and should also be re-examined.

PAY GRADES AND BANDING

A **pay grade** refers to a compensation job grouping, by level, with similar responsibilities, authority, and experience. This grouping means that within an organization, similar jobs have approximately the same relative value and are therefore paid at similar rates within a pay range. Some compensation structures break out pay grades or ranges into separate **bands** (or levels) so the company can maintain pay equity and stay within budget. This is done by conducting a job analysis and grouping titles into families. For example, those that fall into the first pay grade may have a pay band of $20,000 to $35,000, the second pay grade may have a band of $30,000 to $50,000, and the third pay grade may have a band of $50,000 to $100,000. Jobs may also be evaluated and ranked based upon overall responsibilities and worth to the organization.

55

Although pay bands are broken out based upon job duty and skill level, it is important to recognize whether the company tends to lead, lag, or match current market rates. Matching or leading the market is best for recruitment and retention. The sizes of pay bands tend to grow as you move up the managerial ladder, with executives having the largest pay levels.

TRADITIONAL SALARY STRUCTURE

A **traditional salary structure** could have multiple pay ranges that correlate to differences in a position. The way it typically works is that a new employee will be offered a salary on the lower end of the pay range, and then hopefully advance to a higher pay range depending on their performance evaluation or other means of evaluating the employee. The benefit of an organization using a traditional salary structure is that it provides the organization and its employees an easy-to-understand "ladder" or hierarchical system for an employee to advance or be promoted from one pay grade to another. Typically, an organization will first set the minimum and maximum salary range for each grouping. Then, based on the number of groupings, the organization will figure out the logical number of pay grades in their salary structure.

BROADBAND SALARY STRUCTURE

A **broadband salary structure** takes multiple pay grades that only have a modest difference between the minimum and maximum pay scale and combines them into a single band with a much broader difference in the spread. In effect, the organization is collapsing multiple ranges in order to obtain a larger spread between the minimum and maximum point for a salary range. An organization might use a broadband salary structure if they wish to remove hierarchical levels and thereby limit the levels of management, a process sometimes referred to as "flattening" an organization. For example, an organization may have had 10 levels of management, with a narrow salary range in each level. They then decide to adopt a broadband salary structure and reduce the levels from 10 to 5, thereby also allowing the organization to increase the difference in the salary range. Existing employees are then moved to the most appropriate level within the five options.

Companies may also choose a broadband salary structure in a large organization if managing too many pay grades becomes complex and difficult to equitably administer.

Traditional Pay Grades Compared to Broadbanding

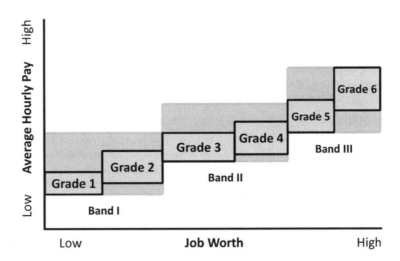

MARKET-BASED PAY STRUCTURES

A **market-based pay structure** can be thought of as a combination of traditional and broadband structures, except market-based pay is a pay scale based on what similar employers in similar geographic locations pay employees. In other words, appropriate pay is determined by an employer evaluating data from various sources in the job market that summarize pay for similar jobs. Sources include the US Bureau of Labor Statistics and some private companies that offer salary surveys for a fee. Like traditional and broadband, the market-based pay structure also has a pay range for specific jobs. However, what usually happens is that the pay range, minimum to maximum, is too slim to be competitive with similar jobs in the external market, while the salary range is usually too high, like the broadband structure. A large majority of businesses utilize a market-based pay structure in their organization.

VARIABLE PAY

Variable pay is employee pay that changes based on predetermined parameters or goals set by an employer. Variable pay is most often used as a monetary incentive to achieve business objectives and reward employees, and is usually a supplement to base salary or wages. An organization that wants to use variable pay to incentivize behavior or performance can accomplish this goal based on criteria such as sales revenue, customer satisfaction scores, percentage increase in clients, and pieces produced. Variable pay is frequently either a dollar amount or percentage based on target objectives and is included in an employee's overall compensation plan. The following are some examples of how variable pay might work:

- An electrician paid hourly could be paid $30 extra for every referral made.
- An account executive could be paid a salary and, for every quarter that his or her team exceeds their sales objective by 10 percent, could receive an additional $5,000.
- An assembly line worker who exceeds his or her pieces built per hour by 10 percent or more (with no defects) could receive an extra $100 per day.

PAY COMPRESSION

Pay compression occurs when a senior employee has a salary that is only slightly more, or in some cases less, than a new hire in the same position. This is a situation in which beginning salaries for new hires are too close to the salaries for existing employees in the same job. In some cases, it is not exactly the same job—this could also occur if a new hire makes more money than their manager. Pay compression can be the cause of high turnover and employee disengagement. Causes of pay compression may include the following:

- An organization increases wages to attract new hires and doesn't adjust wages for existing employees according to market changes.
- Internal compensation is not aligned with real-world market salary data.
- There are issues with existing organizational pay grades, levels, and bands.

The answer to pay compression is easy, but its implementation and fallout are challenging. The answer is to adjust the inequities and pay employees fair market-value wages. This is a costly proposition for most organizations, but if they do not adjust wages accordingly, they risk losing good workers and facing the challenges and costs that come with replacing them.

JOB EVALUATION/CLASSIFICATION

Job evaluation is the process a company uses to identify the relative worth (in terms of monetary value) of each position.

Common methods used to evaluate and classify jobs include:

- **Ranking method**—Ranking begins by listing all an organization's jobs in order, from the highest value or difficulty to the lowest value or difficulty. Those that have the highest value or difficulty receive the highest pay, with compensation adjusted accordingly as the level of value or difficulty decreases.
- **Classification method**—Rather than starting with individual jobs, classification involves establishing multiple pay grades and writing a broad description for each grade. Next, each job description is compared to the description of each grade and assigned to the closest match.
- **Point method**—The point method involves identifying various compensable factors that will be evaluated to determine how much individual jobs should pay. Points are assigned for each compensable factor and compared to benchmark positions within the company.
- **Factor comparison method**—Factor comparison involves evaluating each job against a benchmark position in relation to a set group of five predetermined factors, which are usually defined as skill level, responsibility, mental requirements, physical requirements, and working conditions.

Ranking and classification are non-quantitative classification methods, while the point method and factor comparison method are quantitative.

PAY ADJUSTMENTS

Pay adjustments are not generally required by law, except when necessary to match minimum wage increases. However, pay adjustments are an important part of a company's compensation strategy for positions at all levels.

Employees expect to be rewarded with pay increases as time goes by as a reward for their hard work, loyalty, and contributions. Without pay increases, employees may feel unappreciated—which can negatively impact job performance, engagement, and retention. A company also needs to consider the fact that the cost of living changes over time, a factor that can reduce the overall value of employee compensation.

It is common for companies to consider pay adjustments on an annual basis, though some employers do so more or less frequently.

- For salaried employees, pay adjustments are ordinarily awarded as a percentage of current compensation, though a company can opt to award a specific dollar amount.
- For hourly workers, an employer may opt to adjust pay as a flat per-hour increase or as a percentage of the current hourly rate.

DIFFERENTIAL PAY

Differential pay is when an organization pays an employee an extra wage for working undesirable shifts or hours. This could mean working through the night or maybe on the weekend or a holiday. Organizations are not legally obligated to offer differential pay; rather, they offer it to incentivize people to work those shifts. However, if a worker works over 40 hours in a week, regardless of shift, then they are entitled to overtime pay according to the Fair Labor Standards Act (FLSA). Most employers offer differential pay as a percentage. For example, suppose XYZ Supermarket offers 20% differential for the overnight shift, and the normal day rate of pay is $15 an hour. Multiplying 20% by the normal rate of pay ($15 \times 0.20 = 3$) indicates that the differential would be an additional $3 per hour, meaning the worker doing the overnight shift would earn $18 an hour.

COST-OF-LIVING ADJUSTMENT (COLA)

A **cost-of-living adjustment** (COLA) is designed to counteract and stabilize inflation by declaring a percentage increase in Social Security and supplemental income. Usually, a COLA is equal to the percentage rise in the consumer price index for urban wage earners and clerical workers (CPI-W) for a predefined period of time, a calculation that frequently aligns with the calculation for inflation. For example, if a person received $20,000 in Social Security and the COLA was evaluated at 3.1%, then their benefits would be $20,620 for the year. COLA began in 1975 in response to high inflation and is evaluated every year. The Social Security Administration uses COLAs to protect compensation-based benefits from inflation.

BONUS PAY

Bonus pay is similar to variable pay in that an employee is paid a sum of money based on criteria set by the organization, but not necessarily linked to a clear objective. For example, at the end of the year, an organization might pay employees a bonus, perhaps a percentage of pay or just a lump sum not based on wages. This type of bonus could be offered because the business or the individual achieved certain goals, or the bonus could be made at a manager's discretion to reward the employee(s). Discretion-based bonuses could be given at any interval of time—perhaps by a manager when an employee successfully handled the closing of a deal. Additionally, a bonus could be shared among an entire department, region, team, etc., for a goal achieved or any other valued display of work.

There is only a subtle difference between bonus pay and variable pay. Bonuses may be linked to an achievement of predetermined metrics or factors, such as a holiday bonus or manager discretion bonus. Generally, bonuses reward past activities or achievements, whereas variable pay encourages future performance.

MERIT PAY

Merit pay is money awarded to an employee, via a base pay increase, based on predetermined and performance-related goals. The FLSA does not require or manage merit pay; the management and distribution of merit pay is between the employer and the employee. The overarching goal of merit pay is to motivate employees to meet and hopefully exceed individual predetermined goals. A merit pay program can drive individuals to be more productive and hence an organization more successful. The difference between merit pay and other incentive pay programs (variable, commission, etc.) is that it is incorporated into an employee's base salary rather than being a one-time occurrence. Merit increases can vary based on the organization and circumstances, but typically are under 5 percent of base salary.

There are many advantages to merit pay, such as monetarily rewarding high performers, assisting with the retention of top talent, and differentiating individual contributions versus team contributions to company goals. On the other hand, there are some issues to be aware of when administering a merit pay program, including making sure there are predefined, clear, measurable performance objectives, as well as managing merit awards in a fair, consistent manner.

INCENTIVE PROGRAMS

In addition to base pay, a company may include incentives in its compensation strategy. Incentives should be strategically aligned with the company's goals and objectives, while also providing a way for employees to increase their earnings.

Some incentive programs are specific to certain types of jobs, while others may be open to all types of employees. Examples of commonly used approaches to incentive compensation include:

- **Sales commission**—Sales professionals often earn a percentage of each sale they make as part of their compensation package.
- **Customer referral**—To encourage non-sales employees to refer customers, a company may incentivize other team members by paying a finder's fee for new customers they refer.
- **Employee referral**—To boost its applicant pool, an employer may incentivize current employees by paying a bonus when an applicant they refer joins the company.
- **Signing bonus**—For hard-to-fill jobs, an employer may induce applicants to join their company by offering a signing bonus.
- **Skill-based pay**—A company seeking to have highly trained employees who are prepared for multiple roles in the company may incentivize employees to master new skills.
- **Shift differentials**—Companies with multiple shifts may incentivize employees to accept hard-to-staff shifts with a higher rate of pay for those time slots.
- **Profit sharing**—Some organizations have structured incentive programs that provide profit sharing bonuses on a quarterly or annual basis.
- **Gain sharing**—A company looking for ways to decrease expenses may incentivize employees to increase efficiency by sharing cost savings with them.
- **Year-end bonus**—Some companies offer a year-end bonus to employees as a way of saying thank you for their hard work and service throughout the year.

SERVICE AWARDS

Service awards can also play an important role in a company's compensation strategy. A service awards program is designed to recognize employees for longevity with a company, so these programs are sometimes referred to as "years of service" awards. These awards may be tangible items or have monetary value, or both.

- **Anniversary recognition**—Some companies recognize team members on each employment anniversary with a mention in an employee newsletter, a certificate of appreciation, a thank-you note from the CEO, logo merchandise, or other items.
- **Milestone awards**—Service award programs often include larger items or more formal recognition, such as acknowledgement at the annual meeting or higher-value items, when employees reach major milestones, such as 5, 10, or 15 years.
- **Longevity pay**—Some compensation systems include longevity pay, which can be a bonus for each year of service or a step raise, which is an increase in pay automatically awarded when employees complete another year of service.

MARKET ANALYSIS

In developing a compensation and benefits strategy, it's important for a company to be aware of what other companies pay for similar positions, or for employees who have the skills and backgrounds that an organization needs. After all, a business must compete with other businesses not just for customers, but also for employees.

Gathering or reviewing market analysis data can help determine whether a company's compensation is similar to that of companies with whom an organization is competing for talent, or if the pay is above or below what other employers are paying. This information can be used to make a business case for keeping compensation where it is, or to support making changes such as increasing pay or adding benefits.

INTERNAL RESEARCH

Compensation-related market analysis data can be gathered via internal research, though it can be quite time-consuming to take this approach. Gathering information for this type of market analysis usually involves scouring job openings posted by companies with similar positions, as well as reviewing position-specific pay data that the Bureau of Labor Statistics (BLS)—a division of the Department of Labor (DOL)—publishes online. Websites like Payscale.com and ZipRecruiter.com can also be helpful resources for finding information on pay for certain types of positions.

EXTERNAL RESOURCES

Rather than conducting a market analysis internally, it is also possible to work with external service providers to gain access to compensation data. While there are fees associated with using external service providers, it's usually possible to get information faster this way as compared to internal research.

- The company's benefits broker may be able to provide access to market analysis data about the types of benefits that employers in the same industry or size category tend to provide.
- Some third-party organizations compile salary data that they make available to employers for a fee. For example, it is possible to purchase access to federal, state, and metro-specific salary survey data and benchmarks via Compensation.BLR.com.
- For data customized to specific interests or needs, a company might engage a compensation and benefits consultant or consulting firm to conduct a custom market analysis.

EXTERNAL SERVICE PROVIDERS

Some companies rely on their own internal resources to develop and administer their compensation strategy, while others engage outside consultants to lead this aspect of operations. In a small business, the HR manager or director, or a member of the executive team, may be responsible for compensation strategy, while the HR team in a larger organization may have one or more compensation specialists or compensation analysts on staff.

In either case, a company may opt to work with an external services provider for a special project or on an ongoing basis. This could involve contracting with an individual compensation consultant or engaging a consulting firm that offers compensation strategy services. There are several reasons it can be beneficial to work with an external service provider, including the following:

- Developing an effective compensation strategy requires time and focus. A consultant can focus solely on this one thing rather than trying to fit it in with the myriad of day-to-day compensation-related matters that require the attention of internal staff members.
- It can be difficult for an internal team member to be truly objective about compensation at the company where they work. As a third party, a consultant will bring an external and objective perspective to compensation strategy.
- Developing compensation strategy requires expertise beyond how to administer a compensation program. A consultant who specializes in compensation strategy will have not only compensation-specific expertise, but also expertise in strategic planning and bottom-line impact.

Benefits and Insurance Programs

Employee benefits are an important aspect of a company's compensation program. They add financial value to the wages and any incentives a company offers, and they meet important health and wellness needs for employees and their families.

Benefits packages usually include access to group health coverage, as well as other kinds of group benefits like dental insurance, vision plans, term life insurance, and more. Without access to group health coverage or other types of group benefits, employees who want coverage would have to purchase individual plans on the open market. Individual plans tend to be much more expensive than group plans.

In some cases, offering benefits also helps employers comply with regulatory requirements. For example, companies with 50 or more employees are subject to financial penalties if they don't offer health insurance that meets the requirements of the Patient Protection and Affordable Care Act (PPACA).

BENEFIT PROGRAMS
NON-DISCRETIONARY VS. DISCRETIONARY BENEFITS

Benefits fit under two basic categories: non-discretionary and discretionary. **Non-discretionary** benefits are benefits that an employer must offer and are mandated under various legal statutes. These benefits can include, but are not limited to, unemployment insurance, Medicare, workers' compensation, Social Security, unpaid family medical leave, and COBRA.

62

Discretionary benefits are those benefits that an employer chooses to offer—and thus are not mandated by legal regulations—in order to attract and retain talent. Generally, discretionary benefits comprise three primary areas:

- **Health benefits**—This includes everything under the healthcare umbrella, including medical, dental, vision, prescription, employee assistance programs, disability insurance, and life insurance.
- **Deferred compensation**—This area includes any type of employer-offered retirement plan whereby the benefit is received at a later date than when work is performed.
- **Other** discretionary benefits—This includes perks that do not fit into health benefits or deferred compensation, such as paid time off for holidays, paid vacation time, flexible work schedule, tuition reimbursement, and childcare.

FLEXIBLE BENEFIT PROGRAMS

Flexible benefits are programs offered by an employer that enable an employee to select and create their own customized benefits based on their preferences. In recent years, employees have come to expect benefits that promote work-life balance and support families. To that end, an increasing number of employers offer telecommuting, flex time, and compressed work week options to help workers juggle all of life's different demands. In addition, many workplaces now offer benefits like paid parental leave and designated lactation rooms, making it easier on new parents. Additionally, some employers have started offering paid caregiver leave, which allows workers to care for parents and other relatives without worrying about their paychecks. Small and large businesses alike recognize that flexible benefits are necessary to remain competitive in the marketplace.

PENSIONS OR RETIREMENT PLANS

Pensions and company retirement plans fund an individual's retirement by providing deferred payments for prior services. These accounts may be funded by the employer through a variety of means. Retirement benefits are accumulated by the total amount contributed plus interest and market earnings. These defined contribution benefit plans are the traditional company-provided plans, such as 401(k)s, 403(b)s, simplified employee pensions (SEPs), SIMPLEs, and IRAs. A defined contribution benefit plan requires separate accounts for each employee participant, and funds are most often contributed by both the employee and the employer.

Some employers will implement an auto-enroll policy in which new employees are automatically enrolled and minimum contributions to the plan are withheld from payroll. The contribution rates may even automatically increase on an annual basis. However, the Pension Protection Act of 2006 provides employees with a 90-day window to opt out of these plans and recover any funds contributed on their behalf.

EMPLOYEE STOCK OWNERSHIP PLANS (ESOPS)

An **employee stock ownership plan** (ESOP) is created by establishing a trust into which the business makes contributions of cash or stock that are tax deductible. Employees are then granted the ability to purchase stock or allocate funds into individual employee accounts. The stock is held in an **employee stock ownership trust** (ESOT), and the business can make regular contributions, typically up to 25 percent of its annual payroll. ESOPs became popular because it is believed that employees who have an ownership interest in the business will work more diligently and also have a vested interest in its efficiency and profitability. Although this logic is debatable, many studies have shown that ESOPs do motivate employees and support business growth.

MEDICARE

Medicare, established in 1965 as an amendment to the Social Security Act of 1935, is healthcare coverage primarily for people 65 years of age or older. Medicare is not dependent on income levels and is also available to individuals under age 65 who are disabled. Employers and employees contribute a percentage of salaries to fund Medicare. There are four types of Medicare coverage:

- Medicare **Part A**: This free coverage is considered mandatory for basic hospital coverage.
- Medicare **Part B**: Optional and additional medical insurance coverage for eligible individuals who pay a monthly fee.
- Medicare **Part C**: Additional healthcare coverage available to those people who qualify for Part A and enrolled in Part B. Typically called Medicare Advantage Plans, Part C provides expanded coverage such as dental, vision, and hearing. There is a fee to enroll in these plans.
- Medicare **Part D**: Prescription drug coverage available to those people who qualify for Part A and are enrolled in Part B. There is a monthly fee associated with this coverage.

> **Review Video: <u>Medicare & Medicaid</u>**
> Visit mometrix.com/academy and enter code: 507454

SOCIAL SECURITY

The Social Security Act was first implemented to force workers into saving a fraction of earnings for retirement and to require employers to match those funds. These funds are now withheld as a portion of the **Federal Insurance Contributions Act (FICA) payroll taxes** and regulated by the IRS. The benefits have since been extended to cover four types of insurance benefits:

- **Old age or disability benefits**—For workers who retire or become unable to work due to disability; based upon eligibility requirements
- Benefits for dependents of retired, disabled, or deceased workers—Paid to certain dependents
- **Lump-sum death benefits**—Paid to the worker's survivors
- **Medicare**—Healthcare protection provided to individuals age 65 and older, consisting of Parts A, B, and D

MANAGED CARE HEALTHCARE PLANS

Employers usually provide managed care healthcare plans, which are defined as care that ensures an individual receives appropriate and necessary treatment in the most cost-efficient manner possible. There are many forms of healthcare insurance plans, and the increasing cost of insurance has forced employers to absorb additional costs, pass more costs to employees, or find affordable alternatives.

- **Fee-for-service plans** allow employees to decide what services they need from any provider; fees are paid by both the employee and the employee's benefits plan through deductibles and coinsurance.
- **Preferred provider organization (PPO) plans** allow insurers to contract with providers of the employees' choosing, with lower fees and better coverage for providers within the organization; fees are paid by deductibles, coinsurance, and co-payments.
- **Health maintenance organization (HMO) plans** emphasize preventative care through fixed costs regardless of the number of visits, but primary care physicians (PCPs) must refer others, and no other providers are covered; fees are paid by deductibles, coinsurance, and co-payments.

- **Point of service (POS) plans** are similar to PPO plans, with certain elements (PCP referrals) of HMO plans; fees are paid by deductibles, coinsurance, and co-payments.
- **Exclusive provider organization (EPO)** is a plan whereby no payments or coverage will be made unless the individual uses a provider within the network of coverage.
- **Consumer-directed health plans** provide tax-favored accounts, such as a flexible spending account (FSA) or a health savings account (HSA), to pay for medical expenses and may allow employees to see any provider of their choosing. However, these plans carry high deductibles and may have low or no coinsurance after the deductible is reached.

CAFETERIA PLANS

Section 125 of the Internal Revenue Code defines a **cafeteria plan** as an employer plan providing participants the opportunity to receive certain benefits on a pretax basis. Funds allocated to these benefits are not included as wages for state or federal income tax purposes and are generally exempt from the Federal Insurance Contributions Act (FICA) and Federal Unemployment Tax Act (FUTA). Unused benefit credits can sometimes be reallocated by the employee to buy more benefits through pretax salary reductions, or the employee may end up losing the unused monies. An employer-sponsored cafeteria plan enables the employee to pick and choose benefits based on their preferences. (This idea of an employee choosing their benefits, like a customer choosing food at a cafeteria, gives cafeteria plans their name; they have nothing to do with actual cafeterias.)

Qualified benefits under these plans might include the following:

- **Medical healthcare coverage**—Plans may include some or all portions of physician services, office visits and exams, prescription drugs, hospital services, maternity services, mental health, physical therapy, and emergency services.
- **Dental coverage**—Plans may include some or all portions of routine exams, cleanings, x-rays, fluoride treatments, orthodontic services, fillings, crowns, and extractions.
- **Dependent care**—Plans may cover some or all portions of on-site childcare, allowances and flexible spending for childcare, daycare information, or flexible scheduling.
- **Short-term disability**—This provides partial income continuation to employees who are unable to work for a short period of time due to an accident or illness. "Short-term" is usually defined as three to six months.
- **Long-term disability**—This provides partial income continuation to employees who are unable to work for long periods of time due to an accident or illness. "Long-term" is usually defined as over six months.
- **Group-term life insurance and accidental death or dismemberment**—This provides financial assistance to an employee or their beneficiaries if the employee has an accident that results in loss of limbs, loss of eyesight, or death. The cost of group plans is frequently lower than individual plans, and payments are based upon the employee's age and annual salary.

WELLNESS PROGRAMS

Employer-sponsored **wellness programs** are implemented for three primary purposes: (1) to assist employees in improving their health in an effort to prevent serious health problems, (2) to help employers offset the expense of increasing healthcare costs, and (3) to improve employers' overall benefit offerings to remain competitive for attracting and retaining talent. Wellness programs indicate that employers are investing in their employees' health and well-being. Some companies create awareness about the available programs by encouraging employees to participate in a voluntary health assessment or screening as an impetus to encourage healthy lifestyle changes. Employers benefit from these changes through decreased absenteeism, decreased healthcare spending, higher employee morale, and improved productivity. Wellness programs can vary tremendously and may include personalized one-on-one health coaching, nutritional counseling, well-being workshops, healthy snacks at work, stress reduction programs, and fitness activities. Some employers will give monetary incentives to encourage participation in wellness programs.

BENEFITS ENROLLMENT

Employers generally make their benefits packages available to full-time employees; some organizations also extend benefits eligibility to part-time employees.

- Some companies allow employees to enroll in benefits at the very beginning of their employment, while others require employees to work for a period of time, such as 30 or 60 days, before becoming eligible for benefits.
- Employees are able to change their benefits elections each year during annual enrollment, which is also referred to as open enrollment. Annual enrollment usually takes place in the fall, with new benefits elections taking effect on January 1.
- Employees who experience a qualifying event, such as losing eligibility for other coverage, getting married, or becoming a parent, may add or remove coverage or dependents outside of open enrollment.

In addition to providing access to group benefit plans, an employer may cover part or all of the cost of some benefits programs for employees; some companies offset the cost of benefits for dependents as well. Company contributions can add significantly to the value of a company's overall compensation, which is often referred to as total rewards.

HEALTH INSURANCE

Health insurance is a very important aspect of a company's benefits package. Employers often pay a portion of employees' health insurance premiums. Some pay the full cost of employee coverage, as well as a portion of the cost for dependent coverage.

Employees don't all have the same needs when it comes to health insurance, so companies often offer multiple plans, with premiums at varying levels. This is to the advantage of the company and its employees alike.

- Employers with 50 or more employees should offer at least one health plan that meets the affordability requirement of the Patient Protection and Affordable Care Act (PPACA) in order to avoid costly penalties.
- Limiting health insurance options to only the plans that meet the affordability requirement of the PPACA would mean that employees wouldn't have access to health plans that offer higher levels of coverage.
- By offering varying levels of coverage at different price points, an employer is providing choices for employees. This helps employees find the right balance between services and cost, letting them get a level of coverage that meets their needs at a price they can pay. It also helps an employer compete for talent with other companies with robust health insurance offerings.

PREFERRED PROVIDER ORGANIZATIONS AND HIGH-DEDUCTIBLE HEALTH PLANS

It has become common practice for employers to offer both a **preferred provider organization (PPO)** plan and a **high-deductible health plan (HDHP)**.

Preferred Provider Organization (PPO)	High-Deductible Health Plan (HDHP)
Higher monthly premiums	Lower monthly premiums
Lower deductible	Higher deductible
Co-pay applies to office visits and prescriptions (rather than full fee) before deductible has been met	Individual pays 100% of costs until deductible has been met
Coinsurance percentage applies after deductible has been met (such as 80% paid by insurance, 20% paid by employee) until out-of-pocket maximum is met	Insurance policy pays all covered costs, once the deductible has been met
May require using an in-network provider or facility; if out-of-network is allowed, fees will be higher than in-network	May require using an in-network provider or facility; if out-of-network is allowed, fees will be higher than in-network
Generally best for people whose primary concern is to minimize out-of-pocket expenses for office visits or prescriptions while also having coverage for major medical events.	Generally best for healthy people who rarely seek medical care or for those who are likely to reach their deductible very early in the plan year, as the policy covers after that point.
Cannot be combined with a health savings account.	Can be combined with a health savings account.

HEALTHCARE ACCOUNTS

Healthcare options offered by employers have shifted in recent years to a more "consumer-directed" initiative in order for employers to reduce costs and allow employees to choose or customize their healthcare spending. As a result of this shift, employer healthcare options tend to be high-deductible plans. For example, an individual employee could have a deductible of $3,000 and a family deductible of $6,000. This means that the employee must pay the deductible out of pocket before medical insurance begins to pay. This is frequently a burden for employees, so many employers have created and administer programs to help offset the employee expense.

MEDICAL COSTS AND CONTRIBUTION LIMITS

Eligible medical care expenses are defined by the IRS and include costs that relate to disease deterrence, diagnosis, or treatment. The costs of procedures undertaken for solely cosmetic reasons are generally not considered expenses for medical care and are not reimbursable. Expenses ineligible under an FSA include procedures and services such as liposuction, Botox treatments, contact lenses, and personal trainers. Eligible expenses do, however, include things like service or guide animals and acupuncture. Employees can also open dependent care FSAs, which allow them to use pretax dollars to pay for dependent care, like daycare.

The IRS determines FSA contribution limits annually. The main drawback to the FSA is that it requires careful budgeting because there is a use-it-or-lose-it provision attached to the benefit. If employees do not use the funds within an account during the given plan year, they may lose the money. Exceptions to this are when the employer opts to offer a grace period, granting an additional 2.5 months to use the funds, or a carryover provision, which is limited to $500.

Employers are not required to offer either and can offer only one of the two. They may also offer a run-out period, which gives employees an additional 90 days to make claims for reimbursement.

Health Savings Account (HSA)	Health Reimbursement Account (HRA)	Flexible Spending Account (FSA)
Requires enrollment in a high-deductible health plan (HDHP)	Some HRAs require a health insurance plan; some do not	Does not require participation in a health insurance plan
Can be funded by employer and/or employee	Funded solely by the employer	Can be funded by employee and/or employer
Contribution can be changed at any time	Employer sets contribution rules	Contribution can be changed at annual enrollment or with a qualifying event
Employee owns the account	Employer owns the account	Employer owns the account
Account is portable; it will stay with the employee after separation of employment	Account is not portable; it will not follow the employee after separation of employment	Account is not portable; it will not follow the employee after separation of employment
Use for qualifying medical expenses	Use for qualifying medical expenses	Use for qualifying medical, vision, dental, and dependent care expenses
Funds do not expire	Employer sets rules for expiration/rollover	Funds expire if not used; limited rollover may be possible

Employees are generally eligible to enroll in an HSA, HRA, or FSA when they become eligible for benefits with their employer or during annual enrollment.

DISABILITY INSURANCE

Health coverage and healthcare accounts help offset the cost of seeking medical care, but they don't provide income replacement for employees who become unable to work due to illness or injury. That's why short-term disability and long-term disability insurance are often included in employee benefits packages.

Disability insurance policies don't provide full income replacement, but they do provide covered employees with a percentage of their ordinary income for a set period of time when they are unable to work due to illness, injury, or other disability.

In a few states, including (but not limited to) California, New Jersey, and New York, employers are required to provide short-term disability insurance to their employees. Most states don't require employers to provide—or even offer—disability insurance, but it is very common for employers to offer both types of coverage to employees.

Some employers pay for a level of coverage and allow employees to purchase additional protection if they want, while others do not offset the cost of disability insurance. Even in that case, it is usually more affordable for employees to sign up for disability coverage available via their employer than to purchase it on their own, because group plans tend to be less costly than individual coverage.

SHORT-TERM DISABILITY (STD)

Short-term disability (STD) insurance provides partial income for a short time, usually between three and six months (depending on the policy). Some STD policies provide coverage from the first day of disability, while others have an elimination period of a few weeks.

LONG-TERM DISABILITY (LTD)

Long-term disability (LTD) is intended to extend income protection beyond the time covered by a company's STD policy, with the length of coverage varying greatly by policy. Most plans provide coverage for a set number of years; some may last until retirement age. This type of policy usually has an elimination period of at least 90 days, though it can be as long as six months.

BENEFIT BROKERS

A **benefit broker** is an external vendor that assists an organization in navigating employee benefit options that are cost-effective and tailored to an organization's needs. Benefit options may include health, dental, vision, financial, and more.

Not all brokers are the same. For example, some might work for a large provider and therefore only offer choices that particular providers offer—think of a large insurance company with only four options for medical insurance to choose from. Others may only specialize in one type of benefit, such as vision. Additionally, some may have a sizable amount of different benefit options in a variety of specialties, but may or may not have extensive knowledge across all benefit offerings. Generally, benefit brokers supply expertise on some or all of the following common offerings:

- Forms of insurance—Most benefit brokers offer some form of insurance, such as medical, dental, vision, disability, and life.
- Compliance expertise—The broker counsels organizations on benefits to stay in compliance with federal laws, including the Employee Retirement Income Security Act (ERISA), Affordable Care Act (ACA), and specific state and local laws and regulations.
- Overall benefit analysis—This could include cost efficiencies, examination of potential changes based on laws or changing environments, and analysis of existing benefits and related claims.
- Direct employee assistance—This assistance could include direct communication with employees about benefits regarding coverage, claim questions, etc. Additionally, they could provide assistance with enrollment and offer training sessions about benefit options.

Benefit broker fees are usually contingent on the type of coverages and services offered. However, there are others that charge a flat fee based on specific services and offerings.

Supplemental Wellness and Fringe Benefits

Many companies offer supplemental benefits beyond health and disability coverage. Most companies that offer employee benefits include standard offerings like dental and vision insurance, as well as at least a basic level of life insurance.

Recognizing that offering additional benefits can boost the value of their total rewards package, employers seeking to gain competitive advantage when it comes to recruiting and retaining employees often choose to go above and beyond standard supplemental benefits.

Popular supplemental benefits offerings include the following.

EMPLOYEE ASSISTANCE PROGRAMS (EAPs)

An **employee assistance program** (EAP) is a program sponsored by an employer that provides confidential counseling services to help employees manage all types of stressful life situations or problems. Because it is sponsored by the employer, an EAP is free to employees. The service is confidential, meaning the employer is not aware of the employee's usage. This confidentiality is primarily due to Health Insurance Portability and Accountability Act (HIPAA) regulations, meaning complete confidentiality is maintained with the third-party vendor contracted to provide the counseling.

An EAP is designed to help the employee, which in turn allows them to be more productive at work. EAP services can vary, but typically include mental health issues, family problems, financial concerns, legal issues, and substance abuse. Usually, the program provides guidance and professional referrals to resources that can help the employee on a short- or long-term basis.

GYM MEMBERSHIPS

Healthy employees tend to be productive employees who are less at risk for on-the-job injury than others, so it makes sense for a company to offer benefits that help employees get and stay as healthy as possible. That's why gym memberships are such a popular component of employee benefits programs.

Employers often sign up for corporate discount programs with local gyms or nationwide fitness networks, as doing so makes it possible for employees to join at a reduced rate and pay via payroll deduction. Some companies even cover all or part of the cost of gym memberships for employees who opt to participate.

HOUSING OR RELOCATION ASSISTANCE

When an employer hires an employee for a job that requires the individual to relocate, the company may offer a relocation assistance program to the employee and their family. Relocation packages vary greatly, but usually include covering the cost of packing up and moving personal belongings and the cost of transporting the employee and their family to where they will be living.

Relocation benefits may also cover additional moving-related costs, such as fees associated with selling a house or breaking a lease, traveling to look for housing prior to the move, temporary housing assistance for a set time at the beginning of the individual's employment, and storage of personal items until a place of residence is secured.

TRAVEL OR TRANSPORTATION STIPENDS

Recognizing that commuting and/or parking can be a significant expense for employees, some employers include benefits designed to help offset such costs in their benefits package. Some companies provide commuting stipends or reimbursement for parking expenses, the use of public transportation (such as subways or buses), or rideshare programs.

Additionally, some employers offer special travel/transportation stipends to employees who commute a long distance to work. For example, a company may provide a per diem to employees who drive more than a certain number of miles or who live outside the county where the company is located. This may be based on what county or state the employee drives in from, or the specific number of miles between an employee's home and the worksite.

Retirement Plans

Retirement plans are an important component of an employee benefits plan. Offering a retirement plan boosts the value of a company's overall compensation plan and helps the organization attract and retain talent. Having access to a workplace retirement plan helps employees save money for retirement via pretax payroll deductions.

PLAN TYPES: 401(K) VS. 457(B)

There are a few different types of retirement programs that a company can offer, with 401(k) and 457(b) being among the most common. Only state and local governments and nonprofit organizations can participate in 457(b) plans. Private-sector employers typically offer 401(k) plans.

Requirements for 401(k) and 457(b) plans are similar, with a few key differences because 401(k) plans are governed by the Employee Retirement Income Security Act (ERISA) and 457(b) plans are not. Because 401(k) plans fall under ERISA, they are considered qualified plans, while 457(b) plans are considered nonqualified. Both offer tax benefits, with 457(b) plans providing greater flexibility.

	401(K)	457(B)
Employer Type	Private-sector employers	State and local governments, nonprofit organizations
Eligibility	Employees only; must be offered to all employees once they reach 1,000 hours of service	Open to employees and independent contractors; does not have to be offered to all employees/contractors
Automatic Enrollment	Permitted	Permitted
Employee Contributions	Permitted	Permitted
Employer Contributions	Permitted	Permitted
Catch-Up Contributions (employees 50+)	Permitted	Permitted
Written Plan Document	Required	Required
Hardship Withdrawals	Permitted	Permitted
Pretax contributions	Permitted; taxable upon withdrawal	Permitted; taxable upon withdrawal
Post-tax (Roth) contributions	Permitted; not taxable upon withdrawal	Permitted; not taxable upon withdrawal
Withdraw without penalty	After age $59\frac{1}{2}$	Upon leaving employer

In addition to being able to offer 457(b) plans, nonprofit organizations and certain governmental entities can offer 403(b) plans. This type of plan does fall under ERISA and largely mirrors 401(k) plans (except for the types of organizations that can participate).

Wage Statements and Payroll Processing

Payroll is an important function that is usually housed in the HR or accounting department. No matter which of these two departments has the primary responsibility for processing payroll, they have to coordinate. After all, payroll involves critical accounting matters, such as money and tax withholdings/filings, as well as critical HR matters, such as wage and hour compliance, benefits payments, and more.

PAYROLL PROCESSES

Payroll processing is a system that an employer utilizes to manage the payment of wages to its employees. Payroll processing is more than just issuing a paycheck. There are other components that need to be addressed, such as legal compliance with all federal, state, and local laws and regulations, including reporting requirements; the time period for record retention of information; and all aspects of control and security. Generally, the major steps involved in payroll processing include gathering the time worked per employee for a designated time period, calculating and applying cost of benefits and deductions, distributing paychecks (direct deposit or paper check), and following retention procedures. The employer must then file and remit payroll taxes. An organization can face expensive penalties if payroll taxes are not accurate and on time. Most organizations use payroll software or outsource to a third-party payroll processing service.

INFORMATION NEEDED TO PROCESS A PAYROLL

There are many documents and information needed to process a payroll. They include but are not limited to the following:

- Completed **W-4** form (for employees)—This form is completed by an employee before or on their first day of work. It documents employee withholding information needed so that the employer can deduct the correct amount of federal income tax from their wages.
- Completed **I-9** form—This form is for employment eligibility verification, and must be completed by an employee's first day of work. It requires showing the employer a combination of identification documents that prove they can legally work in the US.
- **Job application**—This contains consistent, detailed information about an employee such as name, address, education, and dates of employment, which are used to enter information into a payroll system.
- **Bank account information**—This is usually used by an employer to directly deposit an employee's pay into their bank account(s).
- **Medical insurance** form—This form details the amount to be deducted from an employee's pay and their permission for the deduction (usually requires a signature).
- **Retirement plan** form—This form details the amount being deducted for various retirement plan options. As with medical insurance, an employee signature is required for an employer to deduct from an employee's pay.

PAYROLL CYCLE

A **payroll cycle** or schedule refers to the frequency that an employer issues pay to an employee. The most common cycle is biweekly, or every other week, for a total of 26 paychecks per year. However, an organization could also offer a weekly cycle, meaning 52 paychecks a year; or possibly a monthly cycle, with 12 paychecks a year; etc. An organization can choose their payroll schedule as long as it is in compliance with all federal, state, and local laws and regulations. Many states require employers to pay their employees biweekly, others have more specific requirements, and some have no specified schedules. However, an organization must also consider what the employees would prefer. Most employees prefer to get paid more frequently as compared to less frequently, especially those employees earning low wages. Employers must also weigh the cost of processing payroll more frequently, because it will cost more. An organization must decide and communicate a consistent payroll schedule.

PAYROLL POLICY

A payroll policy is a set of guidelines and protocols established to ensure that payroll is accurate, processed on time, and conducted with strict adherence to all payroll laws and regulations.

- To comply with the Fair Labor Standards Act (FLSA), a **standard work week** needs to be defined and usually constitutes seven consecutive 24-hour periods. A work week doesn't have to start on Monday, but can begin on any day of the week.
- There should be a system in place, electronic or paper, to **accurately record employee hours** worked, with an approval process to verify the information is correct. State laws and regulations may require employers to give breaks from work for rest, meals, etc., after a given number of hours worked. These breaks also need to be reflected in total hours worked.
- **Overtime hours** must also be outlined, including who is eligible and how much they will be paid for hours worked over 40 in one work week. Overtime is usually paid at a rate of one and one-half times the regular pay rate per hour. However, this can vary from state to state—usually in favor of the employee receiving more wages.
- **How often employees are paid** should be detailed—whether biweekly, weekly, monthly, etc.—and what days they will receive their pay.
- A **payroll policy** should also explain deductions: mandatory deductions, such as Social Security and other taxes, and voluntary deductions, like health insurance and retirement plans. In addition, it should give further explanation of pre- and post-tax information. All the different wage structures should be explained, such as hourly pay, salary, bonuses, commission, and stock options.
- Finally, all time periods for **payroll recordkeeping** should be documented, as well as applicable security measures.

GROSS PAY

Payroll starts with gross pay, which is the total amount an employee has earned during the pay period. This includes salary for exempt employees, as well as straight-time and overtime earnings for nonexempt employees. Gross pay must include base pay and additional pay owed to employees, such as shift differentials for working a challenging shift or hazardous assignment, as well as other compensation such as incentive compensation or bonuses.

TAXATION

When processing payroll, it's very important to properly deduct taxes from each employee's compensation, including federal income tax; Federal Insurance Contributions Act (FICA) tax, which funds Social Security and Medicare; and any applicable state or local taxes that an employer is required to withhold. Tax withholdings must be paid to appropriate government agencies, and appropriate paperwork must be submitted in the required time frame (which varies based on the type of tax and agency).

An employer must also keep track of, properly file, and report company-paid taxes. For example, the company makes FICA contributions in addition to what employees themselves pay. The employer also has to pay Federal Unemployment Tax Act (FUTA) and state unemployment insurance (SUI) premiums.

DEDUCTIONS

Processing payroll involves making sure that deductions are properly withheld from each employee's paycheck. This involves a lot more than just making sure that an employee's tax deductions are correct. Employees may pay for a number of items via payroll deduction, including voluntary deductions for employee benefits, mandatory deductions such as income tax, and—in some cases—other financial obligations.

MANDATORY DEDUCTIONS

In addition to payroll taxes, mandatory deductions may include things like court-ordered child support or alimony, as well as wage garnishments for unpaid debts, payments ordered due to bankruptcy, or unpaid income tax. An employer is obligated to withhold mandatory deductions and submit the funds to the organization or agency specified on the court order or judgment received. Most states allow employers to charge employees a small fee (generally between $1 and $5) for each garnishment, to offset the administrative burden of processing them. This fee would also be withheld as a deduction.

VOLUNTARY DEDUCTIONS

The most common voluntary deductions include benefits premiums paid by the employee; contributions to a health savings account (HSA), health reimbursement account (HRA), and/or flexible spending account (FSA); and contributions to an employer-sponsored retirement plan.

Employees may authorize other voluntary deductions, such as:

- Contributions to a charitable organization
- Payment for on-site parking at the workplace
- Gym membership fees as part of a corporate membership
- Other programs for which the company allows payroll deduction

LEAVE REPORTING

Wage statements also include information about employee leave, including how much paid time off (PTO), vacation time, or sick leave an employee currently has available to use, and how much (if any) of each type of leave the employee used during the current pay period. Wage statements may also show how much leave an employee has used so far in the current year.

An employer may also show other types of leave on wage statements, including Family and Medical Leave (FML) or leaves of absence for personal or other reasons. Reporting leave on wage statements helps employees know where they stand in terms of their accrued leave at any given time.

PAID TIME OFF

Employees will need to take time off from work to attend to various life circumstances and events. There is no simple formula for an organization to follow when developing guidelines for PTO. PTO varies tremendously from one organization to another, and much depends on the needs of the business as well as what employees need. Furthermore, PTO must comply with all federal, state, and local laws and regulations. Some organizations, like the federal government, have rigid guidelines; others have looser, almost employee-determined PTO days. For instance, some companies might give employees 12 vacation days, 6 sick days, 3 bereavement days, and 10 holidays, then let the employee choose and categorize their PTO days. A PTO policy usually states the guidelines and processes for an employee to request PTO and obtain necessary approvals.

EXAMPLES

There are many categories for PTO. The following are some common examples:

- **Personal** time—Time off to attend to various life activities.
- **Sick** time—Time off for personal illness, injury, or general medical care. Sick time may also be covered under the Family and Medical Leave Act, ADA, short- and long-term disability, or workers' compensation.
- **Vacation** time—Time off from work for recreation or fun.
- **Holidays**—Time off to celebrate recognized holidays.
- **Floating holidays**—Time off to celebrate holidays that might not be recognized by the organization.
- **Bereavement**—Time off due to a death in the employee's immediate family. Some organizations even have bereavement PTO days for the death of a pet.
- **Jury duty**—Time off from work for compulsory jury duty.
- **Compensatory (comp)** time—Credited time off from work for eligible employees who would prefer time off instead of payment. Not all employees are eligible for comp time because FLSA mandates that all nonexempt workers must be compensated for time worked, both standard and overtime.
- **Maternity and paternity** leave—Time off following the birth or adoption of a child.
- **Military** leave—Time off for military service obligations. Includes the US Armed Forces, the National Guard, and state defense forces. The Uniformed Services Employment and Reemployment Rights Act (USERRA) provides certain job protections, and employers also frequently offer a supplement to offset the difference between regular pay and military pay.

UNPAID LEAVE

Unpaid leave is time off from work that is approved by the employer, but not compensated in any way. There are many reasons an employee may need to take unpaid leave. Every employee request and situation must be carefully considered by an employer to make sure it is consistent with organizational policy and legally compliant with all federal, state, and local laws and regulations. If an employee is requesting unpaid leave under the parameters of the Family and Medical Leave Act (FMLA), then the employee's unpaid leave is mandatory, and the employee is guaranteed to keep their job and benefits upon returning to work. An unpaid leave of absence can also occur when an employee has used up all of their paid time off. Assuming the request does not have to be granted under federal, state, or local laws and regulations, it is up to the employer's discretion and policies.

In some instances, the employer can also force an employee to take unpaid leave if the workplace does not have enough work, a practice sometimes referred to as a **furlough**. During a furlough, employees typically have access to benefits. Furloughs are sometimes implemented to avoid a staff reduction such as layoffs. Another example of when employees could be furloughed is when coming to work is temporarily unsafe, like during a national pandemic. Paying or not paying employees during such a furlough is up to the employer's discretion and is dependent on many other factors.

FINAL PAY

The final paycheck for an employee who is exiting the company should include all compensation owed to that employee, including their final salary or wages, any commissions or incentives owed to them, and the payout for any accrued paid leave due to them per company policy.

Regulations regarding final pay vary by state. In some states, the final paycheck can be issued with the next regular payroll cycle, such that the employee receives the check at the same time they would have gotten it if they were continuing to work for the company. However, in some places, an employee must be given their final paycheck on the last day they work for the company.

TOTAL REWARDS STATEMENTS

A total rewards statement is a document that shows the full value of an employee's compensation, which is usually much higher than the actual wages or salary paid to an employee. Employers are not required to produce this kind of statement, but it is considered best practice to periodically provide each employee with an individualized total rewards statement. Many organizations provide employees with a total rewards statement annually; some do so quarterly or even monthly.

Why should an employer consider producing yet another statement to share with employees? Because employees tend to think about their pay solely in terms of their hourly rate of pay or their monthly or annual salary. However, that's only part of the true value of their compensation. A total rewards statement shows the full value, including what the employer pays above and beyond the rate of pay, such as employer benefits contributions, FICA payments (employees pay half; employers pay half), unemployment insurance, retirement plan contributions, and more.

When employees see all of this summed up in a single statement, this helps to clarify the full value of their total rewards package above and beyond their pay rate. Having this information can contribute positively to employee satisfaction and retention. After all, the more that employees know about the full picture of their compensation, the less likely they are to consider leaving their current employer for a small difference in pay; at least, they should know the full picture of how another employer's offer compares with the total value of their current position. Often, a marginally higher pay rate is worth less when other factors are taken into consideration.

Employee Relations

Mission, Vision, and Values Statements

VISION STATEMENTS

A **vision statement** provides a concise assertion that captures what the leadership team foresees as the future of the organization. This long-term, result-driven declaration serves as a guiding, inspirational force for the organization. A vision statement is aspirational and usually contains several of the following key elements: it is inspirational, it is future-oriented, it captures the organization's culture, and it strives to articulate its benefits in the future. Here are a few examples of notable organizations and their vision statements:

- Disney—"To make people happy."
- Ben & Jerry's—"Making the best ice cream in the nicest possible way."
- Apple—"We believe that we are on the face of the earth to make great products and that's not changing."
- TED—"Spread ideas."

A vision statement is vital for the planning and execution of organizational strategies. As an organization grows and evolves, a vision statement might be altered over time.

MISSION STATEMENTS

A **mission statement** describes an organization's purpose and the activities an organization will pursue to achieve its vision. This declaration is designed to offer three basic elements: (1) an overall description of who the company is, (2) a description of what the company does, and (3) an explanation of why the company exists. The statement also serves as a communication tool explaining, at a high level, how an organization will achieve its goals with its customers, its employees, and all other stakeholders. A mission statement also explains to suppliers, customers, and clients why they should want to do business with an organization. In fact, organizations frequently use their mission statement theme in advertising and marketing collateral. A mission statement could also be thought of as the guiding force of an organization's operating manual, helping employees and other stakeholders better understand its central purpose. A mission statement might be altered over time as an organization grows and evolves.

VISION VS. MISSION STATEMENTS

A vision statement and mission statement are essential components of an organization's strategic planning process. They both help the organization directionally prepare for the future and achieve its goals. However, a mission statement highlights what the organization is currently doing, while a vision statement highlights what the organization strives to achieve in the future. As such, a mission statement is more short-term, usually one to three years, detailing the organization's purpose and current activities. A vision statement, on the other hand, is a long-term declaration that is more inspirational, highlighting the organization's hope for the future. Additionally, a vision statement is directional and may or may not be crystal-clear about what the future state will look like. In contrast, a mission statement is crystal-clear in its goals, objectives, and desired performance for successful achievement. A vision statement can only be achieved if the mission statement is successfully implemented.

ORGANIZATIONAL VALUES

Values are part of an organization's strategic plan and define what is important to a particular business. Organizational values are frequently referred to as the "heart" of the organization, helping form the culture and playing a significant role in directing employee behavior. Some organizations choose to document their values and include them with their vision and mission statements. In other organizations, values are more informal and/or unwritten. Organizational values help drive decision making in the organization and ultimately signify what it stands for. These values serve as a filter, defining how organizational tasks should be accomplished. When organizational values and employee behavior are not in sync, conflict can develop, causing negative consequences and possibly interfering with the achievement of strategic goals. Values should be understood by all employees and serve to enhance employee contributions and commitment to the organization.

ORGANIZATIONAL CULTURE
PURPOSE OF ORGANIZATIONAL CULTURE

Organizational culture is the way activities are accomplished. It is a tone set by leaders for everyone in the organization to share basic beliefs that support an overall direction and strategy. Employees play a pivotal role in achieving organizational goals by behaving in a certain way, knowing they will be rewarded for displaying the organization's values. Organizational culture is the foundation that drives how an organization operates. It is often referred to as the force behind an organization's mission attainment and success. There is no specific model or formula to develop a culture. A robust culture is grounded in shared beliefs and common goals and is supported by strategies and processes in an organization. However, it is often challenging to define an organization's specific culture. Some keywords that might capture an organization's culture include: family-oriented, innovative, customer-focused, motivating, fast-paced, rewarding, ethical, fun, technology-driven, inclusive.

CONNECTION BETWEEN STRONG ORGANIZATIONAL CULTURE AND SUCCESS

In order to sustain a strong culture, an organization's values and beliefs must be shared and adhered to by every employee. Maintaining a strong sense of culture can lead to enhanced collaboration among employees and more efficient decision making, and can ultimately drive competitive advantage—all of which contribute to making an organization successful. In other words, behavior is supported or justified by the common denominator of a culture developed by organizational leaders and driven by leaders and employees into all aspects of work. All members in an organization have the framework of culture to guide their behavior and act as an informal control system. Often, an ineffective culture can lead to employee disengagement, high employee turnover, poor customer relationships, and loss of revenue and business. For some enterprises, culture has been a significant factor in their ability to implement strategies and successfully execute the mission statement.

HR AS CARETAKER OF ORGANIZATIONAL CULTURE

One of the most important assets of an organization is its people. HR plays an essential role in ensuring that an organization's culture is built and cultivated in order to gain or maintain a competitive advantage. HR must work with leaders not only to understand strategic direction and monetary goals, but also to influence leaders by showing them how an organization's culture can drive the achievement of these priorities. HR can influence this by doing the following:

- Communicating and reinforcing an organization's values
- Building and maintaining communication and continuous feedback
- Ensuring ethical standards are defined, understood, and practiced

- Providing professional development and training
- Defining roles and responsibilities for employees
- Developing and maintaining a recognition and/or rewards system
- Observing and recognizing organizational and specific employee relations problems, and facilitating solutions
- Motivating employees in order to maintain job satisfaction
- Establishing external professional relationships that benefit the organization

UNWRITTEN CULTURE

Mission and vision statements are literally documented with specific words. However, an organization's culture is about behavior and what is observed, heard, and felt—in other words, it is unwritten. Culture is about the degree to which an organization subscribes to or pursues its mission, be it aggressively or slow and steady; about the value placed on people and their work-life balance; or about the hierarchy of the organizational structure. Some unwritten cultural cues could include dress code, size or location of offices, open doors, hallway or breakroom conversations, friendliness, laughter, or facial expressions. Unwritten rules are simply the way an organization operates, and are deep-rooted in its culture. Other unwritten rules are operational and can easily be learned by observation. For example, in some organizations, employees feel it is in their best interest to always agree with the organization's leaders or else possibly face negative consequences. Other organizations may encourage open and honest feedback with company leaders and reward new or alternative ideas. Employees usually learn to adapt and alter their behavior based on observations.

CONNECTION BETWEEN TRADITION AND ORGANIZATIONAL CULTURE

Usually, an organization's culture is based on factors that contributed to its success in the past, and thus became tradition. In its early stages, an organization's leaders play a significant role in establishing its culture, thereby planting the seeds of behavioral norms that are closely aligned with their values. These norms will blossom and grow over time to become tradition, shaping an organization's culture. Tradition, when embedded in an organization's culture, can take many forms. How conflicts are resolved—whether respectfully, quietly, privately, or perhaps in the open with raised voices—serves as an example of culture. Decision making is another example; one organization might make all decisions in a hierarchical manner, while another organization might have a more ad hoc decision-making process. "Culture" is an all-encompassing term that includes beliefs and an organization's traditions that are passed down over time. HR should be aware of an organization's traditions and their positive or negative impacts on the organization.

THE INFLUENCE OF MISSION, VISION, AND VALUES STATEMENTS

The mission/vision/values statements of an organization serve many purposes, but primarily they serve as the heart of the organization and its guiding principles. If an organization is dedicated to equity and diversity, those elements will be present in all aspects of the workplace, from hiring to advertising to sourcing. Equity and diversity would not exist merely as enrichment programs or feel-good declarations. These statements would define what the organization stands for and how people within that organization are expected to behave.

When organizational behavior embodies the statements listed in the values, vision, or mission, the influence on the company culture is undeniable. Employees feel as though the organization has followed through, and it stands for what it says. There truly is support and buy-in from the top down. These principles help individuals, teams, and departments to collaborate to meet a common purpose, facilitating a culture of support and teamwork. When the workforce is aligned with and inspired by these principles, it can lead to greater employee engagement and motivation toward achieving goals and objectives. These statements influence how employees feel about the organization, and how they communicate about the organization to others.

When a company fails to live by the guiding principles, it sends a poor message to the work base that the organization cannot be trusted and does not believe in its own message. Employees may wonder why they must abide by the statements when they don't see others doing the same. This can negatively influence the company culture and create a toxic workplace where unethical and immoral behaviors, actions, and attitudes can flourish.

Supporting Organizational Goals and Objectives

HUMAN RESOURCE INFORMATION SYSTEMS (HRISs)

A **human resource information system** (HRIS) is a computer system designed to help HR professionals carry out the day-to-day HR functions necessary for an organization to continue functioning normally. Most HRISs are designed to collect and store data related to the use of employee benefits, hiring, placement, training and evaluations of employees, payroll, and information about the work performed by employees during a given period of time. An HRIS is designed to help an HR professional carry out all primary functions associated with HR needs, which include benefits administration, payroll, time and labor management, and human resources management. An HRIS not only aids the HR department, but also helps the entire organization function effectively. Some HRIS functions could include the following:

- **Tracking basic employee information**—May include name, address, salary, and emergency contact information.
- **Keeping company documentation**—May include items such as employee handbooks, emergency procedures, and safety guidelines.
- **Benefit administration**—Could include enrollment capabilities, insurance changes, attendance and time off, and the ability for employees to look up and track information.
- **Payroll integration**—Reduces duplication of efforts with payroll and increases efficiencies.
- **Applicant tracking**—Allows recruiters to manage an applicant's information, then move the applicant to employee status and retain information.
- **Performance management**—Could include performance evaluations; possible improvement plans can follow the employee throughout the organization.
- **Tracking disciplinary issues**—May include the recording of demotions, suspensions, or other negative actions taken, all of which may be important to retain even after an employee leaves the organization.
- **Training**—Retains records of required certifications, licenses, and/or other compliance training.

BENEFITS

There are many benefits afforded by an HRIS:

- **Productivity**—The primary purpose of an HRIS is to improve HR productivity. An HRIS enables HR to quickly access information, thereby increasing the speed of decision making.
- **Reduced errors**—Whenever the manipulation of data occurs, the opportunity for error can increase, which in HR could lead to financial loss, unwanted legal issues, and/or possible damage to the brand or image.
- **Metric analysis**—Analyzing employee-related metrics such as recruiting costs, attendance, and benefit usage is an essential HR function. An HRIS allows for the proper storage and retrieval of needed data for calculations and statistical analysis impacting the organization.

- **Attendance management**—Tracking employee time off, whether for illness, PTO, or vacation, reduces the need for HR to manually capture and track all time-off situations.
- **Payroll management**—Capturing payroll-related information, such as time off or certain benefit selections, makes it easier to keep accurate records and expediently retrieve information for analysis.
- **Benefit administration**—Keeping records of health insurance, pension information, bonuses, and any other benefits enables HR to not only quickly retrieve data, but also efficiently analyze trends.
- **Training management**—An HRIS may store relevant training information for an organization. Employees, depending on their occupation or position, may be required to have current training credentials; training may be legally required; or training may enhance an employee's skill set, thereby increasing an organization's competitive advantage.
- **Communication**—Some HRIS software enables an organization to quickly distribute information or changes to everyone, or segments of a population. This communication could include procedural changes, handbook updates, weather-related closings, warnings, and policies. Some HRIS programs are even designed to distribute and analyze surveys.
- **Self-service**—Some HRIS programs have the capability to respond to employee questions about things like benefits, time off, and policies, thereby reducing the amount of time HR professionals spend answering simple questions.
- **E-signature capabilities**—As information and communication have become more digitized, so has the need for electronic signatures (e-signatures) on contracts, forms, etc. Many HRIS products have a feature whereby an electronic signature can be stored, which reduces a tremendous amount of paperwork.

DISADVANTAGES

The purpose of an HRIS is to safely store employee-related information, retrieve it efficiently, and analyze the data, allowing for more expedient organizational decision making. In other words, it is a system that is used to enhance the quality and efficiencies of management's decision making. Sometimes these advantages come at a cost and could become a disadvantage. The following are some of the possible disadvantages of an HRIS:

- **Human error**—There is an old adage: "Garbage in, garbage out." If a human error is made in data input, then there will be an error in the output, putting the organization at risk of making a decision based on false information.
- **Expense**—An HRIS can be costly to purchase, maintain, and update. Also, depending on the system, it could require an organization to hire an HRIS specialist to efficiently administer and maintain it. Additionally, new systems and updates require training. The time spent on training needs to show a positive return on investment for the HRIS to be cost effective.
- **Technical malfunctions**—System downtime can occur, which takes time and effort to resolve, possibly costing the organization time and money.
- **Unauthorized access**—As with any technology system, necessary precautions such as encryption and firewalls need to be taken so that only those with a "need to know" have access to HRIS information.

PREDICTIVE ANALYTICS

Predictive analytics is a type of technology that uses reliable current or historical data to forecast future behavior. These analytics technologically apply the old adage that "past behavior is the best indicator of future behavior." However, predictive analytics uses science and technology to make predictions that are usually very specific. Predictive analytics uses many different statistical techniques that scrutinize reliable current or historical data and related outcomes. The goal is to generate a formula or algorithm that best replicates the outcomes. This information can then be leveraged to forecast reliable future outcomes.

HR captures a tremendous amount of data about employees, and the data is usually stored in its HRIS. This data could be used to generate predictive models for HR professionals to enable better organizational decision making instead of relying on an unquantifiable feeling or some other non-science-based metric. HR analytics is being used more frequently to help an organization predict and respond to a variety of people policies. Some of the areas to which predictive analytics is being applied include improving employee turnover, predicting revenue through employee engagement measures, improving hiring decisions, and evaluating employment risk.

COMMUNICATION TECHNIQUES

Workplace communication is the exchange of information and ideas in an organization. Good workplace communication is necessary in order to have a high-performing organizational culture and operate with maximum efficiency. The most important aspect of communication is not simply saying or technically communicating information, but rather ensuring that the information is received accurately and is correctly understood by the intended audience. Effective communication is critical in order for an organization to achieve its goals. The goal of effective workplace communication is to avoid confusion or ambiguity, build collaboration among employees, shape a positive culture, and create accountability. Frequently, the best measure of effective communication is to observe what works and what doesn't work. Additionally, workplace communication is a strong mechanism for all members of an organization to provide input and come away feeling that their thoughts were heard and valued.

BASIC COMMUNICATIONS FLOWS

Organizational communication flows follow five main paths. Those paths are downward, upward, lateral, diagonal, and external.

- *Downward* communication flow occurs when communication travels from a higher level within the organization to a lower level. This type of communication takes place when leaders communicate to direct reports. Downward communication is made up of work-related information that employees need in order to understand expectations and complete tasks. Examples include providing feedback on performance, communicating the organizational mission and vision to employees, and detailing job instructions.
- *Upward* communication flow occurs when communication flows through to a higher level. Direct reports use upward communication to address issues, report problems, and ask questions of leaders. Upward communication can also be used to foster a collaborative decision-making process. Open expression and dialogue regarding ideas, opinions, feelings, and views can also be facilitated through upward communication. Pulse surveys, satisfaction surveys, and suggestion boxes are all ways to facilitate upward communication.
- *Lateral* communication flow occurs when communication is exchanged at the same hierarchical level within the organization. This type of communication takes place when peers or same-level leaders communicate with one another. This can foster cooperation between team members, share information, resolve conflicts, and solve problems. It can help build teams and develop relationships. Lateral communication is also important in providing emotional and social support and assistance within the workplace.

- *Diagonal* communication flow occurs when managers or leads communicate with employees from other departments or workgroups. This takes place often when working on projects, initiatives, or training, to ensure each area is accurately included and represented. When utilized effectively, diagonal communication can help eliminate misunderstandings and promote a culture of open dialogue.
- *External* communication flow is communication between leaders and external groups like suppliers, vendors, and service providers. This occurs when seeking new products or services, negotiating contracts, or ordering materials and supplies. External communication is critical to ensure that an organization has the materials and items needed to function successfully.

CHANNELS OF COMMUNICATION

Communication can be transmitted through a wide variety of channels or media, such as phone, email, face to face, reports, presentations, or social media. The chosen method should fit both the audience and the type of communication. **Information-rich communication channels** include phone, videoconferencing, and face-to-face meetings or presentations. **Information-lean communication channels** include email, fliers, newsletters, and reports. When trying to sell a product or service, a salesman might use a series of phone calls, face-to-face meetings, and presentations. This is because information-rich media are more interactive, which is more appropriate for complex messages that may need clarification. Rich and verbal communications should be used when there is time urgency, immediate feedback is required, ideas can be simplified with explanations, or emotions may be affected. Lean and written communications should be used when the communicator is simply stating facts or needs information permanently recorded.

ORAL COMMUNICATION IN THE WORKPLACE

Oral communication is the art of using speech to deliver information about ideas, feelings, and opinions. Good communication skills are not only a necessity in personal life, but extremely important in the workplace. In fact, most job offers require or at least prefer applicants with "excellent written and oral communication skills." Oral communication is how relationships and trust are formed among employees. Poor oral communication can lead to misunderstandings and conflict, and results in a loss of workplace productivity.

Oral communication is a combination of which words a person chooses to use and how those words are communicated. The marriage of what and how a person communicates while speaking allows for the smooth flow of communication among employees and a more productive work environment. Additionally, this marriage of "what and how" is significant in HR because critical information is frequently communicated by speaking, as with job offers, performance improvement, compensation changes, and layoffs. Usually, for information that is more emotional in nature, oral communication is the preferred method, although sometimes the same information is contained in a written follow-up. The right words, tone, and speed of oral communication impact how something is understood. Another critical component of good oral communication is active listening, as the workplace is more successful if opinions are heard and employees feel engaged.

USING EMAIL, TEXT, OR INSTANT MESSAGING (IM) AS A FORM OF COMMUNICATION

Emailing, texting, and instant messaging (IM) are increasingly popular forms of workplace communication because they are simple and efficient. The workplace is becoming more technology-driven, and many companies have implemented written communication policies that dictate what types of workplace communication are allowed via text and email versus phone and face-to-face. These policies vary by company, but they frequently outline or offer guidelines as to which form of communication is appropriate situationally. In general, email, texting, and IM are excellent forms of communication for information that is clear, brief, and actionable. Examples include asking a coworker if they can attend a meeting at a particular date and time, requesting someone to review information and respond, or asking for specific information. When writing via any form of technological communication, one must consider whether the communication is necessary and if it is appropriate. For instance, a phone call might be more efficient if there is going to be a lot of dialogue. Additionally, email, texting, IM, or really any form of writing might not be appropriate if sensitive or bad news needs to be communicated, because it can be challenging to communicate compassion, empathy, and tone. Information shared in this format could be misinterpreted, causing further harm. Similarly, anything put in an email, text, or IM could inadvertently be shared, potentially causing harm or embarrassment.

PASSIVE AND AGGRESSIVE COMMUNICATION STYLES

Communication styles vary by individual, and there is not one communication style that is correct because so much depends on the situation and individual preference. Someone with a **passive communication** style frequently acts indifferent, may not express their feelings, and prefers to listen to others as opposed to objecting or disagreeing. A passive communicator usually wants to avoid causing any conflict, even to the point of remaining silent when they should speak out. In fact, sometimes their silence causes a misunderstanding. In the workplace, a person with this style of easygoing, patient communication can be effective at calming nerves and putting others before themselves. They almost never complain and rarely object to work.

By contrast, someone with an **aggressive communication** style has no problem voicing their opinion at every opportunity, and frequently is rude and hurtful when speaking. The key for an aggressive communicator is to get their opinion heard and listened to, no matter the consequences. "I'm right, you're wrong" could be the motto of an aggressive communicator. They put their needs ahead of others. Despite these often-unwanted characteristics, aggressive communicators who can temper or control their more negative tendencies often make excellent leaders because of their ability to attract attention and convince others to follow them.

PASSIVE-AGGRESSIVE COMMUNICATION STYLE

A **passive-aggressive communication** style is challenging to describe, but easy to recognize. While the passive-aggressive communicator doesn't literally state their feelings of anger, disagreement, or dissatisfaction, they will communicate their true thoughts in subtle ways. This communication style is covert because the passive-aggressive person desires to suggest their discontent without overtly stating that they are upset or disagree about something.

Examples of this communication style in the workplace might include blaming others for personal issues or problems, starting rumors or gossip to distract or undermine leadership, facially expressing their opinion instead of using words, being quick to embarrass others, perhaps using words like "whatever" or sarcastically saying "fine," or verbally agreeing to something with no intention of doing whatever was agreed to. Frequently the goal of a passive-aggressive communicator is to cause others to convey the feelings that the passive-aggressive person is feeling. This gives the passive-aggressive person the satisfaction of exerting their power over someone else.

ASSERTIVE COMMUNICATION STYLE

An **assertive communication** style is defined by honest, direct verbalization about one's thoughts or opinions without judging others for their beliefs. The premise of an assertive communicator is to communicate in a polite manner while demonstrating respect for one's own beliefs or ideas as well as the opinions of others. When others deal with an assertive communicator, they feel comfortable and welcome to express their feelings because they know civility and consideration for all is an objective that will be met.

An assertive communicator will try to find a solution that benefits all parties, allowing everyone to benefit or at least letting them feel as though their opinion was heard and valued. For example, an assertive communicator might respond with, "I really think this is the way to proceed, but I'm genuinely open to hearing your opinion." Those with an assertive communication style frequently use "I" statements when conversing. An "I" statement allows someone to be assertive without putting the listener on the defensive. It permits communicators to take ownership of their feelings without implying they are the cause of the problem. For example, instead of saying, "You never listen to me and probably aren't listening now," one could say, "I feel my concerns are not being heard." In the workplace, an assertive communicator is excellent at building and maintaining productive teams and collaboratively solving conflict.

DELIVERING CLEAR MESSAGES

Delivering messages can be difficult, especially if the context is serious. The message content should be tailored to fit the audience. This requires understanding the roles, expectations, and perspective of recipients. First, focus on eliminating any barriers or vague wording that may interfere with interpreting the message. Once the proper channel for delivery is selected, it may be important to focus on nonverbal signals and ensure that they coincide with the mood of the message content. Finally, messages should allow for feedback that will lead to follow-up discussions. If a message is complex, such as a business change or new benefits offering, it may be critical to share repeated reminders and have open lines of communication to reduce confusion and ensure success.

ACTIVE LISTENING

Active listening is an important component of communication that requires paying close attention to what is being said. It often involves making eye contact and appropriately nodding to show engagement. To gain a better understanding, listeners should try to understand things from the speaker's point of view, or visualize what they are saying. It is important to be considerate, avoid distractions or interruptions, and respond appropriately. Additionally, listeners should try to pick up on emotional cues beyond the literal words that are used. Even if the message differs from the active listener's own opinion, the listener will try to focus on accepting what the other person has to say rather than being critical. Active listeners should make sure to fully hear what the other person is saying before formulating their own response. When compared to passive listeners, active listeners are more connected and conscientious.

ORGANIZATIONAL STRUCTURE

Organizational structure allows organizations to carry out their goals in the most efficient and productive manner possible. Basically, organizational structure is the way work flows through an organization. There is no such thing as a one-size-fits-all organizational structure; it is dependent on what work needs to be accomplished, and by whom. Organizational structure can be formal or less formal as well as flexible depending on the organizational goals. Typically, organizational structure is aligned with the organization's strategy.

Interdependencies between business functions and output need to be carefully examined. This requires looking closely at the relationship among the following: leadership, which is responsible for strategy and results; the organization, which determines how processes and operations strategy are implemented; the jobs and the responsibilities needed to perform key organizational roles; and the people whose experience is needed to execute operations and achieve strategic goals.

Understanding and maintaining the sync between these interdependencies is what drives the type of organizational structure that will work best for a business.

The creation of an organization reporting structure is based on several factors:

- Job departmentalization—How jobs are grouped together to complete work
- Span of control—Number of people who report to a supervisor or manager
- Centralization—Decision making that is conducted by upper-level management
- Decentralization—Decision making that is conducted by lower- or middle-level management

FLAT ORGANIZATIONAL STRUCTURE

A **flat organizational structure** can be represented as a list of company employees, usually managers and supervisors, who report to a single leader. It is sometimes called a horizontal organizational structure because the list is usually arranged horizontally along a single line below the leader. This type of organization chart is most often used by small or startup companies. Also typical of this structure is that middle management is eliminated, thereby allowing employees to more easily make independent decisions and change direction quickly. This structure also provides employees with more responsibility, which increases employee involvement and leads to a freer exchange of ideas and communication. However, this type of structure can also make it challenging for employees because supervision is sometimes not so clear. Overall, a flat organizational structure is very difficult to maintain as a company grows larger.

Flat (Horizontal) Organization Chart

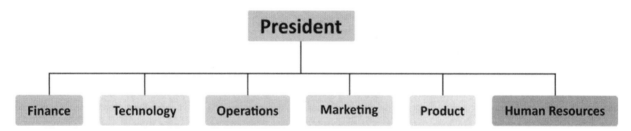

HIERARCHY ORGANIZATION STRUCTURE

A **hierarchy organization chart** looks like a tall pyramid and is sometimes called a functional or functional hierarchical organizational chart. The top portion of the chart is almost always a single person, usually the president or CEO. The chart widens slightly on the second level with employees who report directly to the leader, possibly vice presidents. It widens further at the next level for employees who report to vice presidents, possibly directors. This pattern continues, with the chart widening as it includes more employees, until it reaches the bottom level with the lowest title designations. Each level is subordinate to the levels above it.

This organization structure is best suited for large organizations, in which supervision and responsibility are clearly established. Typically, the hierarchical environment utilizes specialists or positions with expertise in a specific area that tend to have a strong allegiance to their area or department within the business. This quality can be good for the individual department, but it makes horizontal communication across the other areas of the business very challenging, especially when decision making may be a benefit for one department and not necessarily for another. Sometimes a hierarchical structure is considered very bureaucratic, thereby possibly causing a slow response to changing market conditions or customer needs, and making the entire structure generally less flexible.

Hierarchy Structure

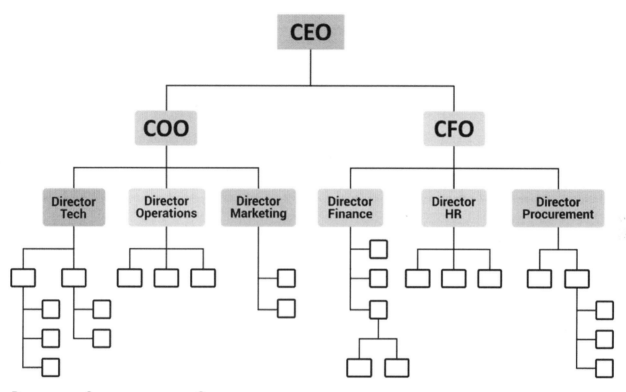

DIVISIONAL ORGANIZATIONAL STRUCTURE

A **divisional structure** basically separates an organization into parts. This could mean organizing a business by product or service and output. Divisions could also be further divided by geographical region. Each division is then responsible for everything related to that product, service, or region, depending upon how the business is structured. For example, a large beverage company might have three divisions: soda, water, and flavored seltzer. Each division would have its own departments, such as finance, marketing, and research and development. In other words, there could be identical departments in each division. Continuing with this example, soda would have separate departments for finance, marketing, and research and development. Water would also have separate departments for finance, marketing, and research and development, as would the flavored seltzer division.

This structure allows for intense focus and attention on each of the specialized services or products a company has and easy coordination within each specialized division, especially when compared with a hierarchical structure. Decision making is also faster in each functional area. The main disadvantage of divisional structure is that there is a duplication of effort, and some efficiencies could be lost between duplicated departments. From a financial perspective, different divisions might be competing against each other for the same customers, and procurement of supplies might cost more than if the divisions purchased together. Additionally, a divisional structure reduces the ability for employees in a certain department to benefit from the knowledge and continuing education from another identical department in a different division.

Divisional Organization Chart

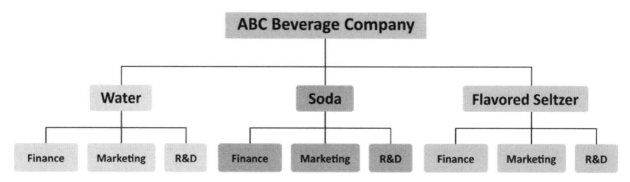

MATRIX ORGANIZATIONAL STRUCTURE

The **matrix organizational structure** is the combination of the flat structure and the divisional structure. Basically, employees are supervised by at least two managers, who are usually equally responsible for the employee's performance depending on which function they perform. For example, an employee might work in a specialized area in a business division dedicated to a product, service, geographical region, or customer. This structure is useful when a product or service is complex or is rapidly expanding. Businesses might choose this structure when the silos that exist within divisions no longer make the organization efficient. Furthermore, it is an optimal structure if rapid change is needed for a business to achieve a competitive advantage, whether that change requires more resources or additional expertise. In this manner, the business can focus more on the work that needs to be completed and a little less on the people in their silos. As a result, cost is typically minimized through the sharing of people and/or resources.

There are also disadvantages to this structure. For instance, reporting to more than one manager can be challenging, as responsibilities may be unclear or complicated. The matrix structure requires constant awareness, communication, and coordination between two or more managers to figure out an employee's work assignments and priorities. This could sometimes lead to conflicting messaging and demands, causing the employee's stress level to rise, resulting in a loss of efficiency as the work assignments are agreed upon. Matrix structures are common in project-driven organizations, or circumstances in which employees from different specialties form a team until the completion of the project, after which they return to their standard functions. From an HR perspective, ensuring fairness and equity can sometimes be tricky in a matrix structure because there are many reporting levels for employees.

Matrix Organization Chart

OPEN BOUNDARY ORGANIZATIONAL STRUCTURE

An organization with an **open boundary structure** is established without traditional boundaries or divisions. In other words, there are none of the boxes or solid lines found in a typical organization chart. Instead, all units or functions are fluid and flexible. Traditional departments are more team-like, and the business—including suppliers—works closely together as one. This means that everyone can participate in decision making, as organizational hierarchy is almost nonexistent. The most important characteristic of an open boundary structure is the organization's ability to quickly adapt and be flexible in order to be as innovative as possible. Additionally, organizations with this structure are usually tech savvy, utilizing the latest and greatest technology, and have flexible working schedules that rely heavily on all forms of electronic communication.

The primary advantage of this structure is that it fully leverages everyone's talent, eliminates bureaucratic bottlenecks, and can adapt and change to market forces quickly. However, this type of structure needs strong leadership and vision because efficiencies based on specialty knowledge may not always be achieved and could be time-consuming to maintain.

PREPARING HR-RELATED DOCUMENTS

HR documentation is a key aspect of a well-functioning department and organization. Accurately preparing and maintaining HR documents can provide evidence and give the rationale behind different organizational decisions. This documentation can be used to help make a case in the event of a legal action or EEOC case.

HR documents encompass a myriad of work activities. When preparing HR-related documents, there are several things to keep in mind, the first of which is what type of document is being prepared. There should be records in areas such as recruiting, hiring, policies, medical files, benefit documents, personnel records, payroll data, disciplinary or performance records, leave records, and training materials. It will be important to understand what the compliance requirements are for the documentation. The individual preparing the document should know how long the documents must be retained, where they should be stored, who will be viewing the documents, and who will have access to them after completion. There are regulations surrounding the storage and retention of many HR documents. For example, an employer must keep an application on file for one year according to Title VII. I-9 forms and verification documents have different retention requirements as well. They should be maintained for three years after an employee is hired or for one year after an employee separates. The person responsible for maintaining documents should determine which of the two has the later date and use that as the guideline. Regarding storage, medical files should be housed separately from personnel files, so knowing which category certain prepared documents fall under is key.

SWOT ANALYSIS

A SWOT analysis is used to identify and define the strengths, weaknesses, opportunities, and threats related to an organization, department, or project. This technique can be applied to a variety of fields. It is frequently used at an organizational level to ascertain how closely a business is aligned with its strategic objectives and benchmarks and to evaluate how it is placed competitively in the market. Strengths and weaknesses are internally focused, and opportunities and threats are external factors.

Strengths are internal factors about the organization that are positive, and that the organization can control. Strengths could include products, qualities, or practices that set the organization apart from competitors. Resources, such as a trained and knowledgeable staff, are considered strengths, as are things the organization does well. Tangible assets like proprietary processes or technology and intellectual property fall under the strengths category as well.

Weaknesses are internal factors about the organization that are considered adverse attributes or that deduct from the strengths. Weaknesses include areas where the company does not perform well. Limited or lacking resources are also weaknesses. Additional weaknesses can include low customer satisfaction rates or high levels of turnover.

Opportunities are external factors that could potentially contribute to success or higher performance. Opportunities can include areas such as potential growth rate in the industry, the ability to provide a new or requested product or service, advances in technology, the ability to hire talent, or the capacity to operate in a location where less competition exists.

Threats are external factors that cannot be controlled and could negatively affect success or lower performance. Threats can include costs of materials and supplies, changes to laws and regulations that impact the business, supply chain issues, and emerging competitors.

SWOT analyses are usually represented visually in a table or matrix with four separate areas.

- Strengths:
    - What does the organization do well?
    - What resources does the organization have?
    - What is the competitive advantage?
- Weaknesses:
    - Where can the organization improve?
    - What limitations to resources exist?
    - What does the organization lack?
- Opportunities:
    - Is there a current need the organization could meet?
    - Are there requested products that could be provided?
    - Is there talent that could be hired?

- Threats
  - Are there regulation changes that could impact the organization?
  - Are competitors offering new products?
  - Is there dependence on a single supplier?

ORGANIZATIONAL STRATEGY AND HR STRATEGIC PLANNING

Organizational strategy is a dynamic plan detailing the necessary actions that will enable the organization to achieve its short- and long-term goals. HR plays a critical role in an organization's strategic plan. Understanding an organization's strategy and how the business operates allows HR to better serve the organization's needs and human asset-related issues. Human capital impacts many aspects of a business, including recruitment, performance management, compensation and training, and development. HR must ensure that the correct people are aligned and performing in accordance with the organizational strategy adopted by the organization. There is a strong connection between HR, strategic planning, and implementation because HR must leverage human capital to optimize the success of an organization.

Strategic planning in HR refers to how HR professionals plan for both risks and opportunities by leveraging resources to meet HR initiatives and organizational objectives. The more closely aligned the HR department is with the business strategy, the closer the organization can get to anticipating and responding to needs, trends, and targets. This allows the organization to better maintain an advantage in its market. Planning, training, metrics, forecasting, and developing the workforce will aid the company in successfully achieving the business objectives and strategy.

Strategic planning in HR can help promote productivity, keep employees aligned with strategic goals, address critical issues in a timely manner to avoid dilemmas, and help guide development and training. When developing an effective strategic plan, HR should be able to assess staffing levels and skills needed to not only meet and keep up with demands, but also keep up with changes in the technology and various processes. Performance management is another key area that needs to be adequately designed, to motivate and engage employees and focus them on the objectives and goals of the department and organization. Compensation is another important element, as competitive total compensation will help retain employees and could aid in attracting new talent.

Prior to developing a strategic plan, the HR department should assess the current situation, identify the desired future state, form and begin to implement frameworks to meet the strategic objectives, and determine how progress toward the objective is measured and evaluated. The SWOT analysis can be a key aid when developing the strategic plan, as the analysis can help provide understanding of the organization's current state. Additionally, a PESTLE analysis (political, economic, social, technological, legal, environmental) can be used to help provide a more detailed look at how external factors may impact the organization in the current state and over the long term. Solid strategic planning helps the organization achieve its mission, objectives, and goals while also maximizing productivity and profit.

Engaging Employees

METHODS AND PROCESSES FOR COLLECTING EMPLOYEE FEEDBACK
CONDUCTING AN EMPLOYEE ATTITUDE SURVEY

An employer would conduct an employee attitude survey to better understand what employees think about the company and its work environment. Employee attitude surveys can measure either employee satisfaction or opinions on specific issues. Some of the information that might be collected and evaluated includes workplace culture, communication effectiveness, management effectiveness, safety at work, and specialized initiatives in the organization. There are many advantages for an organization to conduct an employee attitude survey:

- Employees like to feel valued, so asking them their perspective on a number of key topics helps them feel their voices count while also helping employers adjust course if necessary. Also, it demonstrates the organization cares about its employees.
- Employee attitude surveys are anonymous, which encourages honesty. Employers gain the honest opinions of employees because of this format. It provides a better understanding of the organization's strengths and weaknesses as viewed by employees.
- New ideas resulting from the survey could lead to better development and training programs.
- These surveys boost employee engagement and two-way communications.

There are also some disadvantages an organization should consider before implementing an employee attitude survey:

- Surveys set the expectation that an employer will act upon its employees' responses. If the employer just wants to know employee thoughts and does not plan to implement changes or communicate rationales, then employee morale could drop.
- It could be time-consuming to design, implement, and evaluate the survey, and execute changes based on the results.
- Completing a survey could be thought of as an annoyance, and employees may choose not to participate, resulting in a low response rate that may not be worth the effort.
- Employees may not give undivided attention to the survey, or perhaps concentrate only on areas they view negatively, which could be misleading for employers.

EMPLOYEE ENGAGEMENT SURVEYS

An **employee engagement survey** is an empirical method for capturing what is in the hearts and minds of employees. It is usually conducted once a year. The survey is designed to measure aspects of employee engagement and is used as a tool to analyze the employee experience and drive change.

An employee engagement survey can be administered on paper or electronically, depending on the environment and employee access to technology. Employee engagement surveys typically range from 20 to 40 questions. There is no exact number of desired questions because that depends on the organization and what information is desired. A balance needs to be achieved between too few questions, which may not yield enough data, and too many questions, which might create an overabundance of data too complicated to summarize in reports. Usually, questions are written to measure engagement, determine what drives engagement, and provide the opportunity for open-ended questions and comments. Except for comments, responses can be indicated on a Likert scale of five ranking points that measures the degree to which an employee agrees or disagrees with a statement.

PULSE SURVEYS

A **pulse survey** is different from an employee attitude or engagement survey in that it is shorter (usually just a few questions), can measure anything, and can be administered more frequently. Hence, it lets an organization assess any specific topic more often. These short, usually easier-to-administer surveys also let an organization evaluate and act upon information quickly. Therefore, there is sentiment among employees that the organization is listening to them more and genuinely trying to implement changes that benefit the employees and the organization. As a result, employees feel valued, and the organization can continuously grow and improve.

Some of the topics a pulse survey might measure include effectiveness of business metrics, effectiveness of specific employer initiatives, and training effectiveness. Additionally, the questions can change from department to department and can be modified over time to measure progress in a specific area. For example, how likely is an employee to recommend the company as a place to work for friends and colleagues?

A pulse survey can be an effective tool to supplement an annual employee engagement survey and/or stand alone to measure specific aspects of progress. Pulse survey results are sometimes viewed as a monitoring tool.

FOCUS GROUPS

Focus groups can be used to glean employee views and concerns. They may be used to assess a new benefit plan or organizational change. Most focus groups contain 5 to 12 voluntary participants, with 3 to 10 groups in total. Participants should be informed about the subject of the focus group, about who will benefit, and that the information will be kept confidential. Participants may be selected at random or through the use of certain applicable filters. Focus group organizers should ensure that power differentials within the group are avoided. It is also important to involve participants from various levels of staff so they can fully represent the affected population. A neutral facilitator should be chosen to lead the discussion and ask open-ended, guided questions. Following the meeting, collected data should be analyzed and reported.

MANAGEMENT BY WALKING AROUND STRATEGY

The **management by walking around** (MBWA) strategy is simply a method in which an organization encourages employee communication and involvement by making managers and supervisors readily available. An organization encourages managers and supervisors to traverse the workspace so they can check on the progress of each employee, discuss questions or concerns, and ultimately handle any problems that the employee or the manager identifies.

This strategy may appear to be extremely straightforward and relatively obvious because most organizations attempt to make sure that managers and supervisors are monitoring the progress of their employees. However, it is an important qualitative methodology for informally collecting information about what employees might be thinking. This is extremely useful during times of rapid changes, when observing and listening captures the essence or tone of issues that other methods of data collection might miss. This form of data collection usually requires active listening training for the manager and the ability to direct or redirect conversations in a nonconfrontational format to reveal the root of a problem or trends.

SUGGESTION BOXES

A suggestion box is a place, either physical or virtual, where employees can give their anonymous opinions about anything in the work environment or working conditions, or ways to improve efficiency or profitability. A suggestion box is a tool to help employees feel more engaged and involved, and to help the organization become a better place to work. A suggestion box improves communication, increases innovative thinking to help solve organizational problems, and could improve employee morale.

If the organization is using a physical box, then the box should be placed in a location where all employees have access. A physical box should also be locked shut, with access limited only to those with keys. If a virtual box is used, then IT needs to ensure suggestions are truly anonymous. Before implementing a suggestion box, an employer should be prepared to take it seriously by being welcoming of suggestions and eager to read and act on them. A program, including guidelines, should be developed to administer and promote the suggestion box. Additionally, incentives could be offered for participating. Employers should read suggestions on a regular basis and be sure to thank employees for their input.

INTERVIEWS

The basic purpose of an interview is to obtain a certain amount of information from the interviewee concerning defined questions and issues. This give-and-take process is not merely words. Information can be gathered from gestures, body language, facial expressions, posture, and other nonverbal communication. Communication with words can be further dissected when tone, speech speed, and inflection are taken into consideration. An interview is a purposeful exchange between the interviewer and the interviewee that can be one-on-one, in groups, or any combination thereof. Generally, interviews tend to be more personal than surveys and allow the interviewer to probe further with follow-up questions and additional clarification if needed.

TYPES OF INTERVIEWS

The type of interview used depends on the situation and the preference of the interviewer. These are the most commonly used types of interviews:

- **Structured** interview—Every interviewee is asked the same questions. Similar information from interviewees can then be fairly compared to others.
- **Patterned** interview—Interviewees are asked different questions, but all questioning the same body of knowledge, skill, or ability.
- **Stress** interview—The interviewer is aggressive in approach to see how an interviewee might respond. Stress interviews are frequently used in law enforcement.
- **Directive** interview—A structured interview in which the interviewer asks very specific questions in a calm, controlled manner.
- **Nondirective** interview—The interviewer asks more open-ended questions in a particular direction, but the interviewees can drive the direction of questions. These are frequently used in counseling.
- **Behavioral** interview—The interviewer asks specific questions about past behavior, performance, and examples as a way to gauge the interviewee's skill set and knowledge. Typically, past performance can be a good indicator of future performance.
- **Situational** interview—The interviewer asks questions that require the interviewee to consider situations he or she may have experienced in a certain role and how it was handled, thereby gauging an interviewee's knowledge and skills.

STAY INTERVIEWS

A **stay interview** is a discussion between a manager and an employee in which the employer ascertains why a valued employee continues to work for the organization and if there is anything the employer can do to improve. The goal is to retain top talent and better understand what the organization is doing poorly, as well as learn what the organization is doing well. While employee satisfaction and engagement can be measured in an attitude survey, a stay interview allows for an immediate two-way conversation, enabling the employer to ask follow-up questions. Generally, stay interviews are conducted by employers once or twice during the onboarding process, typically over a six-month period; and then annually, usually six months apart from an employee's annual performance appraisal. The following are some questions an employer might ask during the approximately 30-minute stay interview:

- What do you enjoy about working here?
- What are a few things you look forward to every day?
- What can we do to make your job more satisfying?
- Do you feel valued and utilized in your current position?

EXIT INTERVIEWS

Exit interviews are opportunities for organizations to gather honest feedback about why an employee is choosing to leave the organization. Exit interviews are almost always encouraged because they yield information that may help the organization improve and retain employees in the future. In most organizations, a member of the HR team, acting as an impartial and neutral party (and not as the employee's direct supervisor), conducts the exit interview to put the employee at ease. The following are ways to make an exit interview as productive as possible:

- Try to make the employee feel comfortable. Remind them that their input is extremely valuable and thank them for their time and expertise.
- Ask open-ended questions and repeat responses to ensure understanding. Yes-or-no questions should be avoided, and notes should be taken about what the employee said and did not say.
- The most important question to ask is why the employee started to look for another job.

Typically, HR analyzes and summarizes the information obtained from an exit interview and shares the information with the organization's leadership team to examine areas for improvement.

WORK-LIFE BALANCE PRACTICES

Work-life balance is generally defined as the competing prioritization between one's personal and professional activities. Advances in technology have meant that a physical office location no longer always needs to be the primary place to accomplish work-related tasks; this, in turn, has made the juggling act of work-life balance an increasingly hot topic. A poor work-life balance can lead to employee stress and burnout, diminished productivity, and lost revenue. Therefore, it is in the organization's best interest to share some of the responsibility for improving the balance between work and an employee's personal life.

Some business leaders maintain that, due to technological advances that everyone should strive for, a "work-life integration" should be the true end goal because complete separation might not be realistic. Achieving a balance then becomes a shared responsibility with the employee and the employer.

HELPING EMPLOYEES ACHIEVE A GOOD WORK-LIFE BALANCE

An employer can help its employees in a number of different ways, depending on the needs of the business. A **flexible work arrangement** could mean working remotely, scheduling outside typical business hours, part-time arrangements, telecommuting on certain days, job sharing, and shift swapping. Businesses that adopt such measures may experience reduced turnover, increased productivity, and the ability to recruit from an expanded talent pool. In some situations, flexible work arrangements are not possible due to the nature of the business. If that is the case, businesses can also promote campaigns to encourage breaks, regularly review workload balance, and take time off; lead by example; provide resources for working parents; or offer other perks to ease the burden for their employees.

There is not a one-size-fits-all approach for employers to assist workers in finding their individual work-life balance; rather, the program should be customized for the business, as well as recognizing that every employee is different with diverse circumstances. Work-life balance programs can give businesses a competitive advantage, but if poorly designed and implemented, or managed incorrectly, the program could unintentionally harm morale and/or be legally detrimental to the company.

VIRTUAL OR REMOTE WORK ENVIRONMENTS

A virtual work environment is possible thanks to technological advancements that have reduced employers' need for a physical, brick-and-mortar presence or office space. Virtual work environments allow employees to work in remote locations, including homes, coffee shops, or anywhere that connectivity can be achieved. Work units or teams can collaborate via virtual networks and accomplish work via many formats, such as video conferencing, phone, and virtual servers to share and store information. Employers are starting to include virtual or remote policies in their employee handbooks that define expectations when working remotely, with new protocols regarding start time, end time, meal breaks, check-in procedures, etc. Some employers have more informal plans, such as a quick video conference in the morning or at the end of the day, casual conversation to see how everyone on a team is doing, or manager office hours. Due to advances in technology and the cost savings achieved from remote work, the trend is that the virtual workplace is growing.

ADVANTAGES AND DISADVANTAGES

There are many advantages to a virtual or remote work environment:

- Cost effectiveness—Working virtually enables companies to have lower operating costs and be more environmentally friendly. Examples include smaller workspace and less commuting, which respectively cost less to maintain and expend less energy.
- Flexibility—Working remotely or at home is a perk for many employees because it eliminates commuting and promotes better work-life balance.
- Improved productivity—Employees who can better balance their work and personal life tend to be happier, and research indicates that happier employees tend to be more productive. Remote work also eliminates many of the distractions that occur in an in-person office environment.
- Bigger talent pool—Virtual work environments mean that recruiting is not restricted by location. This enables an employer to cast a wider net for top talent.

There are also some disadvantages to virtual or remote work environments:

- Preference—Some employees may not like working remotely or do not have a space or environment that is conducive to productively accomplishing work. Remote work can be isolating, and many have a hard time separating work and personal life when working from home.
- Difficulties collaborating—Sometimes there is no substitute for face-to face collaboration. It could take time to figure out ways to make virtual collaboration work well.
- Trust—Employers can monitor technology to see if an employee is active, but there needs to be a level of trust between the employer and employee for this work arrangement to work.

Legal Considerations When Devising and Managing Work-Life Balance Programs

Generally, the US Equal Employment Opportunity Commission (EEOC) supports work-life balance programs. However, if the program is not implemented fairly, it could violate Title VII of the Civil Rights Act, requiring equal treatment and preventing discrimination. Some work-life balance programs are left to the discretion of a manager or HR representative. If an employee requests a flexible working arrangement and the manager is not consistent and fair in administering these requests, the disappointed employee may claim unlawful discrimination. Furthermore, there is the risk of an inconsistent or unfair decision resulting in disparate treatment or disparate impact against a protected class or classes. In addition, an employee could ask for a flexible work arrangement due to a family or medical condition that would otherwise be covered under the Family and Medical Leave Act (FMLA). If the request meets the specific requirements of FMLA, then it should be processed accordingly to avoid legal consequences. Another legal consideration is whether the employee is making the request due to a disability. In this case, the employer may be in violation of the Americans with Disabilities Act (ADA), and the request should have been processed and determined via a reasonable accommodation. Lastly, flexible work arrangements carry the potential for Fair Labor Standards Act (FLSA) wage and hour issues or violations, especially when calculating hours worked. These types of legal matters, along with ongoing changes in federal, state, and local laws, should always be considered when a business implements a work-life balance program.

Sabbatical Leave

A **sabbatical leave** is generally a paid leave from an organization to work on a long-term project. This is typically a four-week to three-month leave to concentrate solely on the project without distraction. Sabbatical leave used to only apply to professors or researchers in academic environments. There has been a slow shift to allow this type of leave in other industries for professional development, authoring articles, etc. Sabbatical leave is usually reserved for more senior, longer-term employees who already have years of experience, but there are no specific legal regulations and few case-law precedents for sabbatical implementation. It is wise for organizations to have clearly defined criteria and guidelines when offering sabbatical leave to employees in order to ensure it is implemented in a fair and consistent manner.

There are many advantages for an organization to offer sabbaticals: they attract top talent; give employers a competitive edge; demonstrate that an employer cares for their employees, thereby promoting loyalty; and promote long-term retention of employees. There are also some disadvantages: cost; decreased productivity due to an employee's absence; administrative challenge to maintain benefits; potential conflict or resentment among employees covering the workload; and the possibility that the employee on sabbatical will not return to work.

Employee Relations Programs
Recognition Programs

Recognition programs are an important part of the employee experience that enhance employee engagement and help positively shape company culture. Recognition should be tailored to the organization and its employees—there is not a one-size-fits-all plan. However, the goal of most recognition programs is to help make employees feel valued or appreciated, and they frequently serve as an incentive to strive toward. Recognition programs can reward any number of desirable attributes or events, such as going above and beyond, team effort, wellness objectives, innovation, quality improvements, and career celebrations. Recognition rewards can vary, but may include the following:

- A heartfelt, verbal (or written) thank-you
- A meal celebration
- A point-based system for employees to choose a reward
- Treats or candy
- Gift cards
- Unique experiences such as concerts, sporting events, or shows

A recognition program provides an employer with the ability to create a workplace of choice where employees thrive. Recruitment and employee retention is positively influenced by an effective recognition program. Successful recognition has the following characteristics: recognition is genuine, all employees have an opportunity to give and receive recognition, the reward is given in a timely manner, it is specific, it is connected to the company's purpose, and it is presented in a public forum. There are also software programs and vendors that can help an organization design and administer recognition programs.

SPECIAL EVENTS

Company-sponsored special events can vary, but all serve as a way to leverage and promote employee engagement and build a positive company culture. Some special events can be recurring, such as holiday dinners, summer picnics, Friday social nights, or Tuesday tacos in the office. These events may be social outings with or without employee family members. However, they serve to build camaraderie among employee team members and give them opportunities to socialize with one another outside of the work environment. This may help build a stronger, more productive work team, as well as improve employee satisfaction. Events can also incorporate an element of community service, including serving food at a local soup kitchen, volunteering at an animal shelter, or building homes for those in need. Some special events might also include wellness-related campaigns, company walking or running teams, weight loss or healthy eating initiatives, or yoga classes at lunch. Special events demonstrate that the employer cares about the employees' health and well-being.

Workforce Management

PERFORMANCE MANAGEMENT PRACTICES

Performance management is the HR function concerned with setting performance standards, evaluating employee effectiveness against those standards, identifying any problem areas, and implementing interventions to correct problems. Performance management is vital because an organization cannot thrive if individuals, teams, and departments aren't effective in their roles.

The performance management process can vary from one organization to another, but most firms follow three basic steps:

- Through activities like goal-setting, needs analysis, and the creation of a corporate value statement and code of conduct, company leaders and HR professionals establish organizational goals. They then identify the knowledge, skills, behaviors, and tasks required to achieve those goals and inform employees how to best work to meet those company objectives.
- The firm's management then needs to monitor employee performance, document any problems, and help employees correct those problems if possible.

- At predetermined intervals, typically once a year, managers will conduct in-depth performance appraisals for each employee. These appraisals measure performance during the preceding period. Often, the manager and employee will set goals for the employee to work toward in the new appraisal period.

SETTING PERFORMANCE GOALS

A performance goal is a written declaration of an anticipated end result in a specified period of time. These goals are usually discussed between an employee and their manager. Performance goals are then chosen and agreed upon based on company objectives and/or the employee's personal aspirations. Goals are desired outcomes that specify defined measures such as time frame, quantity, quality, or a percentage. Employee performance goals should link into and support the overall strategic plan of the company or unit, and at the same time should assist in keeping the employee engaged and motivated. It is an opportunity for an employee to formulate a plan with their manager to focus on those job duties, responsibilities, and tasks that will best enable individual achievement of goals that carefully integrate with company goals. To be effective, performance goals should be evaluated and re-evaluated in a timely fashion, perhaps every quarter, six months, or annually. Performance goals are not written in stone and can be updated or revised as needed to maintain motivation over time.

SMART PERFORMANCE GOALS

SMART is an acronym that stands for "specific, measurable, achievable, relevant, and timebound." The idea is that every goal an employee sets should be SMART:

- **Specific**—The goal should clearly define what is to be achieved as specifically as possible. For example, a goal to "improve diversity in the company" is not specific at all, but a goal to "begin an electronic diversity awareness monthly communication about a different aspect of diversity" is very specific.
- **Measurable**—Performance goals should be quantifiable in some unit of measurement. For example, "reduce return processing" isn't measurable, but "reduce return processing time by 10 percent before December 31" has a clear and unmistakable deadline.
- **Achievable**—A goal should be a challenge for the employee and require a high level of effort, but should also be reasonable and realistic.
- **Relevant**—All performance goals should link to organizational goals.
- **Timebound**—There needs to be a due date or period of time in which the goal will be achieved. Time is usually reflected as a specific date or numeric period, like December 31 or the end of the third fiscal quarter.

IMPORTANCE OF DOCUMENTING EMPLOYEE PERFORMANCE

Up-to-date performance documentation is important to maintain in an employee's personnel file, as it frequently demonstrates the reasoning behind why decisions, both positive and negative, were made. This documentation is especially useful in an employee's performance appraisal because it demonstrates performance with examples. Some managers find it useful to keep a performance diary, documenting a record of key activities or tasks executed by the employee.

Employee performance documentation is essential in the event of a lawsuit. Furthermore, the documentation must be accurate, objective, and specific. The following are some guidelines to maintain when documenting employee performance:

- Document right away to avoid anything being forgotten.
- Keep notes on all employees.

- Separate fact from opinion.
- Make sure notes are objective.
- Remove emotion from documentation.
- Be respectful when writing.

Performance documentation is not only useful to avoid possible legal issues, but it can also be leveraged to improve an employee's performance and to create a professional development plan or possibly reward outstanding performance.

BENCHMARKING

Benchmarking is a process or system by which an organization measures its performance against other similar business groupings considered to have best practices, sometimes called "best in class." In order to grow, companies must compare given functions and practices to the best in class in order to improve efficiencies and productivity. In HR, benchmarking is frequently used to compare an organization in the areas of recruitment, employee retention, salary, performance, employee engagement, HR strategies, etc.

An organization can choose to conduct **internal benchmarking**, whereby they closely examine and compare the efficiencies realized in their own organization, or **external benchmarking**, which involves an organization comparing its functional information against other industries. The objective is to discover what areas of the business could benefit from improvement to hopefully maintain a competitive advantage and cultivate a culture of continuous improvement. Some specific benefits of benchmarking may include lowered labor cost, increase in sales and profits, operational efficiencies, increased productivity, and quality improvements. Benchmarking may be the impetus that drives change, so organizations must prepare accordingly with change management education in the organization.

BALANCED SCORECARD

The **balanced scorecard** is a strategic performance management tool that was developed by Robert Kaplan and David Norton in 1996. The tool is designed to identify, report, and improve an organization through four perspectives in time:

- **Financial**—How various stakeholders view the organization
- **Customer**—How customers view the organization
- **Business process**—What the organization excels at
- **Learning and growth**—How the organization continuously improves

This tool and subsequent reports can be used by leadership and management to better monitor the actions or activities within their span of control and keep track of the results.

PERFORMANCE FEEDBACK TECHNIQUES

How performance feedback is delivered plays a vital role in how it is received and subsequent outcomes. First, whenever possible, feedback should be given in private and always in a respectful manner. It is important to remember that feedback is not negative. Rather, performance feedback is an opportunity for a supervisor to discuss information that should help make the employee more productive and provide clear direction and priorities moving forward. This should be a two-way discussion and not a supervisor speaking at length to a silent employee. It is important for a manager not to come across as overbearing or cruel, but rather approach feedback in a manner that is sincerely helpful. The manager giving feedback should actively listen to the employee and recap or clarify what the employee is saying if needed, as well as empathize with the employee's point of view.

A manager should be cognizant that the words used to describe an undesired behavior are factual, not judgmental. For example, "Ann, could you just stop making so many errors on the same XYZ activity? Try harder!" is judgmental. However, "Ann, it seems there are some issues doing XYZ. What are your thoughts?" is better. A manager should be specific when providing feedback, both positive and negative. For example, "Derrick, you are doing a good job!" isn't specific; instead, a manager should say something like, "Derrick, your closing numbers are great, 35 percent above the department average, and with 98 percent customer satisfaction ratings. That's awesome!"

PERFORMANCE MANAGEMENT SOFTWARE

The performance management process needs to be effective to be productive. If the process is too cumbersome, then there is the risk it becomes a "check-the-box" routine and not as productive as it could be. The end goal is to improve the performance of employees. Many companies utilize various forms and formats of performance management software, both web-based and mobile, to augment the process for efficiency. Software can vary, but most programs enable the manager to easily keep a record of all performance-related discussions, track progress against goals, and illustrate how progress against goals is linked to the company's strategic objectives. Most also provide a way of capturing skills for each employee, which in turn can assist with succession planning in case an employee leaves the organization. Many even have the capability to facilitate 360-degree feedback between managers, employees, and peers. Additionally, most software packages can produce helpful dashboards, illustrating progress and standard and customized reports to assist management when evaluating performance. Performance management software can be a stand-alone product or part of a more integrated and robust HR system.

PERFORMANCE APPRAISAL METHODS

There are many different performance appraisal methods. Some involve feedback from the immediate supervisor, and some involve the feedback of peers, clients, or subordinates. Many organizations begin the process with self-appraisals. **Self-appraisals** are most beneficial when used for personal development and identifying training needs, but less beneficial when they are used as a basis for the formal evaluation process. Good supervisors are able to evaluate performance and give meaningful feedback. Hence, it should not be surprising that **supervisor appraisals** are typically required as at least one major component of the overall performance appraisal process. One type of appraisal that considers feedback from multiple sources is a **360-degree appraisal**. These appraisals have rapidly grown in popularity and are expected to share a broader perspective of performance because they include feedback from everyone the employee interacts with—managers, peers, clients, and subordinates.

FORMS OF RANKING

Ranking procedures put employees in order from highest to lowest based upon evaluation characteristics such as performance. There are three main forms of ranking:

- **Straight ranking** involves listing all employees in order, with number one being the best, number two being second best, number three being third, and so on.
- **Alternate ranking** entails choosing the best and the worst from a list of all employees, removing these names from the list, and repeating until there are no names left.
- **Paired comparison** consists of evaluating only two employees at a time, deciding which is better, and continuing until each employee has been paired against every other employee.

Ranking procedures assist with distributing budgeted pay increases that are more clearly tied to performance, and they eliminate some of the biases found in traditional review criteria. The forced-distribution method, also known as **forced ranking**, uses a bell curve in which the majority of employees will receive an average score and a small group will receive extremely high or extremely low performance scores.

RATING APPRAISAL METHODS

There are a variety of rating appraisal methods, but the two most common are the checklist method and the rating scale method. The **checklist method** is a series of statements describing a certain level of performance. The performance evaluator can then check a box next to the statement that best describes the individual's performance in each performance area. The **rating scale method** rates an individual's performance on a point scale, usually a 1–3, 1–4, 1–5, or 1–10 scale, with higher numbers representing better performance.

BEHAVIORALLY BASED APPRAISAL METHODS

Greater focus on accountability and results has led to new approaches for appraising performance. The three main **behaviorally based appraisal methods** are management by objectives, behaviorally anchored rating scales, and behavioral observation scales.

Management by objectives is proactive rather than reactive. It focuses on predicting and shaping the future of the company, accomplishing results rather than simply following directions, improving competence and effectiveness, and increasing the participation and engagement of employees.

Behaviorally anchored rating scales (BARS) assign numerical values to performance based on a given range, such as a five-star system or a scale from 1 to 10. The BARS method analyzes the job description for a particular position and identifies the tasks that must be performed for the organization to function effectively. Once the tasks are identified, a determination is made about the specific way the individual should behave to perform each task. For example, if communication is identified as a necessary skill for a management position, then an individual in that position must be able to keep others informed. A series of ranked statements are then designed to describe how effectively the individual performed. Performance appraisers can choose the statement that best describes the employee's behavior. The key benefits of BARS are that they create agreement by being less subjective and more based upon observations.

Behavioral observation scales are similar to BARS, but with greater focus on frequency of behavior than on quality of performance, such as a sliding scale of "always," "sometimes," and "never."

NARRATIVE APPRAISAL METHODS

The three most common narrative appraisal techniques are the critical incident method, the essay method, and the field review method.

The **critical incident method** documents each performance problem related to an employee occurring during a set period so that the evaluator can discuss problems with the employee at the end.

The **essay method** requires performance evaluators to write a short essay about each employee describing their performance during the period in question.

The **field review method** is a method in which an individual other than the employee's direct supervisor or manager performs the appraisal and writes down a series of assessments and observations about that employee's performance.

ERRORS OCCURRING IN THE PERFORMANCE APPRAISAL PROCESS

Errors can occur when assessing employee performance. It is important to be aware of and hopefully avoid the following common errors:

- **Recency and primacy error**—A **recency** error is when the appraiser evaluates an employee on their more recent activities and not earlier performance. A **primacy** error is when an appraiser values an employee's earlier performance with greater emphasis than their more recent performance.
- **Halo and horn effect**—A **halo** effect is when an employee is exemplary in one area and rated outstanding because of the one area of expertise, ignoring other categories. A **horn** effect is just the opposite, where one area of weakness overshadows all other areas.
- **Strictness and leniency**—Some appraisers may believe the agreed-upon standards for performance are too low and therefore do not rate performance in a fair manner. In other words, they are reluctant to give the highest rating because, from their perspective, no one is ever that good. **Strictness** gives no room for failure. Conversely, **leniency** is when an appraiser gives an undeserving employee an inflated appraisal.
- **Bias**—This occurs when an appraiser's prejudices and values cloud their judgment, causing them to evaluate someone's performance through their own belief system and not necessarily the organization's.

BIAS AS IT RELATES TO PERFORMANCE APPRAISALS

Performance appraisals are a key part of employee feedback and development. However, it is very difficult to be 100% objective when completing such an evaluation, and inevitably, some bias may seep in. Both conscious and unconscious bias during the review process can have a negative impact on the employee and on the organization. Reviews that are inflated or deflated can lead to skewed metrics, with unreliable readings on true performance levels in the organization.

In order to combat bias in performance appraisals, there are several things to keep in mind. Those responsible for rating others should be reminded to think critically about their own biases and assumptions so they can avoid having them affect their assessments. Leaders should provide their team members with regular feedback, which will help prevent recency bias. Regular feedback also provides contextual information to refer back to during formal appraisals and ensures nothing during the appraisals comes as a shock.

Previous appraisals should be reviewed to check for patterns and trends that might indicate bias. Leaders need to be mindful and review the language used in the appraisal, as certain adjectives and phrases can demonstrate various types of bias. Metrics should be gathered to support feedback and should be incorporated in the report. Having hard data can eliminate some of the emotions involved in evaluations and can help eliminate bias. Feedback should be gathered from various sources such as peers, direct reports, and departments the employee may work with closely. Employees should also be asked to complete self-assessments, which can provide insights into areas where the rater might not have much knowledge or oversight.

LEGAL CONSIDERATIONS IN THE PERFORMANCE APPRAISAL PROCESS

The EEOC clearly explains that performance appraisals, in accordance with Uniform Guidelines, must be job-related. Additionally, in a performance appraisal, careful attention is necessary to avoid any form of discrimination covered under Title VII of the Civil Rights Act of 1964 and related anti-discrimination laws. Evaluation criteria should be formally assessed in a structured format that limits subjective responses and increases the validity of data about performance. The goal is for performance to be rated against objective, predefined standards. Information and documentation must be based on genuine interaction with the employee being appraised. Furthermore, the actual appraisal meeting should have some mechanism or protocol in place to prevent one manager from dominating the discussion and unfairly influencing employee rating. Overall, the performance appraisal process should be equitable and fair for all employees.

WORKPLACE BEHAVIOR ISSUES
ETHICAL AGENTS

Ethics are the moral principles, values, and accepted standards of behavior that determine whether an action is right or wrong. The Society for Human Resource Management (SHRM) Competency Model defines ethical practice as "the knowledge, skills, abilities, and other characteristics needed to maintain high levels of personal and professional integrity and to act as an ethical agent who promotes core values, integrity, and accountability throughout the organization."

Ethics and compliance officers ensure that business is conducted in accordance with rules, legal regulations, and industry standards of practice. Additionally, an ethical agent makes moral judgments based on fundamental ethical principles that are rooted in their personal character, not based on a situation's potential gains. Ethical dilemmas occur when a corporation or individual is faced with a conflict of interest, or actions that are blatantly wrong, deceptive, or may have uncertain consequences. Many ethical conflicts value profit over moral principles. Over the past few decades, ethics and business conduct have received increasing attention that has led to more stringent compliance regulations, like the Sarbanes-Oxley Act.

CODE OF CONDUCT

A **code of conduct** is a set of behavioral rules rooted in moral standards, laws, and best practices that a company develops, adopts, and communicates to employees. It outlines expected behavior and defines what behavior will not be tolerated. The document should also state what disciplinary actions employees could face if they violate the code.

Employee involvement in the development of a code of conduct will lead to greater employee buy-in and adherence. The code should be written in clear language that can be applied to specific situations as they arise. Upon finalization, the code should be shared with all employees. Employees should then be required to sign a document acknowledging receipt and understanding of the new code.

> **Review Video: Ethical and Professional Standards**
> Visit mometrix.com/academy and enter code: 391843

ABSENTEEISM

Absenteeism is when employees do not arrive at work when scheduled. **Tardiness**, a form of absenteeism, occurs when an employee arrives late for work. Absenteeism and tardiness both negatively impact an organization's productivity, financial performance, and administrative cost to operate. Taking pre-approved time off for personal reasons or vacation is a benefit, and time for an employee to "recharge" away from work is beneficial. Additionally, the organization's management team knows in advance and can plan accordingly. Time off for illness usually cannot be predicted and is generally encouraged in order to not make an entire office sick. Also, there are many legal protections afforded an employee for illness-related absences.

Absenteeism is usually regarded as habitual time off for either legitimate or illegitimate reasons. Employers can develop policies for absenteeism that might involve improving communications about their excusable and inexcusable absences, one-on-one discussions with the employee, and recognition programs to reward good attendance. However, an employer should be careful when disciplining an employee for excessive absenteeism to ensure the discipline is not in violation with federal, state, or local laws and regulations, such as USERRA for military leave, occurrences covered under the Family and Medical Leave Act (FMLA), and other protected activities depending on state laws (voting, children's activities, medical).

AGGRESSIVE BEHAVIOR IN THE WORKPLACE

Aggressive behavior in the workplace is typically a response to stress that should be recognized and handled immediately before it causes more harm. Aggression and violence could be displayed in any number of ways, such as physical assault, intimidation, threats, stalking, property damage, or verbal or written abuse. It can also occur between employees, between an employee and customer, between an employee and a family member, or from an outsider who has ideological differences with the business, among other possibilities.

The US Department of Labor maintains that some people work in and around circumstances that present a greater danger of violence than others: people who handle cash, work in high-crime areas, or deliver services or goods. There are many triggers for aggression to occur, including money issues, job loss, demotion, personal loss, and holidays. Sometimes, there is nothing an employer can do to prevent aggression or violence, like a terrorist incident. Other times, there are warning signs that an employee might become aggressive at work, such as unexplained drastic changes in behavior, absenteeism, performance decline, chatter about unfair treatment, overly emotional reactions to situations, or expressions of paranoia. The goal is to recognize the signs and address them, usually with a zero-tolerance policy for aggressive or violent behavior. The following are some options for organizations addressing aggressive behavior:

- Educate employees about safety and zero tolerance for violence, including resources such as an HR contact, a company security group, and key phone numbers or websites for help. Tell employees not to do anything or go anywhere they feel unsafe.
- Maintain vigilant security at the work site—surveillance cameras, identification tags, electronic entry, etc.
- Conduct training programs or offer resources to de-stress.

There is not a specific remedy if aggressive behavior is observed because it is dependent on a number of factors. Nevertheless, when encountering aggressive behavior, try to stay calm and de-escalate if possible, and never hesitate to call the police for assistance.

DEALING WITH EMPLOYEE CONFLICT

Employee conflict, or disagreement among employees, will occur. Not all conflict is unproductive. Many times, employee disagreement or conflict that occurs in a constructive, respectful manner leads to innovation, increased creativity, and ultimately improvements. However, there are times when the opposite occurs and employee conflict is a negative experience for all involved. The following are some strategies for an organization to address negative employee conflict:

- Ask questions and gain a complete understanding of the problem. First, evaluate whether the conflict involves any EEOC violations, such as discrimination or harassment. Assuming no EEOC violations, gain an understanding of the root cause of the problem, not the fallout. Depending on the situation, encourage employees to work it out on their own, if possible. This is a judgment call.

- If intervention becomes necessary to prevent escalation, do so immediately. Listen to both sides, ask questions, and restate issues for clarification. Make sure both parties understand that they must let each other speak uninterrupted and address each other with respect. Encourage both parties to devise a way to manage going forward, and assist in devising a written plan that both agree to follow. Reference the employee handbook for behavioral expectations.
- Offer training or personality assessments to help conflicted employees improve their communication style, and encourage managers to lead by example.

INSUBORDINATION

Insubordination is when an employee overtly refuses to do or comply with a reasonable work request from their manager. The manager's request must meet two basic criteria: (1) the employee must thoroughly understand the request, and (2) the request cannot be dangerous or unethical. Claims of insubordination must be thoroughly investigated by HR from a position of neutrality, and a conclusion must be drawn as to why the employee is refusing to complete the assignment. The incident should be documented.

If this is a one-time occurrence that is unlikely to happen again, then a discussion of ways to behave going forward is appropriate. However, if insubordination becomes a pattern, then disciplinary action should be followed—possibly a verbal warning, a written warning, a suspension, or a combination of other similar alternatives. Termination is even possible if no other remediation helps to rectify the situation. Insubordination should always be thoroughly investigated, documented, and addressed immediately and appropriately, before it leads to a decline in productivity, possible employee turnover, or a hostile work environment.

ILLEGAL HARASSMENT

Illegal harassment usually involves unwelcome verbal exchanges, unwelcome physical contact, or unwelcome actions that are based on a person's race, religion, gender, sexual orientation, national origin, age, disability, genetic information, military membership, or veteran status. The action(s) taken must meet the threshold of a "severe and pervasive" work environment, characterized as hostile, abusive, or intimidating for "a reasonable person." If this type of harassment is present, it could be a violation of the following federal regulations: Title VII of the Civil Rights Act of 1964, the Americans with Disabilities Act (ADA), the Age Discrimination in Employment Act (ADEA), the Genetic Information Nondiscrimination Act (GINA), or the Uniformed Services Employment and Reemployment Rights Act (USERRA). Additionally, many states and local laws provide even more enhanced legal protections against harassment. Harassment interferes with an employee's ability to accomplish their work. All allegations of harassment should be reported, investigated immediately, and acted upon appropriately by the employer.

CONDUCTING HARASSMENT TRAINING

Companies should conduct regular harassment training because employers must exercise reasonable care to avoid and prevent harassment. Several states have mandatory harassment training for certain types of employees. Otherwise, employers may be found liable for the harassing behaviors of vendors, clients, coworkers, and supervisors. **Harassment** is defined as any demeaning or degrading comments, jokes, name-calling, actions, graffiti, or other belittling conduct that may be found offensive. Any form of derogatory speech can be considered harassment, including neutral words that may be perceived in a vulgar or intimidating way. Furthermore, the Civil Rights Act of 1964 protects individuals from harassment on the basis of race, color, religion, gender, or national origin. Damages awarded under Title VII can total anywhere from $50,000 to $300,000, depending upon the size of the employer.

BULLYING IN THE WORKPLACE

Bullying is a form of aggressive behavior in the workplace that includes numerous forms of mistreatment that allow the bully to assert control and attack another person's self-confidence or self-esteem. Bullying can be overt, such as yelling, obscene language, and public humiliation. However, bullying can also be much more subtle, such as failing to invite a targeted employee to an essential meeting, withholding needed resources, sabotage, micromanagement, and inequitable treatment. In either case, while bullying is obviously detrimental to the victim, it may also damage the business by harming productivity or incurring legal costs. Many organizations have modified their harassment policies to specifically address bullying. Changing the policy needs to be combined with an awareness campaign so that employees understand what bullying is, what its consequences are, and how to report it. There should be a process for reporting claims of bullying—such as a contact in HR—so that the victim feels comfortable. All reported bullying incidents should be investigated immediately and, if necessary, met with action. Also, Title VII of the Civil Rights Act of 1964 and the EEOC could offer protections against harassment in the form of bullying, depending on the circumstances and investigative findings.

GUIDING PRINCIPLES WHEN APPROACHING EMPLOYEE DISCIPLINE

Discipline in the workplace is necessary, but should always be fair and within the constraints of federal, state, and local laws. To paraphrase an old proverb, "the punishment should fit the crime." All discipline should be applied consistently, or the organization is at risk for a legal violation. Additionally, it is a good practice to document a record of facts, including dates, leading to the disciplinary action, and steps taken to remedy the situation. An HR professional should be in a position to support any disciplinary actions. Asking questions to clarify when in doubt is an important step. An employee may not always agree with the action, but they must understand why corrective actions are needed. Being firm and consistent, and showing respect and empathy toward the employee, are necessary when discipline must be deployed.

IMPORTANCE OF TRACKING EMPLOYEE GRIEVANCES

A **grievance** is a complaint, by an employee to an employer, of some type of unfair treatment or violation. An employee grievance can be formal, like a written report, or informal, like a verbal discussion. Generally, a grievance can be from an employee against an employer or management official, from an employee against another employee, or any combination thereof. Some examples of grievances might include harassment, discrimination, safety concerns, workplace relationships, and organizational changes.

HR is often involved and tracks grievances, both for awareness and to determine if there are trends in grievances pointing to a bigger issue in an organization, such as a large number of grievances against one manager. Tracking grievances based on subject matter can assist in implementing quicker corrective actions. Measuring the time it takes to close a grievance could also impact employee satisfaction with the organization. If the problem is quickly addressed and resolved in a fair and expedient time frame, then the employee will feel more valued and satisfied. Tracking grievances also provides the organization a picture of whether employee complaints and grievances are rising or falling, which is another measure of organizational health.

PROGRESSIVE DISCIPLINE

Progressive discipline is a method to inform an employee about behavior, conduct, or job performance that is unsatisfactory and to gradually implement actions designed to improve their behavior or performance. This gives the employee the opportunity to correct the undesired behavior or poor performance through a gradual progression of disciplinary responses. The goal of this process is to get the employee back on track toward becoming a more productive member of the organization.

There is not a specific formula for implementing progressive discipline. Usually, the seriousness of the infraction and number of incidents factor into the implementation of progressive discipline. Progressive discipline is typically a five-step process:

1. A **verbal warning**, or a one-on-one session with a manager reviewing the issues and the corrective action
2. A **written warning**, in which a manager documents the issue and lack of improvement
3. A **performance improvement plan (PIP)**, which is a documented plan that is time-bound and details what will happen if corrective action is not achieved
4. **Suspension**, for when a corrective action is not achieved and the employee is given time away from work to reflect on the situation
5. **Termination**, at which point the progressive discipline is labeled a failure and the employee is terminated

The overall rationale behind progressive discipline is to ensure employees are treated fairly and to help nurture a positive organizational culture.

POLICIES, PROCEDURES, AND WORK RULES

The goal of an organization's policies, procedures, and work rules is to help an organization achieve its goals in an equitable and efficient manner. However, there is a difference between the three terms:

- **Policy**—An overarching or broad statement describing the company's basic philosophy and standards for all related management and employee activities. For example, a company might have a policy stating that "The company will reimburse for educational tuition if the course is related to work the employee performs. All coursework must be pre-approved by the management team." This is a broad statement that explains the policy for tuition reimbursement, but doesn't give specifics—it only states that there is an educational reimbursement policy.
- **Procedure**—This specifies very specific steps or methods to process or handle employee activities. For example, if an employee wants reimbursement for taking a course, they might have to follow these steps: (1) Meet with immediate supervisor to discuss, (2) obtain form XYZ and have it signed by the supervisor with supporting attachments, (3) supervisor must obtain approvals from certain department heads, etc.
- **Work rule**—These rules stand as a guide for clear action to be taken or not taken in a specific situation. These rules are usually black and white, designed to leave no room for ambiguity or interpretation. For example, "Educational reimbursement will be granted only if an employee takes a class at a college accredited by the following institutions ..."

DELIVERING DISCIPLINARY ACTION

Disciplinary actions, whether part of a union contract or not, should always be fair to all. Therefore, employees should have a process or ability to defend their actions against any accusation of wrongdoing. In other words, employees should be given the opportunity to present their side of the story in their words. An employer should be consistent in delivering discipline, meaning that treatment is similar to what others have received for equivalent offenses. A manager should always be able to produce strong, preferably documented, evidence of an employee's wrongdoing.

Disciplinary actions are rarely straightforward, and are usually complicated by other factors that must be taken into consideration. HR usually reviews disciplinary actions before they are implemented, trying to mitigate risk for the company. The following are some considerations HR should examine: any EEO violations; consistency in treatment; potential tort or other legal liabilities; compliance with union contracts (if applicable); and compliance with federal, state, and local laws and regulations.

WARNINGS IN A PROGRESSIVE DISCIPLINE PROCESS

A **warning** is usually a clear indication that a supervisor or the management team is dissatisfied with an employee's work or attitude. A warning is typically the first step in a progressive discipline process, with the goal being to correct the undesired action(s). A warning can be either verbal or in writing.

- **Verbal**—A verbal warning could be an informal discussion with the employee about their undesired actions and what should be done to improve. It is important that the employee leave the conversation with a clear understanding of the corrective action that must be taken, and what could happen next if the action is not corrected.
- **Written**—A written warning is similar in tone to a verbal warning, except the manager delivers a document or letter detailing the issue with an employee's actions or attitude, and clear expectations about what specifically needs to be corrected. A written warning will also document possible consequences if the issue is not corrected.

ESCALATING CORRECTIVE ACTIONS

Escalating corrective actions are measures taken by an employer, usually a manager, to fix a problem or wrongdoing that an employee is continually repeating even after initial interventions are taken, such as a verbal and/or written warning. An employee issue can be behavioral or can involve any other aspect of their work that impacts performance. When initial interventions do not produce the desired results, escalating corrective actions need to be taken. Employers may document these specific measures in their employee handbook, or they can be unique, and consequences may need to be altered slightly. Also, in the case of a union environment, there may be very specific disciplinary actions that contractually must be adhered to because they are specified in the collective bargaining agreement. Escalating corrective actions is a logical sequence of discipline that could include required training, suspensions with or without pay, demotions, and sometimes termination. The following is an example of escalating corrective actions:

- Verbal warning
- Written warning
- Mandatory training (if applicable)
- One-day suspension
- One-week suspension
- Two-week suspension
- Termination

Every step needs to be documented: what was incorrect or unacceptable, the expected behavior or performance measure going forward, the discipline being dispensed, and consequences if the corrective actions are not taken.

TERMINATION IN THE PROGRESSIVE DISCIPLINE PROCESS

Termination is when an employee is removed from their job. It is often described as a separation from employment. Involuntary termination can result from the employee's failure to abide by the progressive discipline plan due to poor performance or behavior, or from a policy violation. Usually, it is preferable for an employee to know well in advance that continued actions which remain uncorrected could result in termination. Managers should ensure employees understand the gravity and consequences of failure to correct wrongdoing.

If a decision is made to terminate an employee, it should be done swiftly, and employers should take necessary measures to make sure managers understand that departing employees must be treated with dignity and respect during the termination process. Typically, a private meeting is held between the manager, an HR representative, and the employee. The manager delivering the termination should get right to the point and be clear, yet remain sympathetic and patient. Additionally, at the termination meeting, the manager or HR representative should be prepared to discuss the employee's last paycheck and any other financial matters that need to be settled. Final pay and other financial matters are sometimes dictated by state law and regulations. As always, employers should adhere to all federal, state, and local laws and regulations when terminating an employee.

WRONGFUL TERMINATION

Wrongful termination occurs when an employee is illegally terminated from employment, or fired in such a way as to violate an agreed-upon contract or public policy. Laws can vary enormously from state to state on criteria for wrongful termination. The following are some more specific reasons a termination could be wrongful:

- Discrimination
- The employer asking the employee to pursue an illegal act
- Breach of contract
- Termination for whistleblowing
- Violation of company policy

There is not a particular law or regulation that specifically shields or protects an employee against wrongful termination; rather, it is usually other laws, such as anti-discrimination laws, whistleblower protections, public policy, or collective bargaining agreement laws. The majority of states recognize some form of at-will employment, meaning the employer does not need a reason to fire an employee, and an employee is permitted to leave employment without reason or notice. However, the employer cannot terminate an employee in a manner that breaks a law or violates the company's own policies. And just because an employer can fire an employee without reason does not mean that they should do so.

OFFBOARDING

The terms "onboarding" and "offboarding" evoke images of getting on and off a vessel for an ocean voyage. Employment is being compared to a journey on the ocean. The complexity of the voyage dictates the steps needed for the onboarding and offboarding processes. The same holds true for employment. Every organization wants the beginning and ending of employment to be a good experience. **Offboarding** is a process that includes all decisions and steps that need to be completed when an employee separates from an organization. Offboarding is also an opportunity to talk with an exiting employee about ways to improve the organization. It is important to remember that, when an employee leaves an organization, he or she could be a loyal supporter of the organization, or could speak negatively about the employer. Offboarding gives an employer one final opportunity to influence how the employee feels when they leave. A good offboarding process can help minimize the chance that potential ill feelings might linger. Offboarding leaves a lasting impression in the minds of employees separating from an employer.

STEPS INCLUDED IN THE OFFBOARDING PROCESS

Employers' offboarding processes can differ depending on the organization and functions of a job. The following are some of the items that might be included in the offboarding process:

- Planning for the transfer of knowledge from the departing employee to their replacement (if appropriate)
- Reviewing final pay, benefits, and financial information, including retirement options, unused vacation, health coverage, and COBRA (if applicable)
- Collecting all computer equipment, phone, and other technology-related items
- Collecting other employer-issued items, such as uniforms, credit card, and automobile
- Collecting physical keys and security badges
- Deactivating access to company intranet and other systems (email, databases, etc.), as well as related rights and passwords
- Verifying accurate contact information—mailing address, phone number, and email address
- Conducting an exit interview—Usually done by an HR representative to understand the employee's viewpoint on their overall work experience and other concerns that will enable the organization to improve going forward

RETENTION

Retention describes the ability of an organization to keep individuals employed within the company. Retention is directly related to the strategies employed by organizations to increase employee engagement and organizational loyalty. These strategies can include competitive compensation strategies, flexibility (e.g., hybrid schedules, working from home, and split shifts), employee recognition and reward programs, positive culture, regular and meaningful feedback, and professional development and advancement opportunities.

Organizations that lack adequate retention strategies—or that have lower levels of engagement and morale—can risk losing members of the organization, including high-potential or top-performing employees. Low retention rates lead to increased recruitment and onboarding costs. Low retention rates can impact organizations from the perspective of the customer and vendor as well. If these individuals deal with a revolving door of contacts, this can cause a loss of trust.

Measuring retention rates and implementing retention strategies will assist the organization with morale, productivity, and consistency. Higher retention rates naturally lead to less turnover. This in turn mitigates the poor morale and poor productivity that likely would have resulted from higher turnover rates. Satisfactory levels of employee retention are critical to organizational success because team building, cohesion, and institutional knowledge come with stability and consistency.

Retention can be calculated using the following formula:

$$\frac{ending\ head\ count\ for\ period}{starting\ head\ count\ for\ period} \times 100$$

Complaints, Investigations, and Conflict Resolution

IMPORTANCE OF HR POLICIES AND PROCEDURES

An **HR policy** is a set of rules that all members of an organization are required to follow, whereas an **HR procedure** covers the steps necessary to implement a policy. Basically, policy states what rules must be followed in an organization, while procedures detail in writing how to adhere to organizational policies. For an organization to be successful, HR policies and procedures should contain the following core elements:

- Employee role descriptions that detail employee expectations specific to each position in an organization
- Rules and regulations that specify what employees can or cannot do, as well as behavior that is or is not acceptable
- A clear description of consequences for unethical or inappropriate behavior or actions

There are many reasons why an organization needs to have HR policies: (1) They give people defined rules to achieve a respectful environment, (2) they reduce conflict and provide an organization with a certain standard to guide acceptable behavior, and (3) they assist an organization in forming an image in the community that is also helpful for recruiting.

WORKPLACE MONITORING PARAMETERS

Workplace monitoring is a documented policy and program that an employer can use to monitor and gather information related to suspicious activity by a person in their organization. This monitoring is conducted if the employer has reason to believe a person in their organization is engaged in some activity that might threaten the interests of the business. Monitoring methods might include reviewing internet content usage, wiretapping, GPS tracking, and interviewing other employees. Many of these surveillance methods are easier if the company requires employees to utilize company-issued phones and computers.

Before any workplace monitoring activities are deployed, two actions must occur: (1) employers must be aware of and adhere to all local, state, and federal laws regarding the desired method of workplace monitoring; and (2) employers must ensure that all employees have been made aware and given documentation of all company rules and regulations at the onset of employment, and changes thereafter. Employees' knowledge of employer rules and regulations is helpful if there is unethical or illegal activity because, when such activity is committed, existing employee knowledge proves the activity was committed intentionally by the employee.

METHODS FOR INVESTIGATING COMPLAINTS OR GRIEVANCES

INVESTIGATING EMPLOYEE MISCONDUCT

The investigation process usually begins when a complaint is received, or when it is determined there is reasonable cause to investigate an employee's conduct. The organization should identify exactly what is being investigated, what sort of evidence is needed to prove or disprove the misconduct, who should be interviewed during the investigation, and which questions need to be asked to gather the necessary evidence. Next, the organization needs to interview the person making the complaint, the individual the complaint is against, and any other employees who have relevant information. Finally, the organization should come to a decision and take appropriate action.

WEINGARTEN RIGHTS

In *National Labor Relations Board v. Weingarten*, the Supreme Court established the right of employees to have union representation at investigatory interviews in which the employee must defend conduct or behavior. If an employee believes that discipline or other consequences might follow, he or she has the right to request union representation. However, management does not need to inform an employee of their Weingarten rights. It is the employee's own responsibility to know these rights and request representation. When requested, management can (1) stop questioning until a representative arrives, (2) terminate the interview, or (3) ask the employee to voluntarily relinquish their rights to representation. The company does need to inform the representative of the interview topic, and the representative does have the right to counsel the employee in private and advise them what to say.

GRIEVANCES

A **grievance** is a work-related complaint or formal dispute that is brought to the attention of management. However, in nonunion environments, grievances may encompass any discontent or sense of injustice. Grievance procedures provide an orderly and methodical process for hearing and evaluating employee complaints, and they tend to be more developed in unionized companies than in nonunionized companies as a result of labor agreement specifications. These procedures protect employee rights and eliminate the need for strikes or slowdowns every time there is a disagreement.

Disagreements may be unavoidable in situations where the labor contract is open to interpretation because negotiators cannot anticipate all potential conflicts. Formal grievance procedures increase upward communication in organizations and make top management decisions more sensitive to employee emotions. The first step to resolving grievances is for a complaint to be submitted to the supervisor or written and submitted to the union steward.

If these parties cannot find a resolution from there, the complaint may be heard by the superintendent or plant manager and the industrial relations manager. If the union is still unsatisfied, the grievance can be appealed to the next step, which may be arbitration if the company is small. Large corporations may have grievance committees, corporate officers, and/or international union representatives who will meet and hear grievances. However, the final step of an unresolved dispute will be binding arbitration by an outside third party, where both parties come to an acceptable agreement.

RESOLVING DISCRIMINATION COMPLAINTS

Resolving discrimination complaints requires an employer to decide between two different paths:

- An employer can follow the process defined by the Equal Employment Opportunity Commission (EEOC) and thus be subject to further investigation by the state or local Fair Employment Practice Agency (FEPA). An employee has 180 days from the date of the incident to file a discrimination complaint with the EEOC. After an investigation, probable cause will or will not be found, and the process can go one of two ways:
  - o Probable cause found—The EEOC will try conciliation, and the employer can agree to settle, or litigation could be pursued with the EEOC or private court.
  - o Probable cause not found—After the 180-day period is over, the employee can ask for a right-to-sue letter, and then has 90 days to file in court. At this point, the EEOC's involvement with the matter ends.
- An employer can make the decision to settle the alleged charges instead of facing an investigation by FEPA.

An employer must contemplate a number of issues before deciding which path is best. Typically, employers will weigh the costs involved in a one-time settlement versus a possibly extended period of legal disruption that could cost both time and money. An open investigation could harm a company's reputation whether the allegations are true or not. Also, if a company believes the claim of discrimination might be truthful, the one-time settlement might make sense in order to quickly pivot, address, and rectify any possible systemic discriminatory practices within the company.

FRONT PAY

When an employer is found guilty of discrimination, the employee who brought forth the complaint is usually permitted to return to their position in the organization. However, the court will sometimes instead rule for front pay. **Front pay** is money awarded to the employee from the employer in a discrimination situation. Generally, the amount awarded is equal to lost wages. There are three situations in which front pay is required from the employer:

- The position left vacant by the employee discriminated against is no longer available.
- The employer has taken no action to rectify the discriminatory practice(s) occurring within the organization.
- The returning employee could be facing an unreasonable, possibly hostile, work environment if he or she were to return to the prior position.

MEDIATION PROCESS

The goal of the **mediation process** is to solve a dispute without having to take more aggressive legal steps. A mediator is specially trained to work with two or more disagreeing parties to reach an agreeable resolution. There is a difference between mediation and arbitration. Arbitration can be the final judgment for a dispute, meaning that if mediation doesn't work, the parties involved can move to arbitration or litigation. Mediation is considered non-binding.

Typically, both parties must mutually agree on a mediator to start the process. A mediator speaks with both parties and there are agreed-upon ground rules, such as logistics, when the negotiation will occur, what specifically will be discussed, who should be involved, and protocol or procedures for discussion. During the agreed-upon negotiations, the mediator will work with both parties to problem-solve and create a reasonable solution to move forward. Frequently, this requires compromise on both sides. If a resolution or compromise is agreed upon, both parties must sign documentation stating they will abide by the agreed-upon plan. If a resolution is not reached during the mediation process, then the parties can either pursue arbitration or litigation to resolve the dispute.

TYPES OF ARBITRATION

Arbitration is a formal way to settle disputes outside of court. Frequently, parties in a dispute try arbitration if mediation does not work. Parties must agree on a neutral, third-party arbitrator, who listens and makes decisions based on the information and facts presented during the questioning and subsequent discussions. There are many types of arbitration:

- **Binding** arbitration—During this type of arbitration, both parties are required to abide by the final judgment. In other words, the party that "loses" the arbitration must carry out the final judgment. Also, in binding arbitration, this is the end of the legal process: both parties have no other legal recourse with regard to the dispute after a decision is rendered in binding arbitration.
- **Non-binding** arbitration—This type follows the same process as binding arbitration, except the decision rendered does not have to be followed and cannot legally be enforced. Additionally, if either party chooses, they can pursue further legal action.
- **Compulsory** arbitration—In this situation, both parties are required by law to enter into the arbitration process. Generally, this occurs due to one of two reasons: (1) a court order dictated that compulsory arbitration is mandatory, or (2) an agreed-upon contract states that disputes require compulsory arbitration to be resolved.

- **Voluntary** arbitration—The parties in dispute mutually agree to willingly participate in the arbitration process in the hopes of avoiding potentially expensive and time-consuming legal alternatives.

TYPES OF ARBITRATORS

There are three different types of arbitrators that could lead the resolution of a dispute. Which type of arbitrator an organization chooses is dependent on the circumstances and previously agreed-upon contracts, if applicable.

- **Permanent** arbitrator—This type of arbitrator usually judges cases for a particular organization or during the life of a contract. In either case, the arbitrator has intimate knowledge of the organization and material being discussed. This knowledge makes arbitration highly efficient, but it is important that both parties continue to believe the arbitrator is unbiased.
- **Ad hoc** arbitrator—In this situation, an arbitrator is mutually agreed upon by both parties, but the arbitrator does not have a previously established relationship with either party. Usually, an ad hoc arbitrator is chosen in one-time situations.
- Arbitrator **panel**—This group of arbitrators, usually three, is similar to ad hoc arbitrators in that they do not have a previously established relationship with the parties involved. This type of panel is sometimes referred to as an arbitral tribunal or a tripartite panel. In the case of a tripartite arbitration panel, the representation is as follows: one arbitrator represents the management, one arbitrator represents the union, and one is neutral. In most cases, the neutral arbitrator is the one who makes the deciding vote.

ESCALATION

Employees need to know what to do when discrimination, harassment, or bullying occurs in the workplace. There are several ways to address these types of issues. If the employee is comfortable, he or she can confront the perpetrator of the behavior directly. The employee can talk with the perpetrator and let that individual know which behaviors, language, or actions are causing the issue. Individuals can be less defensive when addressed about a possible issue privately.

If the concerning behavior, commentary, or actions continue, escalation will be required. Escalation involves bringing the complaint or issue to the next level up. If confronting the perpetrator directly is not successful, the individual can bring the complaint to a team lead, supervisor, or manager. This allows an outside party with a particular level of authority the opportunity to help work through the issue. The leader can mediate between the two parties or address the perpetrator directly.

If the behavior persists after escalating to a leader within the organization, or the leader fails to address the complaint satisfactorily, the individual can then escalate the complaint to HR. HR is required to address and investigate complaints of harassment, bullying, or discrimination. HR should meet with the individual raising the complaint to get as much information as possible. HR should also meet with anyone who may have seen or overheard, or has knowledge of, the concerns raised. The person responsible for the areas of concern should also be interviewed. Once the interviews or conversations are complete, the HR department should review all company policies and regulations, as well as employment laws, to determine whether a violation has taken place. If a violation is found, it should be handled according to policy and law. If the concerning behavior persists after HR intervention, if retaliation occurs, or if HR fails to adequately address the issue, the next step in escalation is to lodge a complaint with the EEOC and allow that process to begin.

Organizational policies surrounding harassment, bullying, and discrimination should clearly state the levels of escalation so that all employees know what to do should they find themselves in that situation.

RETALIATION

Within an organizational setting, retaliation can take place when an employer takes adverse action against advocacy of protected rights. Retaliation is usually seen on an individual level. The action taken by the employer could come from an administrator, team lead, supervisor, or manager. Adverse actions can include demoting the employee, passing him or her over for a promotion, excluding that employee from meetings or events, giving unwarranted and excessive negative reviews, transferring the employee to a lesser position, harassing the employee, or even terminating the employee.

Retaliation in the form of adverse actions can result when an employee communicates with an individual of authority within the organization about harassment or discrimination, resists sexual advances, requests a religious or disability accommodation, or refuses to follow directives that could result in some type of discrimination. Retaliation stemming from an employee exercising his or her rights within the workplace is prohibited under law.

When an employee feels that the employer utilized retaliatory acts, he or she can file a charge with the EEOC for investigation. Should the EEOC validate the charge, the employee may receive money for damages (such as a settlement, backpay, or reinstatement to a position) from the employer. Additionally, the employer might be required to change policies and procedures, to complete training, or to take other measures to prevent further issues.

DOCUMENTATION

Documentation in HR is critical, as proper and detailed documentation keeps the organization compliant and protected from questionable lawsuits and legal actions. There must be a clear and consistent documentation process for all HR departments. In the event of official complaints and allegations, those interactions must be written down. Official conversations or interviews related to the complaints must also be documented. When complaints are substantiated, those results need to be written down as well, along with which regulations, policies, or laws were violated. Official counseling, warnings, or disciplinary actions stemming from complaints or concerns should also be recorded. All documents surrounding the complaint should be stored in a central location. This could be in the personnel file or in a separate area for complaints. There are many different templates for investigations, complaints, and employee contact available for use. Thorough documentation illustrates the process and intent behind different actions and can be used to provide evidence for both progressive discipline and termination actions.

IMPORTANCE OF CONFIDENTIALITY IN THE WORKPLACE

Confidentiality is vital in HR practices. Maintaining the confidentiality of all employee records is imperative. Information to be safeguarded includes, but is not limited to, Social Security numbers, birth dates, addresses, phone numbers, personal emails, benefits enrollments, medical or other leave details, garnishments, bank account information, disciplinary actions, grievances, and employment eligibility data. When employee record information is requested for legitimate purposes, a written release signed by the employee should be obtained and kept on file. Examples of these requests include employment verification for bank loans and mortgage applications.

Further, HR should internally disclose this sensitive data only to those who are authorized and have a need to know based on the scenario at hand. For example, a supervisor should know employees' disciplinary histories so that they can manage them more effectively. But that supervisor doesn't need to know what benefit plan the employee chose, or that the employee has a tax lien.

However, HR cannot always promise complete confidentiality. For example, if an employee makes a harassment allegation, HR will move to investigate immediately. HR should inform the complainant, and anyone involved in the investigation, that the situation will be handled as discreetly as possible; the nature of an investigation dictates that information obtained during the process may be shared with those who need to know, including the accused.

Diversity and Inclusion Initiatives

CORPORATE SOCIAL RESPONSIBILITY (CSR)

Corporate social responsibility (CSR) refers to an organization's effort to improve its environmental and social impact on the community at large. This is based on the premise that organizations can make the community (and the world) a better place. At the very least, the goal of CSR is to avoid causing damage that will ultimately harm the community. Typically, CSR programs can benefit the organization and its shareholders. Examples of CSR initiatives include, but are not limited to, donating to local charities such as soup kitchens, offering job training or mentoring programs for disadvantaged populations, reducing the organization's negative footprint on the environment, and helping in the event of natural or human-caused disasters.

There is evidence supporting the idea that CSR programs can benefit the organization financially, as well as establishing the organization as a reliable, upstanding member of the community. From an HR perspective, CSR programs could assist in recruiting, as potential employees may seek to work for a socially responsible company. CSR programs may also improve customer relations, brand management, and public relations, which may lead to competitive advantages and the possibility of improved profits.

SOCIAL RESPONSIBILITY INITIATIVES

CSR initiatives often focus on the external community of an organization, while diversity, equity, and inclusion (DEI) is more internally focused. However, CSR initiatives and DEI are closely related, reinforcing one another, and they can be combined to create an even more engaged and motivated workforce. These two areas can be merged to address both internal and external needs. Organizations can review existing company initiatives to determine whether CSR initiatives capture the diverse and varied perspectives of stakeholders. Do existing CSR initiatives leverage the traits, skills, and contributions that make the organization and the surrounding community unique? Does the organization support disadvantaged or underrepresented groups? Do organizational CSR initiatives help redistribute power in tangible ways? How do organizational behaviors and programs promote values and behaviors that make stakeholders feel like members of the community? How does the organization include unique and diverse points of view when developing CSR initiatives?

These are all important frames to review when looking over CSR implementations. Ways to ensure a blending of CSR and DEI can include utilizing diverse suppliers, such as minority- or women-owned businesses. This particular framework is even more successful if small and locally owned organizations are used as suppliers. When researching outside vendors, suppliers, and resources, the organization should investigate where the company is from, what their labor practices are, and what their employee population looks like. Doing business with other organizations that support women and minorities, do not practice unfair labor standards, and do not directly or indirectly

promote questionable activity, is a statement in itself and can help the organization build a reputation and commitment as a group that values DEI and CSR.

CULTURAL SENSITIVITY AND ACCEPTANCE

Cultural sensitivity can also be referred to as cultural awareness. Cultural sensitivity occurs when individuals understand that people come from a myriad of diverse cultures and backgrounds. Developing cultural sensitivity and acceptance requires individuals to reflect on and identify their own beliefs, values, attitudes, and behaviors that are specific to their own culture. The next step is for individuals to identify values, attitudes, beliefs, and behaviors of other cultures, aimed at gaining a deeper understanding and acceptance of diverse cultures. Differences are recognized, but no one culture is given specific value. One is not better than another; they are simply different. Cultural sensitivity and acceptance require individuals to recognize that not all experiences are shared; in fact, people's experiences differ based on their own upbringing, background, and culture. These experiences can impact both the way an individual interprets information and actions, and how he or she behaves in various instances.

In a professional setting, cultural sensitivity and acceptance are crucial for employees, especially those working on diverse teams. These practices allow communication to not only be effective, but flourish, and will promote an inclusive setting. Cultural sensitivity and acceptance are also important for relationships and exchanges with vendors and business partners. Organizations or individuals who lack cultural sensitivity and acceptance can cause customers, vendors, and partners to feel uncomfortable, marginalized, or disrespected, which could negatively impact the organization.

APPROACHES TO AN INCLUSIVE WORKPLACE

The first step toward establishing an inclusive workplace is to identify any areas of concern. An internal workforce should reflect the available labor market. Examine the corporate culture and communications to ensure that they advocate for a diverse and inclusive workplace. Review or amend policies and practices to support an inclusive culture. Focus on the behavioral aspects of how people communicate and work together. Are all perspectives respected and input from all positions valued? Address any areas that might not welcome protected classes or disabilities. Then brainstorm approaches and ideas for an inclusive workplace.

Once a diverse culture is established, target recruiting efforts to reach a broad audience. Some ideas may include college recruiting, training centers, career fairs, veteran's offices, and state unemployment offices or career centers. Set business objectives for areas that can be improved upon, document what changes will be implemented, and review progress.

DIVERSITY AND INCLUSION TRAINING

Although people most often think of diversity as being inclusive of minorities, diversity may also embrace a robust variety of traits such as generation, gender, sexual orientation, race, ethnicity, language, religious background, education, or life experiences. Diversity is the ability to consider and value the perspectives of all people. It is important for HR practitioners to recognize that everyone has both conscious and unconscious biases. **Diversity and inclusion training** supports establishing a nonjudgmental and collaborative workforce that is respectful and sensitive to differences among peers. Additionally, it can teach humility and self-awareness. Training program methods may be extensive or may address specific gaps. Moreover, diversity and inclusion training may introduce new perspectives to the workforce, promoting creativity and innovation.

ADVOCATING FOR A DIVERSE AND INCLUSIVE WORKPLACE

Diversity fosters the potential for more perspectives, creative ideas, and innovation. **Inclusion** involves realizing and accepting the benefits and competitive advantages to be had when everyone feels welcome and respected. This environment can be developed with openness, cultural sensitivity, and equal support. HR practitioners can advocate for a diverse and inclusive workplace by reflecting how it can align with business objectives. Building diverse teams can improve problem-solving and productivity and may increase customer satisfaction by providing better representation of an employer's stakeholders. Once buy-in has been gained from upper management, a diversity committee can collaborate to design and communicate initiatives.

OPERATING IN A DIVERSE WORKPLACE

HR practitioners should identify whether there are any areas of concern or need in the organization. Do current employees fairly represent the available talent pool? HR should work to address any unconscious biases or prevailing attitudes in policies or practices that do not support diversity initiatives. They can further support diversity by drawing attention to and eliminating discriminatory perspectives or prejudices. They should train managers on how to fairly and consistently conduct interviews and how to supervise employees from various backgrounds. Moreover, providing appropriate accommodations to employees in need can increase safety, efficiency, and team morale.

UNCONSCIOUS BIAS

Bias occurs when a judgment, decision, or assumption is made about an individual or group of individuals based not on objective fact or evidence, but on one's own perceptions and feelings associated with traits such as gender, physical ability, age, sexuality, ethnicity, religion, or race. Unconscious bias, also called implicit bias, occurs when the person making the judgment is unaware of their prejudice.

Unconscious bias can be rooted in learned stereotypes that happen unintentionally or automatically. Unconscious biases can form over time without being detected. They can start as early as childhood and can be learned through environmental and social interactions.

These biases can be present in the workplace and seen throughout the hiring process. For example, when reviewing resumes, a person could reach a conclusion about an individual based only on their name. Another form of unconscious bias seen in the hiring process relates to gender. Individuals may be prone to prefer one gender over the other. To help avoid these biases, it would be beneficial to provide resumes without names or identifying characteristics, instead highlighting skills, experience, qualifications, and education.

To help uncover and eliminate unconscious bias, training and education can be utilized by the organization or the individual. This type of training and education can include teaching individuals how certain factors and behaviors can alienate colleagues, and such education can challenge the individual to recognize prejudices or stereotypes he or she might hold. Incorporating diverse hiring tactics, like resume samples, phone interviews, and standardized questions, can help reduce bias during that process. Organizations should also set hiring goals designed to target diverse individuals, leading to a robust employee pool.

STEREOTYPES

Stereotypes are overgeneralized, exaggerated, fixed beliefs about a person or a group of people. Stereotypes do not account for individual differences and are used to make assumptions about individuals or groups. These beliefs can be based on traits like sexual orientation, religion, race, gender, ethnicity, education, background, or age. Stereotypes can also form as a result of past experiences. Stereotypes are harmful because they can lead to overt discrimination or more subtle unconscious bias, either of which can, in turn, marginalize certain individuals or groups of people.

Stereotypes exist in all areas of life, including in the workplace. An example of workplace stereotypes could be the belief that women are not able to perform the same roles as men. A woman might be passed over as a machine operator because she is viewed as less physically able than a man might be. Or a woman might be passed over for a promotion, because she isn't viewed as being as competent as a male competitor. Another example is stereotyping based on age. An interviewer may be hesitant to hire an older person, assuming he or she may struggle with technology or may not remain with the organization long due to the proximity of retirement.

Diversity and inclusion initiatives are key to reducing or eliminating stereotyping in the workplace. These initiatives can include DEI training, employee resource groups, and revisions to the interviewing and hiring processes. Individuals can also combat stereotyping by being more self-aware, intentionally collaborating with others from varied backgrounds, and addressing such behaviors and attitudes as they appear.

Compliance and Risk Management

Laws and Regulations: Talent Acquisition, Training, and Rights and Responsibilities

HELPING AN ORGANIZATION TO ABIDE BY LEGAL REGULATIONS IN THE WORKPLACE

Compliance with all laws and regulations is mandatory for all aspects of HR programs, practices, and policies. The HR professional must stay current with applicable federal, state, local, and possibly international laws impacting their organization. Basically, HR professionals work to ensure a safe and fair workplace at all times. At the same time, they should also be aware of and ready to communicate the cost of noncompliance with legal regulations, including fines, possible lawsuits, and other liabilities. This means it is necessary to coach managers and employees with regard to applicable laws in such matters as hiring, terminations, and employee relations issues.

HR professionals can assist their employers in hanging legally required posters in common areas, detailing Fair Labor Standards Act (FLSA) and Occupational Safety and Health Act (OSHA) information. The legal requirements for what should be displayed on these posters may differ based on local, state, or federal guidelines. Understanding and complying with all local, state, and federal laws helps the organization and its employees do the right thing and reduce costly legal liability.

EMPLOYMENT REGULATIONS OVERSEEN BY THE US DEPARTMENT OF LABOR

The US Department of Labor (DOL) has established and actively enforces hundreds of employment laws and regulations. The following are three major acts administered by the DOL:

- Fair Labor Standards Act (FLSA)—An act administered by the DOL Wage and Hour Division. Establishes basic wage requirements for employment in the private sector, such as wages, overtime pay, recordkeeping, and employment standards for children.
- Family and Medical Leave Act (FMLA)—An act administered by the DOL Employment Standards Administration. Requires covered employers to provide employees with job protection and unpaid leave in the event of qualified medical and family reasons. Such reasons include pregnancy, adoption, foster care placement of a child, personal or family illness, or family military leave.
- Occupational Safety and Health Act (OSHA)—An act administered by the DOL Occupational Safety and Health Administration. Ensures that employers provide safe and healthy working conditions for employees. Employers covered under the act must comply with legal safety and health standards, ensuring that the workplace is free from hazards.

KEY ANTI-DISCRIMINATION LAWS

Employment laws and regulations detail the legal parameters under which an organization must operate. The application of laws may vary depending on the size of an organization, the type of organization, and many other factors. Additionally, requirements can vary based on local, state, and federal laws. A large percentage of employment laws are overseen by the Equal Employment

121

Opportunity Commission (EEOC), a federal government agency that interprets and enforces federal laws prohibiting discrimination.

- Equal Pay Act (EPA) of 1963—Prohibits wage discrimination based on gender for anyone in the same organization, performing the same or a similar job, in the same or similar conditions.
- Title VII of the Civil Rights Act of 1964—Prohibits discrimination based on race, color, religion, gender, or national origin.
- Age Discrimination in Employment Act (ADEA) of 1967—Prohibits discrimination against anyone 40 years of age or older as it relates to hiring, termination, promotion, compensation, and benefits.
- Uniform Guidelines on Employee Selection Procedures (1978)—Procedures that cover all aspects of employee selection decisions (recruiting, testing, interviewing, etc.) designed to achieve equal employment opportunities without any form of discrimination. Note that these are guidelines and not a law.
- Americans with Disabilities Act (ADA) of 1990 and ADA Amendments Act (ADAAA) of 2008—Prohibit discrimination against people with disabilities and guarantee that people with disabilities have the same opportunities as those without disabilities.
- Lilly Ledbetter Fair Pay Act of 2009—Implements a somewhat flexible time frame for filing wage discrimination claims.

EQUAL EMPLOYMENT OPPORTUNITY COMMISSION (EEOC)

The **Equal Employment Opportunity Commission (EEOC)** was formed by Title VII of the Civil Rights Act to protect certain groups of individuals from unlawful discrimination. The EEOC is a federal agency designed to encourage equal employment opportunities; to train employers to avoid practices and policies that could cause unlawful discrimination; and to enforce the laws included in the Civil Rights Act, the Age Discrimination in Employment Act, and laws included in other similar anti-discrimination legislation.

Discriminatory practices by an employer are either intentional (like an employer advertisement saying they will not hire a certain race) or unintentional (such as banning hats for reasons unrelated to safety, being discriminatory against those who wear a head covering for religious purposes). Equal opportunity laws prohibit both intentional and unintentional discrimination. The EEOC attempts to obtain settlements from employers for actions that the commission deems to be discriminatory. If the employer will not settle with the EEOC, the EEOC will continue their attempt to enforce the law by filing a lawsuit against the employer on behalf of the victim of the discrimination.

EEO REPORTING

The **Equal Employment Opportunity (EEO) Act**, passed by Congress in 1972, strives to ensure that any person in the US may not be discriminated against based on age, gender, race, ethnicity, or religion when applying for a job. The EEOC, which enforces the EEO Act, requires annual workforce reporting for any employer with 100 or more employees, and federal contractors who have 50 or more employees as well as contracts of at least $50,000. In addition to reporting, employers must post EEO posters in workplace common spaces in their offices. The reason for the reporting requirement is to calculate and capture the workforce composition and ensure there is no discrimination against a protected class. There are various EEO reports that must be completed if an employer meets the EEO reporting criteria, and none of it is voluntary. EEO reports capture information in nine categories:

- Senior-level officials and managers—Highest-level workers who set strategy, develop policies, and direct.
- Professionals—Jobs that do not always, but usually, require degrees. Includes engineers, accountants, and teachers.
- Technicians—These jobs require very specialized skills for a specific form of work. Includes emergency medical technicians and dental hygienists.
- Sales workers—Workers who list sales as their primary function. Includes retail, real-estate agents, and telemarketers.
- Administrative support—Office and clerical workers. Includes secretaries and payroll clerks.
- Craft workers—Specific skill with advanced knowledge or skills. Includes carpenters, plumbers, and auto mechanics.
- Operatives—Jobs that require minimal training. Operatives are sometimes called semi-skilled. Includes bakers and butchers.
- Laborers—Jobs that require a marginal amount of training. Laborers are referred to as unskilled. Includes assistants and freight movers.
- Service workers—This ranking does not imply that this is the lowest level of work, and some make more money than other categories. Includes janitors, hairstylists, and police.

EEO-1 REPORTING

Private employers with 100 or more employees, and federal contractors with 50 or more employees as well as contracts of at least $50,000, must complete and submit an EEO-1 report each year. This report organizes employee-specific data by race, gender, and job category for an employer. The completed report is submitted to the EEOC and the Office of Federal Contract Compliance Programs (OFCCP) for adherence to federal laws against employment discrimination. This is a mandatory report. If it is not filed, if false information is provided, or if an employer discriminated against an employee, then there are monetary and legal consequences and/or penalties. While there are other EEO reports (EEO-3, EEO-4, EEO-5) that apply to unions, governmental entities, public schools, etc., the EEO-1 report is the reporting mechanism most utilized by the EEOC.

AFFORDABLE CARE ACT (ACA)

The Affordable Care Act (ACA) requires employers of 50 or more employees to offer healthcare options providing minimum essential coverage that is affordable and gives at least a certain minimum value. This act requires employers with a self-insured health plan to annually complete the following IRS forms:

- **Form 1094-C**—Employer information, including number of full-time employees and total number of employees by month, minimal coverage offered to 95 percent of eligible employees for each month, and whether a 4980H safe harbor (line 16) was used each month.
- **Form 1095-B**—Employee proof of insurance—Employees' share of the lowest-cost monthly premium, and whether a 4980H safe harbor was used each month.

Additionally, employers are required to give a copy of form 1095-B to all employees. Included on this form is information for the IRS and for employees who are covered by the ACA-mandated essential health benefit. Reporting is mandatory for employers with 50 or more (on average) full-time employees. Employers who fail to comply with all ACA requirements and deadlines could be subject to substantial penalties and steep fines.

TITLE VII OF THE CIVIL RIGHTS ACT OF 1964

Title VII of the Civil Rights Act, which was originally passed in 1964 and amended in 1972, 1978, and 1991, is designed to prevent unlawful discrimination in the workplace. This section of the Civil Rights Act makes it unlawful to discriminate against or segregate any aspect of an individual's employment based on any of the following:

- Race
- Color
- National origin
- Religion
- Gender

In other words, Title VII legislation prevents an employer from discriminating with regard to any condition of employment based on these criteria, including recruiting, hiring, and firing. Furthermore, Title VII prohibits an employer from limiting the opportunities for an employee with regard to compensation, career promotions, training, and other employment avenues for advancement or progress. Title VII also makes it unlawful for an employer to discriminate against individuals who are pregnant, are about to give birth, or have any similar medical condition.

Title VII of the Civil Rights Act applies to any employer who has more than 15 employees. Exceptions include religious organizations, which can choose to hire only individuals within that religion, or to consider individuals of that religion for employment before individuals of other religions; and Indian reservations, which can choose to hire or consider Indians living on or near a reservation for employment before other individuals.

CIVIL RIGHTS ACT OF 1991

The Civil Rights Act (CRA) of 1991 made the Civil Rights Act of 1964 stronger, but did not replace it. The CRA of 1991 primarily reduced the burden of proof the victim, and made liability for the employer difficult to circumvent, making it easier for employees to sue employers for unlawful discrimination. For example, if an employer is found guilty of intentional unlawful discrimination, the damages awarded to victims could be both compensatory (for emotional distress) and punitive (for breaking the law).

There is a limit on how much juries can award per person. If there are four individuals suing, then the amount awarded increases fourfold. Moreover, the CRA of 1991 offers plaintiffs a jury option in alleged cases of intentional employment discrimination. Prior to the CRA of 1991, the only option was a judge's decision. The CRA of 1991 clarified statutory guidelines for disparate-impact cases (actions that are nondiscriminatory at face value, but negatively impact a member of a protected class under Title VII). Additionally, the CRA of 1991 enhanced the strength of civil rights that were, at the time, losing power by unfavorable Supreme Court decisions, thereby increasing protection for employees from discriminatory treatment.

AGE DISCRIMINATION IN EMPLOYMENT ACT (ADEA)

The Age Discrimination in Employment Act (ADEA), which was originally passed in 1967 and then amended in 1991, is designed to prevent discrimination against individuals over the age of 39. This act makes it unlawful to base decisions related to an individual's employment—such as pay or benefits—on the age of the individual if that individual is at least 40 years old. This act applies to

any business, employment agency, labor organization, or state or local government agency with more than 20 employees. Exceptions include individuals age 40 or over who do not meet the occupational qualifications required to perform the tasks reasonably necessary to the business's operations; termination due to reasonable cause; employment of firefighters or police officers; retirement of employees with executive positions; and tenured educators under certain conditions. Pre-employment inquiries about an individual's age are not recommended because it could deter an older worker from applying for a position, and could indicate discriminatory intent by the employer on the basis of age. Someone's age can be determined after the employee is hired.

REHABILITATION ACT OF 1973

The **Rehabilitation Act** of 1973 is similar to the Americans with Disabilities Act (ADA) in that the Rehabilitation Act is designed to prevent discrimination against individuals with disabilities. However, the ADA expands the protections granted by the Rehabilitation Act, which was only designed to prevent discrimination against individuals with disabilities if those individuals were seeking employment in federal agencies or with federal contractors that earned more than $10,000 a year from government contracts. Employers were not required under the Rehabilitation Act to make the organization's facilities accessible to individuals with disabilities, so there was no legal remedy for individuals who were employed but unable to access their place of employment.

PREGNANCY DISCRIMINATION ACT OF 1978

There are two main clauses of the **Pregnancy Discrimination Act** (PDA) of 1978. The first clause applies to Title VII's prohibition against sex discrimination, which also directly applies to prejudice on the basis of childbirth, pregnancy, or related medical conditions. The second clause requires that employers treat pregnant women the same as others for all employment-related reasons. In short, the PDA makes it illegal to fire or refuse to hire or promote a woman because she is pregnant; to force a pregnancy leave on women who are willing and able to perform the job; and to stop accruing seniority for a woman because she is out of work to give birth. If a pregnant woman is not able to perform her job because of a medical condition related to the pregnancy, the employer must treat the pregnant woman the same way it treats all other temporary disabilities, which includes providing reasonable accommodations. In addition to the PDA of 1978, employers should be aware of any other state regulations that may afford pregnant women more protections.

AMERICANS WITH DISABILITIES ACT (ADA)

The **Americans with Disabilities Act** (ADA), which was passed in 1990, is designed to prevent discrimination against individuals with disabilities. A disability, as defined by the ADA, is a mental or physical impairment that impedes one or more life activities. Examples might include, but are not limited to, mobility and personal hygiene. A qualified person with a disability should be able to perform the essential functions of a job with or without reasonable accommodations. This act makes it unlawful to base decisions related to aspects of an individual's employment (such as pay or benefits) on whether the individual is disabled. This act also requires the business, employment agency, or labor organization to ensure the disabled individual has access to his or her place of employment unless making these changes will cause the business significant harm.

ADAAA OF 2008

The **ADA Amendments Act** (ADAAA) of 2008 amends the ADA of 1990 in areas that further clarify protections and definitions of a disability. The following modifications were made in the ADAAA:

- Prohibits the display of so-called "mitigating measures" in assessing whether a person has a disability. Basically, a person will be assessed without certain measures used to manage their impairment, such as prosthetic devices or hearing aids, taken into consideration. Notable exceptions to these measures include eyeglasses and contact lenses.
- Further clarifies the ADA wording of "regarded as" having a disability if employees can prove that they have been discriminated against because of actual or perceived disability. In other words, if employees feel they have been discriminated against for being "regarded as" having a disability and were discriminated against by an employer, the organization could be in violation of the ADAAA of 2008. Note that there could be a true disability or a perceived disability. Examples of discrimination include being denied training or not receiving a promotion.
- Expands the definition of "disability" to include a listing of life activities and conditions, including physical movement, cognitive functions, and medical conditions. The act states that "homosexuality, bisexuality, transvestitism and compulsive gambling" are not considered impairments. In general, most disabling conditions that are temporary in nature are also not included under this act.

VIETNAM ERA VETERANS' READJUSTMENT ASSISTANCE ACT (VEVRAA)

The Vietnam Era Veterans' Readjustment Assistance Act (VEVRAA) is designed to prevent discrimination against veterans. This act makes it unlawful for federal contractors or subcontractors with $25,000 or more in federal contracts or subcontracts to base employment decisions on the fact that the individual is a veteran. It also requires federal contractors or subcontractors meeting these requirements to list open positions with state employment agencies and requires these employers to institute affirmative action plans for veterans. However, in order for this act to apply, the veteran must have served for more than 180 days, with at least part of that time occurring between August 5, 1964, and May 7, 1975; have a disability or group of disabilities that are rated at 10-30 percent or more, depending on the severity or circumstances of their disability; and be eligible for compensation from the Department of Veterans Affairs; or have served on active duty for a conflict with an authorized campaign badge.

JVA OF 2002

The **Jobs for Veterans Act** (JVA) of 2002 amended the VEVRAA by raising the amount of a federal employer contract from $25,000 to $100,000 and further clarifying the categories of protected veterans. The JVA of 2002 applies to a contractor with contracts that began before December 1, 2003. The JVA made the following changes:

- Eliminated the category of Vietnam-era veterans, but still provided coverage under a new category titled "campaign veterans."
- Added a new category of "Armed Forces Service Medal" veterans.
- Expanded disability-related coverage to include all veterans with "service-connected disabilities."
- Changed coverage from one year to three years after discharge from active duty.

Federal contractors and subcontractors are still required to post open positions (except top management jobs) on state and local job databases.

IMMIGRATION REFORM AND CONTROL ACT

The **Immigration Reform and Control Act** (IRCA) is designed to prevent discrimination based on nationality. This act makes it unlawful for an employer to base employment decisions (such as pay or benefits) on an individual's country of origin or citizenship status, as long as the individual can legally work within the United States. This act also makes it unlawful for an organization to intentionally hire individuals that cannot legally work in the United States and requires completion of the I-9 form for all new employees. This act specifically requires the employer to obtain proof of the employee's eligibility to work in the United States for the I-9 form, but the employee must be allowed to provide any document or combination of documents considered acceptable by the IRCA.

I-9 FORM COMPLETION

I-9 forms are completed for any employee hired in the United States after November 6, 1986. The form must be completed by the employer, as required by the IRCA, and is used to verify eligibility to work in the U.S.

The I-9 form has three parts:

- Section 1: This section is completed by the employee, and it must be done on the first day of employment. Within the first three days of employment, the employee must prove both identity and eligibility to work in the United States by providing documents that are deemed acceptable as identified on the I-9 form.
- Section 2: This section is completed by the employer (or their representative). The employer must physically examine the employee's acceptable documents and complete the appropriate fields on this section of the form within the first three days of employment.
- Supplement B on the I-9 form should be completed by the employer if a legal name change has occurred, a work authorization has expired, or a previously terminated employee is being rehired.

E-Verify is an electronic/remote internet-based system for confirming employment eligibility.

VOCATIONAL REHABILITATION ACT

The **Vocational Rehabilitation Act** was intended to increase occupational opportunities for disabled individuals and to prohibit discrimination against qualified individuals with disabilities. In this case, "qualified" means that the person applying for the job can perform the essential function with or without reasonable accommodations. The act applies to federal government contractors and subcontractors holding contracts or subcontracts of $10,000 or more. Contractors and subcontractors with greater than $50,000 in contracts and more than 50 employees must develop written affirmative action plans that address hiring and promoting persons with disabilities.

There are regulations that protect those engaged in addiction treatment; however, this act does not protect individuals who currently suffer from substance abuse that prevents them from performing the duties of the job, or whose employment would constitute a direct threat to the safety and property of others. The primary focus of the act is to extend grants to states for vocational rehabilitation services with a heightened emphasis on those individuals with severe disabilities.

UNIFORM GUIDELINES ON EMPLOYEE SELECTION PROCEDURES

The **Uniform Guidelines on Employee Selection Procedures** (UGESP), passed in 1978, is a procedural document that helps employers to comply with several federal anti-discrimination laws, such as EEO, with an emphasis on Title VII. The primary purpose of these guidelines is to define the specific types of procedures that may cause disparate impact and are considered illegal. These

127

guidelines apply to all aspects of the selection and hiring process: recruiting, interviewing, testing, performance appraisals, and any other factor of consideration used to make employment decisions. The UGESP relates to unfair procedures that make it much less likely that an individual belonging to a protected class would be able to receive a particular position.

GENETIC INFORMATION NONDISCRIMINATION ACT (GINA)

The **Genetic Information Nondiscrimination Act** (GINA), passed in May 2008, protects people from discrimination based on their genetic information. The act specifically offers protection in two areas: (1) it prohibits discrimination with regard to healthcare coverage based on genetic information, and (2) it protects against discrimination based on genetic information in employment. Employers, under GINA, are not permitted to request any type of genetic information about prospective job candidates or employees, except for a few extreme situations. For example, an employer cannot ask a prospective job candidate about their family medical history. In fact, employers are strongly encouraged to ask healthcare providers not to collect genetic information in the case where an employee needs a medical exam for employment or ADA-related leaves of absence and possible accommodations. Additionally, GINA forbids any type of harassment based on genetic information.

EXECUTIVE ORDERS

An **executive order** is a written declaration made by the president of the United States establishing a policy for enforcing existing legislation. Executive orders are legally binding and are treated as law if the order remains in the Federal Registry for more than 30 days. Executive Order 11246, which was published to the Federal Registry in 1965, states that federal contractors are not only required to avoid employment discrimination but are also required to take steps to ensure equal opportunities are available to individuals belonging to protected classes. This executive order established the concept of affirmative action and required federal contractors with more than $10,000 in government contracts during a single year to implement affirmative action plans, and federal contractors with $50,000 or more in contracts and 50 or more employees to file written affirmative action plans with the Office of Federal Contract Compliance Programs (OFCCP).

EXECUTIVE ORDER 11246

Originally, Executive Order (EO) 11246 applied only to employment discrimination based on an individual's color, national origin, race, or religion. However, EO 11375, EO 11478, EO 13152, and EO 13279 amended the policy and changed the groups that were covered. EO 11375 made it unlawful to discriminate based on gender, EO 11478 made it unlawful to discriminate based on disabilities or age if that individual is over age 40, EO 13152 made it unlawful to discriminate based on parental status, and EO 13279 excluded federal contractors who were religious and community organizations providing services to the community from the need to adhere to the policies.

AFFIRMATIVE ACTION AND AFFIRMATIVE ACTION PLANS (AAPs)

Affirmative action is a set of written procedures designed to correct discriminatory practices from the past and prevent the continuation of such practices now and in the future. Affirmative action plans (AAPs) were first established by Executive Order 11246, and it is required for those entities doing business with the federal government to have AAPs in compliance with equal employment opportunity laws. In other words, an AAP is supposed to help make sure that every person has equal opportunities when it comes to recruitment, selection, promotion, and training. Moreover, organizations with an AAP must prioritize a quantifiable grouping of qualified candidates who are disabled, minorities, female, and/or covered veterans.

An AAP includes a list of action-oriented programs, an availability analysis of employees from protected classes, a section that designates the individual responsible for the organization's AAP, a job group analysis, an organizational profile, placement goals, a system for internal audits and reports related to analyzing barriers to equal employment opportunities, and a utilization analysis of the number of protected individuals employed by the company compared to the number of protected individuals available. The Office of Federal Contract Compliance Programs (OFCCP) oversees and enforces regulations for those organizations that comply with AAPs. Organizations with AAPs must file their AAP document and report related metrics with the OFCCP annually.

DISPARATE IMPACT

Disparate impact is a type of discrimination in which an employer institutes a policy that appears to be reasonable, but prevents individuals of a certain color, national origin, race, religion, or gender, or individuals with certain disabilities or military status, from receiving employment or any of the benefits associated with employment, such as promotions or pay. It refers to a policy that may seem to make sense, but is unfair because it makes things more difficult for individuals of a certain group to receive the job or benefit. For example, a policy stating that individuals applying for an office job must be at least 5'10" and weigh at least 185 pounds may create a disparate impact if it makes it more difficult for women to get the job. However, a physical attribute directly linked to the work that must be performed is not discriminatory so long as it correlates with the essential job requirements. For example, a firefighter has to fulfill certain physical requirements to perform the essential functions of the job. Disparate impact discrimination was first identified by the Supreme Court in *Griggs v. Duke Power Co.*

DISPARATE TREATMENT

Disparate treatment is a type of discrimination in which an employer deliberately treats an individual differently because of that individual's age, color, disability, military status, national origin, race, religion, and/or gender. It refers to any instance in which an employer uses a different set of procedures, expectations, or policies than they would normally use simply because the individual belongs to a particular group. For example, a business that requires female employees to follow a strict dress code, while the male employees can wear whatever they like, would be guilty of disparate treatment because of treating employees differently based on gender. In general, an individual claiming disparate treatment must prove that they are a member of a protected class. They must then prove they were qualified but were not hired. If the employer then continues the application process after rejecting a qualified candidate because of a protected class criterion, then this might be considered unlawful discrimination, and thus, disparate treatment. This type of discrimination was first identified by Title VII of the Civil Rights Act.

COPYRIGHT ACT (TITLE 17)

The term **"copyright"** refers to protection from the US government for original works being copied, duplicated, or distributed, and for cases where someone takes credit for someone else's creative expression. **Title 17** of the United States Code includes the **Copyright Act**, first passed in 1976 and amended many times since. The Copyright Act automatically grants protections once the original work is expressed in a medium. In other words, original works are copyright-protected once they are printed, created into an object, in a form of technology, etc. However, it is usually recommended that a person or organization register copyrighted material. To be clear, ideas cannot be copyrighted; rather, it is the tangible expression of the idea in some medium that is copyrighted.

The five primary rights or protections afforded to copyright owners are the ability to authorize others to do the following:

- Reproduce the work
- Distribute the work
- Use the work as a basis for new creations
- Publicly display the work
- Publicly perform the work

The owner of a copyright may be the person who created the work, but if it is a work made for hire, the copyright is given to the person or organization that ordered or commissioned the work. In the commissioned-work scenario, an employer could be the copyright owner.

US PATENT ACT

The **US Patent Act** (Title 35 US Code) grants protection for new inventions whereby no one other than the owner of the patent is allowed to do anything that involves using or selling the invention. Article 1, section 8 of the US Constitution gives Congress the power "to promote the progress of science and useful arts, by securing for limited times to authors and inventors the exclusive right to their respective writings and discoveries." Congress created the United States Patent and Trademark Office (USPTO) to assess and process applications for two types of patents:

- **Utility** patent—This type of patent is issued for inventions that are new and have a use, such as a new machine, process, or manufacturing system. The USPTO qualifies utility patents in five categories: (1) composition of matter, (2) improvement of an existing idea, (3) machine, (4) manufacture, and (5) process. Approximately 90 percent of all patents are utility patents.
- **Design** patent—This type of patent is issued for original designs on an existing product. Sometimes organizations apply for a design patent when the look of a product is changed.

Whoever creates the invention is the owner of the patent. However, if the patent was obtained through work, the inventor often contractually agrees to turn over all rights of the patent to the employer.

TRADEMARK ACT

The **Trademark Act** was passed in 1946 and amended several times. A trademark is any "marking," meaning a logo, slogan, phrase, company name, or combination of attributes, that distinguishes a product or service from others. This distinction enables the product or service to have a competitive advantage in market recognition. In some way, a trademark makes a product or service unique or authentic. The Trademark Act gives certain rights to the owner of the so-called "marking" to prevent other individuals or organizations from using it without authorization. Trademarks, both registered and unregistered with the USPTO, are protected from infringements. In other words, if an organization uses a trademark that is similar to—or likely to be confused with—a widely recognized trademark, it is considered infringement and grounds for legal action.

EMPLOYMENT AT WILL

The **employment-at-will doctrine** states that an employer can terminate an employee without reason or warning, and also that an employee can choose to resign or leave an organization without reason or warning. An employer's employment-at-will policy should appear in the employee handbook and be clearly communicated to all employees. Additionally, the policy is usually in the contract for employment, if applicable. This type of employer-employee relationship offers ultimate flexibility.

However, it is very important to note that just because an employer or employee can do something—like abruptly terminate an employee or unexpectedly quit a job without notice—does not mean that they should. Wrongful termination in at-will employment situations is protected by federal and state laws, and state laws can vary tremendously. Some of the areas protected in a case of wrongful termination can include termination because of age, gender, sexual orientation, race, religion, disability, or whistleblowing, or termination as retaliation for a legally protected act. All states have some type of at-will employment, but many states place stipulations and limits on how it is interpreted.

EXCEPTIONS TO THE EMPLOYMENT-AT-WILL DOCTRINE

There are a few exceptions to employment at will, and they too can vary in execution from state to state:

- **Employment contracts**—If an employee is working under a collective bargaining agreement or other type of specified employment contract, then the employee may have more rights than typical at-will employees.
- **Public policy exception**—Some states prevent an employer from firing an employee in violation of state public policy. For example, in some states with this exception, an employer cannot terminate an employee who was injured on the job and is filing a workers' compensation claim.
- **Implied contracts**—Some states prevent an employer from firing an employee if an implied contract for employment is established between the employer and employee. Cases of implied contracts, where nothing is directly stated or written, are challenging to prove, and the burden rests with the employee. The employee can reference the employer handbook or historical proof that termination is for cause.
- **Good-faith and fair-dealing exception**—Some states specify this exception to prevent an employer from terminating employees to circumvent an employer obligation, such as paying workers for earned commissions, retirement agreements, or healthcare.

Laws and Regulations: Employment in Union Environments

LABOR UNIONS

A **labor union** is a group of workers who organize together as a collective to negotiate with an employer to advance their rights and interests. This negotiation process with an employer is called "collective bargaining." The concept is that a group of individuals banding together is more powerful than a single person fighting for more rights. The formation of unions began in the 1790s and reached its prime in the 1940s and 1950s. Union contracts typically specify safe working conditions, health benefits, compensation in the event of an injury, and retirement stipulations. Additionally, labor unions were extremely influential in ending the practice of child labor. Organized labor unions have diminished since the 1950s, but have meaningfully impacted the economic, political, and workplace environment since their inception. Unions have been partially responsible for a significant amount of federal legislation protecting worker interests and rights, as well as the creation of the US Department of Labor.

COLLECTIVE BARGAINING

Collective bargaining is a process during which unions work to negotiate contracts with employers to help decide the terms and conditions of employment agreements. Employment agreements cover such issues as wages, hours worked, leave policies, health benefits, and conditions of employment such as rules and policies. The National Labor Relations Act has established three types of discussion topics in contract negotiations:

- Mandatory topics, including hours, discipline procedures, wages and overtime pay, processes for firing, layoffs, and reductions in force
- Permitted topics, including how the union board of directors is formed and other matters internal to the union operations
- Illegal topics (topics that cannot be discussed), including unlawful discrimination and unlawful union membership procedures

At the conclusion of the collective bargaining process, the union and the employer reach a collective bargaining agreement (CBA), which is a legal written contract. Both the union and the employer should seek legal advice and counsel, because once the CBA is signed, it is a binding agreement that both parties must abide by.

Norris-LaGuardia Act

The **Norris-LaGuardia Act**, which was passed in 1932, protects the right to unionize. This act grants employees the right to form unions and initiate strikes. In addition to granting the right to unionize, this act also prohibits the court system from using injunctions to interfere with any nonviolent union activity and prohibits employers from forcing employees to sign "yellow-dog" contracts. A **yellow-dog contract** refers to any contract that prohibits an employee from joining a union, or any contract that requires an employee to agree to be terminated if it is discovered that they are a member of a union or intend to become a member of a union. The act stated that members belonging to a union have "full freedom of association," meaning they are free to strike, picket, or initiate boycotts without legal penalty.

National Labor Relations Act (NLRA)

The **National Labor Relations Act** (NLRA) was passed by Congress in 1935 after a long period of conflict in labor relations. Also known as the Wagner Act, after New York Senator Robert Wagner, it was intended to be an economic stabilizer and to establish collective bargaining in industrial relations. Section 7 of the NLRA provides employees with the right to form, join, or assist **labor organizations**, as well as the right to engage in **concerted activities** such as collective bargaining through representatives or other mutual aid. Section 8 of the NLRA also identifies five **unfair labor practices**:

- Employers shall not interfere with or coerce employees away from the rights outlined in Section 7.
- Employers shall not dominate or disrupt the formation of a labor union.
- Employers shall not allow union membership or activity to influence hiring, firing, promotion, or related employment decisions.
- Employers shall not discriminate against or discharge an employee who has given testimony or filed a charge with the NLRA.
- Employers cannot refuse bargaining in good faith with employee representatives.

Taft-Hartley Act

Because many employers felt that the NLRA gave too much power to unions, Congress passed the Labor Management Relations Act in 1947. More commonly known as the **Taft-Hartley Act**, it sought to avoid unnecessary strikes and impose certain restrictions over union activities. The act addresses **four basic issues**: unfair labor practices by unions, the rights of employees, the rights of employers, and national emergency strikes. Moreover, the act prohibits unions from the following:

- Restraining or coercing employees away from their right to not engage in union activities
- Forcing an employer to discriminate in any way against an employee to encourage or discourage union membership
- Forcing an employer to pay for work or services that are not needed or not performed
- Conducting certain types of strikes or boycotts
- Charging excessive initiation fees or membership dues when employees are required to join a union shop

LANDRUM-GRIFFIN ACT

The government exercised further control over union activities in 1959 by the passage of the Labor Management Reporting and Disclosure Act. More commonly known as the **Landrum-Griffin Act**, this law regulates the **internal conduct of labor unions** to reduce the likelihood of fraud and improper actions. The act imposes controls on five major areas: reports to the secretary of labor, a bill of rights for union members, union trusteeships, conduct of union elections, and financial safeguards. Some key provisions include the following:

- Granting equal rights to every union member with regard to nominations, attending meetings, and voting
- Requiring unions to submit and make available to the public a copy of their constitution, bylaws, and annual financial reports
- Requiring unions to hold regular elections every five years for national organizations and every three years for local organizations
- Monitoring the management and investment of union funds, making embezzlement a federal crime

> **Review Video: US Employment Law: Employee and Labor Relations (NLRA)**
> Visit mometrix.com/academy and enter code: 972790

NATIONAL LABOR RELATIONS BOARD (NLRB)

The National Labor Relations Board (NLRB) is a federal agency that protects the right of employees to choose whether they want to be represented by a union or not. It is designed to handle activities related to investigating and preventing employers and unions from taking part in unfair labor practices. The NLRB can take a number of actions related to unfair labor practices by employers, including requiring employers to rehire or return positions to employees who were affected by an unfair labor practice, requiring employers to resume negotiations with a union, and disbanding unions that are controlled by an employer. The NLRB may also take a number of actions related to unfair union labor practices, including requiring unions to refund membership fees with or without interest to union members who have been charged unreasonable fees, requiring unions to resume negotiations with an employer, and requiring unions to accept the reinstatement of any employee if the union specifically discriminated against that employee.

WORKER ADJUSTMENT AND RETRAINING NOTIFICATION ACT (WARN)

The **Worker Adjustment and Retraining Notification Act** (WARN), passed in 1988, states that companies must give 60 days' notice in advance of closings and mass layoffs. WARN applies to union and non-union environments, employers with 100 or more full-time employees, or those with total employees cumulatively working 4,000 hours per week at all locations. WARN

133

specifically states that notification must be given to the following: local government, state dislocated worker units, and the workers or their representatives.

There is a difference between a closing and a mass layoff. A closing is a temporary or permanent shutdown of one or more sites or business units at one location in a 30-day period, impacting 50 or more full-time employees. A mass layoff, sometimes called a reduction in force (RIF), is also defined as occurring in a 30-day period, but it is always an employment loss for 50 or more full-time employees, if the layoffs comprise 33 percent of the workforce at the site, or impact 500 or more full-time employees. It is important to note that this is an involuntary employment termination for 6 months or a 50-percent-or-more reduction of hours worked each month for 6 months. There are a few exceptions to the WARN Act, such as natural disasters and "other unforeseeable business circumstances."

Laws and Regulations: Compensation and Benefits

EMPLOYEE RETIREMENT INCOME SECURITY ACT (ERISA)

The Employee Retirement Income Security Act (ERISA) outlines the standards for private health and pension plans offered by an employer. This act specifies what an employer must do, what they are not permitted to do, and what they might be able to do as it relates to private health and pension plans. This is a complicated statute, but the goal is for employees to receive the benefits promised and outlined by the employer, and to be protected against any type of funds mismanagement.

Most employees who have worked at least 1,000 hours per 12 months, for two consecutive years, are eligible to participate in private pension plans. Employees have the right to receive some portion of employer contributions when their employment ends. Employees must be allowed to transfer pension funds from one retirement account to another. Sufficient funds must be available from the employer to cover future payments. Employers must appoint an individual to be responsible for seeking ideal portfolio options and administering pension funds. Employers must adhere to extensive reporting requirements, provide summary plan documents, and notify participants of any changes. Employers are required to complete annual minimum coverage, actual deferral percentage, actual contribution percentage, and top-heavy testing to prevent discrimination in favor of highly compensated employees. Administration of ERISA is handled by the Department of Labor's Employee Benefits Security Administration, the IRS, and the Pension Benefit Guaranty Corporation.

The employer has three primary regulatory obligations as it relates to ERISA:

- Obligation to file Form 5500. The IRS, the Department of Labor, and the Pension Benefit Guaranty Corp. developed **Form 5500**, which is for reporting financial conditions, investments, and operations. This form must be completed annually and filed by an employer to satisfy reporting requirements outlined under ERISA and the IRS.
- **Dissemination and disclosure information** for all participants in the employer-sponsored plan.
  - Must have an easily accessible, documented plan
  - Must annually receive a summary plan description (SPD) within 90 days for new participants and 120 days for new plans
  - Must receive (in a timely fashion) a summary material modification (SMM) if the plan is altered no later than 210 days after changes and no later than 60 days if there is a material reduction in coverage

134

- o Must be given a summary annual report (SAR)
- **Standard of conduct obligation** that requires fiduciaries (trusted individuals) to conduct activities for the sole benefit of the participants and beneficiaries, not in their own self-interest.

If an employer fails to comply with any requirements of this mandate, they could face severe civil and criminal penalties.

FAIR LABOR STANDARDS ACT (FLSA)

The **Fair Labor Standards Act of 1938 (FLSA),** also known as the Wage Hour Bill, sets minimum wage standards, overtime pay standards, and child labor restrictions. The act is administered by the Wage and Hour Division of the Department of Labor. The FLSA carefully classifies employees as exempt or nonexempt from provisions, requires that employers calculate overtime for covered employees at one and one-half times the regular rate of pay for all hours worked in excess of 40 hours during a week, and defines how a work week should be measured. The purpose of minimum wage standards is to ensure a living wage and to reduce poverty for low-income families, minority workers, and women. The child labor provisions protect minors from positions that may be harmful to their health or well-being and regulates the hours minors can legally work. The act also outlines requirements for employers to keep records of hours, wages, and related payroll items.

> **Review Video: US Employment Compensation Laws**
> Visit mometrix.com/academy and enter code: 613448

EXEMPT EMPLOYEES

An **exempt employee** is not entitled to minimum wage or overtime pay as defined by the FLSA. FLSA regulations do not apply to exempt employees. It is usually decided by the employer whether they wish to compensate an employee for working more than 40 hours, and this is usually achieved through bonuses or extra benefits; it is not mandatory. Additionally, exempt employees must meet certain tests based on job duties performed and must earn no less than $684 per week.

It is not job title alone that determines exempt status, but rather the tasks performed on the job. An exempt employee is paid by salary, not hourly, and spends more than 50 percent of their time performing bona fide exempt functions, usually falling into three general categories:

- Executive employees—Responsibilities include directing the work of two or more full-time employees. The primary focus of their job is management and having direct input into the hiring, ongoing management, and firing of employees.
- Professional employees—This category is most often associated with learned professionals; it requires knowledge and education in a specific field, as with doctors, engineers, and accountants. This category also includes roles in more creative fields that rely on invention, creation, imagination, or artistic talent, such as writers, actors, and graphic designers.
- Administrative employees—Duties include using judgment and discretion with regard to the management of an organization and/or handling high-level interactions with customers.

However, these three categories are not an all-inclusive list; many other types of jobs may be classified as exempt, such as outside sales or computer systems management. Another exempt category could be highly compensated employees, if they do non-manual work, if their salary is $107,432 or higher, and if they also perform work in one of the three main categories. State and local wage and hourly rate laws may have their own requirements in addition to the FLSA.

Nonexempt Employees

Nonexempt employees fall under the regulation of the FLSA. Nonexempt employees are hourly workers who earn wages less than $684 a week or $35,568 annually. Nonexempt workers must receive at least minimum wage up to 40 hours a week, and must receive overtime pay for any time above 40 hours of work. Overtime pay requires employers to pay at a rate of one and one-half times the employee's regular rate of pay. Generally, nonexempt positions do not require special education, independent judgment or discretion, and/or supervising others; they could work in almost any field. Typically, nonexempt workers have work that is routine and utilizes their body or skills; examples include carpenters, plumbers, craftsmen, mechanics, first responders, park rangers, emergency medical technicians, and correctional officers. Some states have nonexempt regulations in addition to the FLSA.

Independent Contractors

An **independent contractor** is not covered by the FLSA and hence not eligible for minimum wage or overtime pay. The most important distinction between an employee and a contractor is whether the worker is dependent on the employer (meaning they are an employee) or conducting business for the sole benefit of himself or herself (making them an independent contractor). The Department of Labor refers to this as an "economic reality test," which takes five factors into consideration:

- Worker's control over the nature of their work, such as schedule, projects, etc.
- Worker's control over profit or loss
- Skill needed by the worker for the work performed, particularly specialized skills that require training
- Worker's relationship with the employer with regard to permanent status
- Whether the worker is part of an existing unit within the organization

The first two factors above carry the most weight and must be examined first. If the worker does have the kind of control described in factors one and two, then there is a substantial likelihood that the worker is an independent contractor. These first two factors are often called "core factors." However, if there is ambiguity, then the next three factors must be examined for clarification. Employers must also comply with all federal, state, and local laws with regard to worker classification, as they may vary.

The Davis-Bacon Act and the Walsh-Healey Act

The **Davis-Bacon Act**, passed in 1931, requires contractors and subcontractors working on federally funded projects or federally assisted projects—contracted for at least $2,000—to pay wages and fringe benefits at a rate equal to or more than the prevailing wage rates of similar projects in the area. Any employer who performs work to which the Davis-Bacon Act is applicable must place a WH-1321 poster in a workplace common area detailing the wage protections offered by this act. Additionally, employers operating under the Davis-Bacon Act who fail to comply risk losing both their existing federal contracts and their new contract eligibility for three years.

The **Walsh-Healey Act**, passed in 1936, is almost an extension of the Davis-Bacon Act in that the prevailing wage principle was expanded to include manufacturers and suppliers of goods to employers of federal contractors with contracts that exceed $10,000. Furthermore, time-and-one-half wages for nonexempt workers must be paid for any hours over 40 worked in a week. Work sites that must comply with the Walsh-Healey Act are required to post an "Employee Rights on Government Contracts" notice, including wage amount, in a common work area. Similar to the Davis-Bacon Act, penalties for noncompliance are monetarily severe, with the potential for federal contractors to lose their federal contracts and not be eligible to receive new contracts for three years.

COPELAND "ANTI-KICKBACK" ACT

The Copeland "Anti-Kickback" Act, passed in 1934 and since amended, prevents federal contractors and subcontractors who perform work on covered contracts from persuading an employee to give up any compensation that he or she is rightly entitled to earn based on their contract of employment. All methods of persuasion are prohibited, including force, intimidation, and threat. Prior to the passage of this act, it is estimated that many employees working under a covered federal contract were unfairly intimidated into returning wage earnings to the federal contractor as a so-called "kickback" for employment. There are steep criminal and civil penalties for violating the Copeland Act, including prison time, fines, or both.

MINIMUM WAGE REGULATIONS

The FLSA established regulations designed to prevent employees from receiving substandard wages, and it established the minimum wage. The federal minimum wage is the smallest amount an employer can pay for each hour of work; employers must pay at least the amount specified by the federal minimum wage to any nonexempt employee. An employee will be considered exempt from this provision if the individual receives a weekly salary of at least $684, if the employee works in a profession not covered by the FLSA or a profession identified as exempt from the minimum-wage provision of the FLSA, or if the employer has received special permission to pay less than the minimum wage as part of a Department of Labor program.

REQUIREMENT TO PAY AN EMPLOYEE MORE THAN THE FEDERAL MINIMUM WAGE

There are two situations in which an organization may need to pay an employee more than the federal minimum wage:

- If the individual has worked more than 40 hours in a single week and is in a position covered by the FLSA
- If the minimum wage for the state in which the organization's employees are located is higher than the federal minimum wage

However, most states have their own list of exemptions and requirements, so a particular organization may be part of an industry covered by the FLSA but not by the regulations set by state law.

PORTAL-TO-PORTAL ACT

The **Portal-to-Portal Act** was passed in 1947 as an amendment to the FLSA to clarify when and under what conditions activities are not considered compensable work time. The general compensation rule is that an employee should be compensated for time worked. This act specified what constituted work time and concluded that activities before work, such as getting ready and commuting, are not compensable. Similarly, activities conducted after work are also not compensable work time. Before- and after-work activities are called "preliminary" and "postliminary" activities.

The Supreme Court interpreted the act to mean that the employer is responsible for compensating employees for activities that are integral and indispensable for principal job functions performed. If a function is integral to the job duties, then the employer must compensate the employee for that work. The following is a non-exhaustive list of situations that would be considered exceptions to the Portal-to-Portal Act, and therefore must be compensated:

- If an employee must travel to various work sites to perform job duties
- If an employee must put on and remove protective clothing for their job
- If a specific type of washing is necessary because an employee is working with toxic or caustic material

EQUAL PAY ACT (EPA)

The **Equal Pay Act** (EPA), which was passed in 1963, prevents wage discrimination based on gender. It requires an employer to provide equal pay to men and women performing similar tasks unless the employer can prove that there is an acceptable reason for the difference in pay, such as merit, seniority, or quantity or quality of work performed. This act also establishes the criteria that must be considered to determine whether a particular position is similar or not. This includes the following equal work factors:

- **Skills**—The necessary training, education, and experience needed for a particular position
- **Effort**—This includes the physical and mental capabilities required for a given position
- **Responsibility**—This is primarily an issue of accountability and the degree to which an employer relies on employees to successfully accomplish their job
- **Working conditions**—The physical working environment (e.g., hazardous, indoors, outdoors, cold, hot)

RETIREMENT EQUITY ACT (REA)

The **Retirement Equity Act** (REA), which was passed in 1984, is an amendment to ERISA designed to establish a number of benefit plan regulations in addition to those originally established by ERISA. These regulations are designed to protect spouses from losing their plan benefits after a plan participant's death or after a divorce, but they also include regulations to strengthen the protections offered by ERISA. Protections established by REA include:

- Regulations prohibiting benefit plan administrators from considering maternity/paternity leave as a break in service regarding the right to participate in a plan or become vested in a plan
- Regulations requiring pension plans to automatically provide benefits to a spouse in the event of the plan participant's death unless a waiver has been signed by both the spouse and the participant
- Regulations that lowered the age at which an employer had to allow an individual to participate in a pension plan

An employer not complying with this act could face severe criminal and civil penalties.

CONSOLIDATED OMNIBUS BUDGET RECONCILIATION ACT (COBRA)

The **Consolidated Omnibus Budget Reconciliation Act** (COBRA) of 1986 requires that all employers with 20 or more employees continue the availability of healthcare benefits coverage and protect employees from the potential economic hardship of losing these benefits when they are terminated, are working reduced hours, or quit. COBRA also provides coverage to the employee's spouse and dependents as qualified beneficiaries. Events that qualify for this continuation of coverage include the following:

- Voluntary or involuntary termination for any reason other than gross misconduct
- Reduction in hours that would otherwise result in loss of coverage
- Divorce or legal separation from the employee
- Death of the employee
- The employee becoming disabled and entitled to Medicare
- The dependent being over 26 and no longer a dependent child under plan rules

Typically, the employee and qualified beneficiaries are entitled to 18 months of continued coverage. There are some instances that will extend coverage for up to an additional 18 months. Coverage will be lost if the employer terminates group coverage, premium payments are not received, or new coverage becomes available. COBRA is a high-cost plan; typically the cost to the employee is the full cost that the employer pays for health coverage, plus an administrative fee that averages around 2 percent. Alternatives to COBRA are purchasing coverage through marketplace offerings, Medicaid coverage if applicable, or switching coverage through a spouse (again, if applicable) because a qualifying event entitles the spouse to special enrollment.

FAMILY AND MEDICAL LEAVE ACT (FMLA)

The **Family and Medical Leave Act** (FMLA) of 1993 is a federal regulation that provides employees the right to take up to 12 weeks of unpaid leave in each 12-month period for the care of specified medical conditions that affect themselves or immediate family members. To be eligible for FMLA leave, an employee must have worked for a covered employer for the preceding 12 months and for a minimum of 1,250 hours during that time. All private employers, public or government agencies, and local schools with 50 or more employees within a 75-mile radius, must adhere to the regulations. Qualifying events covered under FMLA include the following:

- The birth or adoption of a new child within one year of birth or placement
- The employee's own serious health condition that involves a period of incapacity
- An ill or injured spouse, child, or parent who requires the employee's care
- Any qualifying exigency due to active-duty foreign deployment by an employee's spouse, child (or children), or parent. Exigencies may include arranging childcare, tending to legal matters, and attending military ceremonies.
- The care of an ill or injured covered service member, as long as the employee is a spouse, child, parent, or next of kin. In addition, time to care for military personnel or recent veterans has been expanded to 26 weeks in a 12-month period.

Additionally, employers covered by FMLA must display a poster in a common area workspace that outlines FMLA provisions, including how to file a complaint.

AMENDMENTS

The FMLA has undergone some significant amendments, and HR practitioners should be aware of the following:

- If an organization fails to denote an employee's leave as FMLA leave, the employee may be eligible to receive compensation for any losses incurred.
- Prior to 2008, all FMLA disputes required Department of Labor or legal intervention. Now, employees and employers are encouraged to work out any issues in-house to avoid the cost of litigation.

- Light duty does not count toward FMLA taken.
- FMLA covers medical issues arising from preexisting conditions.
- Due to their unique scheduling, airline employees are eligible for FMLA after 504 or more hours worked during the preceding 12 months.

HEALTH INSURANCE PORTABILITY AND ACCOUNTABILITY ACT (HIPAA)

The **Health Insurance Portability and Accountability Act** (HIPAA) was passed in 1996 to provide greater protections and portability in healthcare coverage. Some individuals felt locked into current employer plans and feared that they would not be able to obtain coverage from a new employer plan due to preexisting conditions. As a result, some of the key HIPAA provisions are pre-existing condition exclusions, pregnancy, newborn and adopted children, credible coverage, renewal of coverage, medical savings accounts, tax benefits, and privacy provisions. Employees who have had another policy for the preceding 12 months cannot be excluded from coverage due to a pre-existing condition or pregnancy, and it must be applied to newborn or adopted children who are covered by credible coverage within 30 days of the event. **Credible coverage** involves being covered under typical group health plans, and this coverage must be renewable to most groups and individuals as long as premiums are paid. **Medical savings accounts** were created by Congress for those who are self-employed or otherwise not eligible for credible coverage. Individuals who are self-employed are also allowed to take 80 percent of health-related expenses as a deduction. Finally, HIPAA introduced a series of several regulations that impose **civil and criminal penalties** on employers who disclose personal health information without consent.

> **Review Video: What is HIPAA?**
> Visit mometrix.com/academy and enter code: 412009

WORK OPPORTUNITY TAX CREDIT (WOTC)

The **Work Opportunity Tax Credit** (WOTC) is a federal tax credit that is provided to employers who hire individuals that are part of targeted groups facing significant challenges or barriers to employment. The tax credit is intended to financially incent employers to hire from these 10 targeted groups:

- Qualified veterans
- Qualified ex-felons
- Designated community residents, meaning individuals living in designated empowerment zones or rural renewal counties
- Vocational rehabilitation referrals
- Summer youth employees living in an empowerment zone
- Supplemental Nutrition Assistance Program (food stamps) recipients
- Supplemental Security Income recipients
- Long-term Temporary Assistance for Needy Families (TANF) recipients
- Qualified long-term unemployment recipients
- Qualified long-term family assistance recipients

There are many stipulations and specific qualifications for all the targeted groups. Generally, the tax credit is based on three factors: the category of the worker, compensation to the employee, and the number of hours they worked. The WOTC is authorized until December 31, 2025 (Section 113 of Division EE of P.L.116-260—Consolidated Appropriations Act, 2021). The Department of Labor (DOL), the Department of the Treasury, and the IRS all play a role in administering the WOTC program with employers.

UNIFORMED SERVICES EMPLOYMENT AND REEMPLOYMENT RIGHTS ACT (USERRA)

The **Uniformed Services Employment and Reemployment Rights Act** (USERRA) of 1994 is applicable to all employers, both public and private. USERRA forbids employers from denying employment, reemployment, retention, promotion, or employment benefits due to service in the Armed Forces, Reserves, National Guard, and other uniformed services, including the National Disaster Medical System and the Commissioned Corps of the Public Health Service. In other words, this statute is designed to prevent those in the uniformed services from being discriminated against or otherwise disadvantaged in the civilian workplace because of their military service or affiliation.

Employees absent in uniformed services for less than 31 days must report to the employer within 8 hours after arriving safely home. Those who are absent between 31 and 180 days must submit an application for reemployment within 14 days. Those who are absent 181 days or more have 90 days to submit an application for reemployment.

Employees are entitled to the positions that they would have held if they had remained continuously employed. If they are no longer qualified for or able to perform the job requirements because of a service-related disability, they are to be provided with a position of equal seniority, status, and pay. Moreover, the escalator principle further entitles returning employees to all of the seniority-based benefits they had when their service began, plus any additional benefits they would have accrued with reasonable certainty if they had remained continuously employed. Likewise, employees cannot be required to use accrued vacation or PTO during absences. USERRA requires all healthcare plans to provide COBRA coverage for up to 18 months of absence and entitles employees to restoration of coverage upon return. Pension plans must remain undisturbed by absences as well. However, those separated from the service for less-than-honorable circumstances are not protected by USERRA.

MENTAL HEALTH PARITY AND ADDICTION EQUITY ACT (MHPAEA)

The **Mental Health Parity and Addiction Equity Act** (MHPAEA), which was passed in 1996, is designed to prevent health plan providers from setting limits on mental health benefits that are stricter than the limits the provider has set for other health benefits. This act prohibits a health plan provider from setting a financial cap on the amount the health plan provider will pay for mental health benefits if that cap is lower than the cap the provider has set for other benefits. For example, if a medical or surgical lifetime cap is $8,000, then the cap on mental health benefits cannot be below $8,000. This act applies to any health plan provider providing coverage for an employer with at least 51 employees, but only if the regulations set by this act will not result in a 1 percent or greater increase in the costs of the provider. Also, health plan providers are not required to offer mental health benefits, and providers may set other limits related to mental health coverage as long as there is no specific payout limit.

LILLY LEDBETTER FAIR PAY ACT OF 2009

The **Lilly Ledbetter Fair Pay Act** overturned the 2007 Supreme Court decision in the *Ledbetter v. Goodyear Tire & Rubber Company* case, which ruled that the statute of limitations to make a discriminatory pay claim was 180 days from the first discriminatory paycheck. Because of the Lilly Ledbetter Act, the statute of limitations now restarts with each discriminatory paycheck. The act applies to all protected classes and covers both wages and pensions. Due to the scope of the act, employers could face claims years after an employee has left the company. This act was designed to make employers more proactive in resolving pay inequities. Additionally, employers should review their compensation record retention procedures in case they need to produce any related documentation for potential pay disparities.

PATIENT PROTECTION AND AFFORDABLE CARE ACT (PPACA)

The **Patient Protection and Affordable Care Act** (PPACA) is a comprehensive healthcare law that was passed in 2010 to establish regulations on medical services, insurance coverage, preventative services, whistleblowing, and similar practices. A few key provisions of the PPACA include the following:

- **Individual mandate**—Requires all individuals to maintain health insurance or pay a penalty. It was removed from the statute effective tax year 2019. However, there are a few states that have an individual mandate.
- **State healthcare exchanges**—Provides individuals and families a portal in which they can shop through a variety of plans and purchase healthcare coverage.
- **Employer shared responsibility**—Requires that employers with more than 50 full-time employees provide affordable coverage to all employees that work 30 or more hours per week or pay a penalty.
- **Affordable coverage**—Does not allow employers to shift the burden of healthcare costs to employees and imposes a penalty on employers if their employees qualify to obtain government subsidies for coverage.
- **Flexible spending accounts (FSAs)**—Imposes a cap on pretax contributions to FSAs, health reimbursement arrangements (HRAs), and health savings accounts (HSAs).
- **Wellness incentives**—Allows employers to provide premium discounts for employees who meet wellness requirements.
- **Excise tax on "Cadillac" plans**—Imposes excise tax on employers that provide expensive coverage.
- **W-2 reporting requirements**—Requires employers to report the cost of coverage under employer-sponsored group health plans on each employee's W-2 form.
- **Summary of benefits coverage**—Requires insurance companies and employers to provide individuals with a summary of benefits coverage (SBC) using a standard form.
- **Whistleblower protections**—Amends the FLSA to prohibit employers from retaliating against an employee who applies for health benefit subsidies or tax credits.

TAX TREATMENT

There are several things to be aware of when considering the implications of taxes for compensation and benefits. The first area to consider is tax treatment of compensation. Employee gross wages, including overtime, are subject to federal income tax (FIT). In addition, Social Security and Medicare are taxed under the Federal Insurance Contributions Act (FICA). Meanwhile, employers pay federal unemployment insurance (FUTA) taxes.

The second area to consider is tax treatment of benefits. The most common benefits that are not taxable are:

- Commuting/transportation expenses
- Health benefits, including care for dependents
- Most group life insurance plans
- Plans such as 401(k) programs that are considered "qualified benefits plans"

The most common taxable benefits are those that can be considered a form of payment for the performance of a service. The following are subject to FIT, FICA, and FUTA taxes:

- Paid vacations
- Using a company-issued car for commuting to and from the workplace

- Company-paid bonuses
- Gym or health club memberships

Laws and Regulations: Health, Safety, Security, and Privacy

WORKPLACE CONFIDENTIALITY

Workplace confidentiality is defined as the policies and procedures created by an organization to maintain confidential, private, sensitive, or compromising information related to the employer and its employees. Confidential or private information may include, but is not limited to, business planning and forecasting, client information and contracts, research and development studies, and employee records. HR plays a vital role in maintaining confidential and private information. There are laws for specific types of data and how they should be maintained, and other data types come with suggested procedures to securely protect an organization from legal risks. A general litmus test in the dissemination of private information is:

- Is sharing the information legal?
- Does the individual or group absolutely need to know because their input is mandatory in order to investigate, settle, or solve the issue?

A breach exposing confidential or private information can result in a broad range of negative consequences legally, financially, and in the court of public opinion.

CONFIDENTIALITY RULES PERTAINING TO EMPLOYEE RECORDS

An organization's HR department collects a substantial amount of employee paperwork: completed job applications, resumes, contact information, completed benefit forms, performance evaluations, and possibly performance improvement plans and medical records. Some documents, whether in paper or electronic form, must remain private and thus protected. Medical records absolutely must be kept confidential, as release of this information in any form could be a violation of the Americans with Disabilities Act (ADA), the Genetic Information Nondiscrimination Act (GINA), and/or the Health Insurance Portability and Accountability Act (HIPAA).

The rationale for confidentiality is that this type of information, if not held private, could result in possible discriminatory decisions by an organization. For example, the ADA maintains that employee medical information must be kept separate—in a locked file cabinet or secured behind a firewall, for instance—from the employee's personnel record. This is a specific legal ruling. However, there are other documents that most organizations should keep secure and private because it is in everyone's best interest, including I-9 forms, background check results, performance evaluations, termination data, and investigative documents (harassment, complaints, etc.). These documents may include information that could potentially be utilized in a discrimination case against the employer if it is released and wrongdoing is suspected.

CONFIDENTIALITY RULES PERTAINING TO COMPANY DATA

Company data must be kept private and only released to those who have been identified as needing to know the information in order to operate the organization. Typically, the following information is considered proprietary and confidential data: client names, sources of revenue, expenditures and losses, trade secrets, and all business processes and operations. Confidentiality applies to paper and electronic company data. Paper documents must be kept in a secure, locked location, and electronic data must have appropriate firewalls and password protection.

Organizations will often have an employee sign a privacy or nondisclosure agreement that clearly documents what information is protected, and how and with whom proprietary information can be shared. This is an important step to avoid potentially negative legal repercussions, loss of business, or competitive advantage. For example, if an employee reveals trade secrets to a competitor, thus causing harm to their employer, they are in violation of their nondisclosure agreement and could face legal consequences. Additionally, some organizations have procedures in place for protecting intellectual property via trademark, patent, and copyright protocols.

PRIVACY PRINCIPLES AND IMPACT IN THE WORKFORCE

With technology now a part of every business transaction, it is essential that companies and employees adhere to strict confidentiality practices and **privacy principles**. From employee monitoring to asking interview questions, employers need to carefully avoid invading personal privacy. Legal regulations that inform best practices and internal privacy policies should be consulted regularly for guidance. On the other hand, companies should consider implementing confidentiality or nondisclosure agreements so employees are aware that databases, client lists, and other proprietary information must be protected and that the sharing of these records externally is strictly prohibited.

EMPLOYEE MONITORING SOFTWARE

An organization may choose to utilize **employee monitoring software** to gain information on how employees are using their time at work. Usually, monitoring software allows the employer to see internet activity and software usage. It can also save random screenshots and track keystrokes. This monitoring is typically done from a central location, but can also capture information from local and remote computers. The rationale behind employee monitoring software is to understand how an employee spends their time while working because it can directly and indirectly impact the organization's productivity and security.

Best practices for the deployment of employee monitoring software includes clearly communicating to employees, usually in an HR handbook or company policy manual, what is and is not appropriate computer usage in a given organization, and possible repercussions for violating such a policy. It is important that the employee know from the beginning of their employment that the organization has the right to monitor all technology use from company-procured or sponsored equipment. The goal is to effectively design and communicate a technology policy that protects the organization from threats such as viruses, hacking, or unethical activity, while at the same time providing employees some balance in internet and/or software usage.

CONFIDENTIALITY DISCLOSURES

Confidentiality disclosures should include definitions and exclusions of confidential information while outlining individual responsibilities. Confidentiality disclosures are used to keep private or secure information available only to those who are authorized to access it. It is important to ensure that only the proper individuals have access to the information needed to perform their jobs. Moreover, legislation mandates due diligence to protect the confidential information of employees and customers. Technological breaches in confidentiality could happen via phone, fax, computer, email, and electronic records. For this reason, some businesses might utilize encryption software, limit the communications that can be sent via email, or include a statement notifying the reader what to do if the email is inadvertently sent to the wrong person.

OCCUPATIONAL SAFETY AND HEALTH ACT (OSHA) REPORTING

The Occupational Safety and Health Act (OSHA) of 1970 set safety and related recordkeeping standards for the workplace. Safety records could include a log of occupational injuries and illnesses related to work while performing a job, a record and summaries of illnesses and injuries, and a record of any toxic exposures for employees. OSHA regulations require compliance by an organization that is engaged in commerce and has one or more employees. OSHA also protects employees who may work in substandard conditions by informing them of their rights and providing training to remedy the situation. An employee can reach out to OSHA to investigate possible substandard conditions without legal fear of retaliation. The following are the OSHA forms that an organization may have to complete, depending on the situation.

- Form 300—Used by an employer to record and keep information about an injury or illness an employee experienced. There are three parts to this form: (1) identification, including name of the person, maybe a case number, job title, and department; (2) description of event, with date, location, and summary of event; and (3) classification of injury or illness, its type, number of days off from work, and any restrictions.
- Form 301—Used if the injury or illness event has supplemental material that needs to be documented. For example, it may contain information about events leading up to the occurrence, or whether an object or substance was involved.
- Form 300A—A summary of illnesses and injuries that occurred throughout the year. Form 300A does not contain any of the personal information that is on Form 300. The primary purpose of this form is to calculate incident rates.

> **Review Video: What is OSHA?**
> Visit mometrix.com/academy and enter code: 913559

SEXUAL HARASSMENT

Title VII of the Civil Rights Act of 1964 prohibits sexual harassment. There are two different types of sexual harassment in the workplace: quid pro quo and hostile work environment.

Quid pro quo literally means "this for that." This type of harassment occurs when a supervisor, manager, or someone with authority demands some form of sexual interaction in exchange for an employment-related benefit, such as more compensation, a promotion, or keeping a current job. In other words, the person with authority basically states, "If you do some sexual favor for me, then I will provide some work benefit for you." A worker is then coerced or forced into unwelcome sexual demands to avoid negatively impacting their job.

A hostile work environment occurs when an employee is confronted with unwelcome, sexually offensive conduct that is severe and in a clear, pervasive pattern, thereby creating an abusive environment. Some of the circumstances that should be examined in a possible hostile environment are as follows:

- How often the offensive, discriminatory action occurs
- How severe the actions are
- Whether the conduct can cause or has caused physical harm, is intimidating, or is more subtle
- Whether it unreasonably prevents the employee from performing his or her job

The goal for organizations is to try and prevent sexual harassment. This can be done by clearly communicating the organization's policy that sexual harassment will not be tolerated, and by providing training. However, if sexual harassment occurs, there needs to be a formal complaint process whereby it is immediately investigated, and swift and fair action is taken to stop the harassment.

EMPLOYER AND EMPLOYEE RIGHTS WITH SUBSTANCE ABUSE

There are federal and state laws outlining policies an employer can develop to combat drug and alcohol abuse in the workplace. Generally, employers implement three policies that address this type of abuse: (1) unequivocally prohibit alcohol and drug use on the job, (2) provide permission to test for drug use (within guidelines), and (3) fire employees who have been proven to use illegal drugs. Employers should document their drug and alcohol policies, including what could happen if someone fails a drug test. Employees also have some protections afforded to them from both federal and state laws, whereby the employer may have to provide some accommodations to address the substance abuse problem. It is important to keep in mind that the Americans with Disabilities Act (ADA) and the Rehabilitation Act of 1973 include drug and alcohol policies, and some states have their own policies. The following are some examples to keep in mind:

- The ADA does not prohibit an employer from testing for illegal drug use, although it must follow any applicable state protocols.
- Some states restrict pre-employment drug testing until the candidate has accepted the job. It is usually a good practice to test all candidates instead of singling out any one individual.
- Some states can randomly test workers for drugs, especially where safety is an issue. However, there are also some states where an employer must have a reasonable suspicion before requiring an employee to be drug-tested.
- An employer—if applicable, and if possible—must offer reasonable accommodations for employees with substance abuse problems, in their past or currently, to attend to medical care.
- Under the ADA, a person considered an alcoholic might be considered an "individual with a disability" and treated accordingly.

EMPLOYERS AND AN EMPLOYEE'S RIGHTS TO PRIVACY

There is no specific federal law that compels employers to inform employees about any type of monitoring in the workplace. Therefore, US employers have the right to monitor employees with such things as surveillance cameras, internet tracking, or email or phone tracking applications. The ability to do this is a double-edged sword for employers. Technology affords employers many ways to monitor, which is helpful for reducing liability and perhaps increasing productivity. However, at the same time, employees have almost no choice other than to surrender most of their privacy while at work.

There is much debate among employers about the ethical, moral, and legal decisions to reduce employee privacy rights. There is also the question of where it ends, such as whether an employer should use a candidate's social media presence when making a decision to hire. The debate continues about how a company can strike a balance between employer rights and employee privacy. Every company is different and needs to evaluate whether the monitoring is worth the effort and what the monitoring is doing to drive better business results. Additionally, a company may want to consider how the monitoring will impact its culture: Will employees want to work for a company that aggressively monitors its employees? There are no right or wrong answers, but it is helpful for companies to be clear and transparent about employee privacy and monitoring activities.

DEFAMATION

Defamation is when a person intentionally makes a false and malicious statement causing harm to a person's reputation in a given community. If harm is caused by speaking, it is called slander. If it is in written form, it is called libel. For example, if someone makes a negative statement during a reference check regarding a former employee, or over-the-top positive comments, then the person giving the reference could be liable for making distorted false claims. Another example of this type of misrepresentation could be when an employee is upset because he or she was passed over for a promotion and decides to spread a rumor that the person who received the promotion lied about their qualifications.

The First Amendment, which protects free speech, does not protect someone guilty of defamation, and as a result, the person can face legal consequences. Many companies have implemented policies to try and reduce the likelihood of harmful gossip and rumors that cause needless stress and negatively impact productivity.

FRAUDULENT MISREPRESENTATION

Fraudulent misrepresentation is an intentionally false statement that deceptively causes someone to enter into a contract. Basically, someone can be accused of fraudulent misrepresentation if a statement of fact is a blatant lie, and this lie creates a false pretense under which another person enters into a contract. For example, suppose an employer says to a prospective applicant that the company is doing great financially and job security is strong. Hearing this, the applicant turns down other jobs for the one with the most job security. He accepts the position and learns three months later that the company has not been profitable in many months and the employer knew the job would only be temporary without any job security whatsoever. This is a case of fraudulent misrepresentation, in which the job applicant entered into a contract of employment with an expectation of job security when the employer knew that was not true.

Fraudulent misrepresentation can occur in any form that results in the other party being deceived with false information, a half-truth, or silence when there was an opportunity to speak up. Also, fraudulent misrepresentation requires the deceived party to enter into a contract; this is different from defamation, which is when an intentionally false statement is made about a person without the involvement of contracts.

DRUG-FREE WORKPLACE ACT

The Drug-Free Workplace Act of 1988 requires that government contractors make a good-faith effort to ensure a drug-free workplace. Employers must prohibit illegal substances in the workplace and must create drug awareness trainings for employees. Any federal contractor with contracts of $100,000 or more, and all organizations that are federal grantees, must adhere to a set of mandates to show they maintain a drug-free work environment:

- Employers must develop a written policy prohibiting the production, distribution, use, or possession of any controlled substance by an employee while in the workplace.
- Employers are required to develop standards of enforcement, and all employees must receive a copy of the policy and understand the consequences of a violation.
- Employers need to implement drug awareness trainings to help employees understand the hazards and health risks of drug use.
- Although drug testing is not required, it is intended that employers have some type of screening in place.

SARBANES-OXLEY ACT (SOX)

The Sarbanes-Oxley Act (SOX) was passed in 2002 to provide accountability, standards, and oversight to prevent corporate fraud. The act was largely in response to major corporate accounting scandals in the early 21st century like those at WorldCom and Enron. In turn, the passage of SOX created the Public Company Accounting Oversight Board (PCAOB) as an oversight agency for the accounting industry. However, the Securities and Exchange Commission (SEC) enforces compliance with SOX.

SOX holds senior executives responsible for any accounting misconduct or manipulation. Additionally, the law protects shareholders from any activity that might mislead or influence investors about the company's financial health and outlook. Under SOX, a public corporation is required to accurately report financial information to both investors and the SEC. If the information reported to the SEC is later found to be inaccurate or altered in any form, there are large financial penalties and stringent white-collar crime consequences. Additionally, SOX offers protection to whistleblowers who report fraud and could potentially testify against their employer.

Risk Assessment and Mitigation

EMPLOYEE RECORDS MANAGEMENT

Workplace employee-related records should have organizational policies that might be regulated by federal, state, and local laws as well as operational necessity. It is sometimes easier to think of a record as the complete, final version of a document so that there is no need to keep every draft or note. The following are key elements of workplace records retention management and access:

- How long to **retain** records—First, all records that are regulated by law should be kept for the prescribed time period according to federal, state, and/or local laws. This can be confusing because certain records might be regulated by more than one law, or the time period may vary. In these cases, records should be kept for the longest period required.
- Who should have **access** to records—Access should be provided (1) only to those people with a legitimate business need, and (2) only where federal, state, and local laws permit such access. For example, HIPAA and many data privacy regulations specify not only who may have access, but how the information may be used.

STORAGE OF RECORDS AND SECURITY NEEDED

Workplace policy should describe specifically where records will be stored and in what format—paper or electronic. Records should be held in a secure, locked location or electronically maintained with necessary technological protections. There is no specific law that dictates how records must be stored, whether paper or electronic, but the law does dictate that an organization must have the ability to quickly retrieve information and supply paper copies if necessary.

It is imperative for HR to always protect employee records and the privacy of the information, regardless of the format. Frequently, an organization will have a documented employee records confidentiality policy to protect all employee information and maintain confidentiality. Furthermore, if an employee feels there has been a breach in confidentiality, then HR needs to investigate the allegation immediately. Alternatively, if an organization feels there was a breach in confidentiality, regardless of how it occurred, the organization usually has an obligation to share the breach and offer corrective actions.

CONCERNS BEFORE DESTRUCTION OF HR RECORDS

Employee records management is critical to comply with federal, state, and local requirements and to reduce legal liabilities. If an organization prematurely destroys HR records, that organization could face criminal liabilities and possible legal penalties or litigation. Additionally, the organization may not be able to adequately defend itself in employment-related litigation due to spoliation of evidence. An organization should only retain the legal HR records that are required to comply with federal, state, and local laws or operational necessity. For example, holding on to every scrap of paper an employee writes on is not necessary; only legally mandated documents are necessary. In some cases, keeping every scrap could turn into a liability for the organization.

The end goal for HR is to keep what is legally mandated and to properly, legally dispose of the rest. Disposal of confidential, personal, or financial information after the legally dictated retention period is over should comply with all federal, state, and local regulations. For example, the Fair and Accurate Credit Transactions Act (FACTA) has specific rules for how to dispose of background check documentation. Usually, if it is paper, this means shredding on-site or hiring a professional vendor that specializes in shredding. In the case of electronic records, the organization must follow protocols so that the information is erased and cannot be read or reconstructed.

PRE-EMPLOYMENT RECORDS RETENTION

The pre-employment phase of a job comprises activities that occur before a candidate is chosen for and has accepted a position at an organization. During this phase, HR posts a job, resumes are submitted, applications are completed, reference checks and/or background checks may be conducted, and interviews may be held. All of these documents should be retained for EEO purposes demonstrating nondiscriminatory hiring, equal opportunity, and overall fairness and equity.

Organizations must retain the following information for all applicants: job posting; resumes; and completed applications, including interview notes related to the decision to hire or not hire an applicant. Based on federal regulations in the Age Discrimination in Employment Act (ADEA), Americans with Disabilities Act (ADA), and Civil Rights Act of 1964 (Title VII), these documents are retained one year after creation of the documents or hire/no-hire decision, whichever is later. In the case of federal contractors, document retention is two years. If the contractor has less than 150 employees or a government contract is less than $150,000, then the retention is, again, one year. These are the federal retention regulations, but retention rates could vary slightly depending on state and local laws.

EMPLOYMENT RECORDS RETENTION

Employee records, whether they are paper or electronic, have specific retention requirements. Retention of employee records could vary according to federal, state, and local laws. Therefore, it is important to understand the legal requirements as well as the system that an organization utilizes. The following is a summary of federal guidelines for the most common HR records.

- **I-9 forms**—Securely retained for three years beginning from the hire date, or one year after separation of employment.
- **Payroll records**—These records, which contain personal information such as name, address, Social Security number, and compensation, should be retained for three years according to federal laws. There are many federal laws that regulate payroll records, including the Age Discrimination Employment Act (ADEA), Fair Labor Standards Act (FLSA), Service Contract Act, Davis-Bacon Act, Walsh-Healey Act (for federal contractors), and Family and Medical Leave Act (FMLA). However, it is recommended for the purposes of the Lilly Ledbetter Fair Pay Act to retain these documents for at least five years after the end of employment. Additionally, under the Equal Pay Act (EPA), employers must retain two years of all payroll records in case they need to justify the pay wage differential between different sexes.
- **Employment benefits**—These records should be retained for six years and are carefully regulated, requiring employer reporting based on the Employee Retirement Income Security Act (ERISA).

- **Background checks**—These are retained for a minimum of one year based on the Equal Employment Opportunity Commission (EEOC) requirements and Title VII of the Civil Rights Act of 1964 to possibly report hiring and selection records. However, it is often recommended to save background check documents for five years after the date the consumer report is accessed because the statute of limitations in the Fair Credit Reporting Act is five years.
- **Tax records**—All related tax records should be retained by the employer for four years after the fourth quarter of the year in order to be in compliance with the Federal Insurance Contributions Act (FICA), Federal Unemployment Tax Act, and Internal Revenue Code.
- **Safety records**—This data, and related reports, should be retained for five years after the year that the record pertains to, based on the Occupational Safety and Health Act (OSHA) and the Walsh-Healey Act (for federal contractors).
- **Family and Medical Leave Act (FMLA) records**—Based on the requirements in the FMLA, these records should be retained for three years.
- **Disability accommodations**—All employee disability and accommodations documentation should be retained for one year from the date of the record or last date of an action. However, for contractors and public employees, the records should be retained for two years. There are many laws that require compliance with disability issues, such as the American Disabilities Act as Amended (ADAAA), Executive Order 11246, and the Vietnam Era Veterans' Readjustment Assistance Act (VEVRAA).

Records retention can be a complex process. However, it is a critical HR function to support and protect an organization.

SEPARATING PERSONNEL FILES INTO TWO CATEGORIES

Not every record in a personnel file should be treated the same. Specific records regarding an employee and their employment history should be kept in their personnel file, while other documents, because of their confidential nature, might need to be protected differently.

- **Personnel file**—This file should include the job description, application resume, offer letter, acknowledgement of organization handbook, emergency contact information, job performance, promotions, transfers, appraisals, awards, training, any disciplinary actions, and all documents related to separation from the organization.
- **Confidential personnel information**—These records should have an added layer of protection because of the employee's privacy rights and, if these rights are breached, to protect the employer from liability. These records usually include any medical information such as ADA accommodations, workers' compensation, drug tests, disability information, Family and Medical Leave Act (FMLA) information, health insurance, COBRA information, all employee credit information, I-9 form, and any documents related to a complaint or investigation.

RISK MANAGEMENT IN THE WORKPLACE

Risk management is a methodical approach an organization engages in to identify, target, and initiate steps to minimize threats that could negatively impact an organization's health, safety, security, and privacy. While employers must abide by all federal, state, and local laws and regulations, they also have an obligation to protect employees from risks that could seriously harm the company, negatively impact morale, or create a financial burden. A **cost-benefit analysis**, or observing the potential cost of an endeavor against the benefit it will bring, is one of the methods an organization can utilize to evaluate risk. This type of evaluation relies on predicting the future based on available current information. Hence, there is an element of uncertainty with cost-benefit analysis that forces an organization to carefully examine all options and possible outcomes. Additionally, there are always unknowns in a situation, such as new obstacles or threats. Accordingly, there is a method to evaluate these risks called **enterprise risk management**. This methodology forces an organization to factor in those risks that have the highest likelihood of occurring, or whose impact is the most drastic. This allows organizations to strategically plan for worst-case scenarios and the possibility of perceived risks becoming realities.

COST-BENEFIT ANALYSIS

Cost-benefit analysis is presented as a ratio that helps an organization determine how certain activities and related costs impact its profitability. The following formula calculates the cost-benefit ratio:

$$Cost/benefit\ ratio = \frac{Projected\ value\ of\ benefits}{Cost}$$

For example, if an HR department made the decision to participate in an employee program that resulted in a cost savings of $10,000, and the cost of the program was $2,000, then the cost-benefit ratio would be 5:1. HR typically performs cost-benefit analyses on a regular basis to justify continuing or ending a particular program or activity.

EMERGENCY ACTION PLANS

All emergency action plans should explain the alarm system that will be used to inform employees and other individuals at the worksite that they need to evacuate. They should also include in-depth exit route plans that describe which routes employees should take to escape the building, as well as in-depth plans that describe what actions employees should take before evacuating, such as shutting down equipment or closing doors. All emergency action plans should also include detailed systems for handling different types of emergencies and a system that can be used to verify that all employees have escaped the worksite.

PREPARING FOR EMERGENCIES AND NATURAL DISASTERS

Because it is an employer's obligation to provide a safe and healthy work environment, many companies have begun to create **emergency and disaster plans** for handling situations such as fires, explosions, earthquakes, chemical spills, communicable disease outbreaks, and acts of terrorism. These plans should include the following steps:

1. The **chain of command** should be clarified, and staff should be informed of who to contact and who has authority.
2. Someone should be responsible for **accounting** for all employees when an emergency occurs.
3. A **command center** should be set up to coordinate communications.
4. Employees should be **trained annually** on what to do if an emergency occurs.
5. Businesses should have **first-aid kits and basic medical supplies** available. This includes water fountains and eye wash stations in areas where spills may occur.
6. An **emergency team of employees** should be named and trained for the following:
   a. Organizing evacuation procedures
   b. Initiating shutdown procedures
   c. Using fire extinguishers
   d. Using oxygen and respirators
   e. Searching for disabled or missing employees
   f. Assessing when it is safe to re-enter the building

151

EMERGENCY EVACUATION PROCEDURES

Emergency evacuation procedures should be designed and developed according to the needs of the company to protect the business assets and the employees of the organization. Evacuation procedures should be comprehensive, covering preparations, building exit criteria, and the care and handling of vulnerable persons or employees who may be in danger. There should be highly visible maps of the building exits and designated employee meeting spots outside the building for accountability.

Emergency simulations that are practiced on a regular basis are critical elements of the evacuation plan. These simulations are more advanced than traditional fire drills or evacuation practices. Simulation runs have specific plans that are modeled on unique potential scenarios to which the team must respond. Responses are measured and scored to validate the plan, procedures, and systems, and are used to improve the plans. Simulations should be developed for many different scenarios to test each response plan.

SAFETY AND HEALTH MANAGEMENT PLANS

According to the Occupational Safety and Health Administration (OSHA), there are four things a safety and health management plan should do to be considered effective:

- Establish a **specific system** that an organization can use to identify hazards in the workplace.
- Establish a **training program** that teaches employees to avoid hazards and perform tasks in the safest way possible.
- Include **specific procedures and programs** designed to eliminate hazards that the organization identifies, or at least minimize the risk that a hazard will injure or kill an employee or cause an employee to become ill.
- Allow employees at all levels of the organization to be **involved in the identification, prevention, and elimination** of hazards in the workplace.

WORKPLACE VIOLENCE

Workplace violence can be a physical act against someone, or it can be verbal abuse, threats, or intimidation. No matter what type, workplace violence is disturbing and dangerous, regardless of whether it is physical or psychological. There are numerous reasons why an employee may exhibit violent behavior, including a history of family abuse, drug or substance abuse, or mental illness. Workplace violence not only causes harm to the victim, but could also cause financial harm to a business, with damage to reputation possibly resulting in loss of clients, suppliers, or advertisers. Sometimes workplace violence is random and difficult to predict and prevent. However, there are steps an employer can take to reduce the chances of workplace violence:

- Establish a zero-tolerance policy against workplace violence that is documented and communicated to employees.
- Provide access to an employee assistance program (EAP) whereby employees can speak to a mental health counselor for referrals and appropriate treatment.
- Have only alcohol-free company events, possibly reducing the chances of workplace violence.
- Incorporate a violence prevention program into onboarding safety training.

BUSINESS CONTINUITY PLANS

A business creates business continuity plans to ensure that the business can continue to operate in the face of a crisis or emergency that interferes with normal daily operations. When a disruption of daily operations occurs, the amount of time it takes for a business to recover data and resume normal operations and service is an indicator of whether that business has a well-planned continuity plan.

Business continuity plans consist of five critical components:

- A list of risks and an analysis of each risk's possible impact on the business
- A response plan for each risk
- Roles and responsibilities assigned for each response plan
- A communication plan to be implemented upon an event occurrence
- A training plan that is tested regularly

The business continuity plan should be fully developed and tested, and employees should all be trained on the implementation of the plan on a regular basis. Roles should be assigned and reviewed annually and when key employees leave the organization.

SECURITY RISKS IN THE WORKPLACE

Employers have an obligation and a responsibility to keep employees and the work environment safe, and should have a security plan in place to help achieve that goal. This includes every contingency from a crisis to an uninvited visitor. A well-conceived security plan can reduce panic and enable employees to calmly respond to different types of crises. A security plan can include any or all of the following: photo badges, keycard access systems, locks on rooms and closets, an alarm system with backup, concealed alarms, visible and hidden cameras, exterior fencing and gates, exterior lighting, and security guards. Typically, security plans are designed with key management team members, including HR, to ensure the plan is comprehensive. Additionally, the security plan should highlight specific roles and backups in the event of a security breach. Having a security plan also helps to prevent panic in the event of a workplace emergency. Organizations should periodically review and practice planned drills to reinforce preparedness.

DISASTER RECOVERY PLANS

Certain information should be included in every organization's disaster recovery plan. The plan should identify equipment and locations that can be utilized temporarily in the event of an emergency. It should also identify agencies and personnel that may be able to help the organization continue functioning immediately after an emergency. It is also wise to establish a set of procedures the organization can use to bring the personnel and equipment together after an emergency. Additionally, disaster recovery plans should identify alternative sources the organization can use to receive supplies or products if the emergency disables the organization's normal supply chain.

INFORMATION TECHNOLOGY (IT) SECURITY

IT security is becoming a more serious topic and rapidly gaining more attention. It is important for HR practitioners to be conscientious of controls to mitigate organizational exposure and risk. Some companies may have IT security policies and acknowledgements in place to identify and document compliance and security controls and to reduce liability. Multiple layers of corporate IT security might include the encryption of data files, firewalls, access controls or logins, systems monitoring, detection processes, antivirus software, and cyber insurance. Implementing stronger IT security can provide companies with benefits such as mitigating lost revenue, protecting brand reputation, and supporting mobilization.

CYBERCRIMES

Cybercrime is when a computer or element of technology is used to commit an illegal act, such as violating privacy or stealing data, money, intellectual property, or identities. Cybercrime is a criminal activity even if the activity does not specifically involve money, for example, spreading viruses or causing other forms of technological harm. In fact, companies could be held liable if they do not impose actions or precautions to prevent cybercrimes from occurring. Furthermore, the financial cost of cybercrime to a business can be astronomical. The reality is that a large majority of work is completed with data and the transfer of data by employees. Therefore, it is extremely important for organizations to conduct background checks that include a look at the possibility of criminal hacking.

Employers should take steps to allow and promote open communication and report any suspected cybercrime the moment there is an indication that something might be wrong. Employers should communicate the importance of not opening anything via email or any other form of technology or software that could be linked to scams, hacking, phishing, etc. Companies should make every effort possible to protect their data, including not transferring data on unsecured or unencrypted servers, not posting company information on public social media sites, and updating antivirus protection software. An organization's best defense against cybercrime is vigilance in monitoring and taking every possible systemic precaution to protect its data.

THEFT AND FRAUD

Theft and fraud in the workplace are extremely costly to an organization, and every effort should be made to prevent them. **Theft** is when property or information is taken without consent. **Fraud** is when some form of deception is utilized to take something for personal gain. Fraud is a form of theft. Employees may steal for any number of reasons: a sense of entitlement, the belief that they are underpaid, because it was easy, and more. Furthermore, theft could include almost anything that belongs to the company. Common types of theft include cash, products, equipment, services, ideas, and data. Fraud is a variation of theft and could include inflation of expense accounts, falsified payrolls, fabricated receipts, unrecorded vacation or personal time, forgeries, entertainment expenses without a legitimate link to a business purpose, or fictitious purchase orders.

Regardless of why or what is stolen, theft and fraud are illegal, and should be investigated by the company if suspected. To help prevent theft and fraud, organizations should consider doing the following:

- Conduct background checks on employees before hiring.
- Maintain an inventory control system (if applicable).
- Establish and communicate an employee theft policy, including consequences if found guilty after an investigation.
- Install security cameras (if appropriate).

EQUIPMENT DAMAGE OR DESTRUCTION

Company equipment is typically provided to employees to efficiently perform the functions of their job. Equipment provided can include laptops, printers, cell phones, or cars. Over time, and for various reasons, equipment can be damaged or destroyed. This hurts a company both monetarily and timewise, via work disruption. There are policies and steps an organization can take to mitigate equipment damage or destruction. To begin, companies should have an equipment property policy. This policy should reinforce that all equipment provisioned to or used by employees is the property of the company and is to be used only for company purposes. There should be a procedure in place of who to notify, and when, in the event that equipment is damaged, lost, stolen, or destroyed. The policy should also state disciplinary actions that could occur if the damage was due to negligence.

Employers should consult all federal, state, and local laws and regulations, as they vary from state to state, with regard to recovering lost expenses for equipment. Additionally, if equipment is damaged or destroyed due to unforeseen conditions such as fire, water, or disaster, companies should consult their insurance policy and/or other federal, state, and local resources.

MINIMIZING PASSWORD BREACH RISKS

Passwords are needed for almost every program that is opened on a computer, and it is critical to develop and maintain them in such a way as to minimize risk to the company. Many companies have developed password policies to help manage the process and ensure it is being monitored and enforced with regularity. Most password policies are developed with the whole life cycle of the password in mind, including the creation of passwords, the interval of time at which they are changed, and guidelines for the prevention of password theft. Research indicates that data breaches involving passwords are more likely to occur with a phishing attack or someone inside the company getting knowledge about passwords—as when passwords are left out on a drawer or written on a piece of paper—than by outside hacking. The following are some guidelines that could be adopted while drafting a password policy:

- Passwords should be strong, complex, and challenging for someone to guess—typically they should be combinations of uppercase letters, lowercase letters, numbers, punctuation marks, and special characters, and preferably over eight characters long. Passwords should not be obvious or easy to determine. For instance, Password123! would be a poor password.
- Default passwords, those given by IT for various reasons, should be changed immediately after logging in.
- Passwords should not be shared with anyone. If this occurs, then the employee should change the password immediately.
- Employers should educate employees on ways to avoid phishing scams that might be used to steal passwords.
- To prevent discovery, passwords should be neither written down nor stored in an employee's workspace.

CORPORATE ESPIONAGE

Corporate espionage is a type of spying between companies that involves taking some type of information that would provide one with an unfair advantage over the other. This type of secret could be (but is not limited to) trade secrets or a competitor's plans for future products, services or endeavors, or strategic plans. Corporate espionage can range from a disgruntled employee leaving a company for a competitor and sharing some type of secret, to hacking into or launching malware on a competitor's system. Obtaining information about competitors is not always a crime. For example, a retail company could send secret shoppers to a competitor's retail company to evaluate how they perform specific functions. In this case, they are obtaining information in a legally acceptable manner. However, intentionally (and often, deceptively) obtaining a trade secret without the owner's consent is not legal. Evaluating legality in corporate espionage is extremely complex. The federal Economic Espionage Act of 1996 essentially makes it illegal to steal commercial secrets. For those found guilty, financial penalties could be severe, possibly including prison time. Additionally, violators could be subject to civil litigation. Some states have even more stringent laws and regulations to combat corporate espionage.

Organizational Restructuring Initiatives

DOWNSIZING

Downsizing, sometimes referred to as "workforce reduction," is a strategically planned and necessary elimination of jobs in order to make an organization potentially more competitive and ideally more profitable. This process is intended to reduce operating costs for the purpose of maximizing production, which is intended to drive profitability in a positive direction. Downsizing can occur for any number of reasons, including a decrease in profits over a period of time, closure in parts or entire lines of the business, or acquisitions that might involve duplication of functions. Downsizing is not linked to employee performance and is usually regarded as a complex process due to all the factors that must be taken into consideration.

Organizations need to identify exactly what downsizing will achieve, create reliable and legally defensible selection criteria, develop a plan for work redistribution (if applicable), and gauge how downsizing will impact the business in the short and long term. Typically, the process of downsizing negatively impacts both productivity and morale. Hence, the employer should communicate with employees throughout the process and keep the lines of two-way communication open in order to minimize disruption to the business.

OPTIONS BEFORE IMPLEMENTING A DOWNSIZING PLAN

The decision to downsize is rarely an easy one. However, it is often a necessity for a business to stay viable. The negative effect of downsizing on a business culture and its brand in the marketplace is challenging. Therefore, many businesses look for alternatives to downsizing before implementing a reduction in force. Some of these alternatives include the following:

- Implement an immediate **hiring freeze** and work with employees on work redistribution if needed.
- Reduce employees' hours.
- Create an **early retirement program**, whereby the company can offer eligible employees financial incentives to leave. Eligibility can be tied to years of service and/or age to incentivize the most senior employees to take early retirement.
- **Reduce pay** in order to avoid layoffs, although the employer must pay careful attention to legal regulations and consistency in implementation.
- Place employees on **furloughs** if the financial distress is temporary.
- Encourage employees to **voluntarily leave with incentives**, which could include a generous severance package and/or outplacement services.

REDUCTION IN FORCE (RIF)

The following are the steps for conducting a layoff or reduction in force (RIF):

1. Select employees for layoff using seniority, performance, job classification, location, or skill.
2. Ensure selected employees do not affect a protected class to avoid adverse or disparate impact.
3. Review compliance with federal and state WARN Act regulations, which require employers to provide 60 days' notice to affected employees while specifying whether the reduction in force is permanent or for a specified amount of time.

4. Review compliance with the Older Workers Benefit Protection Act, which provides workers over the age of 40 the opportunity to review any severance agreements that require their waiver of discrimination claims. The act allows a consideration period of 21 days if only one older worker is being separated, and 45 days when two or more older workers are being separated. They also must receive a revocation period of seven days after signing the agreement. Additionally, they must be informed of the positions and ages of the other employees affected by the layoffs so that they can assess whether or not they feel age discrimination has taken place.

5. Determine if severance packages, including salary continuation, vacation pay, employer-paid COBRA premiums, outplacement services, or counseling, might be available to affected employees. Typically, employees laid off in a RIF will sign a document called a separation and general release, whereby the employee signing the document accepts a severance package and agrees to not sue or make any claims against a company. A company is never required to offer a severance package.

6. When conducting meetings with employees, be empathetic, have tissues, ensure that all required documentation is available to the employee, and review all information in detail.

7. Inform the current workforce by communicating sustainability concerns, methods used to determine who would be selected for the reduction in force, and commitment to meeting company goals and objectives to maintain morale and productivity.

OUTPLACEMENT FIRMS

An **outplacement firm** is an external vendor that is contracted by an organization in the event the organization needs to reduce its workforce and lay off a large number of employees—sometimes referred to as a "reduction in force" (RIF). Outplacement firms, sometimes called career transition services, offer services to outgoing employees to cope with the loss of a job and assist in finding a new job. Usually, outplacement firms are contracted and paid for by the organization that is laying off its employees. This service is typically part of an employee severance benefit and is therefore offered at no cost to the exiting employee.

Services provided by an outplacement firm can vary, but some of the most common offerings are career assessments, career coaching, job search programs, and resume and networking workshops. Depending on the options selected by the organization, services can be in-person, one-on-one, group, and/or video appointments. An organization may choose to utilize the services of an outplacement firm because it is the moral or conscientious and responsible thing to do, because it may reduce the risk of litigation, or because it protects the employer's reputation by assisting their displaced employees.

MERGERS AND ACQUISITIONS

Mergers and acquisitions are similar in many ways, as both terms refer to a type of structural change in which two organizations join together to form a single organization. However, the two terms refer to different ways in which an organization's structure changes. A **merger** refers to a situation in which two or more organizations agree to combine into a single organization because both organizations will benefit from the merger. An **acquisition**, on the other hand, refers to a situation in which an organization purchases enough of another organization's stock to take control of the organization's operations. This is an important difference because all of the organizations involved in a merger must agree to the merger, while the organizations involved in an acquisition do not necessarily need to agree to the acquisition in order for it to take place.

The most vulnerable time period of a merger or acquisition is the transition through the first year, when roles and responsibilities are still being sorted out, employees are feeling vulnerable, and emotions are typically running high. With this in mind, it is critical that a new business continuity plan be created during the process of defining organizational structure.

As executives are seated in new roles, the management staff is shuffled and reassigned, and organizations are realigned, the team responsible for the business continuity plan must work closely with the teams to reassess the plan and the roles and responsibilities, and to develop a new communication plan. The executives must be briefed on the new business continuity plan, and once it is approved, it must be rolled out to employees, who must be trained, and the plan must be tested.

If a crisis or emergency occurs during the transition time frame or within the first few years of merger or acquisition activity, and a business continuity plan has not been very clearly defined, roles have not been assigned, and plans have not been tested, the organization will be at high risk for failure.

DIVESTITURES

A **divestiture** is the opposite of an acquisition, whereby a company separates a portion of itself, usually a division or subsidiary, in a form of restructuring.

A company that initiates a divestiture typically seeks to remove a business line that is unrelated to its core operations or is simply a poor fit that requires inordinate management attention. A subsidiary that operates in an aging business with modest growth prospects may be sold or spun off in order to focus on more promising opportunities.

Alternatively, the divestment may be required by a regulatory authority, such as to comply with an antitrust adjudication.

During a divestiture process, it is critical to update the business continuity plan for the organization. As elements of the business are separated from the core and sold off or removed and data is separated, workflows are adapted, processes are changed, and employees are moved out and around the company, it will be critical to readdress the risks, requirements, and roles and responsibilities that have been altered and rework and reassign them. In the event of an emergency, the transitioning company cannot afford to have a lack of plans that could result in a failure in service or the inability to reconstitute the organization.

During the divestiture process, the business continuity plan should be reviewed, updated, rewritten, and tested, and employees trained, as quickly as possible during the transitioning of the company.

UNPAID LEAVE

Unpaid leave is time off from work that is approved by the employer, but not compensated in any way. There are many reasons an employee may need to take unpaid leave. Every employee request and situation must be carefully considered by an employer to make sure it is consistent with organizational policy and compliant with all federal, state, and local laws and regulations. If an employee is requesting unpaid leave under the parameters of FMLA, then the employee's unpaid leave is mandatory, and the employee is guaranteed to keep their job and benefits upon returning to work. An unpaid leave of absence can also occur when an employee has used up all of their paid time off. Assuming the request does not have to be granted under federal, state, or local laws and regulations, it is up to the employer's discretion and policies.

In some instances, the employer can also force an employee to take unpaid leave if the workplace does not have enough work, a practice sometimes referred to as a **furlough**. During a furlough, employees typically have access to benefits. Furloughs are sometimes implemented to avoid a staff reduction such as layoffs. Another example of when employees could be furloughed is when coming to work is temporarily unsafe, like during a national pandemic. Paying or not paying employees during such a furlough is up to the employer's discretion and is dependent on many other factors.

FURLOUGHS

When considering implementing a furlough, or forced unpaid leave, for employees within the company for some period of time, the organization must consider the impact on the business continuity plan. The business continuity plan has very specific roles and responsibilities for reconstituting operations, data, and services in the event of an emergency or crisis. If the employees that the company is considering furloughing are essential to the restoration of the organization's business, the organization should either reconsider which employees are furloughed or reassign roles and responsibilities in the plan. Leaving the organization at risk when furloughing essential employees would be a detrimental decision. Many organizations have a list of "essential employees" who are protected from furloughs or reduction-in-force actions. In governmental agencies, essential employees must work even during government shutdowns.

INTEGRATION

Integration of organizations can be external, like mergers and acquisitions, or internal. Internal integrations would be the coming together of components of the organization in a new structure to better align the company to its mission; its customer base, products, and services; or its market.

There are several types of company integrations, including the following:

- Supply chain integration (also known as vertical integration)—acquiring businesses within the supply chain.
  - Backward integration—acquiring businesses that provide goods and services earlier in the supply chain.
  - Forward integration—acquiring businesses that provide goods and services later in the supply chain.
- Combination integration—acquiring functions or activities—or entire firms—that are external to the company and integrating them into the organization.
  - Conglomerate integration—acquiring functions or firms from unrelated business activities.
  - Horizontal integration—acquiring functions or firms in the same industry.

When integrating businesses, it is critical to address business continuity plans early in the process. The most vulnerable time in the integration is during the transition, and if a crisis or emergency were to take place during the transition and a business continuity plan was not established and in place, the ability of the organization to reestablish business operations would be severely compromised. Roles and responsibilities, processes, and methods for recovery must be established for the new entity or entities as quickly as possible, and responsible parties must be identified and notified.

OFFSHORING

Offshoring is a common practice that results in a company sending some aspects of their business or business practices to a different country to be executed. The services must be executed in a different country for it to be an offshore arrangement. An example of offshoring that is frequently encountered in the United States is companies that offshore their IT support to large call centers in India, where labor and talent can be more readily available.

When considering the impact of offshoring on business continuity plans, companies must consider the requirement to reconstitute access to servers of data, storage of information, computers, tools, and communication during emergencies and crises. It may be expedient to offshore the business continuity plan itself if the crisis or emergency scenario involves the loss of capability within the entire country in which the company operates. Offshoring for reconstituting a business can improve the resiliency of the business.

aPHR Practice Test #1

Want to take this practice test in an online interactive format?
Check out the bonus page, which includes interactive practice questions and
much more: **mometrix.com/bonus948/aphr**

1. The Drug-Free Workplace Act is applicable to which of the following groups?
   a. Most federal contractors and grant recipients
   b. Most workplaces with 100 or more employees
   c. Most federal and state employees
   d. Most employees within a blue-collar industry

2. Which of the following recruiting methods is the MOST cost-efficient?
   a. Referral programs
   b. Internships
   c. Alumni networks
   d. Online job boards

3. Weak passwords can pose a threat to Internet security and sensitive organizational data. Which of the following security measures can HR consider to eliminate the use of passwords in the workplace?
   a. Multifactor authentication
   b. Biometric technology
   c. Virtual private network
   d. Random password generator

4. If a Human Resources professional makes decisions and regards other business functions as dynamic, interactive teams rather than silos or independent entities, which of the following skills are they utilizing?
   a. SWOT analysis (environmental analysis)
   b. Systems thinking
   c. Strategic thinking
   d. Growth-share matrix analysis

5. Which of the following types of organizational culture is at the HIGHEST risk of innovation stagnation?
   a. High-Performance
   b. Mechanistic
   c. Learning
   d. Authoritarian

161

6. Which of the following HR functions is LEAST likely to utilize an external provider?

    a. Workforce planning
    b. Workers compensation administration
    c. Workforce recruiting
    d. Payroll processing

7. When designing a recruiting strategy for a reception desk attendant, which workforce team or individuals will be the most critical to collaborate with to determine the information needed for the number of positions to fill?

    a. Executive leadership
    b. Finance and administration
    c. Line managers
    d. Incumbent reception desk attendants

8. In a company that is expanding in size and geography, which of the following areas of expertise will be MOST critical to consider when selecting a benefits broker?

    a. Insurance coverage
    b. Direct connection with employees
    c. Insurance compliance
    d. Existing benefit analysis

9. Which of the following technologies or technological services facilitates an organization's integration of IT needs across multiple business functions such as HR information systems, front line operations, sales and marketing, and customer history?

    a. Software as a service
    b. Best of breed systems
    c. Enterprise resource planning system
    d. Employee self-service technologies

10. Which of the following would be an example of disparate impact during the recruiting process?

    a. Selecting only male applicants to interview for a position that requires strength and stamina
    b. Requiring a college degree for an entry-level position at a department store
    c. Rejecting job applicants who report to an interview with a religious headdress
    d. Offering higher compensation rates to applicants who look similar to the interviewer

11. Which of the following mitigation methods would be the most appropriate to give employees the power to hold one another accountable to stopping theft in the workplace?

    a. Strong whistleblower policy and practices
    b. Transparent surveillance practices
    c. Frequent team meetings to review theft prevention
    d. Trainings that simulate how to confront theft in the workplace

12. The MOST proactive and effective way to improve an organization's response to workplace emergencies is:

    a. Facility signage directing appropriate emergency response
    b. After-action debriefs
    c. Clearly communicated policies and procedures
    d. Practical exercises and drills

Mometrix

13. Pay for performance style compensation structures improve performance as a result of a(n) _____ and a(n) _____

    a. Incentive effect; spillover effect
    b. Competitive position; sorting effect
    c. Incentive effect; sorting effect
    d. Competitive position; spillover effect

14. Which of the following conditions must be met to require a medical exam as a post-offer employment opportunity?

    a. The prospective employee must display clear signs of illness or impairment
    b. A company physician must perform all exams
    c. There is a bona fide business necessity to require an exam for the position
    d. All data related to exam results must be safely and securely stored with the prospective employee's personnel file

15. Which of the following recruitment sources has the potential to reach the greatest number of possible candidates?

    a. Company intranet posting
    b. Job fair at local educational institution
    c. Open house hiring event
    d. Social media job posting

16. Which performance appraisal method involves categorizing employees according to the mean (or average) performance and labeling approximately 20% of employees as exceeding expectations, 70% as meeting expectations, and 10% as not meeting expectations?

    a. Relative Percentile Method
    b. Paired Comparisons
    c. Alternation Rank Order
    d. Forced Distribution

17. While labor strikes are generally protected by the National Labor Relations Act (NLRA), there are limitations. Which of the following limitations to labor striking refers to the potential of a strike's impact affecting national health or safety?

    a. Duty to bargain
    b. Secondary strikes
    c. Taft-Hartley injunctions
    d. Healthcare institutions

18. When determining an organization's pay practices for its national headquarters in a US city where the national minimum wage is $7.25, the state minimum wage is $12.50, and the city minimum wage is $15.00, which of the following levels of law supersedes the others?

    a. Municipal
    b. State
    c. Federal
    d. International

Copyright © Mometrix Media. You have been licensed one copy of this document for personal use only. Any other reproduction or redistribution is strictly prohibited. All rights reserved. This content is provided for test preparation purposes only and does not imply an endorsement by Mometrix of any particular political, scientific, or religious point of view.

19. Which of the following exceptions to at-will employment is applicable in all states?

a. Good faith and fair dealing exception
b. Implied contracts
c. Public policy exception
d. Employment contracts

20. When an HR practitioner is informing an organization's employees of their rights as workers, which of the following is required by federal law to be displayed as a detailed poster?

a. Health Insurance Portability and Accountability Act (HIPAA)
b. Genetic Information Nondiscrimination Act (GINA)
c. Equal Pay Act (EPA)
d. Fair Labor Standards Act (FLSA)

21. Which of the following law sources MOST closely impacts how an organization will design and enact its workforce policies and practices?

a. Statutes
b. Agency guidelines
c. Regulations
d. Executive orders

22. When selecting employees for developmental opportunities, which of the following is the LEAST appropriate factor to consider?

a. Amount of time that has passed since the employee was last offered a developmental opportunity
b. Consistently positive performance evaluations
c. Family or personal circumstance that may prevent the employee from benefiting from the opportunity
d. Amount of time employee has been part of the team being considered for the opportunity

23. Which flexible staffing practice would be the MOST appropriate to accommodate difficult-to-predict spikes in staffing needs?

a. Job sharing
b. Temporary employees
c. On-call workers
d. Contract workers

24. When considering different styles of learning, which of the following approaches of training would be MOST effective when teaching employees to use a new piece of equipment?

a. Sending all employees a training video detailing the functions of the equipment and how to operate it
b. Issuing a printed copy of the equipment manual to all departments to read and review as a team
c. Bringing in an equipment technician to demonstrate the equipment functions to each team of employees
d. Issuing employees a how-to guide to read on their own and then following up with hands-on training sessions conducted in teams

25. For how long must an organization retain pre-employment records such as the original job posting, resumes, and interview notes?
   a. 6 months
   b. 12 months
   c. 24 months
   d. 36 months

26. In addition to performing a job analysis, which of the following organizational tools is MOST valuable to utilize when updating job descriptions?
   a. Environmental scans
   b. Employee timesheets
   c. Performance appraisals
   d. Customer feedback

27. When performing a job analysis, which of the following data sources can provide the most strategic view of job tasks and conditions?
   a. Accounts from job incumbents
   b. Accounts from direct supervisor
   c. Observations from HR professionals
   d. Vision description from senior management

28. Which is the MOST effective way to gain employee buy-in when defining and introducing organizational values?
   a. Manager compliance and leadership during the introduction phase
   b. CEO town hall with interactive question and answer segment during the introduction phase
   c. Executive guidance and expertise during the design phase
   d. Employee input during the design phase

29. Which of the following is TRUE about an employee's Weingarten rights during an investigation?
   a. An employee does not have to be part of the union to exercise his or her Weingarten rights
   b. A union representative is permitted to object to intimidation or confusion tactics taken by the employer during an investigatory interview
   c. An employer is required to approach collective bargaining meetings with a genuine intent to reach an agreeable resolution
   d. An employee may elect to have an attorney present in lieu of a union representative during investigatory interviews

30. When having a difficult conversation with an employee regarding company policy, the employee appears highly agitated when stating his or her viewpoint. What is the FIRST communication technique that a Human Resources professional can utilize to improve the potential outcomes of the interaction?
   a. Respond by explaining the benefits of the policy that the employee does not understand
   b. Listen intently without preconceived opinions or responses
   c. Ask open-ended questions to improve his or her understanding of the employee's viewpoint
   d. Tell the employee to calm down if he or she wishes to continue the conversation

31. Which of the following is an advantage of a matrix-style reporting structure?

   a. Increased partnership between functional and product processes
   b. Consistent expectations for employee outcomes
   c. Clear reporting lines and responsibilities
   d. Reduced time spent in meetings

32. When measuring the impact of a new wellness initiative, which of the following metrics could suggest a successful initiative when negatively correlated?

   a. Employee grievance rate
   b. Employee satisfaction ratings
   c. Employee retention
   d. Employee absence rate

33. Which of the following tools found in performance management practices can BEST inform an appraisal or evaluation design that aligns with a team or organization's financial and non-financial objectives?

   a. Competency Clusters
   b. Organizational Vision
   c. Balanced Scorecard
   d. Work Analysis

34. Which of the following workplace practices is the MOST effective at preventing defamation lawsuits against the employer?

   a. Instituting a strict no-referral policy
   b. Closely monitoring all written workplace interactions
   c. Training managers on fact-based communication methods
   d. Avoiding all types of opinions when writing performance reviews

35. A 'no vacation policy' vacation policy can also be referred to as an unlimited vacation time policy and describes a work-life balance practice that does not limit time spent away from work based on a pre-determined bank of vacation days. In addition to high quality communication practices and fully committing to the policy, which of the following is an important building block for a successful 'no vacation policy' vacation policy?

   a. Compensation
   b. Progressive Discipline
   c. Performance Management
   d. Data Analysis

36. Which of the following career development practices is MOST closely aligned with an organization's strategic plan?

   a. International assignments
   b. Succession planning
   c. Employee mentoring
   d. Tuition reimbursement programs

37. When recruiting for an open nursing position, the HR manager receives 64 applications. After reviewing the following application breakdown information, what is the yield ratio of highly qualified candidates?

Application Sources		Application Quality		Application Progression	
Internet Job Board (IJB)	42	Not Qualified	14	Invited to Interview	12
		Qualified	24		
		Highly Qualified	4	Accepted Invitation to Interview	8
Local Nursing College Job Fair (JB)	22	Not Qualified	7		
		Qualified	7	Job Offers Extended	3
		Highly Qualified	8		
Total	64	Total	64	Job Offers Accepted	2

    a. 0.125
    b. 0.188
    c. 0.286
    d. 0.484

38. If an organization's compensation philosophy states that the base pay structure for jobs deemed critical to the organization's overall mission will be set at the 50th percentile of the market and that their total possible performance incentives will be set at the 75th percentile of the market, what does this mean?

    a. A job deemed critical will be compensated a higher rate than 50% of the other positions within the company.
    b. An employee in a critical position can earn 25% more through incentives in addition to their base pay.
    c. The organization's compensation philosophy suggests a market match strategy for jobs deemed critical to the organization's overall mission.
    d. A job deemed critical will likely share similar base pay practices with external jobs of a similar nature.

39. Which of the following conditions may suggest that a contracted worker should be reclassified as an employee?

    a. When the contracted worker changes their working hours to match company employees
    b. When the contracted worker performs similar tasks alongside regular employees
    c. When the contracted worker loses money on a project
    d. When the contracted worker takes on another project with the same company

40. Total rewards statements can communicate a variety of compensation details. Which of the following is LEAST likely to be found on a total rewards statement?

a. Employee stock options
b. Health benefits
c. Social Security deductions
d. Work-life balance policies

41. Creativity in benefits plans can create appeal for both current and prospective employees while also increasing the costs of total compensation. Which of the following practices would be MOST effective at balancing employee appreciation and rising costs?

a. Passing part of the benefits costs onto employees
b. Tying benefit availability to employee tenure
c. Only offering benefits for full-time staff
d. Personalizing benefits options

42. Unemployment insurance programs are intended to support all of the following EXCEPT:

a. Engagement of unemployed workers during short-term layoffs
b. Stabilization of the working environment by employers
c. Income for unemployed workers to maintain quality of life
d. Finding and securing of a new job by unemployed workers

43. If a company is planning to introduce new remote work opportunities for its workforce, which internal business partner would be the LEAST critical to collaborate with when designing the new policy?

a. Line Managers and Employees
b. Information Technology (IT)
c. Legal
d. Marketing and Sales

44. Which of the following is FALSE about the potential effects of a dual career ladder program for career development?

a. A dual career ladder gives high-performing employees the ability to advance without becoming supervisors
b. A dual career ladder may increase the turnover of senior staff who have nowhere left to advance
c. A dual career ladder program is more common in technical fields like medicine, science, and engineering
d. A dual career ladder may foster resentment from other organizational leadership who feel the compensation practice does not fit the responsibilities

45. Which form of data collection would be the MOST effective to collect qualitative and multi-perspective information regarding employee opinions?

a. Online survey
b. One-on-one interview
c. Focus group
d. Workplace observation

46. Which of the following interview questions is an example of a question that could be used in a behavioral interview?

    a. What do you value in a workplace environment?
    b. In the event that you encounter conflict with a coworker, how would you respond?
    c. Can you tell me about a time when you made a mistake in the workplace?
    d. Tell me why you are the best fit for this position?

47. In a company with a competitive culture and a strategy that emphasizes growth and desired outcomes as a result of increased production rates, which of the following appraisal methods would be MOST effective for line workers?

    a. Behavior observation scale
    b. Behaviorally anchored rating scale
    c. Field review
    d. Straight ranking

48. Which of the following career development practices would be MOST appropriate for a supervisor to consider when guiding an employee who has expressed interest in advancing into a leadership position one day?

    a. Job enlargement
    b. Job rotation
    c. Job enrichment
    d. Job transfer

49. Which of the following classifications of workers are NOT covered under the Fair Labor Standards Act (FLSA)?

    a. A part-time store clerk at a large grocery chain
    b. An independent contractor completing a project for a local hospital
    c. A full-time teacher's aide who is paid an hourly wage
    d. A full-time exempt director who oversees a local childcare facility

50. Which of the following retirement plan options incurs the highest financial burden for employers?

    a. Employee pension
    b. Employee stock ownership plan
    c. 401(k)
    d. Profit-sharing plan

51. Which of the following organizational structures most closely aligns with an authoritarian style organizational culture?

    a. Virtual
    b. Modular
    c. Matrix
    d. Vertical

52. Which of the following HR metrics would be the MOST useful for measuring the financial effectiveness of a team's structure and size?

    a. Cost per hire
    b. Revenue per employee
    c. Time to hire
    d. Retention rate

53. When measuring the effectiveness of a training program, which of the following measures best indicates the level of training optimization?

    a. Usage or training participation
    b. Knowledge retention of training material
    c. Return on investment
    d. Measurable change in behaviors based on training material

54. What is one DISADVANTAGE to utilizing a group interview style?

    a. Group interviews take additional time and resources to execute
    b. Group interviews are less effective when assessing multiple candidates
    c. Group interviews are ineffective at determining how well candidates work together
    d. Group interviews can be intimidating for candidates

55. What is the primary benefit to utilizing an enterprise risk management method when working to mitigate risks in the workplace?

    a. It accounts for the potential financial implications of risk occurring or not occurring
    b. It is a strategic approach to assessing the likelihood and impact of potential risks
    c. It eliminates the potential for certain risks to occur
    d. It spans across an organization's functions and locations

56. Unless otherwise stated by the Equal Employment Opportunity Commission (EEOC), an EEO-1 Component 1 report must be filed annually by private employers with over 100 employees. The primary data collected in this report includes all of the following information EXCEPT:

    a. Job category
    b. Sex
    c. Religion
    d. Race

57. Which regularly updated tool can Human Resources utilize to clearly and concisely communicate organizational policies and procedures?

    a. Company Mission Statement
    b. Employee Handbook
    c. Job Descriptions
    d. Organizational Chart

58. Which of the following is FALSE when referencing an employee's rights to participate in concerted activities?

    a. Concerted activities and an employer's rights to activities on their private property must be balanced

    b. Protected concerted activities are only applicable to union members

    c. Employees discussing and sharing wage and compensation information is considered a concerted activity

    d. Employers prohibiting discussion of a pending sexual harassment investigation is considered an unfair labor practice

59. Which of the following learning activities would be most effective to teach one-on-one communication techniques for customer service representatives?

    a. Concept mapping

    b. Case studies

    c. Role-play

    d. Video example

60. Which of the following post-offer activities helps to protect the employer from future negligent hiring claims?

    a. Drug testing

    b. Background check

    c. Medical exam

    d. Aptitude assessment

61. The primary goal of progressive discipline is to:

    a. Punish an employee for poor decisions

    b. Reshape employee behavior to align with business expectations

    c. Remove the employee from the workforce

    d. Set an example for the employee's team of the consequence of poor performance

62. Payouts from workers' compensation insurance assist an employee who is injured or has fallen ill as a result of his or her job in all of the following ways EXCEPT:

    a. Medical expenses

    b. Dependent benefits

    c. Wage replacement payments

    d. Death benefits

63. Prior to downsizing or restructuring, an organization can take steps to curb the potential fallout to employees and to the company. Which of the following workforce actions would be MOST appropriate for a situation in which a company is planning a major restructure?

    a. Furloughs

    b. Hiring freeze

    c. Pay reduction

    d. Early retirement options

64. When transforming an in-person training into a virtual training, which of the following is the biggest strategic difference to consider in the training design?

    a. Learning tools and materials
    b. Facilitator consistency
    c. Content visualization
    d. Student attention span

65. When designing a compensation system or practice, during which step of the design process would a salary and benefits survey be most useful?

    a. Job Analysis
    b. Job Documentation
    c. Job Evaluation
    d. Pay Structure

66. While similar in purpose and function, orientation and onboarding are two distinct processes for new employees. Which of the following is NOT one of the differences between the two processes?

    a. Orientation typically covers administrative processes and introductions whereas onboarding covers more strategic topics and introductions
    b. Orientation typically spans from a few hours to a few days whereas onboarding can last as long as several months to a year or more
    c. Orientation typically covers the specific duties and role of the new employee's position whereas onboarding can provide a wider view of the organization's culture
    d. Orientation typically is a formal process where onboarding is a strictly informal process

67. During a workforce reduction, expansion, or restructure, which of the following is the MOST critical responsibility for the HR team?

    a. Completing any associated hiring or layoff paperwork
    b. Honest and timely communication with the workforce
    c. Designing the new workforce hierarchy
    d. Salary negotiations with incoming employees

68. Which of the following workplace incidents would NOT require an organization to record the details on the OSHA Form 300?

    a. A remote worker falling down the stairs in his or her home while on the clock and breaking a limb
    b. A change in hearing test results for a worker in one or both ears
    c. An employee calling in sick from work due to exposure to chemicals while on the job
    d. A temporary change in job duties as a result of an injury experienced in the workplace

69. An "Employee Records Confidentiality Policy" may include all of the following EXCEPT:

    a. Standard procedures for protecting employee data
    b. A guarantee that employee data will not be compromised
    c. Contact information or reporting procedures that employees can utilize if they have questions or concerns regarding their personal data
    d. The type of information collected by the organization

70. The Consolidated Omnibus Budget Reconciliation Act (COBRA) set what benefits standards for employers?

    a. Employer rules when providing a pension
    b. Required leave rules for companies with 50 or more employees
    c. Continuing health care coverage for employees who are laid off or resign from their positions
    d. Prohibition of discrimination on the basis of a protected class in the administration of benefits

71. Which of the following is TRUE of an employer's responsibilities when regarding employees and substance abuse?

    a. Alcoholism can be considered a disability and may require reasonable accommodations
    b. Employers are not permitted to randomly test employees for drugs
    c. While employers do not need to tolerate poor or unsafe performance, illicit drug use is protected under the ADA
    d. It is best practice to only test candidates suspected of drug use during pre-employment drug screening

72. Which of the following pay structure designs can be MOST helpful for an organization that is transitioning from a vertical organizational hierarchy to a more horizontal organizational design?

    a. Broadband salary structure
    b. Market-based salary structure
    c. Pay grade salary structure
    d. Outcome-based salary structure

73. When designing the onboarding experience for a new employee, which training tool would be MOST impactful for a new professional entering their desired field?

    a. Mentor system
    b. Role-specific training
    c. Teambuilding event
    d. Job rotation

74. When determining the match accuracy of data from an external compensation survey, which characteristic best indicates the data's comparability to existing internal pay practices?

    a. Job Coverage (Job Comparability)
    b. Geographical Origin
    c. Effective Data Age
    d. Labor Market Coverage

75. Which US federal regulation sets the legal standards and expectations for child labor standards, minimum wage, overtime pay, and recordkeeping?

    a. Sarbanes-Oxley Act
    b. Fair Labor Standards Act
    c. Lilly Ledbetter Fair Pay Act
    d. The Patient Protection and Affordable Care Act

76. Which of the following employee relations programs would be most effective at connecting employees across the company who share a diversity dimension (such as race, ethnicity, religion, etc.)?

a. Employee assistance program
b. Diversity council
c. Company wellness program
d. Employee resource group

77. What holistic business statement reflects the desired future state of the organization?

a. Mission Statement
b. Vision Statement
c. Organizational Values
d. Business Goals and Objectives

78. Which of the following communication media would be most effective for a Human Resources Representative to assist a supervisor struggling to get along with a new employee on their team?

a. Peer review
b. Mediation
c. Arbitration
d. Grievance hearing

79. An employee has been working with a company for four months. In that time, he or she has reported five to ten minutes late to work on five separate occasions. The employee's manager did not address the specific instances of tardiness with this employee but has included the organization's late policy in monthly team-wide emails. When the employee shows up late for a sixth time, what is the most appropriate step along the progressive discipline process for the manager to take with this employee?

a. Verbal Counseling
b. Formal Warning
c. Final Warning
d. Termination

80. Which of the following is FALSE as it pertains to retaliation in the workplace?

a. Retaliation does not need to affect the terms and conditions of the job
b. Retaliation charges must be connected to a corresponding discrimination charge
c. Retaliation is the leading charge filed with the Equal Employment Opportunity Commission (EEOC)
d. Treatment does not need to be discriminatory in nature to be considered retaliation

81. Which of the following is the MOST appropriate goal to set as a result of diversity and inclusion training in the workplace?

a. To demonstrate to shareholders the organization's commitment to an inclusive workplace
b. To eliminate discrimination and harassment in the workplace
c. To change what employees believe about other ways of life
d. To increase employee awareness of diversity issues and improve collaboration skills

82. An employer has scheduled and arranged a special training opportunity for the sales team members as a reward for increased revenue in the previous quarter. One member of the team is unable to attend the training as scheduled due to a physical handicap that prevents him or her from entering the facility. Which of the following responses would be the MOST appropriate for the employer seeking to provide reasonable accommodations for the employee?

    a. Securing an alternate location for the training with handicap accessibility.
    b. Providing the employee with a self-guided virtual training option that teaches the same material.
    c. Sending the employee to a different training that takes place in an accessible facility.
    d. Building the required accessibility features at the training facility.

83. Which of the following internal recruiting sources would be the MOST appropriate when gauging the interest in a future position opening?

    a. Job bidding
    b. Employee referral
    c. Social media
    d. Succession planning

84. According to the Worker Adjustment and Retraining Notification (WARN) Act, how many days in advance must an organization with 100 or more employees notify the affected individuals prior to a mass reduction in force?

    a. 14
    b. 45
    c. 60
    d. 90

85. When designing the benefits package, which of the following benefits is the MOST likely to improve employee turnover rate?

    a. Paid time off
    b. Pension plan
    c. Tuition reimbursement
    d. Profit-sharing

86. A large corporation with a wide array of services and products is seeking to define its strategic position by 'changing the way customers experience' those services and products. Which of Michael Porter's competitive business strategies does this approach reference?

    a. Low-Cost Leadership
    b. Differentiation
    c. Focused Cost Leadership
    d. Focused Differentiation

87. Which of the following is NOT a benefit of outsourcing staffing needs?

    a. Increased access to certain skills or expertise
    b. Improvement in data security
    c. Reduction in staffing costs
    d. Increased free time to focus on core business functions

88. Which of the following is NOT an advantage when an organization shifts from the traditional annual process of performance appraisals to a more frequent and ongoing schedule of performance reviews?

    a. Increased individual and organizational agility
    b. Time and money savings
    c. Development of a feedback culture
    d. Enhanced employee engagement

89. There are a variety of practices for flexible working arrangements within work-life balance practices. Which of the following refers to an employee's ability to determine his or her start and end times for each workday?

    a. Telecommuting
    b. Variable workweek
    c. Job sharing
    d. Flexible work hours

90. While recruiting for a manager position, the HR team states that it is looking for "highly qualified candidates who are available on weekends and who will bring new energy and a fresh face to the team." Which of the following laws is the most likely to be cited if a candidate feels these search criteria are discriminatory?

    a. Americans with Disabilities Act
    b. Age Discrimination in Employment Act
    c. Civil Rights Act of 1964
    d. Immigration Reform and Control Act

Answer Key and Explanations for Test #1

1. A: The Drug-Free Workplace Act requires federal contractors with contracts valued at or in excess of $100,000 and any federal grant recipient to establish policies that prohibit unlawful use, possession, or distribution of controlled substances in the workplace. The Drug-Free Workplace Act also sets standards for drug-free awareness programs, notification standards for employees to inform employers of a breach in policy, and consequences for policy breach.

2. A: Referral programs can run in the background of day-to-day operations for low to no cost and yield high-quality candidates. Internships and alumni networks can be cost-efficient when recruiting new and experienced candidates but require time and resources to design and maintain. Online job boards can reach a broad audience but can be expensive to post and maintain and do not always yield high-quality or relevant candidates.

3. B: Multifactor authentication can utilize biometric scanning, passwords, or other means of access verification but rely on any combination of two or more means in total. A virtual private network (VPN) can be used in addition to heightened login protections to redirect Internet traffic through more secure channels. A random password generator may help to create stronger passwords for users but that still requires remembering or recording the passwords somewhere. Biometric technology such as face scans, fingerprint scans, or voice recognition eliminates the use of passwords for logging into systems or accessing organizational data or property.

4. B: SWOT analyses and growth-share matrix analyses can be utilized as part of systems thinking, but are specific tools used to scan the external environment for conditions that may affect internal processes and outcomes. Strategic thinking aligns decisions and actions with the organization's overall strategy and goals but does not always span a variety of departments or teams. Systems thinking involves focusing on how various business functions interact with and influence each other.

5. B: A mechanistic organizational culture is defined by its formal policies, rules, and procedures. This strict definition of communications and operations fosters consistency and stability, but can serve as an obstacle to innovation. While authoritarian organizational cultures may also lead to slower innovation rates, this potential trait is dependent on the organization's leaders and industry.

6. A: External HR service providers are useful for reducing the administrative workload of an HR team and increasing the time and attention available for the strategic responsibilities of HR. Workers compensation and payroll processing are each administrative in nature and furthest in function from strategic HR functions. Workforce recruiting can be either administrative or strategic in nature, depending on the roles being recruited and goals of the team recruiting. Workforce planning is a purely strategic HR task that focuses on the style, skills, structure, and business alignment of an organization's workforce.

7. C: Line managers are directly in charge of front-line staff teams and will have the most up-to-date information regarding the number of roles to fill for each team that they supervise; line managers may also report to senior managers in regards to their staffing needs and operations. Line managers may also work closely with the current reception desk attendants so they can collect data regarding current attendant opinions and attitudes. Executive leadership can advise to the general philosophy of staffing and workforce structure but are typically too far removed from front line workers to advise regarding the specific number of positions to fill. Finance and administration staff can advise regarding recommended salary rates and staff team budgets but will not always be able to adjust that data to the real-time needs of the team in question.

8. C: While each option represents a benefits broker function or area of expertise, an organization that has or is currently expanding geographically will need to take extra care when ensuring insurance compliance. Laws and requirements for insurance can vary from federal to state to local levels and selecting a benefits broker with a proven track record of providing services across a wide range of regions will be important to support new and continued company growth.

9. C: Employee self-service technologies focus on the needs of the employee such as benefits management or time-off requests. Software as a service refers to the service being delivered remotely instead of as product installed onto a device or computer. Best of breed systems and enterprise resource planning systems refer to varying degrees of system integration across organizational functions. An enterprise resource planning system connects different functions across the organization but may sacrifice functionality for that integration. Best of breed systems offer a higher level of specification to the needs of each business function but may sacrifice each function's ability to communicate with the other.

10. B: Disparate treatment and disparate impact are both types of discrimination. Where disparate treatment is outright discrimination based on a protected class like sex, religion, or color, disparate impact is when a job condition or requirement is not discriminatory in text but can have discriminatory outcomes. An entry level position at a department store does not likely require college level education to be completed, but can be an obstacle to employment for members of a protected class who may not have the same access to education as other applicants.

11. A: Video surveillance can be an effective mitigation method but can also cause discomfort or legal challenges in the workplace. Team meetings that review theft policies can help to mitigate theft but does not necessarily provide employees with the means to hold one another accountable. Encouraging employees to confront theft in the workplace may be appropriate in some situations but can also potentially lead to unhealthy conflict or violence in the workplace. Strong whistleblower policies and practices can give employees the means to anonymously report unethical behavior in the workplace while maintaining their personal safety.

12. D: Signage and policy communication are essential parts of establishing and teaching the desired response to an emergency. However, employees learn best by doing and by practicing the various responses. Practical drills and exercises give employees the visual experience and muscle memory to respond more quickly in the event of an emergency. After-action debriefs are a critical piece to assessing an organization's response to an emergency but take place after the emergency has already occurred.

13. C: Pay for performance has been shown to improve performance by motivating current employees to improve their overall output or results (incentive effect). Additionally, this compensation plan can lead employees to self-select out of the organization who are not able to or do not desire to improve their performance (sorting effect). Competitive position refers to how an employer's compensation plan compares within the market and the spillover effect occurs when union benefits or working demands spill over into nonunion environments in an attempt to discourage unionization.

14. C: Post-offer medical exams can only be required as a result of the physical demands of a job's essential functions. The exam must be performed by a third-party medical provider, the exam results may not be used to discriminate against a candidate due to a disability, and the exam data must be kept separate from the employee's personnel file.

15. D: The Internet can be a powerful tool for reaching a wide audience that is geographically and demographically diverse. Utilizing the company intranet would be more appropriate if the position to be filled was best done by an internal candidate. In-person job fairs and open houses can limit potential candidates based on availability and awareness of the event, but may produce candidates who are a good fit depending on the details and design of the hiring event.

16. D: A forced distribution system of performance appraisals utilizes a bell curve with forced performance labels to identify top performers, middle of the road performers, and performers who must improve. Relative percentile methods of performance appraisal also use the 50th percentile as the midpoint when comparing employee performance but can vary based on the competency measured and determine a specific percentile placement for each employee. Paired comparisons and alternation rank order are systems that compare individual employee performance to the performance of others: paired comparisons pit one employee's performance against each individual performance of other employees and alternation rank order determines the top performer, then the bottom performer, followed by the second top performer and the second bottom performer, and so on and so forth.

17. C: Both employers and union members must give effort during collective bargaining, a principle known as the duty to bargain. Secondary strikes occur when employees from a related industry who are not involved in the labor dispute participate in a strike. Healthcare institutions require specific notification and consideration time frames before striking to determine the potential damage that may occur locally if healthcare is affected. A Taft-Hartley injunction occurs when the size and/or scope of a strike poses a threat to national health or safety.

18. A: When determining compensation practices, an employer is required to comply with all applicable laws. According to the pay rates described in the question, the employer must pay the highest required rate across the three, which is the municipal law of $15.00 per hour.

19. D: Written and mutually agreed upon employment contracts can set an agreed-upon time for the employment relationship to last or can set the standards that termination can only occur for cause or under predetermined circumstances. Public policy exceptions, implied contract exceptions, and good faith and fair dealing exceptions are considered or not considered according to various state laws and precedents.

20. D: The posters required for organization can vary by state, organization size, and other factors. Under federal regulation, a Fair Labor Standards Act poster is required to be posted in a conspicuous area for employees to review details. Other posters that may be required depending on the organization include the Occupational Safety and Health Act, Family and Medical Leave Act, Migrant and Seasonal Agricultural Worker Protection Act, and more.

21. B: While all organizations should ensure compliance regardless of the law source, guidelines are the specific interpretation of statutes and regulations as they pertain to an organization's day-to-day operations. Guidelines explain regulations and statutes and can provide additional material directly related to how the law will be enforced.

22. C: When selecting employees for training or development opportunities, it is essential to do so in a fair and consistent manner in order to avoid possible discrimination or unfair treatment. Time between training opportunities, performance appraisals, and seniority are all work-related qualifications for selecting an employee for training. Selecting or not selecting an employee for training based on what is perceived to be happening outside of the work environment may involve judgment based on a protected class and can lead to a discrimination charge. For example: if a manager knows that one of his subordinates is a mother with small children at home, he may favor her male counterpart for a development opportunity because he assumes the mother will not be able to travel due to her childcare responsibilities. While the manager may see this as being considerate for the mother's home life, it deprives her of the opportunity for development and advancement.

23. C: Job sharing and temporary employees are appropriate alternative staffing practices for predictable and stable work needs. Contract workers should only be utilized for specialized jobs and projects and are not appropriate to fill in for positions typically manned by part- or full-time employees. On-call workers are the most appropriate for difficult-to-predict spikes in staffing needs as they can be brought in at the last minute and are able to step in for regular employee positions.

24. D: Each of the options caters to different styles of learning; however, the most effective approach to teaching combines a variety of learning styles regardless of what the student perceives their individual learning style to be. By combining independent learning with team learning and reading materials with hands-on training, the trainer exposes the students to the new material in a variety of mediums and learning environments.

25. B: Per guidance set forth in the Civil Rights Act of 1964 (Title VII), the Americans with Disabilities Act (ADA), and the Age Discrimination in Employment Act (ADEA), employers must retain pre-employment documentation for one year in order to demonstrate fair and non-discriminatory hiring practices.

26. C: An employee's performance appraisal can reveal a wide variety of data points such as what work the employee performed, how this work contributed to the team or organization at large, and supervisor comments on the role played by the employee, as well as comments on the work challenges and successes by the employee themselves. This data can suggest which jobs and which job tasks most closely align with desired organizational outcomes. Environmental scans and customer feedback can provide valuable data but the data is limited to external conditions and views. Employee timesheets can be a valuable tool to assess working conditions but lack the qualitative data required for substantive job description information.

27. D: Direct accounts of the job functions from incumbents and supervisors of the position in question are the most accurate data sources for the current day-to-day tasks, environment, and expectations of the job. HR observations of the job in question can provide a more objective account of the job functions as well as context as to where the job does or should fit within the workforce as a whole. The senior management vision gives a strategic context to work being performed as it relates to the goals and direction of the organization as a whole.

28. D: The most effective way to elicit employee buy-in to new policies, procedures, practices, and other company messages is to utilize interactive (and genuine) workshops, focus groups, and other feedback mechanisms between organizational leadership and the organization's front line. High quality communication in the form of supervisor role models and town halls can be effective but may take longer for the intended employee buy-in effect. Executive expertise is an important part of crafting organizational values that align with the organization's strategy, but without employee feedback, it may be challenging for employees to develop a sense of ownership over the organizational values.

29. B: An employee's Weingarten rights refers to a union employee's right to request a union representative be present during an investigatory interview. While a union representative present for an investigatory interview is not permitted to cause severe disruption to the investigation process, he or she may protect employees by clarifying questions or objecting to intimidation attempts by the employer. An employer is not required to bargain with the union representative during the investigation process.

30. B: The first step to effective communication is listening to the other party in a genuine and non-judgmental manner. Asking open-ended questions can be a highly valuable tool to better understand the other party, but questions should be informed by the data collected while listening (as well as any data gathered or confirmed when using reflection techniques as well.) Pre-planning a response to the employee regarding the policy benefits does not acknowledge the message that the employee is trying to communicate and can create additional frustration if used too soon (or inappropriately) during the conversation. While taking a break can be a viable tool during heated conversations, giving the employee an ultimatum early in the conflict sends the message that what the employee has to say is not important; this can do more damage than good.

31. A: Matrix-style reporting structures set employees at a cross between a functional and a product-based supervisor. However, reporting to two different supervisors with varying perspectives can create reporting inconsistencies and unclear communications, and lead to increased time spent in meetings to create cohesive plans and expectations.

32. D: A negative correlation between data points means that as one data set increases, the corresponding data set decreases (it is also important to note that a correlation suggests a link between the two data sets and not necessarily a causal relationship). As the roll out and use of a wellness initiative increases, a decrease in the employee absence rate may suggest increased health outcomes for current employees, improved engagement outcomes from current employees, or a shift in the health demographics of newly hired employees. A decreased rate of grievances may be indicative of a positive shift in the working environment but it is not as strongly linked to a wellness initiative as the absence rate. Decreased employee satisfaction ratings and retention rate are each indicative of negative outcomes that may or may not be linked to the wellness initiative.

33. C: Each of the tools listed can be helpful in their own way to inform the design of a performance appraisal but a balanced scorecard is unique in its holistic approach to measuring organizational performance. The balanced scorecard, informed by an organization's strategy and vision, breaks performance down into four main categories: customers, learning and growth, financial, and internal business processes. These categories each list the metrics and indicators of success associated with the big picture of organizational operations. Employee performance evaluations that are derived from their organization's or team's balanced scorecard are subsequently aligned with the organization's financial and non-financial objectives.

34. C: Mitigating defamation risks can be a challenging task that is best met with adequate training, practice, honesty, and discretion. A no-referral policy may backfire and result in negligent referral lawsuits and discontent among the workforce. Closely monitoring written workplace interactions can help to discover libel-related risks but can also negatively impact workplace culture and camaraderie. While opinions on performance reviews and in referrals can present tricky legal waters, in general this is protected speech if the opinions are fact-based and business-focused.

35. C: Successful unlimited vacation policies are built on high quality communication regarding behavior expectations, individual work outcome expectations, and team outcome expectations. A high-quality Performance Management approach clearly defines what 'high performance' looks like and gives individuals and teams the leverage needed to focus more on actual business outcomes instead of the number of hours spent in the office.

36. B: International assignments may be an important aspect of the strategic plan if global expansion is deemed of high strategic importance, but international assignments can also be factored within succession planning if that is the case. Employee mentoring and tuition reimbursement programs can help to improve the quality of individual employees (and consequently their organizational outcomes), but that is a small piece of the strategic plan. Succession planning identifies and develops employees whose work specialties and leadership potential align with the organization's strategic vision for the future.

37. B: In order to calculate the yield ratio of highly qualified candidates, one must add the total number of highly qualified candidates (12) and divide it by the total number of candidates (64) and multiply by 100. This indicates an 18.8% yield of highly qualified candidates.

38. D: By setting the base pay at the 50th percentile of the market, the organization is stating that, of the similar jobs within the labor market, approximately 50% of the jobs will have base pay rates below the determined rate and 50% of the jobs will have base rates above the determined rate. Despite being set at the 50th percentile of the market, the compensation philosophy suggests a lead pay-level strategy (as opposed to a lagging or matching strategy) strategy due to the total incentive pay being set at the 75th percentile of the market.

39. B: Independent contractors are free to set their own work hours, purchase their own work tools, and take on whichever projects they are offered—regardless of whether they will make money or not. One key difference between contractors and regular employees is the type of work being completed. Regular employees typically perform work that is a function of the organization's mission and is closely tied to the organization's day-to-day operations. Contractors, on the other hand, specialize in project-type work as opposed to core operations and maintain their own autonomy as workers.

40. C: A total rewards statement is a tool that organizations can use to communicate the rewards available to employees. Total rewards statements can communicate direct compensation practices like base pay as well as indirect compensation like dental plans and material perks. Social Security deductions, while related to compensation practices, are not perks offered by the employer but required federal taxes and would not be highlighted in a total rewards statement.

41. D: While each of the options may have various levels of effectiveness at balancing the cost-reward balance of benefits, personalizing the benefits options to the needs of employees is the most effective. The personalization process can be accomplished by catering offerings based on the workforce demographics, gathering data through employee surveys, or offering cafeteria-style benefits plans. Reducing the availability of the benefits by passing on costs, tying availability to tenure, or restricting which employees are eligible can positively affect the cost-reward balance, but can also lead to tension from employees who may feel they are missing out or that there is inequity in benefits administration.

42. C: Unemployment insurance is intended to assist employees who are involuntarily unemployed as they transition to a new job and to encourage employers to create a more stable work environment. Unemployment insurance is paid out at a fraction of what the worker's salary was with their previous employer and is only intended to assist the transition, not to support the unemployed worker for an extended period of time.

43. D: While Marketing and Sales may contribute to building and advertising the employer brand in some scenarios, the other options have direct contact with a remote working policy. Line managers and employees will be utilizing and supervising the policy and can lend knowledge to the practical needs and considerations of teleworking. The IT department will be a critical collaborator in the necessary hardware and possible software needed for teleworking. The Legal department will be an essential partner to advise regarding any best practices to avoid disparate treatment in selecting which employees may telework; additionally, the Legal team will be essential to partner with when tackling unforeseen outcomes of a telework policy such as employees moving out of the local area.

44. B: Dual career ladders provide alternate journeys of advancement for high-performing employees who do not have an interest in or would not perform well at supervising others. Dual career ladders are designed to give senior staff somewhere to advance internally so they are not forced to leave the company in search of better opportunities.

45. C: While all of the options are capable of collecting qualitative data, a focus group data collection method elicits not just the viewpoint from one observer or interviewee but back-and-forth dialogue between interviewer and interviewees regarding the topic at hand. Interviewees can react to and build on the opinions and observations of each other to paint a more dynamic and integrative picture of the data being collected.

46. C: Behavioral interview questions focus in on past behavior and experiences that the applicant has had that may demonstrate a good fit for the open position. The other questions may be more appropriately used for attempting to gauge the applicant's work values, approach to work relationships, and self-confidence.

47. D: Field reviews and behavior observation scales can provide valuable qualitative data regarding the work an employee is doing, but do not cover the quantitative data from production over time. A behaviorally anchored rating scale asks the supervisor or manager to rate the frequency or volume of different employee behaviors on the job. This rating scale can be useful for providing quantitative data, but the data is subjective to the opinions and experiences of the rater. Each of these appraisal methods is an absolute system, with the exception of straight ranking. By using a comparative system, the competitive culture is enforced and production volume can be used as a simple metric to anchor the ranking scale.

48. C: Job enlargement entrusts employees with a larger quantity of work but does not necessarily require leadership or additional critical thinking skills. Job rotations and job transfers can be useful to give employees a wider perspective of the organization from a different role or location but do not necessarily develop leadership skills. Job enrichment gives employees additional decision-making responsibilities and leadership experiences that can be valuable for employees hoping to climb the organizational ladder.

49. B: With few exceptions, the FLSA covers workers in both the public and private sector in organizations that report at least $500,000 in sales annually or who do business across more than one state. Employers are not responsible under the FLSA for independent contractors who are utilized for project-based work, provide their own tools, training, and expertise, and who set their own work hours and standards.

50. A: A pension program is a type of defined benefit plan in which the employer is responsible for a predetermined payout amount or rate once the employee retires. Stock ownership plans, 401(k)s, and profit-sharing plans are all types of defined contribution plans in which the employer is responsible for a predetermined contribution rate during the time that the employee is working. In a defined contribution plan, the employer and employee contribute at different rates and in different ways, depending on the program, but it is the employee's burden to make the financial decisions that will lead to their desired retirement date and lifestyle.

51. D: Virtual and modular style reporting structures lack a formal chain of command and do not resemble typical reporting hierarchies; also referred to as a boundary-less structure, these styles are utilized to increase speed, collaboration, and flexibility among work teams. Matrix style reporting structures create a cross-function reporting structure where an employee works for both a functional and a divisional supervisor. Traditional vertical reporting structures most closely align with an authoritarian organizational culture as both value power and decision-making coming from the few leaders at the top of the structure.

52. B: Cost per hire and time to hire measure the efficiency and effectiveness of hiring processes but not necessarily the efficiency or effectiveness of the jobs themselves. Measuring retention rate can be suggestive of effective management policies and workplace environments; however, a team's retention rate does not necessarily indicate whether there is the correct number of jobs and/or types of jobs on a given team. Revenue per employee can be a leading indicator as to what number of employees per team is the optimal level to maximize financial returns.

53. C: Each of the options are metrics that can suggest a certain level or scope of success in training outcomes. However, return on investment best demonstrates a training optimization as it translates participation, learning, and behaviors into tangible business outcomes. Measuring return on investment empowers an organization to efficiently plan and fund the most effective training methods and programs for positive organizational outcomes.

54. D: Group interviews with multiple interviewers can help to combine the time and resources of hiring managers and organizational leaders, especially when assessing multiple candidates for a position that interacts with a variety of organizational functions. Group interviews can also involve multiple candidates to demonstrate in real time how candidates work with one another. Situations with multiple interviewers or candidates interacting with one another can be a stressful and intimidating experience if a welcoming tone is not set.

55. B: Weighing possible costs of mitigation against costs of the risk itself is an element of cost-benefit analysis. Enterprise risk management may eliminate or reduce the likelihood of certain risks and may also be executed in a way that accounts for a variety of organizational functions and locations; however, these outcomes are a product of the strategic approach to assessing a variety of risk characteristics such as the probability of risk, speed of risk onset, and the potential severity of risk if it were to occur.

56. C: The EEO-1 Component 1 report collects data for the EEOC and the Office of Federal Contract Compliance Programs (OFCCP) to utilize when determining hiring and employment patterns for women and minorities.

57. B: While mission statements can be updated over time to reflect the direction and strategy of an organization, this is not an annual process and the mission statement content does not cover policies and procedures. Job descriptions detail the duties, skills, and knowledge required of different positions but are not an inclusive picture of organizational policies and procedures. Organizational charts demonstrate the chain of command and team structure within the organization but not necessarily how the teams or reporting relationships operate with one another.

58. B: Concerted activities are considered actions taken or communications participated in by employees in regards to working conditions or seeking to improve working conditions. Protected concerted activities are applicable to both union and nonunion employees. Limitations to a protected concerted activity can arise when it interferes with an employer's right to conduct business on his or her personal property; therefore, employers and employees alike must stay aware of what is and what is not considered a protected activity. Employers are not permitted to issue blanket bans on or policies intended to prevent employees from discussing pending sexual harassment investigations.

59. C: Role-playing is the most effective example, as it gives students the chance to practice their skills with other live humans. In role-playing scenarios, the instructor can posit a variety of situations so that the students can go back and forth to practice their skills under different conditions and stressors. A video example or case study may be more useful when taught prior to the role-play as it can introduce the new skills or extreme scenarios not appropriate to act out in the classroom (such as if a customer were to become violent). Concept mapping is more useful in complex learning environments that require understanding of multiple factors and overlapping scenarios.

60. B: Negligent hiring refers to an employer failing to do his or her due diligence to protect employees, customers, and the community from new hires who may cause harm or damage to those around them. Background checks can reveal potential threats to the workforce and should be conducted within federal, local, and state regulations.

61. B: Progressive discipline should be conducted privately and with the intent to give the employee an opportunity to improve and succeed. Progressive discipline conducted with the intent to remove or punish an employee hurts both the employee and the organization as a whole.

62. B: Workers' compensation claims can be paid out in medical benefits, wage replacement payments, death benefits, and/or rehabilitation benefits for an injury or illness sustained at work. Benefits for dependents are part of Social Security payouts and can cover benefits for the dependents of disabled or retired workers.

63. D: Furloughs and pay reductions would be more appropriate in situations where there is financial strain that requires a downsize in staffing levels and not necessarily a restructure. A hiring freeze may be appropriate in some situations where the restructure calls for reduced numbers of positions at certain jobs but can also lead to frustration or confusion by the current workforce if that freeze negatively impacts the workflow or work outputs. Early retirement options can give experienced, long-standing staff the option to choose whether or not they want to stay on through major change. Early retirement options can create a situation where there is natural downsizing prior to the restructure and may result in a smoother transition if the staff left behind are more open to change.

64. D: The importance of the learning tools and materials and content visualization is going to vary based on the training content; additionally, adapting the tools and visuals can be considered part of the structure of the training and less so the strategic impact of the training. It is essential that facilitators are able to reach and interact with students over learning platforms, but depending on the content and facilitator, this difference may not always require consideration for consistency. When moving from an in-person training to a virtual training, student attention span (and the lack thereof in a virtual environment) is the greatest strategic threat to a poor training design. Students in a virtual learning environment can struggle with the unchanging environment, lack of peer interaction, and accessibility of other work materials that can divide their attention. Virtual learning opportunities can overcome this by breaking up the learning material into digestible bites, introducing asynchronous learning opportunities they can engage in on their own time, and utilizing other presentation methods that break up the monotony of web conferencing as a training method.

65. C: The Job Evaluation step of compensation design assesses a position's relative value within an organization and/or within the job market. An internal or external compensation and benefits survey can provide a Human Resources professional with the data required to compare the relative value of multiple positions.

66. D: Orientation is typically one piece of the onboarding process. New employee orientation takes place over a few hours or a few days and covers the most immediate details of what the new employee can and should expect: position duties, direct contacts, tools and systems to be used, etc. Onboarding is a more strategic process that takes place over a longer period of time and depending on the organization can be either a formal or an informal process. Informal onboarding processes consist of the employee figuring out the company culture and his or her place by him/herself, whereas formal onboarding processes can include structured training and events that cover the organizational culture, policies, relationships, and expectations.

67. B: Change, especially organization-wide change, can be frightening for employees who are unsure for their futures. In order to successfully navigate that change, HR and organizational leaders must build trust and understanding with the workforce through honest and timely communication practices—even when the message may be bad news. Strong communication practices build strong relationships with employees who remain with the organization, demonstrate strong organizational culture for any incoming employees, and can ease the process of leaving for outgoing employees.

68. A: The OSHA Form 300 details specific information from all work-related injuries and illnesses throughout a year. Hearing loss during employment is a required condition for documentation on the form. Additionally, any illness or injury deemed work-related in a work-related establishment requires documentation. For an employee working from home, the worker's establishment is considered the office to which they report and therefore injuries sustained in the home do not need to be documented on the OSHA Form 300.

69. B: With the evolution of technology and the subsequent transformation of cybercrimes, employers are not able to 100% guarantee the absolute safety of employee records. In order to demonstrate the employer's dedication to data protection, their confidentiality policy should outline what data gets shared when and with whom, what type of data is collected and how it is stored, as well as to whom employees should reach out if they have questions or suspect a breach of data.

70. C: Employer rules when providing a pension were set by the Employee Retirement Income Security Act (ERISA). Standards for leave for companies with 50 or more employees were set by the Family Medical Leave Act. Prohibition of discrimination in benefits administration is addressed in a variety of legislation pieces such as the Civil Rights Act, the Pregnancy Disability Act, or the Age Discrimination in Employment Act.

71. A: Addiction such as alcoholism can be considered a disability and, therefore, may require the employer to provide reasonable accommodations for the employee. However, the ADA does not protect employees under federal law who are using illegal drugs. Employers may establish random testing procedures for current employees so long as the procedures comply with federal and state laws. When requiring drug tests as part of a pre-employment screening, it is best practice to require all candidates of a certain job to get tested and not just some.

72. A: Market- and outcome-based salary structures can be appropriate for some industries and organizations but do not necessarily aid the transition to a flatter organizational design. A broadband salary structure takes the traditional pay grade structure typically found in a vertical organizational hierarchy and combines various grades to create differ pay bands. This combination of pay rates and options gives employees more opportunity for growth where there is no longer a figurative ladder to climb within the organization. Broadband structures can also encourage employees to move laterally and potentially increase the skills, retention rate, and flexibility of a workforce.

73. A: It is important to cater the onboarding experience to the individual joining the company in order to improve engagement and retention. An assigned mentor from a leadership role can be highly impactful for a new professional with aspirations of growing within the industry and company. Role-specific training and teambuilding events can be effective tools for teaching the day-to-day operations and introducing the new employee to team members, but they do not hone in on the employee's background. Job rotation can be a unique onboarding tool for new managers overseeing a new team but is less effective with entry-level individuals or positions.

74. A: While each answer can indicate possible comparability between internal and external positions, comparing positions with similar leadership responsibilities, daily duties, and long-term goals will yield the most specific comparison. Data compared by geographical origin, effective data age, and labor market coverage can be leveled to create a more accurate comparison.

75. B: The Sarbanes-Oxley Act of 2002 limits the potential stock profits of executives based on ethical conduct and reporting standards. The Lilly Ledbetter Fair Pay Act of 2009 was passed in response to Ledbetter v. Goodyear Tire Supreme Court ruling that employees who wish to sue for pay discrimination must do so within 180 days of the initial pay decision (the 180-day limit to file suit restarts with each discriminatory act, consequence, or paycheck). The Patient Protection and Affordable Care Act sets standards for employers and individual to maintain essential health insurance coverage and other health care, coverage, and availability-related standards.

76. D: An employee resource group (ERG) is a type of networking group in which employees can choose to participate that links employees who share a particular dimension of diversity. Employee resource groups can contribute to a variety of organizational functions such as employee development, recruiting, diversity training, and product or services advisement. A diversity council is a formal group that is led by a high-ranking executive and is responsible for aligning goals, operations, and processes with diversity and inclusion goals and needs. Employee assistance programs and company wellness programs can contribute to employee engagement and support, but do not include a social element for diversity-linked connections.

77. B: An organization's mission statement describes the organizational strategy in terms of its primary actions, processes, and stakeholders. Business Goals and Objectives are typically limited to measurable, financial outcomes. An organization's Vision Statement describes the desired future state of the organization as a realization of the organization's strategy. The vision statement may include the organization's future impact on its community, future desired financial or operational states, or future achievements for internal and external stakeholders as a whole.

78. B: For a low-level conflict between a newly introduced supervisor and employee, the legal process of arbitration and the formal process of a grievance hearing would be inappropriate. While involving peers in a type of peer review may be appropriate in the future if it is discovered that the conflict is systemic across the team, it would not be appropriate in in the initial stages of conflict resolution. Acting as the mediator, the Human Resources representative can help to guide conversation between the manager and employee. Mediation empowers the conflicting parties to communicate more effectively, discover the root of disagreements, and create the solutions that best fit each party without having solutions imposed on them by a third party.

79. A: Consistency is a key element in effective progressive discipline (especially across a team). Because the employee had not been previously counseled for a relatively mild transgression, it is essential to acknowledge the undesired behavior prior to formal counseling or warnings. Ideally, the verbal counseling step can serve as an opportunity to problem solve and improve overall communication.

80. B: Retaliation does not need to be filed with a corresponding discrimination charge and can be filed individually. Because retaliation does not need to affect the terms and conditions of the job and does not need to be discriminatory in nature, it can be easier to prove. Any negative change in the treatment of an employee from how they were treated prior to filing a discrimination charge can be considered retaliation and can lead to a retaliation charge.

81. D: In a perfect world, diversity and inclusion trainings would eliminate discrimination and create understanding empathetic workplaces; unfortunately, deeply held beliefs and ingrained behaviors are unlikely to be changed due to diversity and inclusion training. However, training can help to raise employee awareness of the challenges faced by people different to themselves and how those differences and challenges can affect productivity and performance in the workplace. This increased awareness can lead to improved workplace relations and communication skills. While demonstrating commitment to shareholders is not a bad goal for diversity and inclusion training, it should not be the primary goal.

82. A: According to the Americans with Disabilities Act (ADA), one of the keys to a successful reasonable accommodation is that the individual is able to experience the same opportunities as his or her peers who do not require accommodations. While a virtual training or separate training still provides the employee with additional knowledge and reward for their part on the sales team, they are ostracized from the rest of their team and miss out on the social learning and interactions that would come of the team-based learning. For a one-time event, building a ramp for the employee may not be financially possible and may also pose a challenge if the training facility is not owned by the employer. By seeking an alternate location for the training, the organization can ensure that the employee is able to learn from the training and also network and build stronger relationships with the team members.

83. A: Job bidding is the process by which employees can communicate their interest in a job that is not currently posted but may be posted in the future. Part of succession planning does include determining the interest for future leadership positions, but the primary goal is to identify the talent needed for these roles. Once the potential talent is identified, candidates are then groomed, trained, and prepared for future roles in leadership.

84. C: The WARN Act sets the standards for employee notification regarding mass layoffs. For organizations with 100 or more full-time staff (or part-time staff who work at least 4,000 cumulative hours in a week), a 60-day notice is required when the downsizing changes affect at least one-third of the facility or team in question and when unpredictable financial strain is not a factor.

85. B: The two benefits proven most effective at improving the employee turnover rate are pensions and medical coverage. The high, long-term impact of each of these two benefits can create scenarios where it would cost an employee more to leave an organization than he or she would stand to make elsewhere.

86. B: Low-Cost Leadership and Focused Cost Leadership strategic positions seek to establish a competitive advantage by offering the lowest possible price for customers by creating efficient processes and reducing waste. Differentiation and Focused Differentiation strategic positions seek to create a competitive advantage by setting their product or services apart from competitors through quality, performance, advanced/new age design, or some other unique or defining characteristic. A Focused Differentiation strategic position seeks to create this competitive advantage within a niche or specialized market or industry.

87. B: Outsourcing certain staffing needs can enable an organization to cut staffing costs, focus on the core business functions, and tap into knowledge or expertise that would otherwise be difficult to hire and maintain. However, outsourcing can also result in damage to employee morale, compromised data security, and relinquishing of control over procedures and processes.

88. B: Companies that effectively shift from annual performance reviews to quarterly, monthly, or weekly performance feedback formats by definition increase the engagement with employees and establish an expectation of a feedback culture. The more frequently managers and employees meet regarding performance, the more quickly they are able to respond to changes in the business and correct performance challenges the employee may be facing. While shifting from an annual review to a regular review method can produce desirable organizational outcomes, the change can bring with it time and financial costs when learning a new system, investing in any required technologies, and finding the time to regularly meet with employees more than once a year.

89. D: Flexible work hours, or flextime, refers specifically to the employee's authority to set his or her start and end times to fit their home needs while ensuring his or her work day includes the core business hours. Telecommuting and a variable workweek can include flextime scheduling but do not guarantee flextime. Job sharing is when two or more employees split the hours and share the responsibilities of one position.

90. B: Using terminology such as 'fresh face' and 'new energy' can be suggestive of discrimination against older candidates. The Age Discrimination in Employment Act protects employees and job candidates who are forty years of age or older from employment decisions based on age.

aPHR Practice Test #2

1. This statement helps to determine acceptable and unacceptable behaviors within the company.

   a. Values
   b. Mission
   c. Vision
   d. Purpose

2. Training for new employees at your organization involves working closely with a more experienced employee as they carry out the everyday duties of the job. What type of training is being described?

   a. Mentorship
   b. On-the-job training
   c. Technical training
   d. Role play

3. Your company has asked you to research average compensation for roles in similar industries in your geographic area. Which term describes the task you are being asked to perform?

   a. SWOT analysis
   b. Workforce analysis
   c. Job analysis
   d. Market analysis

4. The HR Manager at your company is constructing a new compensation structure and has suggested freezing the pay of employees who are being compensated above the established salary range for their positions. What is the HR Manager most likely trying to address?

   a. Discriminatory pay practices
   b. Skills gap
   c. Red-circle rates
   d. Green-circle rates

5. You have been tasked with updating job descriptions for a department within your organization. You will need a very thorough understanding of the roles and responsibilities that are being performed. What is the best way to gather the information you need?

   a. Perform a job analysis.
   b. Perform a job evaluation.
   c. Research similar roles within your industry.
   d. Conduct a skills assessment.

6. What is the key difference between a furlough and a layoff?

   a. A furlough affects part-time employees, while a layoff affects full-time employees.
   b. A furlough is a leave of absence, while a layoff is separation from employment.
   c. A furlough is temporary, while a layoff is permanent.
   d. A furlough is sometimes part of a reduction in force, unlike a layoff.

7. How does sensitivity training support an organization's diversity, equity, and inclusion efforts?

    a. It gives employees the opportunity to work with others that have the same biases.

    b. It raises employee awareness of their own biases and how they impact the way they treat others.

    c. It teaches employees to accept and deal with stereotypical behaviors at work.

    d. It allows the company to publicly showcase its diversity, equity, and inclusion efforts.

8. What is the difference between a job description and a job posting?

    a. A job description is used internally to document details of a job, while a job posting is used to attract candidates to an open position.

    b. A job posting includes salary information, while a job description does not include this information.

    c. A job description is an agreement between the employee and employer, while a job posting simply advertises the job.

    d. A job description and a job posting are actually the same thing.

9. Your organization wants to look for ways to elicit more feedback from employees in order to see what changes can be made to improve employee morale and understand why employees continue working for the organization and what might cause them to leave. Which is the best method to gather the information management is seeking?

    a. Exit interviews

    b. Stay interviews

    c. HRIS data analysis

    d. Engagement surveys

10. What population does the ADEA protect?

    a. Union employees

    b. Anyone in a protected class

    c. People with disabilities

    d. Workers aged 40 or older

11. Which of these situations is an example of progressive discipline?

    a. An employee is terminated for arriving late to work multiple times.

    b. After recently receiving a verbal warning for arriving late to work, an employee receives a written warning for the same offense.

    c. An employer makes improvements to its disciplinary action policy to best meet the needs of the workforce.

    d. An employee makes gradual improvements to performance after receiving a verbal warning.

12. When federal and state wage and hour laws differ, which standard should employers follow?

    a. Federal

    b. State

    c. Whichever is more protective to the employee

    d. The employer has a right to choose the most convenient standard.

13. While developing an organizational training program, your HR team wants to first define the qualities needed to be successful in each role. What are these qualities known as?

a. KSAs
b. Objectives
c. Skills
d. BFOQs

14. In which of the following situations would a catch-up contribution to a retirement plan be admissible?

a. A 50-year-old new hire becomes eligible to enroll in the employer's retirement plan.
b. An employee chooses to delay enrollment in the 401(k) plan until age 35.
c. An employee has withdrawn from their 401(k) early and now wishes to replenish funds.
d. A 48-year-old employee wants to contribute retirement funds beyond the annual limit.

15. In reference to the Fair Labor Standards Act, what is a major difference between exempt and nonexempt employees?

a. Exempt employees are paid a salary, while nonexempt employees are paid on an hourly basis.
b. Nonexempt employees must be paid overtime wages at a premium rate of 1.5 times their regular pay. Exempt employees are not entitled to overtime pay.
c. Nonexempt employees generally earn more money than exempt employees.
d. Exempt employees don't have federal taxes withheld from their pay.

16. An employee at the manufacturing plant where you work tells you that he has been experiencing hip pain and is having difficulty standing for extended periods of time. He is not sure he can continue working as he spends much of his workday standing. As the HR representative at your company, what is the most appropriate course of action for you to take?

a. Accept the employee's resignation to avoid risk of injury.
b. Request that a first aid certified employee examine the employee to figure out the reason the employee is experiencing hip pain and recommend treatment.
c. Engage in the ADA interactive process to decide whether a reasonable accommodation can be provided.
d. Send the employee home immediately and advise him to return with a doctor's note.

17. An employee is purchasing their first home and has asked to withdraw funds from their 401(k). Which term describes this type of request?

a. Hardship distribution
b. Elective contribution
c. Early withdrawal
d. 401(k) loan

18. After employees at your company completed a diversity training course, you sent a survey out to participants to gather feedback that will help you measure the effectiveness of the training program. What is this process called?

a. Summative evaluation
b. Assessment of training
c. Training metrics
d. Performance evaluation

19. Prior to acquiring another firm, a company researches the seller's customers, finances, contracts, pending lawsuits, and other important business information. Which term does this process describe?

a. Procedural justice
b. Workplace investigation
c. Sound investment
d. Due diligence

20. In your company, employees are grouped into departments based on their area of expertise. Each group operates independently of the others to meet organizational needs. What type of organizational structure is this?

a. Functional
b. Matrix
c. Divisional
d. Learning

21. You run head-count reports at the beginning, middle, and end of each month. Your company had 63 employees on January 1, hired 3 employees on January 12, and had 1 involuntary termination on January 20. There were no additional hires or separations through the end of the month. What was your company's turnover rate for January?

a. 1.55%
b. 1.0%
c. 0.015%
d. 0%; Involuntary terminations don't count as turnover.

22. Management at your company would like to assess ways to increase employee satisfaction, morale, and motivation. Which of the following options will allow you to collect feedback from the workforce to help identify areas of improvement?

a. 360-degree review
b. Engagement survey
c. Needs analysis
d. Employee recognition program

23. Your HR Manager would like you to research ways technology can make the recruitment process more efficient. You need to be able to track candidates through the hiring process and run reports that will tell you how long it takes to fill open positions. What type of system should you consider?

a. HRIS
b. LMS
c. ATS
d. HRMS

24. When comparing 401(k) and 457(b) plans, which of the following is true?

a. Unlike a 457(b) plan, employees have the option to make pretax contributions to a 401(k) account.
b. 401(k) plans are offered by private employers, while 457(b) plans are offered by public employers and some nonprofit organizations.
c. Both 401(k) and 457(b) plans are subject to ERISA.
d. 457(b) plans do not allow for Roth contributions, unlike 401(k) plans.

25. New hire paperwork sometimes includes the signing of an NDA. What is the purpose of this document?

    a. To prevent employees from going to work for the company's competitors
    b. To give the company permission to run a background check
    c. To prevent employees from accepting a counteroffer from their current employer
    d. To prevent employees from sharing the company's confidential or proprietary information

26. Your company's performance appraisal method involves a 5-point rating scale. You notice that one supervisor has rated most employees in the department at a 3, or average. What type of bias is the supervisor most likely displaying?

    a. Leniency bias
    b. Central tendency bias
    c. Recency bias
    d. Primacy bias

27. Which of the following terms describes the component of a job description that outlines the duties that the employee should be able to perform with or without reasonable accommodation?

    a. Responsibilities
    b. Essential functions
    c. Competencies
    d. Objective

28. Which of the following protects certain employment rights of people that serve in the military?

    a. USERRA
    b. ADEA
    c. EEOC
    d. EGTRRA

29. What is the purpose of a formative evaluation?

    a. It helps HR design the training program based on needs and objectives.
    b. It helps HR determine if a training program was successful.
    c. It helps training participants form an opinion about the program.
    d. It helps trainers understand how they can improve the training program.

30. Which of the following pre-employment screenings can help a company avoid a claim of negligent hiring?

    a. Background check
    b. Skills assessment
    c. Credit check
    d. Cognitive assessment

31. Which of the following laws placed more stringent regulations on businesses' accounting and financial practices?

    a. FLSA
    b. ERISA
    c. SOX
    d. FCRA

32. Your company is organizing a leadership development training series for up-and-coming leaders. You have been asked to help identify skills gaps around which training will be developed. Your company is in which stage of the ADDIE Model?

    a. Development
    b. Design
    c. Analysis
    d. Assess

33. Mediation and arbitration are common forms of what?

    a. Alternate dispute resolution
    b. Negotiation
    c. Litigation
    d. Collective bargaining

34. Which of the following is important at every stage of a successful organizational change initiative?

    a. Rewards
    b. ROI
    c. Communication
    d. Acceptance

35. What is OSHA's General Duty Clause?

    a. Employers must have a written safety program, which includes emergency evacuation procedures, incident reporting processes, and a drug and alcohol policy.
    b. Employees have a duty to report all workplace injuries, no matter how minor they appear.
    c. Employers must provide a workplace that is free from recognized hazards that are causing or likely to cause death or serious physical harm.
    d. Employees have a duty to return to work as soon as they are physically capable following a work injury.

36. On her first day of work, a new employee is completing new hire paperwork and supplies two forms of identification so you can complete her I-9 form. The two forms of identification she provides are a social security card and a birth certificate. Are these documents acceptable?

    a. Yes. Both the social security card and birth certificate are on the list of acceptable documents for the completion of Form I-9.
    b. Yes. Form I-9 only requires a document from List B or List C. Since both items can be found on List C, either form of identification would be acceptable.
    c. No. Both documents are "List C" documents, and Form I-9 requires a combination of one "List B" document and one "List C" document.
    d. No. Neither of these documents would be acceptable.

37. What type of pay increase is tied directly to an individual's favorable performance on the job?

    a. Cost-of-living
    b. Merit
    c. Promotional
    d. Incremental

38. Your HR team is looking to implement new technology that will streamline all HR processes, including benefits, time and attendance, payroll, performance management, recruiting, and reporting. What type of software will be most appropriate for the HR team's needs?

    a. Applicant tracking system
    b. Human resource information system
    c. Professional employer organization
    d. Performance management system

39. You are trying to reduce the amount of time it takes to recruit new employees to your company. What metric will determine whether your efforts are effective?

    a. Cost-per-hire
    b. Time-to-fill
    c. Return on investment
    d. Turnover rate

40. Which of these options best describes the benefits of a strong employer brand?

    a. A strong employer brand makes customers more likely to buy from the company.
    b. A strong employer brand helps the company define their mission, vision, and values.
    c. A strong employer brand can boost recruiting and retention efforts.
    d. A strong employer brand will increase the company's social media followers.

41. What is the purpose of a SWOT analysis?

    a. To identify a company's competitors and potential threats to the business
    b. To analyze internal businesses processes and their effect on business outcomes
    c. To analyze the company's performance and identify potential threats and opportunities
    d. To identify workplace hazards and develop a plan to address them

42. Which of the following is considered a discretionary bonus?

    a. Referral bonus
    b. Performance bonus
    c. Spot bonus
    d. Attendance bonus

43. Which of the following options measures the extent to which an employee is meeting the expectations of the job?

    a. Job analysis
    b. Skills assessment
    c. Performance appraisal
    d. Job evaluation

44. While completing Form I-9 on her first day of work, a new hire tells you that she left her forms of identification and employment authorization at home. What is the best next step to take?

a. Have the employee complete section one of the I-9 and request that she supply the acceptable documentation within three business days.
b. Send the employee home immediately and allow her to return when she can provide the necessary documentation.
c. Allow the employee to continue working but request that she email you a photo of her driver's license and social security card when she gets home.
d. Give the employee until the end of the week to supply the documentation.

45. Which of these is a proactive approach to safeguarding employee data and personal identifiable information?

a. Restrict access to this information to only those who need it in order to perform their jobs.
b. Insist that employees share personal information through company email only.
c. Notify employees if there has been a data breach.
d. Offer identity protection services to anyone whose personal information has been compromised.

46. While preparing an offer letter for a candidate, you want to be careful not to inadvertently create an employment contract. What information should you include in the offer letter that will accomplish this?

a. Reasons the employee could be terminated
b. A statement that employment is at-will
c. Pre-employment screening procedures
d. Details of the employee's job duties

47. Which of the following factors are considered when determining whether an employee is exempt from the overtime rule of the Fair Labor Standards Act?

a. Job title and pay rate
b. Job title and work state
c. Salary and hours worked
d. Salary and job duties

48. Which term describes the actions businesses take to benefit various aspects of society?

a. Business ethics
b. Diversity initiatives
c. Corporate social responsibility
d. Affirmative action

49. You have received a letter in the mail requiring your company to deduct an employee's child support payments from their pay and remit the payments to the proper authority. What is this an example of?

a. Tax lien
b. Debt repayment
c. Wage garnishment
d. Childcare assistance

Copyright © Mometrix Media. You have been licensed one copy of this document for personal use only. Any other reproduction or redistribution is strictly prohibited. All rights reserved. This content is provided for test preparation purposes only and does not imply an endorsement by Mometrix of any particular political, scientific, or religious point of view.

50. According to Peter Senge, in which of the following learning disciplines does the learner demonstrate a high level of expertise in their chosen field?

    a. Mental models
    b. Personal mastery
    c. Systems thinking
    d. Continuous improvement

51. Your company is opening a second facility 75 miles from the main location. The staffing plan includes reassigning a group of employees to the second facility, and most of those employees plan to move closer to their new work location. Which of the following benefits should be considered for these employees?

    a. Cost-of-living adjustment
    b. Travel stipend
    c. Employee assistance program
    d. Relocation assistance

52. Which term describes the process of setting organizational goals and objectives and developing a plan to achieve those goals?

    a. Organizational development
    b. Human capital management
    c. Benchmarking
    d. Strategic planning

53. How long must payroll records be kept?

    a. 1 year
    b. 3 years
    c. 5 years
    d. 10 years

54. Your new hire training program includes the completion of training modules within the company's learning management system, classroom training led by an instructor, and mentorship from an experienced peer. What type of training is being described?

    a. Virtual
    b. On-the-job
    c. Blended
    d. External

55. Which of the following recruiting methods is best for sourcing passive job candidates?

    a. Job fairs
    b. Job advertisements
    c. Social media postings
    d. Resume mining

56. What kind of bias occurs when an applicant is rated favorably based solely on their level of competency in one area?

    a. Implicit bias
    b. Nepotism
    c. Horn effect
    d. Halo effect

57. Which phase of Kirkpatrick's evaluation model measures how effectively training participants are able to apply their new knowledge?

  a. Reaction
  b. Learning
  c. Behavior
  d. Results

58. Your exit interview data reveals that many employees are leaving the company because they do not feel challenged at work. To increase employee satisfaction in this area, management provides opportunities for individuals to take on more responsibilities in their roles. What is this method called?

  a. Job enlargement
  b. Job sharing
  c. Job enrichment
  d. Job ranking

59. Your organization offers employees annual pay increases to help workers keep up with rising costs of daily living. What type of increase is this?

  a. Standardized increase
  b. Cost-of-living adjustment
  c. Merit increase
  d. Promotion

60. What are the three stages of Lewin's Model of Change?

  a. Communicate, Develop, Assess
  b. Assess, Change, Grow
  c. Design, Transform, Evaluate
  d. Unfreeze, Change, Refreeze

61. In which of the following scenarios would the WARN Act most likely apply?

  a. The majority of a company's management staff is affected by a mass layoff.
  b. A company with 150 employees is conducting a mass layoff.
  c. More than 10 percent of a company's hourly workers are affected by a layoff.
  d. An employer is being acquired by another company.

62. How does an anti-retaliation policy protect employees?

  a. It prevents an employee's manager from demoting or terminating the employee for performance issues.
  b. It protects an employee who retaliates against an employer for allowing unfair labor practices.
  c. It protects an employee from negative consequences of conduct outside of the workplace.
  d. It prohibits employers from retaliating against employees who report workplace concerns.

63. Which description best describes the vision statement of a company?

  a. The desired future state of the company
  b. The reason the company exists
  c. The behaviors, morals, and beliefs of the company's people
  d. The company's outline of the strategic plan

64. What type of test measures the ability to learn new skills?

    a. Aptitude
    b. Integrity
    c. Emotional intelligence
    d. Skills assessment

65. What is a major difference between a preferred provider organization (PPO) and a health maintenance organization (HMO)?

    a. HMO plans typically come with lower costs, but PPO plans offer greater flexibility in choosing a health care provider.
    b. PPO plans typically come with lower costs, but HMO plans offer greater flexibility in choosing a health care provider.
    c. HMO plans typically do not require referrals to see a specialist, while PPO plans often do.
    d. PPO plans do not cover visits to out-of-network providers, while HMO plans will cover out-of-network services at a higher cost.

66. Hiring a more diverse workforce, providing career advancement opportunities for women and people of color, and establishing employee resource groups are examples of what?

    a. DEI initiatives
    b. Cultural sensitivity
    c. Disparate treatment
    d. Social responsibility initiatives

67. If an interviewer describes a scenario and asks the candidate how they would respond to the situation, what type of interview technique is being used?

    a. Situational
    b. Competency-based
    c. Behavioral
    d. Structured

68. When making hiring decisions, employers are prohibited by the EEOC to consider factors such as a candidate's age, sex, and religion. Which option below provides an exception to this rule?

    a. The employer is a privately held organization.
    b. The employer has been granted an exemption.
    c. The employer proves a bona fide occupational qualification exists.
    d. The employer has a voluntary affirmative action plan.

69. The HR department at your company would like to create a visual that breaks down each component of the employee compensation package, including insurances, paid time off, EAP, and retirement benefits. What is this visual known as?

    a. Wage statement
    b. Pay stub
    c. Summary of benefits and coverage
    d. Total rewards statement

70. How are flexible spending accounts (FSAs) and health savings accounts (HSAs) similar?

 a. Both allow pretax contributions and have annual limits.
 b. Both require participation in a high-deductible health plan.
 c. Both may be used to pay for qualifying medical expenses and dependent care.
 d. Neither may roll over into the following plan year.

71. Which of the options below best describes a mission statement?

 a. Briefly states the overall purpose of the organization
 b. Details strategies for achieving organizational goals
 c. Describes the desired future state of the company
 d. Describes attitudes, beliefs, and standards of behavior for employees

72. If an employer has a policy that prohibits employees from discussing their wages with each other, what is the employer most likely violating?

 a. Fair Credit Reporting Act
 b. National Labor Relations Act
 c. Sarbanes–Oxley Act
 d. WARN Act

73. What type of bias occurs when a person unconsciously judges others based on factors like gender, race, sexual orientation, and national origin?

 a. Halo effect
 b. Implicit bias
 c. Similar-to-me bias
 d. Confirmation bias

74. Security awareness training at your company consists of multiple lessons which the learner completes at their own rate. What type of training is being described?

 a. Virtual
 b. Synchronous
 c. Performance-based
 d. Self-paced

75. The management team at your company is developing a plan detailing how the business will resume operations in the event of an emergency, such as natural disaster or cyberattack. What is this type of plan called?

 a. Disaster recovery plan
 b. Emergency response plan
 c. Business protection plan
 d. Business continuity plan

76. Which of the following issues would trigger a workplace investigation?

 a. Two employees are not getting along and are having trouble working together.
 b. A supervisor wants to give an employee a written warning.
 c. An employee complains to HR about their workload.
 d. An employee complains to HR about a hostile work environment.

77. Your organization has been experiencing higher-than-average turnover recently. Which of the options below is the best first step in addressing this issue?

    a. Offer retention bonuses

    b. Increase pay rates

    c. Improve the benefits package

    d. Conduct exit interviews

78. What aspect of employee relations is aimed at solving disagreements between employees?

    a. Investigation

    b. Conflict resolution

    c. Sensitivity training

    d. Progressive discipline

79. What is the first step the human resources department should take when developing a staffing plan for the organization?

    a. Look at job boards to see who else is hiring in your industry.

    b. Meet with leaders to understand goals and needs.

    c. Review labor market data.

    d. Research local staffing agencies that have experience in your industry.

80. While interviewing candidates for an open position in his department, a supervisor learns that one of the candidates attended the same college he did. When the interview is over, the supervisor tells you he would like to offer the position to the candidate. Which type of interview bias may be occurring based on the information presented in the scenario?

    a. Similar-to-me

    b. Halo effect

    c. Recency

    d. Comparison

81. Your organization is going to be ramping up recruiting and decides to offer a reward to current employees who invite qualified candidates to apply. What recruiting strategy is being implemented?

    a. Job bidding

    b. Internal job posting

    c. Attending a local job fair

    d. Employee referral program

82. Which of the following is true regarding a health savings account (HSA)?

    a. Employees can contribute unlimited funds to an HSA.

    b. If an employee leaves the company, they lose the HSA.

    c. HSA funds can be used to pay for monthly health insurance premium costs.

    d. Only employees enrolled in a high-deductible health plan may contribute to an HSA.

83. Which of the following statements is true regarding confidentiality in a workplace investigation?

    a. If an employee asks HR to keep the information confidential, HR must agree to do so.
    b. The employee never has a right to confidentiality.
    c. HR may not be able to promise confidentiality, depending on the information that is shared.
    d. HR and the employee should both sign confidentiality agreements prior to having the conversation.

84. Your 24/7 organization operates on three shifts. Employees on second shift earn $1.00 per hour more than employees on first shift, and third-shift employees earn $1.50 more than first-shift employees. What does this difference in pay demonstrate?

    a. Unfair pay practices
    b. Production-based pay
    c. Shift differential pay
    d. Competitive wages

85. Which statement is true regarding the Patient Protection and Affordable Care Act?

    a. Young adults may stay on their parent's health plan until age 24.
    b. The insurance company may not cancel a participant's coverage.
    c. Insurance companies cannot deny coverage to an individual based on their pre-existing conditions.
    d. Preventive care is not covered by most health plans.

86. Which of these laws protects the privacy and security of an individual's personal health information?

    a. ERISA
    b. HIPAA
    c. PPACA
    d. ADA

87. What is the purpose of an employee assistance program?

    a. To provide assistive technology to employees with disabilities
    b. To supply resources that support employees' mental health and well-being
    c. To guide new hires through the orientation process
    d. To help employees improve their performance

88. Your company would like to invest in software that will help the HR department implement, track, and assess training throughout the organization. What type of software would accomplish this?

    a. HRIS
    b. CBT
    c. EPSS
    d. LMS

89. What is the overall purpose of a new hire orientation program?

    a. To measure a new hire's career readiness and ability to learn new skills

    b. To welcome new employees, set performance expectations, and acclimate them to the company culture

    c. To complete new hire paperwork, review the organizational chart, and discuss benefit offerings

    d. To teach safe work practices and discuss workplace policies

90. Which of the following questions should not be asked during an interview?

    a. Are you legally authorized to work in the US?

    b. What year did you graduate high school?

    c. What languages do you speak?

    d. Are you able to perform this job with or without reasonable accommodations?

Answer Key and Explanations for Test #2

1. A: A company's values help to guide desired actions and behaviors within the company. The mission statement defines the action and direction of the company, while the vision statement helps to envision the future of the company. The company's purpose is the reason it exists.

2. B: On-the-job training (OJT) is a popular method of training which involves hands-on learning on the job. OJT is beneficial for learners because it exposes them to real-life challenges they will encounter in the workplace. Mentorship generally focuses on growing your career by learning from a more experienced employee. Technical training focuses on a specific skill or tool. Role play is an interactive type of training which involves acting out common scenarios with one or more coworkers.

3. D: Market analysis relies on the use of external data to compare an organization's practices, including compensation, against industry benchmarks. A SWOT analysis examines strengths, weaknesses, opportunities, and threats to organizational success. Workforce analysis uses data to understand trends and possible outcomes related to the organization's current workforce. The purpose of a job analysis is to understand the functions and skills requirements of a job.

4. C: Red-circle rates apply to employees who are paid above the pay range for the job grade. The opposite is true for green-circle rates, wherein employees are paid below the minimum established pay range. Red-circle rates are commonly addressed by making affected employees ineligible for pay increases, or freezing their pay, until conditions allow the pay range to move upward. While discrepancies may occur as a result of discriminatory pay practices, there is not enough information to determine whether that is the case in the scenario described.

5. A: A job analysis may be conducted for several reasons, including creation of job descriptions. A job analysis may consist of questionnaires, employee interviews, and observations, with the goal being to understand the functions of the job and the requirements to perform them. A job evaluation is used to compare jobs within the organization. While researching similar roles within your industry may be helpful in crafting a job description, a job analysis will give you a more thorough understanding of how the job is performed in your organization specifically. The goal of a skills assessment is to evaluate an employee's abilities.

6. B: Furloughs are mandatory temporary leaves of absence or reductions in employees' schedules. Employers use this tactic when they want to avoid terminating employees but are unable to pay their wages. Furloughs allow employees to stay on the company's payroll with the expectation of returning to their normal work schedule once work is available. Layoffs can be temporary or permanent, but in both cases are considered a separation from employment. When the employer has no intention of rehiring a laid-off employee, it is considered a reduction in force.

7. B: The purpose of sensitivity training is to help employees understand their own biases and beliefs about people from diverse cultural backgrounds. Topics covered in sensitivity training may include cultural awareness, unconscious bias, and microaggressions. Sensitivity training is sometimes part of a company's diversity, equity, and inclusion (DEI) efforts, which focus on building an inclusive workplace and fostering a sense of belonging.

8. A: A job description contains key details about a job, including responsibilities, essential functions, and competencies needed to perform the job. Job descriptions are internal documents that help set guidelines, compensation, and reasonable accommodations for a job. Job postings contain much of the same information as job descriptions, but they are used to advertise open positions. Job postings may or may not include salary information, although some state laws require that this information be included.

9. B: The purpose of a stay interview is to gather feedback from individual employees as to what makes them stay with the organization and what may cause them to leave. This retention tool allows employers to understand and resolve issues before their best employees leave. An exit interview is similar in the way it is conducted, but the interviewee is an employee who has already made the decision to leave the organization. You will not find this information in your HRIS system. Engagement surveys help measure the workforce's level of engagement with and commitment to the company.

10. D: ADEA stands for Age Discrimination in Employment Act. It was put in place to protect workers over the age of 40 against discriminatory employment practices.

11. B: Progressive discipline refers to gradual steps an employer takes to address issues concerning employee conduct, performance, or policy violations. The method typically begins with counseling or a verbal warning, then progresses to a series of written warnings before resulting in more extreme measures like suspension, demotion, or termination. Progressive steps and other details should be clearly defined in the employer's policy. The goal of progressive discipline is to address problems at the earliest possible stage.

12. C: When state and federal laws differ, the employer must generally follow whichever wage and hour standard is more protective to the employee.

13. A: KSA stands for knowledge, skills, and abilities. Knowledge is based on what the employee has learned from books, obtaining certifications, and courses. Skills refer to the practical application of knowledge, such as coding, writing, and critical thinking. Abilities are based on the inherent capacity to perform the job, like the ability to communicate verbally and in writing. The objective is the goal of the training plan. A BFOQ, or bona fide occupational qualification, allows employers to consider factors such as a candidate's sex or religion in making an employment decision.

14. A: Catch-up contributions to a retirement plan are permitted in certain circumstances outlined by the Economic Growth and Tax Relief Act (EGTRRA). This provision was designed to allow older workers to save more for retirement, so the option is only available to workers who are at least 50 years old. There is an annual limit to the catch-up contribution, on top of the regular annual contribution limit. These limits depend on the type of retirement plan and may vary year to year.

15. B: Under the FLSA, nonexempt employees must be paid an overtime rate of time and a half for all hours worked over 40 in a workweek. Most nonexempt employees are paid on an hourly basis, although some are compensated by salary, at piece rate, commission, or a combination of pay methods. There is no way to generalize whether exempt or nonexempt employees earn more money, as this will depend on each individual situation. Finally, the FLSA does not determine an employee's tax withholding.

16. C: While employers should be sure to avoid the risk of workplace injuries, there is enough information to trigger an ADA request, so accepting the employee's resignation is not the best response. Answer B is not appropriate, as a first aid certified employee is not qualified to make medical diagnoses or recommendations. According to the Americans with Disabilities Act, employers must provide reasonable workplace accommodations to employees with disabilities. The interactive process may include job analysis and consulting with the employee to discuss limitations and possible accommodations, as well as obtaining medical documentation. While a doctor's note may be helpful in this situation, as suggested in answer D, the interactive process is a more thorough approach.

17. A: An individual may be able to withdraw funds from a 401(k) before age 59 ½ to pay for financial hardships, which are immediate major expenses such as the purchase of a primary residence. Absent a qualifying financial hardship, an early withdrawal from an employee's 401(k) will have a 10% penalty attached to it. Not all 401(k) plans allow for hardship distributions, so it's important to refer to the plan document for guidance. A 401(k) loan differs from a hardship distribution in that participants must pay the money back within a specified period.

18. A: A summative evaluation occurs after training has been completed to gather feedback and help determine the effectiveness of a training program. A formative evaluation, on the other hand, is conducted while the training program is being developed. For a thorough evaluation, it is best to use both types in conjunction with each other.

19. D: Regarding mergers and acquisitions, due diligence refers to the investigatory process businesses follow to ensure they are making a sound investment before the transaction is finalized. The purpose of due diligence is to raise the buyer's awareness of potential risks.

20. A: This is an example of a functional structure, in which employees are grouped based on specialization, such as human resources, finance, and marketing. This structure is typically centralized, meaning that decisions are left to upper management. In a matrix structure, employees report to more than one manager based on several factors like job function, geographic location, and product line. A divisional structure typically groups employees by output, market, or region. In a learning organization, the company is committed to continuous learning and taking action to apply new knowledge.

21. A: Turnover rate is calculated using the following equation: number of separations / average number of employees x 100. To calculate average number of employees, you would total up the head-count fluctuations throughout the month, in this case 63+66+65=194 and divide by 3 = 64.67. Then, calculate the turnover rate using the formula: 1 (number of separations) / 64.67 (average number of employees) x 100 = 1.55.

22. B: An employee engagement survey is a way to collect employee feedback that will measure engagement levels. Data from these surveys can help HR formulate strategies to improve the work environment. A 360-degree review is a method of collecting performance feedback from multiple people who work with an individual, including supervisors and peers. A needs analysis is conducted to identify training needs by comparing current knowledge, skills, and abilities to the desired future state. An employee recognition program may increase engagement by rewarding employees for exceptional performance and behaviors.

23. C: An ATS, or applicant tracking system, is a tool used to automate key aspects of the recruitment process. Depending on the system, it can be used to store resumes, coordinate interviews, and run reports. While a human resources information system (HRIS) or human resources management system (HRMS) can also assist with recruitment, both systems often include other HR functions, such as payroll, benefits, and training. A learning management system (LMS) is used to conduct training, store training materials, and report on learning and development.

24. B: 401(k) and 457(b) are relatively similar in that they both allow participants to make pretax contributions. The major difference between the two is that 401(k) plans are often offered by private employers, while 457(b) plans are offered by public employers and sometimes nonprofits. Also, since 401(k) plans are considered qualified retirement plans, they are administered by the

Employee Retirement Income Security Act (ERISA), whereas 457(b) plans are not. Both types of plans allow for Roth contributions, which are taxed currently rather than at the time of withdrawal.

25. D: NDA stands for nondisclosure agreement. Some companies will have employees and visitors sign such an agreement to protect their proprietary information from being shared outside of the company. A noncompete agreement, as described in answer A, restricts exiting employees from working for competitors within a defined time frame and geographic range. Finally, candidates are free to accept counteroffers at their discretion.

26. B: Central tendency bias occurs when a supervisor tends to rate all employees toward the middle of the rating scale, regardless of individual performance. The other types of biases listed may also occur during the performance appraisal process. Leniency bias occurs when an employee receives positive ratings even when there are areas that need improvement. Recency bias occurs when supervisors consider only recent performance while preparing an appraisal. Primacy bias is the opposite, where supervisors rely on performance from early on.

27. B: Essential functions are the duties that an employee should be able to perform on the job with or without reasonable accommodation. You may also see competencies on a job description, which refers to the knowledge the employee should possess to be successful in the role.

28. A: The Uniformed Services Employment and Reemployment Rights Act, or USERRA, allows military service members to be reemployed in their same jobs upon return from military leave. USERRA also protects health and pension benefits of employees on military leave. The specifics of this protection will vary depending on duration of leave.

29. A: A formative evaluation is done while designing the training program. It helps program designers determine appropriate content based on feedback from participants. Formative evaluation may be accomplished through means such as needs assessments, surveys, and pretests.

30. A: Background checks are often conducted after an employment offer is made to a candidate. One of the main reasons employers conduct background checks is safety. A negligent hiring claim can occur if an employee causes harm to others in the workplace, and the employer did nothing to prevent it. In this example, an employer can assess a background record to determine the risks of hiring the individual. Depending on the position, pre-employment screenings may also include skills assessments, credit checks, and cognitive assessments.

31. C: The Sarbanes–Oxley Act, or SOX, was enacted in 2002 to prevent fraudulent activity in businesses' financial statements and recordkeeping practices. The Fair Labor Standards Act (FLSA) provides guidelines regarding minimum wage, overtime, recordkeeping, and child labor. The Employee Retirement Income Security Act (ERISA) provides protection for participants in retirement and health plans. The Fair Credit Reporting Act (FRCA) establishes protection of the information contained in an individual's credit report.

32. C: The ADDIE model consists of five stages: Analysis, Design, Development, Implementation, and Evaluation. In this example, the training program is identifying skills gaps and analyzing the current state to help formulate training goals.

33. A: Alternate dispute resolution, or ADR, refers to procedures that help to resolve disputes before more drastic measures, such as litigation, would take place. Mediation involves a neutral third party to assist the conflicted parties in reaching a voluntary agreement. Arbitration also involves a neutral third party, although arbitrators are authorized to make a binding decision on the dispute.

34. C: To help overcome resistance to change, the plan for change must include strong communication at every stage of the process. This will make it more likely that employees will accept and adapt to the changes.

35. C: OSHA's General Duty Clause requires employers to protect their employees from recognized hazards in the workplace, even when there is no OSHA standard that addresses the hazard specifically. While a written safety program as described in answer A is not a requirement, it can be an effective way to prevent work-related injuries and illnesses. It is a good idea to have a policy which outlines injury reporting procedures and requires employees to report all injuries as soon as they occur. An employer may also have a return-to-work policy with the goal of bringing employees back to work as soon as possible following an injury, although such policies are not required by OSHA.

36. C: To complete Form I-9, the employer must inspect an employee's identification to support eligibility to work in the United States. Employees may choose to provide either one item from List A (such as a passport), or a combination of one item from List B (such as a driver's license) and one item from List C (such as a social security card or a birth certificate). Employees must complete section one of the I-9 by the first day of work. Employers have three business days from the employee's start date to complete their portion, which includes visually inspecting the employee's identification and employment authorization documents.

37. B: Merit increases are those that reward good performance on the job. Compensation may also be increased to align with cost-of-living adjustments or advancements to one's career, such as with promotional increases.

38. B: A human resource information system, or HRIS, would be the most appropriate solution in this scenario because it would cover all areas the HR team is trying to address. Other solutions listed here, like an applicant tracking system and performance management system, only focus on those specific areas. A professional employer organization, or PEO, is a company that partners with an employer to handle payroll, benefits, workers' compensation, and other HR functions.

39. B: Time-to-fill measures the amount of time it takes to fill a position, from posting the job to the acceptance of an offer. Other HR metrics are listed above. Cost-per-hire measures all costs associated with hiring an employee, including advertising costs and recruiter salaries. Return on investment, or ROI, measures the value of an investment against its cost. Turnover rate calculates the percentage of employees separating from a company within a given time frame.

40. C: The employer brand is different from the corporate brand in that it focuses on the employee experience and the company's reputation as an employer. A strong employment brand is especially beneficial to recruiting and retention efforts.

41. C: The SWOT analysis is performed to identify strengths, weaknesses, opportunities, and threats to a business. Identifying competitors, as suggested in answer A, is often part of the threat portion of the analysis. Answer B describes the balanced scorecard, which is also a strategic planning tool. Answer D describes a job safety analysis.

42. C: Discretionary bonuses are those that are unplanned and awarded at the discretion of the employer. There is no promise or expectation that a bonus will be awarded. An example of a discretionary bonus is a spot bonus, which is a spontaneous reward for a specific action. The other bonuses listed are nondiscretionary bonuses, which an employee expects to receive once they meet the employer's criteria to earn them. An example is a referral bonus, which is promised to employees who successfully refer new employees to the company. It is important to know the difference between the two, as nondiscretionary bonus amounts must be calculated into overtime pay.

43. C: A performance appraisal is a review of an employee's work performance, typically completed by the employee's supervisor. It is intended to provide the employee with meaningful feedback needed to successfully perform the job. The goal of a job analysis to understand the functions of a job and the requirements to perform them. A job evaluation is used to compare jobs within the organization. The goal of a skills assessment is to evaluate an individual's skills and abilities in relation to the job.

44. A: Employers must complete their portion of Form I-9, which includes visually inspecting forms of identification, within three business days of the employee's start date. The employee must complete section one of the I-9 by their first day of work. Because the employer must visually inspect the documents, answer C is not an acceptable solution. Further, the employer may not specify which documents the employee must present. Instead, they must allow the employee to choose from the list of acceptable documents.

45. A: Access to employee data and personal identifiable information should be heavily restricted to only those who need such information to perform their jobs, such as HR and finance. Answers C and D are appropriate steps to take in response to a data breach but are not preventive measures.

46. B: At-will employment means that the employee can be terminated or resign from employment at any time for any or no reason. Employment contracts often contain details such as specific job duties, duration of employment, and reasonable causes for termination or resignation. An offer letter may include a statement regarding the conditions of employment, such as passing a pre-employment background check.

47. D: The Fair Labor Standards Act considers the following "white-collar" exemptions from the overtime rule: executive, administrative, professional, computer professional, outside sales, and highly compensated employee. If the employer claims the employee is not entitled to overtime pay under the FLSA, the burden is on the employer to prove that an exemption exists. HR professionals must be familiar with the salary and duties tests to ensure eligibility for exemption.

48. C: Corporate social responsibility, or CSR, emboldens companies to consider the impact of their business practices outside of the company and commit to actions that will benefit society. Examples of CSR initiatives include environmental efforts, supporting volunteerism and philanthropy, and promoting visibility for underrepresented groups. Business ethics are standards of moral conduct specifically for businesses. Diversity initiatives are voluntary actions an employer takes to create and empower a more culturally diverse workforce. Affirmative action refers to the actions an employer takes to support hiring and advancement of people from underrepresented groups.

49. C: A wage garnishment is a court order to deduct money directly from a person's paycheck to pay a debt. Certain situations may result in an employee's wages being garnished, such as in the repayment of a student loan or child support payments. Similarly, in cases when employees owe back taxes, tax liens are often resolved by payroll deductions.

50. B: As defined by author Peter Senge, the five disciplines in a learning organization are systems thinking, personal mastery, mental models, building a shared vision, and team learning. Personal mastery occurs when the learner has expert knowledge in a particular area.

51. D: Relocation assistance is sometimes offered to employees who are relocating to benefit the employer. Depending on the employer's policy, this benefit may include travel expenses for visiting the new location, reimbursement of moving costs, a relocation bonus, or other miscellaneous relocation expenses. A cost-of-living adjustment refers to a pay increase that will help employees keep up with rising costs of daily living. A travel stipend is an amount of money offered to employees who are traveling for business reasons. An employee assistance program is a wellness benefit that typically includes counseling options and work/life balance support.

52. D: The process described is referred to as strategic planning. It's critical that the HR functions, policies, procedures, and goals align with the organization's strategic plan. Organizational development is a change management term that examines all processes and structures within a company. Human capital management includes all processes related to hiring, developing, and advancing workers within the company. Benchmarking is the process of comparing an organization's processes to standard practices or leading competitors.

53. B: The Fair Labor Standards Act (FLSA) requires that employers keep payroll records for three years.

54. C: Blended training is a format which combines a variety of training methods. The example described above combines virtual, instructor-led, and on-the-job training.

55. C: Passive candidates are those who are not actively seeking employment but may be open to the right opportunity. Social media is an effective tool for targeting passive job candidates, whereas the other options listed are better suited for those actively seeking employment opportunities. For example, someone who is not looking for work is unlikely to attend a job fair.

56. D: The halo effect describes bias that occurs when one positive trait of an individual influences someone's entire impression of them. It may occur in the interview process when an applicant displays a high level of competency in one area, and the interviewer rates the person favorably based on this information alone. The opposite of the halo effect is the horn effect, where the rating is based on one piece of negative information, such as incompetency in one area. Implicit bias refers to unconscious bias or prejudice that affects the way an individual is perceived. Nepotism is a term for favoritism that is given to family or friends in the workplace.

57. C: All four options are levels of evaluation in Donald Kirkpatrick's summative training evaluation model. In the behavior level, behavioral changes that take place as a result of the training are measured. In this phase, participants are applying what they learned to the work they are doing. The reaction level measures how the training was initially received by participants. The learning level measures whether learning took place as a result of the training. The results level measures the overall outcome of the training.

58. C: Job enrichment allows employees to stay in their current roles but with increased responsibilities. The purpose is to make employees' roles more meaningful to them, thereby increasing job satisfaction. Job enlargement is similar but refers to increasing the number of tasks or activities the employee completes in their role. Job sharing occurs when a full-time role is shared by two part-time employees. Job ranking is a form of job evaluation which places an organization's jobs in order of importance.

59. B: A cost-of-living adjustment, or COLA, is a pay increase offered to employees to help them stay in alignment with the rising cost of living. Unlike a merit increase, a COLA is not tied to an employee's performance.

60. D: Kurt Lewin developed his Model of Change in 1947. It consists of three stages: unfreezing, changing, and refreezing. According to Lewin, change begins with unfreezing, or understanding that there is a need for change and preparing for it. The next stage is change, in which the necessary changes begin to activate. The final stage is refreezing, during which the changes made become normal practice.

61. B: The Worker Adjustment and Retraining Notification (WARN) Act requires most companies with 100 or more employees to provide at least 60 days' notice in the case of a plant closure or mass layoff during a 30-day period. The WARN Act applies when at least 50 employees lose their jobs due to a plant closure, or when a mass layoff results in 500 or more employees losing their jobs for companies with 500 or more employees, or 50-499 employees if they make up at least 33 percent of the workforce. The purpose of the WARN Act is to give workers the opportunity to seek other employment or skills training that will allow them to compete in the job market. Managers, supervisors, and hourly and salaried workers are covered by the act.

62. D: Retaliation occurs when an employer takes adverse action against an employee for exercising their rights to a workplace free from discrimination. An example would be an employee who is demoted after reporting a harassment concern. An anti-retaliation policy is a proactive way for employers to prevent these types of situations, as it explicitly states that retaliation will not be tolerated.

63. A: The vision statement is a concise but inspirational statement of how the future of the company is envisioned. Answer B describes the mission statement, and answer C describes the values statement. Mission, vision, and values statements are often essential pieces of a company's strategic plan.

64. A: An employer may use aptitude testing to assess the likelihood that a candidate will be capable of learning any new skills which might be required of them if placed in a particular role. Integrity tests are used to measure an individual's tendency to display honest and trustworthy behaviors. Emotional intelligence testing measures the ability to recognize and manage emotions. The goal of a skills assessment is to evaluate an individual's abilities.

65. A: Participants in health maintenance organization plans may have lower out-of-pocket costs, but out-of-network services are typically not covered under the plan. Preferred provider organizations tend to have higher monthly costs in exchange for greater flexibility in choosing a provider. PPO plans include a network of providers, although a participant may choose to see an out-of-network provider at a higher cost. PPO plans also generally do not require a referral from a primary care physician to see a specialist, unlike HMO plans.

66. A: These are elements of diversity, equity, and inclusion (DEI) initiatives. DEI initiatives are voluntary actions an employer takes to create and empower a more diverse workforce and create an inclusive environment for women, people of color, and people with disabilities. Cultural sensitivity is the awareness and acceptance of other peoples' cultures. Disparate treatment is arbitrarily applying work rules to different groups of employees. Social responsibility initiatives are actions an employer takes to benefit society as a whole, such as its environmental and philanthropic efforts.

67. A: The goal of a situational interview is to understand how a candidate will use their knowledge, skills, and experience to respond to situations they may encounter in the role. Behavioral and competency-based interviews both focus on how the candidate actually did respond to situations they encountered in past positions to help the interviewer predict how they will handle similar events in the future. Structured interviews are those in which the interviewer asks every candidate the same set of questions.

68. C: A bona fide occupational qualification, or BFOQ, allows an employer to consider the factors mentioned above when making employment decisions. Employers should be able to prove that the BFOQ is job-related and consistent with business necessity. An example of a BFOQ is the requirement that a women's locker room attendant be female. Affirmative action plans exist to encourage the hiring and job advancement of minorities. Affirmative action plans are required for federal contractors, but some companies initiate them voluntarily.

69. D: A total rewards statement brings forward the less obvious elements of an employee's compensation, allowing the employee to see the complete package. The total rewards statement can be a useful tool in recruiting and retaining employees. This is different from a wage statement or pay stub, which show an employee how their earnings, taxes, and deductions are calculated. A summary of benefits and coverage, or SBC, summarizes the covered services, benefits, and costs associated with a health care plan.

70. A: Participants in either a flexible spending account or health savings account benefit from pretax contributions. Both types of accounts have annual contribution limits, although HSA funds roll into the next year while FSA funds are "use it or lose it." Employees must be enrolled in a high-deductible health plan to contribute to an HSA, but this is not a requirement of an FSA. FSA funds may be used to cover certain dependent care costs, but this is not true of an HSA.

71. A: A mission statement concisely describes why a company exists. It is often used in conjunction with the vision statement (described in answer C) and the values statement (described in answer D).

72. B: The National Labor Relations Act (NLRA) contains a provision that protects workers' rights to discuss their wages in person or electronically. The Fair Credit Reporting Act (FCRA) protects accuracy, fairness, and privacy of information contained in consumer reports. The Sarbanes–Oxley Act (SOX) mandates that companies maintain proper financial recordkeeping and reporting practices. The WARN Act outlines requirements certain employers must follow when conducting mass layoffs.

73. B: A person is not aware of implicit bias that inherently affects their opinions of others. This is also called unconscious bias. The halo effect occurs when a person judges another person based on one positive trait. Similar-to-me bias occurs when a person forms an opinion about someone based on shared interests or characteristics. Confirmation bias occurs when a person makes a judgment and then seeks information that will support their opinion.

74. D: This describes self-paced training, where the learner advances through predetermined lessons at their own pace. Virtual training uses virtual tools as a training platform rather than a classroom or on-the-job setting. Synchronous refers to training that occurs at the same time with an instructor and other learners. Performance-based training focuses on a skill the learner needs to practice until performance expectations are met.

75. D: A business continuity plan proactively strategizes on getting the business back up and running as quickly as possible following a disaster or disturbance. A BCP may consider several types of scenarios depending on numerous factors. For example, a business that operates in a location prone to earthquakes may include how they intend to respond to such a situation in their business continuity plan.

76. D: A hostile work environment exists when there is pervasive and/or severe harassment or discrimination occurring that affects an individual's ability to perform their job. Complaints that suggest a hostile work environment would call for a workplace investigation. Employee conflicts, as described in answer A, may be solved through conflict resolution techniques. A written warning is often part of a performance management plan and does not normally lead to a workplace investigation. An employee's complaint about their workload should be documented and discussed, but likewise does not warrant an investigation.

77. D: Exit interviews are performed to get feedback from employees choosing to leave the company. While options A through C may help to improve employee retention, exit interviews can provide insight into specific reasons why employees are leaving your organization. That insight can be used to develop relevant retention strategies.

78. B: An HR professional may use conflict resolution techniques to help two parties confront and solve a disagreement in the workplace in a healthy manner. An investigation involves a series of interviews to obtain information regarding workplace misconduct. Sensitivity training focuses on making employees aware of their own beliefs, biases, and prejudices in order to treat others respectfully in the workplace. Progressive discipline refers to gradual steps an employer takes to address issues concerning employee conduct, performance, or policy violations.

79. B: While all responses may be part of an organization's staffing plan, it is best to start by identifying needs. One way to do that is to speak with department leaders to discuss goals, upcoming projects, or any other factors that may require staffing changes.

80. A: Similar-to-me bias occurs when an interviewer favors a candidate because of shared interests, experiences, or other similarities. Other interview biases listed above include the halo effect, which occurs when good qualities about a candidate negate the undesirable qualities, and recency bias, which occurs when an interviewer recalls only the most recent interviews when considering candidates.

81. D: An employee referral program typically offers employees some form of incentive for referring new employees who are subsequently hired to the organization. It is often a cost-effective method of both recruiting and retention, as referred employees are more likely to stay with the organization longer.

82. D: When combined with a high-deductible health plan (HDHP), health savings accounts allow participants to use pretax earnings to pay for qualifying medical expenses, such as deductibles and copayments. HSA funds may not be used to cover monthly premium costs; however, monthly premiums are often lower with an HDHP. HSAs have annual contribution limits. Employees may take the HSA with them, even if they leave the company.

83. C: While there is plenty of employee information that must be kept confidential within the HR department, there are certain situations that should not be kept completely confidential, such as a harassment claim.

84. C: Shift differential pay is sometimes offered to employees who work undesirable hours, such as second or third shift. It is a common practice in industries that operate around the clock, such as manufacturing and health care, and helps to resolve staffing issues that employers typically face regarding these shifts.

85. C: One objective of the PPACA, often shortened to Affordable Care Act (ACA), is to prevent health insurance companies from charging more or denying coverage to individuals based on pre-existing health issues. The PPACA also requires that most plans cover certain preventive care, such as cancer screenings and vaccinations, at no cost to the insured. Additionally, under the PPACA, young adults may remain on their parent's health plan until they reach age 26. Insurance companies may cancel coverage in certain situations, such as falsifying an application or failure to pay premiums on time.

86. B: The Health Insurance Portability and Accountability Act (HIPAA) provides regulations that must be followed by health plans and health care providers to protect peoples' personal health information. The Employee Retirement Income Security Act (ERISA) provides protection for participants in retirement and health plans and sets rules for disclosing certain health plan information to employees. The purpose of the Patient Protection and Affordable Care Act (ACA) is to make health care more affordable and accessible. The Americans with Disabilities Act (ADA) protects individuals with disabilities, including in the workplace.

87. B: An employee assistance program (EAP) provides a wide range of services to support employees' well-being. Services may include a limited number of counseling sessions at no cost to the employee and resources for supporting financial health, addressing substance use, or improving job performance. Offering an EAP may result in fewer absences, improved performance, and lower overall health costs.

88. D: A learning management system, or LMS, is used to manage training within the organization. LMS capabilities range from tracking training attendance to reporting on training results. An HRIS, or human resources information system, stores employee information and may assist in various HR duties, like payroll and benefits. Computer-based training (CBT) and electronic performance support systems (EPSS) are virtual training tools.

89. B: While answers C and D are often embedded in the orientation, the overall goal of new hire orientation is for new employees to feel welcome, become familiar with the company culture, and grasp their performance expectations.

90. B: Asking what year an applicant graduated could reveal their age. Since making hiring decisions based on age is discriminatory, this is information that should not be sought out during the interview process. An employer has a right to ask if an applicant is eligible to work in the United States but should avoid comparable questions such as "Are you a US citizen?" An employer may also inquire about languages the candidate speaks, as well as if they are able to read, write, and speak fluently in English. Finally, an employer should not ask questions that may reveal whether a candidate has a disability. The question "Are you able to perform this job with or without reasonable accommodations" is appropriate because it is focused on the functions of the job rather than the employee's physical or mental capabilities.

aPHR Practice Test #3

1. The manager at ABC Company wants to run an advertisement for a laborer position. HR has been instructed by the manager to list several desired skills in the job advertisement. Which of these desired skills should NOT be listed in the ad?

    a. Ability to lift 50lbs
    b. Possess a high school diploma or GED
    c. Must be born after 1959
    d. Must be able to read and write the English language

2. John, the owner of ABC Company, wants to hire one of his good friends, Dan, for a security guard position at the company. John instructs the HR manager to hire Dan even though he was convicted of felony aggravated assault three years ago. This concerns the HR manager. What would be the HR manager's best response regarding hiring Dan?

    a. The company should hire Dan on the condition that he signs an agreement stating he will not harm anyone while performing his duties.
    b. The company should not hire Dan, because the violent crime conviction could impede his ability to be an effective security guard.
    c. The company should hire Dan but put him in a position away from other workers.
    d. The company should hire Dan as the security guard, as ordered by the owner.

3. The HR manager recommends to the manager of ABC Company that an ethics policy be adopted. The manager asks why this would be necessary. What is the best answer the HR manager can provide?

    a. Ethics policies are required by federal labor regulations.
    b. An ethics policy will set a standard for lawful and appropriate behavior that all members of the organization should follow.
    c. Adoption of this policy will make the company appear more professional.
    d. An ethics policy will eliminate the need for a disciplinary action program.

4. A female and male employee begin a romantic relationship while working together. The female employee is the male employee's supervisor. When the HR department learns of this, what would be their best course of action?

    a. Terminate the female employee for engaging in a relationship with a subordinate.
    b. Contact both parties to confirm the relationship and warn both to not let it influence work decisions.
    c. Reassign one of the parties to another department after the matter is addressed to the couple.
    d. Do nothing. Asking about their romantic relationship is a violation of their privacy.

5. An employee is injured while working on the assembly line at ABC Company. The injury was caused by another employee operating a machine against company policies. Is the company liable for the injury? Why or why not?

    a. Yes. Since the injury occurred on company property, the company is responsible.

    b. No. The company established policies to keep the workplace safe; however, the policies were violated.

    c. Yes. The policies should have been more robust to help prevent any workplace injuries from occurring.

    d. No. This is only an accident.

6. Caroline is an employee at ABC Company, a paper company with 200 employees. Her son has been hospitalized, and doctors tell her that he will need constant care for three months after he is released. Caroline asks the HR manager about what will happen to her employment if she must be out of work that long. What should the HR manager tell Caroline?

    a. Caroline should use all her paid time off but must return to work once that is expended.

    b. Caroline should use all her paid time off. Her job will be held for her until she is able to come back.

    c. Caroline must arrange for someone to care for her son. She will be terminated if she does not report to work.

    d. Caroline should take whatever time she needs. She will continue to receive her salary.

7. There are many termination situations an HR manager may encounter. Out of the answers listed, what is the one termination situation that may be readily disputed by the employee?

    a. Business closure

    b. Outsourcing of labor

    c. Unionization activities

    d. Insubordinate behavior

8. Which of the following answers would NOT be part of a successful workforce planning process?

    a. Forecasting the organization's future needs

    b. Identifying qualified employees

    c. Job analysis and descriptions

    d. The organization's risk management procedures

9. Which of the following would be the best way to minimize the act of employee embezzlement?

    a. Have multiple roles in the finance/accounting department.

    b. Have written policies warning against any unethical behavior.

    c. Computerize all financial data.

    d. Audit the finance/accounting departments regularly.

10. ABC Company wants to bid on a project for the U.S. Air Force. The contract will be for more than $100,000. The project is to build a new playground located on an air force base. ABC has 20 employees and has never performed any government work. Based on this information, should ABC Company implement an Affirmative Action policy? Why or why not?

    a. No. ABC has less than 20 employees, which exempts them from the Affirmative Action requirement.
    b. Yes. All federal contractors must have an Affirmative Action policy.
    c. Yes. The contract is for over $50,000, which means ABC is required to implement an Affirmative Action Policy.
    d. No. A playground is not a government facility, so they would be exempt from the Affirmative Action requirement.

11. The manager of ABC Company is concerned that increased cell phone usage by employees will lead to accidents in the workplace. The manager asks you, the HR representative, if it is proper to institute a no-phone policy while working. Can this legally be implemented? Why or why not?

    a. No. A cell phone is an employee's property, and they cannot be told to put it away.
    b. Yes. Asking employees to set aside their phones while working would be considered a reasonable policy.
    c. No. The employees' right to a fair workplace prohibits this type of rule.
    d. Yes. The company is free to institute any rule it desires, and employees must abide by all company rules while working.

12. Two employees at a steel mill agree to work for one another on different weeks. They do this so that each can be off work during certain times they need for family events. This agreement will cause the employees to work their normal shifts plus an additional forty (40) hours in one week. The company has approved the swap and sent this approval to both employees' supervisors. How should the employees be compensated for their hours worked?

    a. The company should pay them overtime based on the actual hours worked over the normal 40-hour workweek.
    b. The company does not owe them overtime pay, since the shift swap was requested by the employees and not mandated by the company. The employees should be compensated for 40 hours only.
    c. The company should pay the employees for the normal 40 hours and give 40 hours comp time to both employees.
    d. The company should pay the employees double-time pay since they will have worked 80 hours in a week.

13. Johnny, a line worker at ABC Company, approaches the HR manager, wanting a pay raise. He believes he is performing better than all workers on his shift and should, therefore, be compensated for his performance. Johnny will receive a scheduled performance appraisal in two months. What should the HR manager say or do in this situation?

    a. The HR manager should speak with Johnny's supervisors and inquire about his performance in order to see if a raise is warranted.
    b. The HR manager should raise Johnny's pay since he is a high-performing employee.
    c. Wait for the scheduled performance appraisal from Johnny's supervisor to determine if an increase is warranted.
    d. Tell Johnny to speak to management about his desire for a raise.

14. An employee is found carrying a pistol onto company property. The firearm is concealed, and the employee has a state-issued permit to carry the weapon. The manager asks the employee to leave the weapon in their vehicle since other employees have voiced their discomfort in being around a gun. The employee refuses, stating that the permit allows them to carry the weapon anywhere in the state. How should the manager respond?

    a. Leave the employee alone since he has a permit.

    b. Demand that the employee remove the weapon from the property. Failure to comply will result in disciplinary action.

    c. Call the police.

    d. Allow the employee to carry the weapon today, but never again.

15. Two employees come to you, the HR manager, and complain that a supervisor has ordered them to perform a task not in their job description. What would be HR's best course of action?

    a. Instruct the employees to perform the tasks. Job descriptions are not employment contracts.

    b. Inform the employees that they are correct and should only be given tasks that fit their job description.

    c. Advise the employees to take this matter directly to their supervisor. This is not an HR issue.

    d. HR should advise the supervisor that he or she must have the employees' consent before asking them to perform duties outside of their job description.

16. Which of the following situations mentions a requirement that is NOT a Bona Fide Occupational Qualification (BFOQ)?

    a. A church requires that their ministers be male.

    b. A law enforcement agency requires that its officers have a criminal history free of felony convictions.

    c. A gas station in a predominantly Caucasian neighborhood posts a job asking for only Caucasian applicants.

    d. A computer software corporation requires its programmers to have computer science degrees.

17. John, the operations manager at ABC Company, has conducted several interviews attempting to fill a vacant position. What question should John NOT ask during the interviews?

    a. Are you a U.S. citizen?

    b. How much experience do you have?

    c. What are your long-term goals?

    d. What is your desired salary if offered the job?

18. An employee comes to you, the HR manager, concerned about not receiving adequate representation from their union representative. What can you, as the HR manager, do in this situation to help the employee?

    a. Nothing. Any issues employees have with the union must be addressed to union management.

    b. Contact the National Labor Relations Board and complain about the union's activities.

    c. Contact the union leader at the site and meet with them about the situation.

    d. Advise the employee to withdraw from the union and stop paying dues.

19. A supervisor comes to you, the HR manager, to report that an employee has been late for work three times in a single week. The supervisor is concerned about addressing the tardiness because the employee performs well. The supervisor believes that addressing the issue may demoralize the employee and inhibit his or her productivity. What is the best advice you can give the supervisor?

   a. Do not address the issue. A high-performing employee is good for production.
   b. Counsel the employee verbally. Written disciplinary actions will go on the employee's record.
   c. This is a Human Resources issue. The HR manager can address the employee.
   d. Issue a written disciplinary action to the employee. The action needs to be documented in case the tardiness continues.

20. The manager of ABC Company wants to suspend the company's successful recruiting program because all positions are full. As the HR manager, what would be the best advice you could give the manager concerning this course of action?

   a. Move forward with discontinuing the program, as this will save on recruitment and advertising costs.
   b. Keep the recruiting program fully funded and staffed.
   c. Scale back the recruiting program, but do not eliminate it completely.
   d. Minimize the reach of the recruiting program by focusing only on internal talent.

21. Of the answers listed, what is the best advantage of an organization adopting a team learning philosophy?

   a. Team learning allows for high-performing members of the group to be identified for future management positions.
   b. Team learning can reduce training costs by engaging large groups at one time.
   c. Team learning can increase employee engagement.
   d. Team learning allows managers to be trained alongside employees.

22. ABC Company has hired James as the HR manager after an extensive search. The company is excited about James's agreement to join the team and has offered to relocate him and his family from three states away. Which of the following is NOT a common practice used by companies to provide relocation assistance to new employees?

   a. Assistance with finding a new home
   b. Moving expense reimbursement
   c. Finding new local physicians the family can see
   d. Assisting with finding employment for an employee's spouse

23. Of the answers listed, which one is NOT an effective strategy when implementing change management?

   a. Developing a plan for implementation
   b. Motivating supervisors to support the change
   c. Ensuring upper management is supportive of the change
   d. Surveying employees about the proposed change prior to implementing it

24. Three employees at ABC Company called in sick on the same day. The supervisor calls an employee, Jacob, and asks if he can come in four hours early to cover the shift. Jacob will be paid his regular hourly wage plus extra pay for coming in early. What is this extra pay called?

    a. Double-time pay
    b. On-call pay
    c. Compensatory time
    d. Call-back pay

25. An employee comes to you, the HR manager of a paper company, and tells you that she witnessed a coworker injure himself while operating a machine two days ago. The worker that was injured has not reported the incident to anyone. What is the best thing you can do in this situation?

    a. Do nothing. The employee has not reported the injury.
    b. Get a written statement from the witness and investigate the incident.
    c. Have the employee's supervisor issue him a reprimand for failing to report an injury.
    d. Give the witness a lie detector test to see if she is telling the truth.

26. The manager of ABC Company is concerned that profits will decrease if two of their top supervisors retire. The two supervisors are three months away from retirement age. As an HR manager, what can you recommend to the manager to mitigate some of the negative effects of the supervisors retiring?

    a. The company should identify current employees that could perform well in the supervisory role and offer them pertinent training.
    b. Offer the supervisors higher salaries if they agree to stay longer.
    c. Post the job outside of the company and try to recruit well-qualified personnel.
    d. Combine as many departments as possible under other supervisors that have shown talent in helping the company profit.

27. Unprecedented inflation has caused some worry among employees at the ABC Company. They are concerned their current wages will decrease their buying power for food and other goods. What type of compensation strategy could the company's management use to help the employees deal with this situation?

    a. Cost-of-living adjustments
    b. Profit-sharing opportunities
    c. More overtime opportunities
    d. Employer-sponsored health plan

28. The HR manager of a retail store sees a need for additional training in customer service. When this recommendation is taken to management, it is rebuffed as too costly. What can the HR manager do that will help management buy into the idea?

    a. Recommend web-based learning so training can be completed when the employee is at home.
    b. Research similar companies that have used customer service training to help increase their profits, then provide these findings to management.
    c. Explain to management that customers will shop elsewhere if the customer service does not improve.
    d. Do nothing. Management has spoken on the matter.

29. Company ABC has four departments: production, logistics, accounting, and safety. All four departments have different performance appraisal systems for their respective employees. As HR manager, what do you recommend doing in this situation?

a. Recommend nothing. The type and form of performance appraisal should be up to the department.
b. All performance appraisals should conform companywide.
c. Have HR approve each department's appraisal forms prior to using them.
d. Have HR conduct all performance appraisals.

30. ABC Company uses a local plumber for all its plumbing needs. The plumber has no other customers and works an average of 38 hours a week at ABC. The plumber uses his own tools when working and does not rely on ABC to provide any equipment. Given this situation, what type of employee-employer relationship exists?

a. The plumber should be classified as a full-time employee.
b. The plumber should be classified as a part-time employee.
c. The plumber is an independent contractor.
d. The plumber does not have any type of employee-employer relationship with ABC.

31. Of the answers listed, what would NOT be an employer benefit of a tuition reimbursement program?

a. Higher recruitment results
b. Lower employee turnover rates
c. Lower administrative costs
d. Increased leadership development

32. The owner of ABC Company is considering laying off some long-serving employees to save on payroll costs. He recommends bringing in entry-level graduates to fill their positions. What would be the biggest drawback of this plan?

a. ABC Company will pay a large amount in unemployment benefits to laid off employees.
b. The company will lose important knowledge, skills, and abilities when it loses these employees.
c. This will cause low morale within the organization.
d. HR costs will rise due to extra onboarding and training costs.

33. A supervisor comes to you, the HR manager, and tells you that he lost his temper with a subordinate. He explains this has happened several times in the past and is concerned that he may have an anger management problem. His work history has been exemplary, and he is considered by management to be a valuable employee. What should you do in this situation?

a. Tell the supervisor to go to the employee with whom he lost his temper and apologize.
b. Issue the employee a written reprimand for being disrespectful to another employee.
c. Offer anger management counseling through an Employee Assistance Program (EAP).
d. Recommend to your manager that the supervisor be reassigned to a position where he does not manage employees.

34. The owner of the company approaches you about instituting a leadership program for current supervisors. Of the four answers given, what should be included in this type of program?

    a. Managerial accounting
    b. Budgeting
    c. Engineering Controls
    d. Conflict management

35. Which of the following would be a positive effect of having diversity in the workplace?

    a. A diverse workforce will be more creative.
    b. A diverse workforce has a greater chance of attracting customers.
    c. A diverse workforce will lead to a larger pool of candidates to hire from.
    d. All the above

36. The manager of ABC Company, a paper mill, wants to find out if the company's hourly production workers are being compensated on the same level as other paper mill workers in the area. What is the best method to find out this information?

    a. Review information from the Bureau of Labor Statistics.
    b. Review information from the state's unemployment agency.
    c. Engage other local paper mills to participate in a salary and wage survey.
    d. Conduct a survey among the current employees to find out if they feel they are being compensated fairly.

37. Trevor is a supervisor at ABC Company. The HR manager has noticed that Trevor has been acting differently lately by becoming more introverted and staying in his office all day. This is out of character for Trevor, as he is one of ABC's best and most personable employees. What should the HR manager do in this situation?

    a. Leave Trevor alone. Trevor's change of attitude is not a concern for HR.
    b. Tell Trevor you have noticed some changes in his behavior and offer your help.
    c. Report Trevor's change in behavior to upper management so they may be aware of the potential for lower productivity.
    d. Contact Trevor's family members and ask if there is anything going on in his personal life that is causing the change.

38. An employee at ABC Company is injured when a box falls from a rack overhead. The employee was not wearing a hardhat when the incident occurred, which violates the company's mandatory hardhat policy. Is the company liable for this employee's injury? Why or why not?

    a. Yes. The injury occurred on company property.
    b. No. The hardhat policy was violated by the employee. If the policy was followed, the employee may not have suffered the injury.
    c. Yes. The box should not have been put in a place where it could have fallen.
    d. No. The company is not liable for unintentional incidents.

39. Rumors have circulated through the company that there will be mass layoffs. The general manager does not know if she should tell the employees that this is false. What response, if any, should you recommend?

   a. Say nothing; rumors will occur periodically.
   b. Have the supervisors tell the employees the rumors are not true.
   c. Find the source of the rumor before taking any action.
   d. The general manager should address the employees personally and explain that the rumor is false.

40. The owner of a paper company wants to implement a supervisory training program. They ask you, the HR manager, what must be included in the program for it to be effective. Of the answers provided, what would be the most important topic to teach in the program?

   a. Budgeting
   b. Accounting practices
   c. Conflict management
   d. Tips for working successfully in each department

41. An organization wants to open a secondary office in another state and plans on keeping it there as part of their long-term goals. Existing managers will be relocated to manage the new office, but several entry-level employees will be needed for adequate staffing. What would be the best way to acquire this talent?

   a. Reassign several existing employees to the new office.
   b. Post the positions and hire externally.
   c. Hire temporary workers to staff the entry-level positions.
   d. Use contract workers to fill the positions.

42. Due to financial duress, ABC Company must lay off 50 employees. The HR manager has been asked for their opinion on how to break the news to the affected employees. What is the best answer the HR manager can provide?

   a. To avoid direct confrontation, have HR tell the affected employees that they have been laid off via email
   b. Have HR meet with the affected workers individually to explain the reason for the layoff and provide them with unemployment information.
   c. Have HR meet with the affected workers as a group to provide reasoning and unemployment information.
   d. Have the affected workers' supervisors tell them about the layoffs and provide them with relevant information.

43. The manager at ABC Company comes to you, the company HR representative, and wants to know how instituting an ethics policy could help the organization. What is the best answer you can provide about the benefits of ethics policies?

   a. Ethics policies keep employee theft to a minimum.
   b. Having an ethics policy will keep government regulators from examining a company's operating practices.
   c. An ethics policy can motivate employees, improve morale, and help boost company profits.
   d. Ethics policies will make the business more attractive to potential clients and customers.

44. A female employee comes to you, the HR manager, and states her belief that she is being paid less than two of her male counterparts because of her gender. All three employees are supervisors in the same department. What is the best course of action in this situation?

   a. Immediately give the female employee a raise so that her compensation matches that of her male counterparts.
   b. Investigate the issue to determine if and why there is a pay discrepancy.
   c. This could be a rumor. Tell the employee to try to confirm the information before bringing it to HR.
   d. Recommend to the employee that she should file a complaint with the Equal Employment Opportunity Commission (EEOC).

45. The HR manager has identified an employee, John, as a potential talent selection for the next supervisory position. John is open to being promoted and has told some of his fellow workers that he is ready to take on additional responsibilities. What is the best course of action for the HR manager in this situation?

   a. Assign John new responsibilities and tasks by using a job enrichment approach.
   b. Place John in a formal education program to develop leadership skills.
   c. Provide John with your thoughts on his performance so he will stay motivated to move up in the organization.
   d. Wait until a supervisory position opens before asking John to apply for the job.

46. James is recruited by the company manager to fill a supervisory position. You, the HR manager, explain to James that he must submit to pre-employment drug testing as per company policy. The manager tells you that James is not a drug user and does not need to be tested. What should happen in this situation?

   a. As per the manager's orders, James does not need to be tested.
   b. Explain to the manager that discriminating between who needs to take the test and who does not could open the company up to civil liability, then suggest that James should be tested pursuant to company policy.
   c. James should be put into the random testing pool after being hired, but he does not need to be tested immediately.
   d. Refuse to obey the manager's orders and immediately order the testing anyway.

47. Jerry, an engineer at a paper mill, has been placed into a project team with other valuable engineers. Jerry is very excited about working with such a talented group. What type of compensation would this be defined as?

   a. Extrinsic compensation
   b. Monetary compensation
   c. Intrinsic compensation
   d. Commission-based pay

48. You, the HR manager, receive information that a supervisor is receiving gifts from a supplier in return for contracts. Is there anything wrong with this situation? If so, what should be done?

    a. No. Gifts from suppliers are common in business so no action is required.
    b. Yes. This is unethical and the matter should be investigated.
    c. Not necessarily. The matter should only be investigated if the supervisor's reception of the gifts is detrimental to the company.
    d. Possibly. The supervisor should disclose whether the gifts are monetary. If they are, no investigation will be necessary.

49. The HR manager at ABC Company, Nick, is interviewing an applicant for an HR generalist position. He asks the applicant to give an example of a risk management tool that is required by law. What would be one example of such a tool?

    a. EEO-1 reports
    b. Employee contracts
    c. Employee handbooks
    d. Retirement contributions

50. Dissatisfied with current talent, the owner of ABC Company wants to hire an experienced manager from outside of the company. Which of the following would NOT be an effective external recruitment method in this situation?

    a. Posting on Internet job boards
    b. Advertising on social media
    c. Participating in college recruitment fairs
    d. Posting on company websites

51. An employee at a paper mill is accused of theft. The HR manager believes that the results of a lie detector test will show if the employee is guilty. The employee is then offered the test and is told that if she does not comply, she will be terminated. Is this the best way to handle the issue? Why or why not?

    a. Yes. Lie detector tests are a respected method of determining guilt in company investigations.
    b. No. Lie detector tests are not admissible in court; therefore, the company should investigate the theft using other means, such as interviewing witnesses or checking inventory counts.
    c. Yes. The lie detector will save time and be cheaper than a lengthy investigation.
    d. No. The employee should be terminated immediately. Occurrences of theft should not be tolerated by the company.

52. ABC Company is opening a second facility to manufacture a product in a different state. The company owner recommends that employees hired at the new facility are compensated on the same scale as employees at the existing facility. As the HR manager, what is the best recommendation you can give to the owner regarding his or her recommendation?

    a. This is a good policy. To maintain fairness, the employees at the new site should be compensated on the same scale as the employees at the existing site.

    b. Research should be done on the regional labor market at the new site to determine appropriate compensation levels prior to hiring new employees.

    c. A salary survey should be conducted at the existing facility to determine if current compensation meets industry standards.

    d. To get the new facility running, offer higher wages than the existing facility. This will bring in applicants quickly so that positions can be immediately filled.

53. Brent has just been hired at ABC Company as a line worker. He asks the HR manager not to withhold any state or federal taxes from his check. Brent explains that he will pay all taxes at the end of the year when he files his income tax return. Should the HR manager allow this? Why or why not?

    a. Yes. It is up to the employee whether to have his or her income taxes withheld.

    b. No. Employers must withhold income taxes by law.

    c. Yes. Not withholding taxes will help the company save on payroll costs.

    d. No. This would be against commonly accepted company policies.

54. The HR manager at a paper mill notices a broken step while going up a staircase in the plant. Although the step is only two feet off the ground, he or she is concerned that the broken step could cause someone to trip and fall. What should the HR manager do in this situation?

    a. The HR manager should immediately notify the safety manager about the hazard so it can be fixed.

    b. The HR manager is not a safety manager, so he or she does not need to take action. This issue should be handled by a different department.

    c. The HR manager should try to eliminate the hazard, if possible, and then contact the safety manager

    d. The HR manager should notify his or her supervisor about the situation immediately.

55. The CEO of ABC Company asks the HR manager how the organization could develop a pool of entry-level managers to choose from. What would be the best strategy for this request?

    a. Allow interested employees to take company-sponsored management training.

    b. Develop a college internship program.

    c. Assign high-performing employees as "fill-in" managers when needed.

    d. Keep a large number of applicants on file in case there is an open spot.

56. The management team at ABC Company wants to make some major changes in the company's culture. They want employees to be focused on quality and customer satisfaction instead of only on production output. This will require buy-in from the whole company, from the executives down to the workers. Of the answers listed, what would best increase buy-in, giving the initiative a better chance of success?

a. Management should adequately prepare employees for the change.
b. Executives should show support for the change.
c. Employees should receive training for the change.
d. Management should demand compliance from the workers.

57. A manager at ABC Company approaches the HR manager and asks about an employee's medical history. What should the HR manager do?

a. Give the manager the employee's file to review.
b. Advise the manager that you are unable to disclose that information based on employee privacy laws.
c. Verbally tell the manager the employee's information, but do not let them see anything in the file.
d. Contact the employee in question and ask if he will allow the manager to have access to their medical records.

58. ABC Company is growing faster than anticipated. The HR department wants to begin a workforce planning program to ensure qualified employees are available to fill new positions when they are needed. Of the following options, which would NOT be used in building this type of program?

a. Job analysis
b. Identification of qualified employees
c. Establishment of a workforce planning goal
d. Employee compensation surveys

59. The owner of a paper company wants to institute the use of an employee suggestion box to better understand how the employees feel about their jobs. What is the best way management can implement this practice for it to be effective?

a. Put a suggestion box in each breakroom so every employee has access.
b. Have management explain the idea behind the suggestion box to the employees and give parameters for the suggestions.
c. Mandate that supervisors order their employees to contribute to the suggestion box regularly.
d. Reward employees who put helpful suggestions in the box with companywide recognition.

60. An employee reports to HR that a supervisor is treating him differently than other employees. The employee states that he is receiving less break time than his coworkers. What should HR do about this situation?

a. HR should investigate the situation to see if there is any discrimination or favoritism taking place.
b. The employee is being insubordinate. HR should order them to report back to work.
c. HR should advise the employee to take the issue up with the supervisor immediately.
d. HR should take no action, but they should still listen to the employee to make him or her feel valued.

61. Of the answers listed, what knowledge management method is most effective in achieving desired results?

    a. Best practice standards
    b. Mandated employee training courses
    c. Formal education requirements
    d. Employee evaluations

62. A union has begun organizing at ABC Company. The HR manager has sent out a list of acts managers should avoid during this process. Of the answers listed, which would be one of those prohibited acts?

    a. Advising employees that the company wants to remain union free
    b. Describing what the union cannot do for employees
    c. Sharing true and factual statements about the disadvantages of unions nationwide
    d. Offering a pledge to raise benefits for employees if the company remains non-unionized

63. Several production employees at ABC Company have volunteered to participate in a training session on how to use a new software. What is the most cost-effective method of getting these employees trained in the software?

    a. In-house group training
    b. Individual, asynchronous web-based training
    c. In-house individual training
    d. Group training after business hours

64. Jason wants to start a marketing business. He believes hiring a sales representative will be the best way to contact prospective customers. He wants to know what the most common compensation structure is for this type of position. What do you recommend as the best option?

    a. Commission-based pay
    b. Salaried, exempt
    c. Competency-based compensation
    d. Hourly, non-exempt

65. The manager of a paper mill changed the shift work schedule for all employees. The change happened overnight, and only supervisors were advised there would be a change. Opposition to the change is widespread among the hourly workers. How could this situation have been handled better?

    a. The manager should have sent out a companywide email, informing all employees of the new schedule prior to the change.
    b. The manager should have offered pay increases to all staff that were affected by the change.
    c. The manager should have met with the staff and explained why the change should be implemented and how it would benefit the company and the employees.
    d. The manager should have left the schedule as it was. This would have caused no opposition.

66. An employee, Emily, has just been hired at ABC Company. She has been given a federal W-4 form to complete. Emily asks you, the HR manager, to complete the form for her. How should you respond?

a. Fill out the form for Emily using information from her HR file
b. Decline to help. It is a federal requirement that the employee complete the W-4.
c. Question Emily about why she cannot fill out the form
d. Assist Emily in completing the form if she provides you with the necessary information and signs the form, acknowledging it is correct.

67. An employee comes to you, the HR manager, and tells you that he is considering taking a position at another company for more pay. This employee has a good employment record and is considered productive by his supervisor. What would be the best course of action in this situation?

a. Wish the employee luck and assure him that you will provide a good employment reference based on his record.
b. Do nothing. The decision to leave the company is solely up to the employee.
c. Ask the employee if he is willing to negotiate a higher wage, in the hopes of getting the employee to stay with the organization. If the employee is willing to stay, take this to management for a decision.
d. Say nothing, and advise management of the employee's intention to leave.

68. Your manager is considering dropping the lowest paid employees' pay to the federal minimum wage to save on costs. The federal minimum wage is less than the state minimum wage where the company operates. What is the best advice you can give your manager?

a. This would be an effective cost-saving measure.
b. This action could lower employee morale and productivity.
c. This act would be illegal, as the company must pay the state minimum wage.
d. Lowering the minimum wage below the state minimum wage will help the company avoid layoffs.

69. ABC Company has had an unusually high turnover rate in the last three months. The manager asks the HR department to recommend a strategy that could explain why employees are leaving the organization. What would be the best tool for measuring this?

a. Exit interviews
b. Employee surveys
c. Employee committees
d. Suggestion boxes

70. An employee is believed to have stolen a tool from his or her workstation before hiding it in a locker. When the employee is asked to open the locker, the employee refuses and states that the search violates his or her fourth amendment rights. What should the company do next and why?

a. The company cannot search the locker. This violates the employee's rights.
b. Management should search the locker. The employee gives up certain rights when at work.
c. The company should call the police and report the crime. Only they would be legally able to search the locker.
d. The employee should be allowed to return to work. There is no proof to corroborate the theft.

71. To attract better talent for management positions, the manager of ABC Company wants to build an employer brand. What would NOT be a successful element to developing this brand?

  a. Publishing a company values statement
  b. Instituting an ethics policy forbidding corrupt behaviors
  c. Promoting a culture that values profitability
  d. Developing and enforcing a health and safety policy

72. Of the answers listed, which is NOT an unfair employer labor practice under the National Labor Relations Act?

  a. A manager calls a meeting with hourly workers to discuss the negative impact unionizing will have on the company.
  b. The CEO orders supervisors to report any employee that is heard talking of unionization.
  c. The company's policy requires all managers to be non-union members.
  d. Management refuses to bargain with the union due to unreasonable requests.

73. Operations Manager Sarah approaches the HR manager about her desire to mentor new managers on the team. The HR manager thinks this is an excellent idea but asks Sarah what "mentoring" means to her. What would be the best definition Sarah could provide?

  a. A mentor measures a new manager's performance based on company-approved metrics.
  b. A mentor watches over a new employee to be sure he or she does not make mistakes.
  c. A mentor trains someone new to the job.
  d. A mentor takes an interest in a coworker's career and guides him or her toward success.

74. An employee comes to you, the HR manager, and states that he or she would like to be moved from a night shift to a day shift because he or she needs to care for a young child. This employee has a good work record and no past disciplinary actions. What would be the best course of action, if any, in this situation?

  a. Explain to the employee that it is not the HR manager's responsibility to get involved in shift designations.
  b. Ask the employee for proof that their child needs daytime care.
  c. Contact management about the situation and encourage discussion on the matter.
  d. Since the employee needs to care for their child, advise management that the shift change request must be granted.

75. Of the answers listed, which is NOT a benefit of having an Employee Assistance Program (EAP)?

  a. Reduction in employee absenteeism
  b. Increased workplace morale
  c. Higher productivity and output
  d. Lower fringe benefit costs

76. The HR manager of ABC Company, Tyler, has reviewed ABC's compensation strategy. He strongly believes that adding a voluntary benefit to the compensation strategy will improve employee morale and retention. Of the answers listed, what voluntary benefit would best achieve the goal?

  a. More paid time off
  b. Dental insurance
  c. Cafeteria plans
  d. Company retirement plans

77. The HR team at your company is debating what type of candidate screening tool is best to use during the next employee search. Out of the four options suggested by the team, which would be best and why?

  a. Employee referral
  b. Job application
  c. Résumé
  d. Screening interviews

78. An HR manager wants to build an onboarding program that focuses on training employees to proficiency prior to putting them in their roles. The HR manager believes this will be good for the company, but the owner is concerned about the cost of the program. What benefit of the program is most likely to persuade the owner to allow it?

  a. Decreased recruitment and job advertisement costs
  b. Increased productivity due to better employee knowledge, skills, and abilities
  c. Decreased chance of employee injury
  d. Increased cooperation between new and experienced employees

79. The new HR manager at ABC Company has just learned that there is no performance appraisal system in place. She is told by management that employees receive a 2% cost-of-living adjustment per year, and that there are no pay raises based on performance. Is there anything wrong with this system? Why or why not?

  a. No. The system is fair since everyone receives the same yearly pay increase.
  b. Yes. There is no incentive for an employee to perform well since there is no reward for higher performance.
  c. No. Performance appraisals are subjective in nature and should not be used to determine pay increases.
  d. Yes. Federal employment laws dictate that employees must receive a yearly performance appraisal.

80. An employer contacts the HR manager of ABC Company asking for an applicant reference. The applicant, Joe, had a poor work record with ABC due to numerous disciplinary actions. Joe resigned his position prior to being terminated by the company. What should the HR manager tell the employer wanting the reference?

  a. Avoid mentioning that Joe was almost terminated but advise the employer not to hire Joe because of his poor work history.
  b. Advise the employer that Joe resigned and provide basic employment information from his HR file.
  c. Decline to speak about Joe.
  d. Advise the employer that Joe would have been terminated if he had not resigned first.

81. You have been asked to sit on an interview board to hire a new operations manager for your company. Which of the following would NOT be an appropriate job-related question to ask the interviewee?

  a. Would you be willing to relocate if asked to by the company?
  b. Have you had any medical issues in the past that would prevent you from properly doing the job?
  c. Is there anything that would prevent you from meeting work deadlines or schedules?
  d. Are you authorized to work in the United States?

82. The general manager of ABC Company wants to conduct an audit of the Human Resources department to ensure there are no deficiencies that need to be corrected. Which answer is NOT a function that would be included in the audit and why?

a. Evaluating HR policies and procedures
b. Determining if all employee records are being kept secure and up to date
c. Identifying employees that are low performers through HR files
d. Evaluating possible cost savings within the HR department

83. The manager is considering putting all sales staff on a commission-based compensation plan. He asks you, the HR manager, what the benefits of having employees on this type of compensation plan would be. What is the correct answer?

a. Commission provides incentive to perform.
b. Commission helps keep payroll taxes low.
c. Commission-based sales staff will always perform better than non-commission-based sales staff.
d. Commission-based sales staff will not perform as well as non-commission-based staff.

84. ABC Company wants to provide workers with non-compensatory benefits. Company management believes this will help recruit and retain quality employees. The HR manager recommends implementing a Flexible Spending Account (FSA) that provides reimbursement to employees for health and wellness activities. Which of the following would NOT be reimbursable under a standard FSA?

a. Acupuncture
b. Psychiatric care
c. Durable medical equipment
d. A gym membership

85. The manager of a marketing firm asks you, the HR manager, to define the term "mission statement." What is the best definition for "mission statement" you can provide the manager?

a. It describes the organization's goals, operations, and how the organization is different from other companies.
b. It inspires stakeholders to believe in the organization and provides information about the organization's future.
c. It communicates the values and ethical policies of the organization.
d. It explains what the organization does best.

86. You, as the HR manager of your organization, are approached by the general manager. He explains that he wants to train office workers on a new computer program that the company has adopted. Time will be made during their normal work hours to perform the training. What is the most efficient and cost-effective type of training in this situation?

a. Self-study
b. Classroom
c. Virtual training
d. Distance learning

87. Which of the following would be the best benefit of promoting from within the organization?

   a. Recruitment costs would be lowered due to less advertising.
   b. Management could evaluate candidates over an extended period.
   c. It would prevent employee morale from being lowered.
   d. Training costs would be lowered since current employees are already familiar with the company.

88. John, a machinist at ABC Company, trips on a hazard in the plant and breaks his leg. The injury requires hospitalization and X-rays. As the HR manager, what should you do and why?

   a. Do nothing. There was no fatality or amputation that would require notification to OSHA.
   b. Log the injury on OSHA's 300A form in the near future. The injury required hospitalization, so this is a recordable injury, but it does not require immediate notification.
   c. Contact the regional office of the Department of Labor and notify them of the incident.
   d. Contact OSHA about the incident immediately. All injuries that happen in the workplace require notification.

89. The CEO of a paper company has decided to shut down one of its mills that employs 110 people. As the HR manager of that mill, what must you do next?

   a. Offer severance packages to senior supervisors.
   b. Give all employees at least 60 days' notice of the mill closing.
   c. Do nothing. The mill closing is an upper management decision.
   d. Offer positions at other mills for high-performing employees.

90. You are the new HR manager at ABC Company. You learn there is no formal performance appraisal system at the organization. The manager explains that all pay increases are based on the opinions of the employees' supervisors. Is this an effective compensation strategy? Why or why not?

   a. No. There should be a formal process for pay increases.
   b. Yes. Since the supervisors witness the employees' work, it is best they determine compensation increases.
   c. No. The company manager should determine if the employees receive a merit increase.
   d. Yes. This method will increase production since employees will be actively trying to impress their supervisors.

Answer Key and Explanations for Test #3

1. C: Answer C, if listed in the job advertisement, would be a form of age discrimination. No job description or advertisement should discourage older people from applying. The other answers would be legitimate and legal questions to be answered by potential applicants. Answer A would be applicable since the laborer position requires lifting and physicality. Answer B would be relevant because an employer is allowed to have educational requirements. Answer D would apply if the employee would be required to read materials or receive orders from their supervisors in English.

2. B: If ABC Company hires Dan as a security guard, this would be negligent hiring. Negligent hiring occurs when an employer either fails to check an applicant's criminal history or disregards knowledge of an applicant's criminal history. Since ABC Company has knowledge of Dan's violent past, he should not be hired as a security guard, contrary to what answer D suggests. Based on the conviction, he should not be in close contact with employees and visitors during his workday, as this might create the threat of a violent altercation. Hiring him for a different position where he would generally be away from others, as answer C suggests, is not advisable. Even in this case, he would inevitably have to work with others periodically, during which times he could still pose a threat. Having Dan sign a promissory letter stating that he will not harm anyone, as answer A suggests, would not be sufficient to protect the company and its employees.

3. B: An ethics policy should be adopted by companies that desire to hold their employees' conduct to a high standard. Ethical policies apply to all members of the organization, including upper management. Should the ethics policy be violated, disciplinary action should be consistent so that the policy is taken seriously. Answer A is not correct, since there are no government regulations concerning ethics policies. It is completely up to the organization to adopt an ethics policy. Answer C is also incorrect. Ethics policies should not be implemented simply for public image. Rather, ethics policies should be implemented because organizations want employees to behave in an appropriate and lawful way. Answer D is not correct, because an ethics policy should never take the place of a disciplinary action program. Violations of the ethics policy should trigger some sort of disciplinary action.

4. C: HR should speak with both parties and advise them that their relationship is a conflict of interest due to the supervisor-subordinate relationship. Once explained, one of the parties should be reassigned so that the conflict no longer exists. Favoritism or ethical violations may occur if the work relationship is not addressed. Simply warning the couple, as answer B suggests, is not advisable. This warning does nothing to help mitigate the risk of the relationship causing disruptions within the organization. Answer A is also incorrect. Unless the organization has a written policy forbidding relationships among employees, no one can be terminated in this scenario. Answer D is incorrect, since it would not be a violation of privacy for the HR department to ask about the relationship. It is the responsibility of HR to inquire about these issues once they are brought to the company's attention.

5. B: The company is not liable for a negligent act when an employee is to blame. If the negligent employee had followed the policies, the injury might not have occurred; therefore, the company was not negligent in this situation. Answer A is incorrect. A company is not responsible for an injury just because it happens on their property. There must be a negligent act by the company before any liability is assumed. Answer C is incorrect because policies cannot physically ensure that no injuries will occur; policies can only establish approved procedures to assist in protecting workers from injuries. Answer D is not correct, since companies can be liable for accidents if there is evidence of negligence or disregard for safety.

6. B: The HR manager should advise Caroline that her job will be held for her until she is able to return. The company should allow Caroline to use all her paid time off so that she may receive some form of compensation. This decision is based on the size of ABC's workforce. Any company with 50 or more employees must comply with the Family Medical Leave Act (FMLA), which states that an employee's job must be held for certain medical occurrences, even if those medical occurrences pertain to family members. Answer D is not correct, because the company is not mandated to pay Caroline if she is not working; they only have to hold her job. Answers A and C are both incorrect because Caroline's situation is clearly covered under FMLA.

7. C: Employers cannot discriminate or terminate employees for engaging in unionization activities. To terminate an employee for this, the company would be willingly violating the National Labor Relations Act. Answer A, a business closure, is common in the world of business and does account for many termination decisions. Employees should expect terminations for this reason. Employees should also expect terminations due to labor outsourcing, as referenced in answer B, when economic conditions make it difficult for the organization to operate. Termination for insubordinate behavior, answer C, is generally expected by employees who engage in that activity; therefore, it is not readily disputed.

8. D: Risk management is a business function commonly relegated to the Human Resources department, but it is not a factor in workforce planning. Forecasting needs (answer A) allows the organization to prepare for larger or smaller workloads and can directly impact the workforce. As expressed in answer B, a process should be in place to identify qualified and talented employees so that a steady stream of potential candidates is available to fill important positions. Only by having detailed and accurate job analyses and descriptions, as outlined in answer D, can an HR or management representative pair the right job with the right candidate. Ambiguous or vague job descriptions may cause the wrong candidates to be selected for the position.

9. A: Having multiple roles within the financial sector of the organization will prohibit a single employee from handling all deposits, invoices, payments, etc. This separation acts as a "checks and balances" system for each role, which will discourage any unethical behavior. Having written policies (answer B) can show that the company is serious about ethics and that they will take action against unethical behavior, but it does not actively suppress any type of unethical behavior. Computerization (answer C) will allow management and supervisors to see the financials and monitor them more closely, but these numbers can be easily manipulated as well. Audits (answer D) can be effective; however, there will be periods of time between these. Much money could be embezzled before an audit is performed, leaving the company in financial duress.

10. C: Any government contractor or subcontractor with 50 or more employees, or $50,000 or more in government contracts, must have an Affirmative Action Policy. Based on this requirement, ABC Company must comply since the contract is for $100,000. Answer A would not be correct, because the number of employees requirement is made null by the monetary value of the contract. Answer B is incorrect because not all government contractors have 50 or more employees or contracts worth more than $50,000. Answer D would also not be correct, because the Affirmative Action Policy covers any contracted work for the government. The type of work does not matter in this situation.

11. B: The company can implement any policy that is reasonable and applicable to the operation. Ordering employees not to bring their phones with them into the workplace is not unreasonable, since management is concerned about the effect phones will have on safety. Because companies have the right to implement reasonable policies like this, answer A is incorrect. Answer C is incorrect because the lack of possessing a phone while at work would not lead to an unfair workplace where the employee is forced to work under harsh or unsafe conditions. Answer D could be correct, but only if the rules are fair and legal. Employees should not be expected to perform any task or behave in any way that is unsafe, unethical, or illegal.

12. A: The company should pay each employee for the overtime hours worked. It is management's responsibility to ensure that the swaps are performed correctly and that the correct compensation is provided to the employees. Answer B is not correct, because the shift swap was approved by the company. This approval is acknowledgement of the swap; therefore, the company is responsible for compensating the employees. Answer C is incorrect because comp time is given by the company when employees work in excess of their normal hours at the direction of the company. This shift swap does not fall into this category, since both employees agreed to work for each other. The employees should not be paid double-time pay as answer D suggests. Double-time pay is given to hourly employees when they must work on an observed holiday. The situation in question would fall under the overtime rules of time-and-a-half compensation.

13. C: ABC Company should have a company policy concerning raises based on performance appraisals. This policy would give set times that employees could expect performance or cost-of-living increases. Doing this would cut down on employees asking for raises throughout the year. Based on these scheduled appraisals, answer A would not be correct. It would not be necessary to speak to Johnny's supervisors if the performance appraisal is conducted in two months. Answer B would not be wise, since it is not an HR manager's direct responsibility to give pay increases. Recommendations for employees' pay increases should come from members of management. Answer D would not apply either due to the scheduled performance appraisal. Johnny could speak with management about a raise at any time, but management should support the performance appraisal pay increase policy.

14. B: The employee should be ordered to remove the weapon from the property. Employees must follow lawful rules of their workplace, and disciplinary action should result if the rules are not followed. If the company does not want firearms on the premises, they have a right to demand they be removed, contrary to what answer A suggests. Answer C could be correct in this situation, but law enforcement should only be called when employees are no longer under control of management. Should this employee refuse to leave the premises after being told to do so or after being terminated, the police should respond to control the situation. Answer D would not be correct, as the policies or rules of an organization should be followed every day. Allowing the employee to disregard the manager's order today will allow other employees to demand they receive the same "warning" in the future.

15. A: A job description is for informational purposes only and is not an employment contract. A supervisor may order an employee to perform a task if the task is reasonable. For instance, a forklift operator may be asked to sweep the area where the forklifts are operating. Sweeping may not be in the forklift operator's job description, but sweeping the floor so the forklifts will not run over debris is completely reasonable. Answer C would not be correct, as an HR representative is expected to investigate employee concerns. Turning the employees away without providing an answer concerning the complaint is not advisable. Answers B and D are not correct, since the complaint is not legitimate. There are no legal reasons for the employees not to perform the task, and the supervisor does not have to have an employee's consent to ask them to perform a task outside of a job description.

16. C: Being Caucasian is not a bona fide qualification for employment as a gas station clerk. Race would not impact the ability of the new hire to perform the job in any neighborhood. Answer A would be a BFOQ since many religions believe that only males can be ministers in the church. Answer B would fall into the same category since convicted felons are unable to carry firearms, pursuant to federal law. The ability to carry a firearm would be a BFOQ in this situation. Having a computer science degree, as mentioned in answer D, would also be a BFOQ. Formal education in the field of programming would be necessary at most software companies. The educational requirement shows the applicant has a working knowledge of programming and software.

17. A: It is unlawful to ask an employee if he or she is a U.S. citizen. The interviewer may, however, ask the interviewee if he or she is authorized to work in the United States. The other three questions are acceptable and commonly used in modern interviews.

18. A: The HR manager cannot discuss union matters with members of the union. There will be clauses in the labor agreement prohibiting management from interfering with union activities. The employee should address the representation issue with higher ranking members of the union. Answer B would not be correct, since the NLRB should be contacted by members of the union. It would not be wise for the HR manager to contact the union leader, as advised in answer C, as this would most likely be seen as interference from the company in union matters. Under no circumstance should the HR manager try to influence the employee to withdraw from the union as expressed in answer D. This would be seen as management interfering with union activities.

19. D: Any violations of company policies and rules should be formally documented. Allowing an employee to disregard rules and policies because of their high performance is not a wise business decision. This action could potentially cause a breakdown in discipline that could work itself throughout the staff. Answer A, which advocates for not addressing the issue, shows a lack of managerial courage. A good manager should address bad behavior so that employees are well-informed of their performance, whether it be good or bad. Answer B, verbal counseling, is not recommended. Since verbal counseling is not documented, anything the employee or supervisor says during the session can be misconstrued. Answer C is not appropriate in this situation. The supervisor that witnessed and noted the violation should administer disciplinary action. Although Human Resources is responsible for administering policies involving human capital, the supervisor is ultimately responsible for maintaining discipline and correcting their subordinates.

20. C: It would be unwise for a company with a recruiting program to abolish it completely. The program can be scaled back to save on costs but kept active to address unexpected staffing needs. Discontinuing the program (answer A) will save the company money in the short term, but restarting it from scratch when the need arises will be costly. Also, eliminating the program may cause talented recruiters to leave the organization in search of other work. Keeping the program fully funded and running when there is a slowdown in hiring, as outlined in answer B, is not recommended. This will incur unnecessary costs that may hurt ABC's profits. Changing the program to only recruit from within the organization, as recommended in answer D, is also a poor choice. Since the program has been successful, it should not be changed. This may damage the value of the recruitment program for future implementation.

21. C: Team learning is based on members engaging with each other. The engagement in the learning atmosphere encourages engagement in everyday work duties. Engaged employees tend to be more productive and enthusiastic about their jobs. Team learning should not be used as an internal recruitment tool as outlined in answer A. If employees find out that the purpose of the team exercise is to showcase their talents, the learning atmosphere will be compromised. An organization should not use team learning solely to save money, contrary to what answer B suggests. Although costs may be lessened by putting employees in large groups, employees will fail to engage in the program if they learn it is only being used to save money. Also, in team learning, the group will be made up of employees from similar positions. It is not advisable to mix management and employees together as answer D suggests. These types of groups generally do not create a good learning environment, as, in them, employees may feel less comfortable sharing their ideas with the group for fear of retribution.

22. C: Although this answer seems like it would help the family, ABC should allow the employee and his or her family to find new physicians themselves. To register the employee and his or her family members with new physicians, the HR department would have to request private medical information and records, which violates health privacy laws. All the other answers are common practices associated with relocation assistance. Many HR departments work with new employees to find them housing, reimburse moving expenses, and provide spousal employment assistance. This type of onboarding policy helps ensure the employee is focused on their new job and comfortable in their new surroundings.

23. D: Surveying the employees about the proposed change will be counterproductive to its implementation, since the employees may formulate uninformed beliefs prior to knowing the plan's details. Answer A is important to change management because any change should be planned and thoroughly researched. It is also important that the organization gets the support of its supervisors prior to implementing the change, as answer B suggests. Employees tend to believe what they hear from their direct supervisors; therefore, supervisors who respond positively to the change will motivate their employees to do the same. Answer C is also important. Upper management should be enthusiastic and openly supportive of the change. Should word get out that management is not supportive of the change, employees will not support it either. This will cause the plan to fail.

24. D: Jacob would receive call-back pay for coming in early. This compensation is provided to employees when they come in before or after normal hours. On-call pay, answer B, is provided when an employee comes in for coverage on their day off. Answer C, compensatory time (or comp time), is not a monetary compensation type; it is an arrangement that allows employees extra time off if they work extra hours. Double-time pay, answer A, would be compensation at twice the employee's hourly rate and not applicable in this situation. This type of compensation generally occurs only if the employee works on company-recognized holidays.

25. B: The incident should be investigated by HR. The witness's statement can be used in connection with other collected information to determine what happened. Answer A is not correct, because every incident involving an injury should be investigated and documented to ensure there are no active safety issues that could harm other employees. Answer C is not appropriate, because the witness's testimony is not enough information to make an informed decision on the matter and begin disciplinary action. Answer D is incorrect because only government employees are subject to lie detector tests. As an employee of a private company, the witness cannot be given a lie detector test.

26. A: Employees with talent for supervision should be recruited from within the company. If an employee is willing to take on the responsibility of a supervisory position, he or she should be offered leadership and organizational training. This strategy ensures that there are qualified employees ready to take the place of exiting supervisors. Answer B would not be advisable, because offering higher salaries to the retiring supervisors is only a short-term solution. The managers must eventually leave, placing the company in the same situation as before. Answer C suggests hiring applicants from outside of the company that may fit into the supervisory roles. This is not the best solution, since current employees know what the company desires and are already knowledgeable in what the company wants from their supervisors. Also, hiring supervisors from outside may hurt the morale of employees wishing to gain promotions. Combining departments, as outlined in answer D, would cause excessive workloads for talented supervisors, potentially causing them to leave the organization.

27. A: Profit sharing would not help the current situation, since this compensation strategy is based on revenues generated by the company. Overtime opportunities would be good for the employees but may cause the company financial hardship due to higher-than-normal payroll costs. Also, more overtime would be detrimental to the employees' work-life balance. A health plan may help the employees during times of sickness, but it does not address the current issue of decreased buying power due to inflation; therefore, answer A would be correct. A cost-of-living adjustment would keep employees' pay consistent with inflation, thereby helping the employees navigate through any financial hardships.

28. B: The HR manager should research similar companies that have employed customer service training programs, then use his or her findings to show the costs and benefits of the training to management. Management's primary focus is growing the organization's value; therefore, to garner management's support for the idea, the HR manager must provide facts and statistics that indicate the program will add value to the organization. Answer A would not be correct, as recommending the web-based training without providing an estimation of its costs and benefits would likely fail to convince management of its usefulness. Answer C is an opinion from the HR manager not backed by statistical evidence.

29. B: Performance appraisals should be standardized companywide. If performance appraisals are conducted differently in each department, as answer A suggests, one group of employees may be appraised higher or lower than another group of employees. This is not a fair practice and should be forbidden.

30. C: The plumber is an independent contractor. Although ABC is the plumber's only customer, he uses his own tools and equipment to perform his job. If the plumber were on ABC's payroll, then the hours worked in this scenario would matter; however, hours worked by an independent contractor are irrelevant to full-time or part-time employment status.

31. C: One major disadvantage of a tuition reimbursement program is that it generates paperwork for the administration. This increased workload leads to higher payroll costs, which can add up for the company. A company with a reimbursement program is attractive to potential hires, as noted in answer A. Applicants will feel that their education is valued and appreciated by an employer who is willing to help pay for it. Current employees may stay just for the tuition reimbursement, lowering employee turnover rates (answer B). This helps retain employees, especially those who are educated. An employee will be more apt to take courses to help them attain leadership positions if the education is paid for, resulting in increased leadership development (answer D). Employees who want to educate themselves may shy away from doing so if the cost of the education is a burden on their finances.

32. B: Losing employees that have been with the organization for many years would be detrimental to a workforce's KSAs (knowledge, skills, and abilities). Losing employees with organizational knowledge is likely to cause higher training costs and lower product quality. Organizations should value and retain experienced employees to maintain a qualified workforce. Although answer A would be true, the monetary costs of unemployment benefits would be fixed, whereas the impact of losing KSAs would be variable and ongoing. While answers C and D are drawbacks to the manager's proposed decision, the overall impact of losing the KSAs of senior employees would be far more detrimental than lower morale or higher HR costs. These two drawbacks (C and D) would be temporary, whereas answer B could have long-lasting, detrimental effects.

33. C: Since the supervisor is described as a valuable employee, counseling through an Employee Assistance Program would be the most effective action. The program would help the supervisor control his anger and learn methods of suppressing undesired behavior. The employee with whom the supervisor lost his temper has not filed an official complaint; therefore, it would not be wise to issue a reprimand, like answer B suggests. There is not enough evidence in the situation to determine if any policies have been violated. Answer A does not address the root of the problem, which is the supervisor's control of his temper. Answer D would not be wise, since the supervisor is valued in his role. Prohibiting him from managing employees could cause a loss of talent within the organization.

34. D: Managerial accounting, budgeting, and engineering controls are all important business operations; however, a leadership program should focus on teaching supervisors how to better lead their employees to a desired goal. Of the answers given, only conflict management focuses on leading employees to adequately handle conflict that arises in the workplace.

35. D: All the reasons listed can help an organization. Having a diverse workforce will allow different ideas and perspectives to aid the organization in decision-making, as answer A suggests. To flourish, an organization must be open to new ways of conducting operations. A diversified workforce will help gain customers (answer B). Clients and customers will be more comfortable dealing with representatives they can relate to. This level of comfort can help elevate sales or increase company visibility. If the organization has a reputation for being diverse, more people will apply to work there (answer C). This is because applicants, especially minorities, will feel confident that they will not be discriminated against in the hiring process. If the organization is known to only hire people of one race or gender, it is likely that the applicant pool will only be filled with people of that race or gender.

36. C: Salary and wage surveys are common tools used by HR departments to compare compensation levels in a certain industry. To conduct the survey, ABC's HR department would contact other paper mills and request compensation information on hourly production workers. Typically, in this situation, ABC would share its compensation information with the other companies as well, so there would be a benefit to other companies participating in the survey. The Bureau of Labor Statistics and the state unemployment agency do not provide specific position or localized compensation information, so answers A and B would not be correct. Answer D would not be correct either, since a survey among the employees would not provide compensation statistics from other businesses. Their surveys would only contain opinions of what their compensation should be.

37. B: An HR professional must be willing to help employees, like Trevor, who are having personal or professional problems. There is nothing wrong or improper with asking Trevor about how he is feeling and offering to help him. Answer A is incorrect since it is HR's responsibility to inquire about and monitor the well-being of employees. As answer C suggests, the HR manager should inform upper management about Trevor's changes, but the priority should be addressing the issue with Trevor, not anticipating his failure. HR can take the lead on addressing the situation with Trevor while keeping management advised of the process. To contact Trevor's family (answer D) would be inappropriate in this situation. This action may be seen as a breach of Trevor's privacy and should be avoided.

38. B: The employee did not follow the hardhat policy; therefore, the employee was acting negligently. The company should not be liable for the injury, since the safety policy was violated. Answer A is incorrect because the company is not responsible for an injury just because it occurs on company property. Answer C is not correct either, because accidents will inevitably occur in the workplace, and the hardhat policy was instituted for this purpose. Answer D would not be correct, since the company could be liable for unintentional incidents if negligence is found on the part of the company. Accidents could potentially happen at any business; however, ABC Company would have to be found acting negligently to be liable for this injury.

39. D: The general manager should tell her employees that there will be no mass layoffs. The employees will believe this since it comes from the highest executive at the company. The supervisors' words of reassurance do not hold as much weight as the general manager's. Not addressing the rumors, as answer A suggests, would cause low morale and possibly even turnover. Finding the source of the rumor, answer C, would be helpful to see why the rumor was started and how to prevent it from happening again. This, however, does not help the rumor stop, which is what would be best for the company.

40. C: Supervisory training should entail some form of conflict management and resolution. This is not something routinely taught in business or management classes, as are accounting (answer B) or budgeting (answer C). Receiving tips for success, as advised in answer D, may help the recruit thrive in each department, but this would not be effective at training employees in the core skill required in a supervisory role, which is managing people.

41. B: Since the positions are entry-level, they can be filled by external talent. Experienced managers on site will be able to train the new workers on how to perform their new jobs. Sending existing employees to the new office, as answer A suggests, will create a staffing shortage at the current site. Employees will need to be hired either way if this plan is used. Hiring temporary workers (answer C) would not be wise. The company should hire full-time employees, since opening this office is a long-term goal. Money would be wasted on training temporary workers who will only be there for a short time. The company should not use contract workers like answer D suggests. Contractors generally cost the company more than employees in labor costs. Rates for contractors are generally much higher because they are specialized in a certain area and need little training. This cost could be detrimental to the company during the startup phase of the new office.

42. B: An HR representative should meet with each employee to discuss the layoff. HR personnel are trained for this task and have available resources about unemployment options to share with the employees. Telling the employees via email about a layoff, as expressed in answer A, would not be professional nor would it be compassionate. Being that a layoff is a major life change for an employee, the proper way to handle one is with face-to-face communication. A group meeting with the affected workers, outlined in answer C, is not recommended. The layoff may affect each worker differently, which will require the HR representative to address individual questions and needs. Having supervisors share the news (answer D) is not appropriate. Supervisors are generally tasked with production and management duties outside the realm of administration. They do not have resources available to help laid off employees, nor do they have employees' personal information that would be necessary to help them create a plan after the layoff.

43. C: An organization that employs and follows an ethics policy will benefit in many ways. Good employees will want to work at an organization that promotes fairness and honesty. This will lower turnover and encourage current workers to try their best to help the company grow. Inevitably, a happier and more productive workplace will lead to higher company profits. Although an ethics policy could make the business attractive to potential clients and customers, as answer D suggests, such a policy should not be adopted solely to lure new business. Answer A is not the best answer either, since the concept of ethics goes far beyond theft, and a company should have separate policies for that behavior. Adopting an ethics policy just to keep regulators from inspecting or investigating the company, as answer B suggests, would not be ethical in itself. If the ethics policy is adopted solely for this purpose, it will be hollow and largely ineffective as a tool for improving the company.

44. B: The issue should be investigated to determine if there is a pay discrepancy based on gender discrimination. Federal laws protect against an employer compensating employees based solely on gender. Answer A would not be correct, since there is no verifiable information confirming or denying the allegation. An HR professional should always investigate a situation prior to recommending a course of action. Answer C suggests that the employee should investigate the matter, but this is a function of the HR department. Rumor or not, this allegation must be investigated by the organization and not the employee. Answer D is not correct, as the HR manager should tell the employee that the matter will be investigated internally. The employee has a right to file a complaint with the EEOC, but this is a decision that should be made solely by the employee.

45. A: Job enrichment is a development approach that will provide an employee with new learning opportunities and experiences. This would be the best way to keep talent within the organization. Formal education, expressed in answer B, may help John learn more general skills, but on-the-job assignments will better prepare him for supervisory positions at the company. Answer C would be good for John's morale, but it would not help him prepare for career advancement. It would not be wise to wait for a supervisory position to open before using the job enrichment approach, as expressed in answer D, since John could lose motivation or even change his mind about accepting a supervisory position if the company waits too long before enriching his job.

46. B: The HR manager should recommend that James be tested just like all other prospective employees. Pre-employment drug testing is important for organizations since it can help identify any potential drug users. This will allow the hiring team to make better and safer hiring decisions. Being selective about which employees do and do not test will open the company up to civil liabilities; therefore, answers A and C are incorrect. The HR manager should not openly disobey a manager's orders as answer D suggests. Although the manager's request requires a policy deviation, the HR manager must follow orders from a direct supervisor. In situations like this, it is recommended that the HR manager documents the order and whom it came from.

47. C: Intrinsic compensation is a type of job fulfillment. Job fulfillment is an employee's feelings of satisfaction and happiness with their position. Jerry's positive emotions about being part of the talented group have intrinsic value. Answer A is not correct, since extrinsic compensation is usually given in the form of monetary benefits such as bonuses or pay raises. Answer B, monetary compensation, is the act of paying wages. Commission-based pay, answer D, is a type of compensation that is based on sales revenue. This type of pay is common among sales representatives.

48. B: This situation is unethical and should be investigated. If the organization can prove that the supervisor is receiving gifts for contracts, the supervisor should be disciplined according to policy. Since this behavior is unethical, answers A and C are incorrect. Answer D is also incorrect, as the gifts being monetary or non-monetary is irrelevant. Any gift reception for contract consideration would be an ethics violation.

49. A: Organizations with over 100 employees must file an EEO-1 (Equal Employment Opportunity) report each year. This report must be sent to the EEOC annually. Failure to do so will lead to civil fines. Answers B and C are not legal requirements, though both tools may be used if the organization deems it necessary. Retirement contributions, as outlined in answer D, are a great way to provide a non-compensatory benefit to employees, but the implementation of such a program is completely optional.

50. C: College recruitment fairs would not benefit ABC Company, since the owner wants to hire an experienced manager. College recruitment is appropriate when trying to fill entry-level management positions. Internet job boards (answer A) and social media advertising (answer B) have become increasingly important recruitment tools due to the growth of the World Wide Web. Employers can reach out to millions of potential applicants by using these mediums of advertisement. Company websites can also be beneficial in this situation, as answer D suggests. Applicants can research the company and position when the job is posted on the company's own website. Also, a job posting on a company website tends to be more detailed than posts on online job boards, giving the applicant a better grasp of what the position entails.

51. B: The Employee Polygraph Protection Act of 1988 protects workers in most private industries from being given lie detector tests. Exceptions to this statute are government employees and persons employed with private security companies. Since the employee works at a paper mill in this example, she should not be given a lie detector test. Answers A and C are incorrect because the employee is protected under the law. Answer D would not be correct, since the company should investigate the accusation prior to making any decisions. An accusation is not enough evidence to terminate an employee.

52. B: Without research on the regional labor market, an informed decision cannot be made on the new facility's compensation structure. Workers who live near the new facility may have higher or lower costs of living than workers at the existing facility. This will have a large impact on determining appropriate pay scales. Although compensating the employees equally seems fair, the value of the wage could be vastly different between the facilities; therefore, answer A would not be correct. Answer C would be appropriate if there were compensation discrepancies at the existing site, but this tactic would not be beneficial in determining pay scales at the new site. Answer D could be a good way to get the facility staffed quickly, but without research on what is considered good pay in that region, there is no way to determine how much to pay the new employees.

53. B: Withholding both state and federal taxes from an employee's paycheck is a legal requirement. Employees and employers have no choice in this matter, which would make answers A and C incorrect. Failure to withhold taxes would cause the company trouble with the state and federal tax authorities. Although company policies should always be followed when dealing with compensation matters, as answer D suggests, the legal requirement in this scenario takes precedent over any company policy.

54. C: The HR manager is like any other employee in this scenario, in that a recognized hazard should be controlled or reported by anyone at the site. If the HR manager could barricade the stairs or mark the step with warning tape, this would help raise awareness of the hazard until the safety department could be notified. Answer A is not the best choice, because simply notifying the safety manager does not eliminate the current danger of the hazard. Answer B suggests that only the safety manager is responsible for eliminating or identifying hazards; however, all employees are obligated to act on safety concerns. There is nothing wrong with the HR manager notifying his or her supervisor as suggested by option D; however, the issue should be addressed to the safety manager immediately. Since the HR manager can contact Safety themselves, the added communication of notifying the supervisor may slow the process of fixing the step.

55. B: An internship program would allow ABC Company to evaluate and monitor potential candidates year-round. As students graduate, new students will enter the program. This would lead to a stream of potential hires who have already shown their talents. Allowing current employees to take training, like answer A suggests, can be costly due to ongoing training and payroll costs. An employee who is not interested may even sign up for the training just to avoid performing his or her normal duties. Answer C has drawbacks as well. Just because an employee is high-performing does not mean he or she wishes to manage other employees. Assigning these employees to fill in as managers may lower their morale or cause lower productivity among the workers. Answer D is not a good idea, because an organization should only take applications for a position during a specified time frame. Allowing applicants to apply indefinitely for a spot that is already filled will lead to fewer applicants in the future. Interested parties seeking employment will choose to work elsewhere if they are not contacted about their application soon after they submit it.

56. A: Management should prepare the employees for the change prior to implementation. This would mean explaining the necessity for the change and providing details on how it would be implemented. These actions would lead to employee buy-in, which would help the change succeed. Answers B and C would help implement the change, but these would not help influence employees to buy into the initiative. Only through employees believing in the initiative will it be successful. Demanding compliance, as outlined in answer D, would cause employees to resist the change. They will not believe in a plan that is forced on them without explanation.

57. B: Under the Health Insurance Portability and Accountability Act (HIPAA), an employer cannot disseminate any information concerning an employee's health records. For this reason, answers A and C are incorrect. Although the employee could give the manager access to their medical records, as answer D suggests, the manager should not ask. In order to preserve medical record confidentiality, the HR manager should dissuade any manager from requesting access to employee health information.

58. D: Although compensation surveys may be a good tool for the HR department in compensation analysis, it does not help with building an effective workforce planning program. A workforce planning program focuses on how the organization can maintain a pool of qualified individuals who can fill important roles. The other three answers can be used during this process. A job analysis, answer A, defines a job so that potential candidates for the position understand its goals and objectives. Identification of qualified employees, answer B, is also important since management should attempt to locate talent within the organization. A talented employee can be trained while on the job for future openings that are crucial to the organization. Establishment of a workforce planning goal, answer C, is the most important step in the process, as no program should be implemented without first stating an intended goal.

59. B: The company must thoroughly explain to the employees that the suggestion box is being used to improve the company. The company should then set clear parameters for its use. These parameters will give the employees an outline for an acceptable submission and deter employees from using the box as a receptacle for complaints and pranks. Having suggestion boxes easily accessible to employees, as suggested in answer A, is only beneficial if the employees have been motivated and encouraged to use them. If supervisors order their employees to use the boxes, as expressed in answer C, the practice will no longer be voluntary for the employees. The suggestion box will then be seen as a commanded responsibility, and it will lose its benefit. The company should not use the suggestion box to reward employees (answer D). If this occurs, some employees may try to use the box to gain status or promotion. This will delegitimize the process, and employees will stop contributing.

60. A: If an employee feels he or she is being discriminated against or being treated unfairly, HR should investigate the matter. These types of allegations should be taken seriously to mitigate the potential risk of civil lawsuits. The employee sharing his concerns about the issue is not being insubordinate, since he is not disobeying orders; therefore, answer B is incorrect. If an employee desires to speak with his or her supervisor about unfair treatment, as answer C suggests, this should be allowed but not encouraged by HR. The employee may not want to do this for fear of retribution or further unfair treatment. Answer D suggests that HR should listen to the complaint but take no action. This is not an appropriate way to handle the situation, since taking no action on a legitimate issue may open the company up for "failure to act" lawsuits.

61. A: Best practice standards are methods that have been proven to produce desired results. Once a process or procedure has been identified as successful, many organizations implement it companywide. Mandating training (answer B) can be an effective knowledge management method; however, employees may have no interest in the training or feel it is not pertinent to their current jobs. This attitude will make the training less effective. Requiring formal education for certain positions, as expressed in answer C, may ensure that the hire is trainable, but job-specific training will still need to be given by the organization prior to seeing any positive results from the employee. Formal education alone is not a guarantee of successful knowledge management. Employee evaluations (answer D) would not be the most effective knowledge management method, since there would be too many opinions from the employees on how to effect positive change. Management should always lead the efforts based on their own research and policies.

62. D: The National Labor Relations Act prohibits management from interfering with unionization by promising workers better compensation. No promises or pledges can be made to employees to attempt to sway them away from trying to unionize. The act of telling employees the company's stance on unionization, as outlined in answer A, is allowed. This would be a true statement from the company; therefore, it is allowed under the NLRA. Answers B and C follow along these same lines, as telling employees factual statements about the union or the union's responsibility to the employee is not seen as interference.

63. B: Since the training can be taken online, it would be most cost-efficient to have each employee take the training when they have, or are allotted, time to do so. Asynchronous training will allow the employees to complete the training at their own pace, and the company will not have to pay an instructor to be present to train each employee. This can be a major cost-saving tool for the company. In-house group training (answer A) would not be advisable, since numerous employees would be tied up during the workday. This may slow production or cause excessive payroll costs due to overtime incurred by covering the shifts for the training workers. Having an on-site instructor to train each employee, as outlined in answer C, would be time-consuming and costly, since the instructor would have to be paid for their time. Group training after normal business hours, suggested in answer D, would force the company to incur overtime costs. If ABC is looking to save money, this would not be a good recommendation.

64. A: Although Jason and the new sales representative can agree on any compensation structure listed in the answer section, the most common form for an employee engaged in sales is commission-based pay. In commission-based pay, an employee is compensated based on the number of sales made. This number may be calculated based on units sold, volume of sales, or contracts signed. It is advisable that the employer and employee agree on how the commission will be calculated before any sales are made.

65. C: The manager should have advised the staff of the proposed change prior to its implementation. Explaining why the change is important to the company and the employees would have fostered employee buy-in. If the employees could have been persuaded that the schedule change was good, there would have been little opposition. Without the employees believing that the change is positive, it will be hard to have a successful transition. Answer A would have let the staff know about the schedule, but it would not have silenced the opposition to the plan. The employees in this scenario would have still been upset with the fact that they were being forced to accept the change. Answer B would have negative long-term effects. Employees would feel that they were paid off to accept the change. The pay increase would keep the opposition silent for the short term, but it would not solve the root cause of the problem. Making no change, as outlined in answer D, is not a good managerial decision. It is the manager's duty to increase profitability and growth. If a new schedule helps this occur, it needs to be instituted; however, the manager in this scenario instituted the change poorly.

66. D: The HR manager can help Emily complete the form; however, the information must be acknowledged by Emily with a signature. It is recommended that the employee complete the form independently if able, but it is not uncommon for employees to request assistance from HR managers or supervisors. Declining to help Emily, as answer B suggests, is not advisable. Some employees may be illiterate or uncomfortable trying to understand the form. Answer A is not correct, because the HR manager should not complete the form for Emily without her involvement. It is also improper for the HR manager to openly question the employee's ability to complete the W-4, as answer C suggests. This could embarrass Emily early on in her career and lower her morale prior to beginning work.

67. C: A Human Resources manager is expected to help retain quality employees. The best course of action would be to speak with the employee and see if there is anything that can be done to keep him employed. If the employee is open to negotiation, management should be advised of this. Doing nothing to retain the employee, as answer A and B suggest, is not a professional response to the situation and would be a disservice to the organization. Answer D would not be an appropriate response to the situation either. At a minimum, the HR professional needs to acknowledge the employee's intentions. Not doing so may make the employee feel underappreciated and cause them to be unwilling to consider wage negotiations.

68. C: It is illegal for a company to pay their employees less than their state's minimum wage. This should never be done. While lowering the employees' pay would save costs, as answers A and D suggest, this would violate state and federal labor laws.

69. A: Exit interviews usually take place between an HR professional and an employee leaving the company. Interviewees can provide their honest thoughts on the organization without fear of retaliation. The company can use this honest feedback to assess the employment situation within the organization. The other three answers can be effective communication tools, but, with them, employees are less likely to give their honest opinions.

70. B: The company has a legal right to search the employee's locker. Fourth amendment rights only pertain to governmental searches; therefore, answer A is incorrect. Answer C, calling law enforcement, should not be management's first choice. Should the employee become combative or refuse to leave the property, law enforcement should be contacted. It is best, however, to try to handle employee theft administratively prior to involving the authorities. Also, law enforcement searches fall under fourth amendment protections. Answer D suggests the issue should be disregarded, but this approach is not advisable. All incidents regarding theft should be investigated so that the company shows it strictly forbids this behavior.

71. C: Companies that promote profit over their employees, customers, or the environment are not socially responsible. Employers wanting to build a successful brand should place ethical and safe business practices ahead of profits. Answer A would be a good element of a branding plan since a published statement shows the company is serious about its values. An ethics policy, as outlined in answer B, would hold employees and managers accountable for bad behavior. This helps branding by showing the employer is serious about the company rules and government regulations. A health and safety policy, referenced in answer D, is good for employer branding as well. Instituting this policy shows the employer is concerned for their employees' well-being. These policies put safety ahead of production, which allows employees to feel more comfortable on the job.

72. C: It is legal for the company to require their managers to abstain from participating in union activities. Most, if not all, unions agree to this policy so there will be no conflicts of interest between the two parties. A manager cannot restrain a group from wanting to unionize like answer A suggests. This is strictly forbidden by the NLRA. Requiring supervisors to report employees who talk of unionization, as outlined in answer B, is not allowed by the NLRA since the NLRA forbids companies from "spying" on their employees. Any talk between employees about unionizing is a protected activity. Refusing to bargain with the union (answer C) is not allowed either. Should the union request a bargaining agreement, the company must meet with the union. Any request must be heard by both parties, regardless of how either group views its reasonableness.

73. D: Answers A, B, and C are all management functions that deal with training or supervising employees. These answers are common functions performed daily by managers. Only answer D properly fits the description of mentorship. A true mentor wants to help the employee grow and be successful with no expectation of reward.

74. C: The HR manager has a responsibility to take the matter to the company's management. Since the employee has a good record, it may benefit the company to switch the employee's shift; however, the company is not legally bound to make any switch. The HR manager should not dismiss the employee without listening to their problem (answer A). Although it is not HR's responsibility to manage shift assignments, bettering the employee's situation may lead them to be more productive while at work. It is not advisable to ask the employee in this situation for proof of the childcare need as answer B suggests. This could be construed as mistrust of the employee, which could lead to low morale. Management is not bound to move the employee because of the childcare need like answer D suggests. The HR manager should advise management of the situation but not demand any change be made, as there is no legal obligation to do so.

75. D: An EAP is a fringe benefit paid for by the company. Implementing this program will lead to increased costs for the company, since much of it is outsourced to licensed professionals. EAPs have been shown to lead to lower absenteeism, higher productivity, and increased workplace morale. Proponents of EAPs state that employees with high morale and good mental health will perform better, which will improve the company's profitability.

76. A: Voluntary benefits are perks that organizations are not required to provide. These are used to increase employee satisfaction and wellness. For this situation, more paid time off (PTO) would raise employee morale and retention. More PTO would improve the employees' work-life balance and provide more rest opportunities. Answers B, C, and D are excellent benefits but are very common among organizations today. Employees expect these as standard benefits, whereas PTO tends to differ in its amount and usage between organizations.

77. B: Any of the answers may be used by an organization as screening tools; however, a job application is best. The job application is filled out on a standard form created by the company so that each applicant is asked for the same information. Résumés can come in numerous forms, which means applicants could leave out information the hiring team may want to see. Employee referrals are not optimal due to the presence of bias. Screening interviews can overburden the hiring team since there is no ability to weed out applicants unworthy of an interview.

78. B: An employee who is trained prior to starting work will be more productive. This increased productivity will inevitably lead to greater profits, which may be attractive to the owner. Also, higher profits will offset the costs of the program. This answer will be the most persuasive to the owner since he or she is primarily worried about costs. Answer A would not be correct, because the onboarding program would have nothing to do with employee recruitment. Answers C and D would be benefits to the program, but answer B is most likely to persuade the owner due to his or her financial focus.

79. B: A performance appraisal allows opportunities for employees to make higher compensation within their respective positions. If ABC only has cost-of-living increases, as answer A suggests, employees have no incentive to perform above minimum standards. C is incorrect because if the performance appraisal is proper and effective, it will not be subjective. If ABC's management decides to use a performance appraisal, they should structure the appraisal so that it does not allow subjectivity in its application. Answer D would not be correct, since there are no federal laws concerning performance appraisals or employee wage increases. The best practice for ABC to employ would be a combined performance appraisal/cost-of-living approach. This would provide raises for high-performing employees as well as an incentive for employment longevity.

80. B: The HR manager should only disclose pertinent information about Joe's work record. Since Joe resigned, the HR manager can make no negative comments about his time at ABC. Doing this, as answers A and D suggest, could lead to civil lawsuits against ABC for defamation or slander. Answer C is not advisable because, although the HR manager does not legally have to provide any information on Joe, HR departments should share relevant information with other employers. This information sharing can help organizations make better hiring decisions.

81. B: Interviewers should not ask any questions pertaining to a candidate's health. If the job is offered to him or her, interviewers may ask if the candidate can perform the job with or without accommodation or request a medical examination as a condition of employment. Asking an applicant if he or she is willing to relocate, as outlined in answer A, is an appropriate question because relocation is often necessary for business. Answer C is also an appropriate question. As opposed to asking the applicant if his or her home life will affect his or her ability to perform tasks, the interviewer should ask if anything will prevent the candidate from doing the job, as answer C suggests. This question will generally illicit a response from the interviewee about any issues concerning his or her responsibilities outside of work. Answer D is an acceptable interview question as well. While interviewers should never ask interviewees if they are legal residents of the country, they can ask if they are able to work legally. Some workers may not have citizenship but are authorized to work via visas or work permits.

82. C: The HR audit should not be used as a guise to identify low-performing employees. Audits should only be conducted for the purpose of determining how well the HR department is performing. All the other answers in this array are legitimate functions of the HR audit.

83. A: Commission-based compensation provides the employee with the incentive to make greater profits for the company. The more a commission-based employee sells or produces, the more he or she makes. Answer B is irrelevant, as any compensation given to an employee will be taxed by federal and state tax agencies. Answers C and D are not correct, since not all sales situations are the same. These broad answers lack statistical evidence.

84. D: Gym memberships are not covered under Flexible Spending Accounts. If employees want to use a physical fitness center, they must pay for the membership themselves or use a center provided by the company. Acupuncture, psychiatric care, and durable medical equipment are not covered under most employer-sponsored insurance plans. Having an FSA covering these benefits would add value to the company's compensation strategy and help them reach their recruitment and retention goals.

85. A: A mission statement is a way for the organization to share what it does and how it will do these things differently from their competitors. This statement provides a standard by which the organization can measure itself. Should the organization find itself operating outside of its mission statement, it should reassess its operations. Answer B defines a vision statement. This statement focuses predominantly on a company's future goals. Answer C defines a values statement. These statements are intended to inform the employees and shareholders of the organization's intention to conduct operations ethically. Answer D defines an organization's core competencies. Core competencies are the operations that the organization feels they do the best.

86. C: Virtual training would be the best way to train the office staff. This would allow them to take the training at their desks in their normal environments. Classroom instruction could work, but that would introduce costs such as transportation or rental equipment fees. Distance learning does not apply here, since the training is being taken on-site. Self-study would only benefit those employees who are disciplined learners; therefore, this type of learning may not be the best fit for all employees.

87. B: Management can evaluate current employees while they work to see if they would be a good fit for promotion. This is a good practice because, with it, managers can know what to expect from the employee once promoted to the new position. Although it does cost the company to recruit, as referenced in answer A, this cost is nothing compared to the cost of a poor hire if management takes a chance on an external choice that doesn't pan out. Though employee morale may be influenced by the promotion of an external applicant, as answer C argues, this may also not be the reason for a lowering of morale. Current employees may be upset that they, themselves, did not get the promotion, or because an external applicant was hired. It would, indeed, cost less to train current employees for the new position since they are already familiar with company policies, as outlined in answer D; however, the value of a successful employee outweighs the costs of additional training.

88. B: Part of HR's common function is to ensure compliance with laws regarding safe workplaces. John's injury is not of the level where OSHA needs to be immediately notified, but the accident should be logged on OSHA's 300A form. The HR manager should also recommend that an investigation takes place to determine if the injury was caused by negligence or a recognized hazard. Answer A is not correct, since all hospitalizations must be recorded. Answer C is incorrect. The Department of Labor does not need to be contacted, as this agency only enforces laws pertaining to the Fair Labor Standards Act (FLSA). Answer D is also incorrect because not all injuries need to be reported to OSHA, and the severity of the injury does not meet the qualifications of a mandatory OSHA notification.

89. B: In accordance with the Federal Worker Adjustment and Retraining Notification Act (WARN Act), employers with over 100 employees must notify affected employees of a mass layoff. The HR manager at the affected mill should be sure to coordinate with management to ensure there is at least a 60-day notice before ceasing operations; therefore, answer C would not be correct. Answers A and D would be potential duties of the HR professional at the mill, but these decisions will be ultimately approved by upper management. Only answer B is a mandated legal requirement of the company.

90. A: There should be a formal process for all compensation increases. Having no HR policy on compensation creates legal liability for the organization. Compensation decisions based solely on a supervisor's opinion will cause too much subjectivity in the process and may even lead to issues of discrimination. For these reasons, answers B and D are incorrect. Answer C is also incorrect, as the manager of a company should be held to the same standards as the supervisors and follow the HR compensation strategy.

aPHR Practice Test #4

1. The manager of a paper mill is concerned about a recent recordable injury that had to be reported to OSHA. He believes there needs to be an Injury and Illness Prevention Plan (IIPP) implemented to help prevent workplace injuries. What is one topic that should NOT be in the plan?

    a. Discrimination
    b. Emergency response
    c. Employee health and wellness plan
    d. Fire prevention

2. Several employees have complained to the human resource manager that the chairs they sit in while working are causing stress injuries to their backs. This would be classified as what type of health hazard?

    a. Physical health hazard
    b. Chemical health hazard
    c. Biological health hazard
    d. Communication hazard

3. What should HR's role be in the termination of employees?

    a. All terminations should be handled by HR.
    b. HR should take no part in employee terminations.
    c. Only upper management should terminate employees.
    d. HR should provide managers with support and information in termination decisions.

4. How does having an effective mission statement increase organizational success?

    a. It can bring greater profits to an organization.
    b. It can provide direction for an organization.
    c. It can make the organization appear highly professional.
    d. It helps hold management accountable for their actions.

5. What law was enacted to ensure that executives of public companies report accurate financial information to their shareholders?

    a. Financial Fraud Act
    b. Sarbanes-Oxley Act
    c. RICO Act
    d. Insider Trading Sanctions of 1984

6. Health insurance premiums should be deducted from which of the following wage categories?

    a. Gross pay
    b. Net pay
    c. Commissions
    d. Bonuses

7. An employee of ABC Company approaches you, the HR manager, stating his belief that the company's accountant is falsifying financial records. The company is a publicly traded company regulated by the Securities Exchange Commission. What is the appropriate response for you to give the employee?

   a. You tell him that whistleblowing is protected under the Sarbanes-Oxley Act and that he should report his findings to the SEC.
   b. You tell your supervisor what is happening and ask for guidance.
   c. You recommend to the chief executive officer that the CFO be terminated.
   d. Both A and B

8. Wesley, a production manager, tells the HR manager that a friend of his would be a great fit for an open position and that she has shown interest in being hired. Wesley vets his friend by praising her knowledge and work ethic. What should the HR manager do in this situation?

   a. Tell Wesley to have his friend fill out an application online.
   b. Advise Wesley that personal vetting is neither professional nor advisable.
   c. Immediately schedule an interview with Wesley's friend.
   d. Do not contact Wesley's friend, because two friends working together would not be productive.

9. During labor contract negotiations, the company offers to raise current workers' pay by 10% but reduce new hire pay for the same positions. What wage system is this an example of?

   a. Banding
   b. Grading
   c. Incumbent
   d. Two-tiered

10. The management of ABC Company wants to improve the work-life balance of employees who are new parents. What would be the best recommendation for an HR professional to give management?

   a. Remind new parents about employee assistance programs (EAPs).
   b. Increase vacation time for new parents.
   c. Offer new parents unlimited unpaid leave.
   d. Offer new parents a flexible work schedule.

11. A local Baptist church has posted a job for a minister. One applicant sends in an application showing experience in preaching, but it was in a Methodist church. Based on the fact that he is not a Baptist minister, the applicant is not given an interview. The applicant believes he is being discriminated against because of his religious faith. Is this legal? If so, what legislation allows the church to deny the applicant an interview?

   a. This is illegal. An organization cannot deny an applicant consideration due to religious affiliation.
   b. This is legal. Nonprofit organizations are not subject to anti-discrimination laws.
   c. This is legal. The Civil Rights Act of 1964 allows employment decisions based on "Bona Fide Occupational Qualifications."
   d. This is illegal. All applicants meeting basic qualifications must be interviewed.

12. Which of the following should be the focus of a talent acquisition program?

   a. Identifying organizational staffing needs
   b. Filling open positions
   c. Identifying potential managers
   d. Future growth plans

13. Which of the following factors should be the primary reason an organization provides employees with cost-of-living adjustments?

   a. The organization is trying to keep pace with competitors who are providing higher wages.
   b. The government mandates yearly cost-of-living adjustments.
   c. Providing COLAs allows for an alternative to performance raises.
   d. Consumer market inflation is higher than anticipated.

14. The owner of ABC Company is concerned about the organization's high turnover rate. They ask you, the HR manager, what the worst outcome could be from this high rate. What is the best answer?

   a. Poor employer reputation
   b. Higher workloads
   c. Higher HR budgets
   d. Loss of profitability

15. Which of the following would NOT be an advantage of an organization having an employee recognition program?

   a. Increased employer commitment
   b. Increased employee engagement
   c. Improved retention
   d. Higher productivity

16. Which of the answers listed would be the best type of profit-sharing plan if the employer needed to immediately increase employee productivity?

   a. Optional stock purchases
   b. Deferred plans
   c. Cash bonuses
   d. Improshare

17. You, the HR manager, are concerned about the absence of an L&D program at your organization. In order for management to agree to start a program, you must provide them with the best reason for implementing an L&D program. Of the following options, what is the greatest benefit of L&D programs?

   a. L&D programs help with internal talent development.
   b. L&D programs result in engaged employees who are more productive.
   c. L&D programs facilitate the alignment of employees' goals and performance with those of the organization.
   d. L&D programs help organizations stay competitive in their industries.

18. What is the main goal of implementing a profit-sharing program?

   a. To maximize tax benefits
   b. To help employees establish a direct link between work and rewards
   c. To attract talent
   d. To retain high performing employees

19. Ted, the owner of ABC Company, wants to give a manager an immediate 10% raise for good production. What should the HR manager recommend to the owner in this situation?

   a. Give the manager the raise. This will encourage other managers to increase productivity.
   b. Postpone the raise until the employee's scheduled performance appraisal.
   c. Change the performance appraisal system to fit this situation.
   d. Give all managers the same merit increase.

20. What document is used to verify an employee's eligibility to work in the United States?

   a. I-9
   b. W-2
   c. W-4
   d. Employment contract

21. What tool can a human resources professional use to determine if a workplace situation is safe or unsafe?

   a. Risk assessment
   b. Environmental health standards
   c. SDS sheets
   d. Chemical labeling

22. ABC Company has an extensive employee onboarding session. Of the answers listed, what would NOT be a benefit to having this program?

   a. Decreased HR department costs
   b. Increased employee retention
   c. Decreased employee anxiety
   d. Increased employee productivity

23. In what situation does OSHA NOT need to be notified of a work-related injury?

   a. Employee suffers work-related hospitalization
   b. Employee killed on jobsite
   c. Employee requires first aid for a laceration
   d. Employee loses an eye during an accident

24. Which of the answers listed would be considered a positive disciplinary technique?

   a. Performance improvement plan
   b. Verbal warning
   c. Reprimand
   d. Demotion

25. How does a successful branding program help an organization's talent acquisition?

a. Branding can decrease recruiting costs.
b. Branding will increase the candidate pool.
c. Branding will create a positive work environment.
d. Branding can help with employee retention.

26. Before implementing a leadership development program, the manager of ABC Company wants to determine the percentage of internal candidates that fill leadership positions. What would be the immediate benefit of this?

a. The manager can measure the effectiveness of the program.
b. The manager can establish a baseline for comparison after the program has begun.
c. The manager can determine if the program is necessary.
d. Inquiries about the program will increase participation.

27. The owner of ABC Company has decided to implement a new training program for hourly employees. What should be the owner's next step to ensure this change will be successful?

a. Prepare the employees culturally for the change.
b. Evaluate the training program for potential effectiveness.
c. Examine the financial cost associated with the program.
d. Conduct a legal compliance review.

28. Which of the following would be the appropriate type of training for an organization that is planning a production expansion?

a. Organizational-level training
b. Task-level training
c. Individual-level training
d. Career planning

29. A construction manager allows a friend to work on the jobsite for one day. The manager agrees to pay the friend in cash to avoid putting him on the company payroll. The friend gets hurt on the job and subsequently files a workers' compensation claim. The manager tries to dispute the claim, saying his friend was not on the payroll and that there was no employment contract. Is the manager's company liable for the claim? Why or why not?

a. No; since the friend is being paid in cash, he is not legally considered an employee.
b. Yes; there was an employee-employer relationship, and the construction company is liable.
c. No; an employment contract must be completed before the friend is classified as an employee.
d. Yes; anyone on the jobsite, regardless of affiliation, can file a claim if injured.

30. The owner of a welding company wants to recruit entry-level welders for his growing operation. What would be the best hiring strategy for this type of worker?

a. Social media job posts
b. Technical school recruitment
c. Employee referrals
d. State or local unemployment agencies

31. Which of the following should be included in a training program for new supervisors?

 a. Conflict resolution
 b. Managerial accounting
 c. Budgeting
 d. Employment law

32. Which of the following processes helps an employee successfully integrate into an organization's culture?

 a. Cohesion
 b. Assimilation
 c. Onboarding
 d. Orientation

33. For an employer to be subject to the stipulations of the Affordable Care Act, how many full-time employees must they have?

 a. 20
 b. 250
 c. 1000
 d. 50

34. Who should make the final decision on a health benefits program?

 a. Human resources
 b. Upper management
 c. Employee committees
 d. Finance

35. Which of the following best defines the process of job bidding?

 a. Requesting quotes from vendors for services
 b. Posting internal job announcements
 c. Allowing current employees to show interest in a job before it is posted
 d. Ranking job applicants

36. What should be the first phase of developing a training program?

 a. Development
 b. Analysis
 c. Evaluation
 d. Identify performance gaps

37. Two employees have been in a non-violent conflict. What is the appropriate level of involvement from HR during the resolution?

 a. HR should handle the incident and decide on the resolution.
 b. HR should advise on how to resolve the conflict.
 c. HR should only be involved if there is a termination decision.
 d. HR should not be involved, as this is a decision for upper management.

38. Which of the following processes is NOT part of a successful workforce planning strategy?

a. Forecasting
b. Employee retention techniques
c. Employee skill evaluations
d. Employee total rewards

39. Of the answers listed, what retirement contribution plan would be most beneficial to someone who is self-employed?

a. Traditional IRA
b. Roth IRA
c. 401(k) plan
d. 457(b) plan

40. Which of the following is the best way to take employee complaints?

a. Personal communication between employees and supervisors regarding all complaints
b. A complaint and/or suggestion box where employees can share concerns
c. Formal complaint forms that are forwarded to HR
d. Scheduled meetings between employee representatives and upper management

41. What would be the best information an HR representative can provide to an employee wanting to draw money out of his HSA?

a. Employees who contribute to an HSA can withdraw money from the account for any reason.
b. Employees who contribute to an HSA can only withdraw funds for medical expenses.
c. An HSA can be used as a normal savings account.
d. The use of money from HSAs is always tax-free.

42. ABC Company wants to improve its managers' decision-making capabilities through a company training program. They ask you, the HR manager, to take the lead on this. What should be your first step in this task?

a. Identify or hire someone to teach the program.
b. Conduct a needs analysis.
c. Research the cost of implementing the program.
d. Determine the ROI of the training program.

43. Which of the following options would be the biggest benefit of implementing a total rewards program?

a. It can help an organization retain employees with necessary KSAs.
b. It will attract more applicants.
c. It can increase employee morale.
d. It can establish a pipeline of internal talent.

44. Which of the following would be an immediate employer benefit of an unlimited time off policy?

a. Employers would be better able to schedule workflow.
b. Employee time recording methods would not be needed.
c. There would be no need for HR to spend time on tracking time off accruals.
d. Employees would have a better work-life balance.

45. What legislative action allows an employer to monitor employee communication during the normal course of business?

    a. Civil Rights Act of 1964
    b. Equal Pay Act of 1963
    c. Electronic Communications Privacy Act of 1986
    d. Fourth Amendment rights

46. After hiring a new employee for an entry-level position, the company puts her through an orientation program. What business function would NOT generally be included in this orientation program?

    a. Company policies
    b. Industry-specific regulations
    c. Job-specific tasks
    d. Team building training

47. What is the most appropriate way for an HR manager to tell applicants they were not selected for a position?

    a. Meet with the applicants to tell them they were not selected.
    b. Mail the applicants a letter.
    c. No notification is necessary.
    d. Call or email the applicants, depending on the level of interaction they had with the company.

48. As the HR manager at ABC Company, what would be the best response to management if asked about the benefits of a work-life balance program?

    a. The program will decrease the number of sick days employees take.
    b. Workers that are happy in body and mind will be more productive and committed to work.
    c. There will be fewer accidents due to employee fatigue.
    d. Managers will be able to focus more on strategy as opposed to personnel issues.

49. The manager of ABC Corporation learns that the company's quarterly profits were below expectations. The reason for the loss was a poorly performing plant within the corporation. This plant has not met expected production goals during the last three quarters. What would be a good workforce goal the manager could use to increase profitability?

    a. Employ corporate restructuring.
    b. Close the plant.
    c. Sell the plant to the highest bidder.
    d. Retool the plant to produce a different product.

50. Stock options for employees at a company would be classified as what type of compensation?

    a. Fringe benefit
    b. Executive benefit
    c. Equity benefit
    d. Intrinsic benefit

51. Which of the following answers would NOT be an example of a valid pre-employment test?

a. Personality tests
b. Drug screening
c. Face-to-face interviews
d. Aptitude tests

52. An HR manager wants to develop a successful training system for current employees. Which type of evaluation should be used to identify the type of training these employees want, know, and need?

a. Formative evaluations
b. Trainee evaluations
c. Summative evaluations
d. Trainer evaluations

53. A manufacturing company's management has learned that the excessively high turnover in its production unit is the result of employees having to work excessively long hours and weekends. What is the best course of action to combat this?

a. Offer employees a remote work option.
b. Develop a better leave/time off policy.
c. Hire more workers so that current workers are not required to work as many hours.
d. Slow down production so as not to overwork the employees.

54. A successful mentoring program should involve which of the following?

a. Monitoring an employee's performance
b. Sponsoring and guiding an employee
c. Providing training to an employee when needed
d. Developing an employee's skills

55. What should be an organization's primary focus when implementing an onboarding program?

a. Increasing retention rates
b. Developing knowledge and positive behaviors
c. Identifying potential talent that could help the organization's growth
d. Providing information about company policies and practices

56. What would be the best way for management to learn if an employee training method is effective?

a. Get feedback from the manager providing the training.
b. Compare pre-training levels of production with post-training levels.
c. Survey workers who have taken the training to see if they found it effective.
d. Compare company profits before and after the training.

57. What is the best way an HR professional can gauge the effectiveness of an employee onboarding program?

a. Supervisor feedback
b. Employee feedback
c. Quality metrics
d. Retention rates

58. What is one way that HR can support an organization's goals during the onboarding process?

    a. Ensure new employees acknowledge that they understand company policies.
    b. Check employees' references.
    c. Require drug testing.
    d. Identify employees for future supervisory positions.

59. What is the term used to describe the situation where a union hires someone to apply for a position at a company to act as an inside organizer?

    a. Inside organizing
    b. Leafletting
    c. Picketing
    d. Salting

60. Of the answers listed, which of the following is NOT classified as a fringe benefit?

    a. Housing assistance
    b. Gym membership
    c. Health savings account
    d. Tuition assistance

61. What recruitment method is best for staffing entry-level management positions at a production facility?

    a. Promotion of senior hourly workers to management roles
    b. Internship programs
    c. External job postings
    d. Internal Job postings

62. An employee that works at your facility is injured while operating a forklift. She does not require hospitalization, and the injury was treated with a small bandage. The employee was performing a task in violation of policy when the injury occurred. As the HR manager, what should you do about this situation?

    a. This is a recordable incident per OSHA regulations, and they should be notified immediately.
    b. Reprimand the employee for violating policy and then retrain the employee on forklift operation.
    c. Move the employee to a department that does not operate forklifts.
    d. Terminate the employee for violating a policy.

63. Which of the following would not be included in a human resource recruiting budget?

    a. Travel expenses
    b. Social media and job board subscriptions
    c. Fees to staffing companies
    d. Commissions

64. When is the best time during the onboarding process to have new employees read and acknowledge that they understand the company's policies?

    a. During their interviews
    b. During their first day of training
    c. During their first day on shift
    d. After their probationary periods

65. An hourly, unionized worker has been found sleeping on the job. This is a gross violation of company policy, and the employee's supervisor intends to discipline the employee. The employee has no history of bad behavior or disciplinary action. The supervisor calls the employee into his office and issues him a written reprimand. What should the supervisor have done differently?

    a. The supervisor should have advised HR of the incident prior to the reprimand.
    b. The supervisor should have verbally counseled the employee, since it was his first offense.
    c. The supervisor should have asked the employee if he wished to have a union representative present during the meeting.
    d. The supervisor should have terminated the employee on the spot for the violation.

66. The human resources manager at an organization learns there is a movement by the mechanics in the plant to unionize. The company executives do not like the idea of unionization. What does the HR manager need to do in this situation?

    a. Terminate any employee wanting to join the union.
    b. Allow lawful unionization activities.
    c. Give mandatory training on how unionizing will harm the business.
    d. Distribute leaflets in the plant denouncing union activities.

67. The manager of your company is concerned that employees may leak confidential information about a new product to some of its competitors. What could be done to mitigate this risk?

    a. Send a company-wide email warning employees about disseminating confidential information.
    b. Require all employees to sign a non-disclosure agreement stating they will not share confidential information.
    c. Only allow certain employees access to important information.
    d. Use email monitoring to check all outgoing emails for sensitive information.

68. The Occupational Safety and Health Administration was established by what legislative action?

    a. The Fair Labor Standards Act of 1938
    b. The OSH Act of 1970
    c. The Civil Rights Act of 1964
    d. The National Labor Relations Act of 1935

69. **An HR manager receives several complaints from female employees stating that one male supervisor continuously makes lewd jokes about women. This has made them feel uncomfortable in the workplace. What is this situation called?**

   a. Hostile work environment
   b. Quid pro quo
   c. Sexual harassment
   d. Company ethics violation

70. **An employee diagnosed with bipolar disorder would be protected from employer discrimination by what legislative act?**

   a. Civil Rights Act of 1964
   b. Americans with Disabilities Act of 1990
   c. Age Discrimination in Employment Act
   d. Equal Pay Act of 1963

71. **What type of business outcome would be best achieved by a company implementing a career management and planning program?**

   a. Business continuity
   b. Employee retention
   c. Higher production levels
   d. Better return on investment

72. **What organization in the United States government is tasked with investigating discrimination complaints against employers?**

   a. Equal Opportunity Employment Commission (EEOC)
   b. Occupational Safety and Health Organization (OSHA)
   c. National Labor Relations Board (NLRB)
   d. Social Security Administration (SSA)

73. **In which of the following situations would a severance package be appropriate?**

   a. To appease an employee threatening a wrongful termination lawsuit.
   b. To reward a retiring worker
   c. To provide compensation for workers who are losing jobs due to workforce reductions
   d. To pay employees who refuse to accept a reasonable alternative employment position

74. **An OSHA inspector arrives at ABC Company for a random compliance inspection. The manager refuses to allow the inspector into the plant. Can the manager legally do this? Why or why not?**

   a. No; the law states that an OSHA inspector is allowed to immediately enter a place of business and perform an inspection regardless of company consent.
   b. Yes; OSHA does not have the legal right to perform random inspections.
   c. No; managers must always consent to random inspections immediately or risk being arrested.
   d. Yes; although the OSHA inspector has the right to perform a random inspection, the manager can refuse entry until the inspector provides a compliance warrant.

75. An employee is late to work for the first time. The supervisor asks you, the HR manager, what should be done in this situation. What is the best answer you can give the supervisor?

a. The supervisor should tell the employee not to be late again.
b. The supervisor should ignore the tardiness, since this is the first time it has occurred.
c. The supervisor should formally document the incident.
d. The supervisor should terminate the employee.

76. What management representative should perform employee performance appraisals?

a. The employee's HR representative
b. The employee's direct supervisor
c. The company owner
d. Mid-level or department managers

77. The HR manager at ABC Company wants to know if the current compensation rates are directly influencing the employee turnover rate. What would be the best way to gain this information?

a. HR-led exit interviews
b. Anonymous employee surveys
c. Salary and wage studies
d. Periodic HR–employee meetings

78. The owner of ABC Company wants to cost out labor rates for future financial planning. Performing this request would be which type of business function?

a. Forecasting
b. Job costing
c. Financing
d. Accounting

79. The manager of a steel mill wants to plan for future growth by implementing a succession planning strategy. What would be the best starting point for this idea?

a. Conducting a job analysis
b. Developing business goals
c. Selecting employees for promotions
d. Conducting performance evaluations

80. Management at ABC Company wants to reduce learning and development costs. The L&D department is a standalone function in the company. What is a measure that can be taken to achieve this goal?

a. Implement a learning management system (LMS).
b. Allow the HR department to take over all learning and development functions.
c. Outsource all training to third-party providers.
d. Train mid-level managers to administer training.

81. Which of the following would NOT be a successful method of boosting employee engagement?

a. Increasing overtime opportunities for employees
b. Creating an employee feedback program
c. Implementing work-life balance programs
d. Conducting stay interviews

82. Which of the following would NOT be a topic taught in a successful supervisor training program?

a. Financial analysis
b. Communication skills
c. Company policies
d. Progressive discipline

83. What would be the best training delivery technique for a current manager moving to a new management position in the same company?

a. Instructor-led training
b. Virtual training
c. Shadowing
d. External classes

84. What should be the primary reason for an organization establishing pay grades?

a. To help support the budgeting process
b. To comply with legal and regulatory requirements
c. To justify paying some employees less than others
d. To establish a compensation range for a group of jobs with similar value

85. What is the best way a company's management can disseminate information to current employees that unionizing will be detrimental to the organization and workforce?

a. Advertise outside of the mill via television, radio, or billboards that unionizing will harm the company.
b. Gather the hourly employees together and explain to them why they should not organize.
c. Layoff the workers who are most vocal about unionizing.
d. Require all new hires to sign a pledge stating they will not join the union.

86. The manager of ABC Company wants to know the biggest financial impact an employee recognition program could have on the company. As an HR professional, what is the best answer you can provide?

a. Recognition programs are a low-cost, high-reward method of improving profits because they improve employee morale and productivity.
b. The program will be detrimental to the company's finances. Beginning this program will incur extra payroll costs.
c. Employee recognition programs will contribute positively to the company's long-term growth by attracting more applicants.
d. Recognition programs may foster resentment among employees that are not picked. This could lead to poor productivity, which will negatively impact the company financially.

87. What is the best recruitment method in terms of cost and efficiency when hiring an experienced industry professional?

a. Social media and job boards
b. Internal recruiting
c. Third-party recruiting companies
d. Advertisements in industry periodicals

88. The owner of a steel mill wants to know if she is paying the engineers a competitive salary. As an HR professional, what would be the best way to obtain the information necessary to provide a good answer to the owner?

    a. Using information from the Bureau of Labor Statistics
    b. Asking regional competitors to participate in a salary survey
    c. Surveying current engineers, asking if they believe they are being paid fairly
    d. Determining if the turnover rate for engineers is higher than other positions

89. As an HR professional, what is the most important reason to evaluate the current economic situation when discussing employee compensation?

    a. Current economics may help HR stay abreast of potential changes in cost-of-living adjustments.
    b. Current economics may require the timely change of the compensation strategy.
    c. Current economics decide if certain benefits should be reduced.
    d. Current economics should not facilitate changes in the compensation structure.

90. An HR manager is asked to investigate a sexual harassment complaint. What should his first course of action be?

    a. Identify witnesses and take statements.
    b. Interview the accuser.
    c. Suspend the accused until the investigation is over.
    d. Assign the accuser and accused to different departments to separate them.

Answer Key and Explanations for Test #4

1. A: Discrimination is not an act that could cause physical harm to employees. The act of discriminating against employees should be strictly forbidden, but it would not be considered an operational safety risk. Emergency response (answer B) would be included, since it details what employees should do if presented with an emergency. Employee health and wellness plans (answer C) can help alleviate physical risks by helping employees stay physically and mentally healthy; therefore, this would be included in the plan. Lastly, fire prevention (answer D) should be a topic of training because fires at a workplace could endanger many lives. Proper fire prevention methods and escape routes should be discussed in this portion of the Injury and Illness Prevention Plan.

2. A: A physical health hazard has the potential to cause bodily injury. In the situation presented, chairs causing stress to employees' bodies could lead to musculoskeletal disorders.

3. D: HR's role should be informational and supportive in nature. HR should not have the sole responsibility of terminations as answer A suggests. Managers should be trained on what violations warrant employee dismissals. It is appropriate for managers to ask for advice from HR on how to handle a termination or whether a termination is warranted; therefore, HR can have a role in terminations, contrary to answer B. Upper management can terminate employees, but they should not be solely responsible for termination decisions, making answer C incorrect. Upper-level managers should focus on business strategy and growth.

4. B: Mission statements provide direction and purpose for organizations. Organizations without these statements may not have a clear operational strategy. Mission statements may help an organization's success, but it does not guarantee profits (answer A). Simply having a mission statement does not make an organization "professional" (answer C). Organizations must follow the mission statement for it to be effective. A mission statement cannot hold management accountable for their actions (answer D). It has no legally binding arrangement for any party.

5. B: The Sarbanes-Oxley Act specifically forbids an executive of a public company from providing false financial reports. This law also provides whistleblower protection to any employee reporting a violation of the act.

6. A: Health insurance premiums should always be deducted from the employee's gross pay. Net pay (answer B) is the employee's remaining wage amount after deductions, such as health care, retirement contributions, or Social Security. Commissions (answer C) and bonuses (answer D) are types of compensation that would be included in an employee's gross pay.

7. D: The Sarbanes-Oxley Act specifically protects whistleblowers from retaliation. The employee in this example should be encouraged to tell what he knows to the Securities Exchange Commission. The HR manager should also notify his or her supervisor of the situation, since there is potential for criminal and civil penalties. Recommendations on termination should come from the CEO or the board of directors; therefore, answer C would not be correct.

8. C: Having someone at the company offer a potential hire is a cost-effective way to recruit. Since Wesley knows the business, he can tell if his friend would be a good fit. Having the friend fill out an online application like other applicants, as answer A suggests, would not appropriately use the knowledge given by Wesley. It would also be detrimental for future employee referrals if the friend is not interviewed. Answer D is incorrect because there is no legal reason two friends cannot work together. The friendship is not a legitimate reason to deny or offer employment. Option B is incorrect because it is acceptable for employees to vet applicants. Since employees are familiar with the business, they will know if potential employees would be a good fit for the organization.

9. D: Two-tiered wage systems benefit certain employees more than others. Lowering the incoming wage is a concession that benefits the company financially, so both parties benefit from the arrangement. Grading (answer B) and banding (answer A) are wage systems that base a worker's pay on either education or job type within the organization. Incumbent wage systems (answer C) are solely based on a current worker's qualifications and skills.

10. D: Flexible work schedules help new parents balance family needs and work requirements. Employee assistance programs (answer A) could help the employees in other ways, but they do not provide the parent more time at home. Increasing vacation time for new parents only (answer B) could be viewed as unfair for non-parent employees. PTO (paid time off) must be allocated fairly to employees. Unpaid leave (answer C) should not be unlimited. This would make the company unable to plan for adequate staffing, which could cause problems for future growth.

11. C: The Civil Rights Act clearly allows certain organizations to base employment decisions on Bona Fide Occupational Qualifications (BFOQ). The applicant needing to be a Baptist preacher would be one of these qualifications. The applicant would need to understand, and be able to preach, the Baptist faith. Answers A and D would not be correct since the church is making the hiring decision based on an applicant's BFOQs. Answer B would not be correct since nonprofit organizations must abide by anti-discrimination laws as well. Their nonprofit status does not allow them to practice discriminatory hiring in lieu of a valid exemption, such as a BFOQ.

12. A: Talent acquisition should be focused on staffing needs. Although filling open positions (answer B) could be viewed as talent acquisition, this process should fall under recruitment functions. Having a pipeline of future managers (answer C) can help an organization plan, but talent acquisition should not be wholly focused on management positions. Talent planning is needed across the entire organization. Growth (answer D) is an important goal of talent acquisition; however, other business goals should be considered as well. For example, profitability and efficiency are goals that should be aided by the talent acquisition process.

13. D: Market inflation is the primary reason for organizations to provide COLAs. Organizations can provide COLAs so their employees' pay keeps pace with elevated living expenses. There is no government mandate to provide COLAs as answer B suggests. This is completely up to the organization. COLAs should not be used in place of performance raises, contrary to answer C. Most organizations provide both performance-based increases and COLAs. A COLA should be given to all employees, whereas a performance increase should only be given as a reward to those who earn it. Competitors providing higher wages (answer A) may lead the organization to reassess their compensation strategy, but this factor has nothing to do with cost-of-living adjustments.

14. D: High employee turnover would be the most detrimental to an organization's profits. Should profits become too low, organizations will be forced to close. Higher HR budgets (answer C), greater workloads (answer B), and poor employer reputation (answer A) can all be negative effects of poor employee retention; however, negative profitability could cause the quickest end to the company's operations.

15. A: An employee recognition program will increase workloads and add duties for some members of management. This must be considered prior to adopting an employee recognition strategy. Options B, C, and D are all advantages of an employee recognition program. Recognizing employees for good work has been shown to boost morale and provide motivating goals for workers.

Employees will also be more engaged and more likely to stay with the company when they feel their hard work is recognized and appreciated by management. When employees believe they are valued and recognized for good results and positive behaviors, studies have shown that their productivity will increase.

16. C: Cash bonuses given to employees will allow them to immediately see rewards for good production. This immediate recognition of monetary gains should help boost efficiency. Neither deferred plans (answer B) nor stock purchases (answer A) would provide an immediate payout. Improshare (answer D) is a gainsharing plan where the company shares profits with the employees. This sharing of profits may cause employees to feel shorted by the company, since they may feel the company already profits from their work; therefore, the profit-sharing plan may not have a positive or immediate effect on production.

17. C: An effective learning and development program bridges the gap between the goals of the employee and those of the organization. With both parties focused on the same performance goals, the organization will be more efficient and productive. The other three answers—internal talent development (answer A), increased employee engagement (answer B), and continued competitiveness (answer D)—are all positive aspects of L&D programs; however, they all play a part in the ultimate goal of performance and goal alignment.

18. B: A profit-sharing program will help establish a direct link between work and rewards for the employees. This will foster better efficiency, higher quality, and higher production across many different business processes. While it is true that profit sharing programs have tax benefits (answer A), can increase talent acquisition (answer C), and help retain employees (answer D), the goal of the program, in this scenario, is to provide employees with an incentive to perform better.

19. B: Following a formal merit increase schedule will ensure the process is structured and fair. Giving raises outside of the performance appraisal may offend and dishearten other managers, contrary to what answer A suggests. Answer C would not be a wise move for the company. Changing procedures for one employee could discredit the system and destroy morale. Giving all managers the same merit raise (answer D) is not wise, since this will fail to incentivize higher productivity.

20. A: Form I-9 is used to determine an employee's work authorization status. Once completed, the form is submitted to the U.S. Department of Homeland Security for verification. The W-2 form (answer B) is used to document an employee's wages for tax purposes. The W-4 form (answer C) is used to determine the amount of taxes withheld from an employee's pay. An employment contract (answer D) is a written agreement between the employer and employee. Unlike the other three answers, the employment contract is not a government form.

21. A: A risk assessment can be performed to determine how an organization could be affected by an identified work operation. Environmental health standards (answer B) only apply to environmental safety issues, whereas a risk assessment assesses all risks and is, therefore, the better answer. Safety Data Sheets (SDS) (answer C) are helpful in determining the dangers associated with chemicals. SDS sheets on site can assist in the risk assessment but should not be used solely to determine risk. Chemical labeling (answer D) is used to identify chemicals. Labeling chemicals is a safety necessity and can assist in the risk assessment, but it does not take the place of the risk assessment.

22. A: Designing and implementing an effective onboarding program will cause increased HR department costs due to the additional training and personnel needed to administer the program.

Effective onboarding programs will save the company money in other ways, such as by increasing employee retention (answer B) and employee productivity (answer D). In addition, the successful onboarding program will make employees feel prepared for the positions they have been offered, thereby decreasing their initial anxiety (answer C).

23. C: Should an employer provide first aid to an employee injured on the job, OSHA does not need to be notified. Injuries and illnesses are recordable if they result in death, days away from work, restricted work or transfer to another job, medical treatment beyond first aid, or loss of consciousness.

24. A: Performance improvement plans can be used to correct behaviors that are counterproductive to the organization. Using performance improvement plans, management can find ways to improve behaviors or produce better results. A verbal warning (answer B) can be viewed by some employees as a formal disciplinary measure. Although not written, the employee is being advised of his or her negative discipline. Reprimands (answer C) and demotions (answer D) are both negative forms of discipline because they contain some form of punishment.

25. B: A successful branding campaign will build the reputation of the organization as being a good place to work. Applicants are more likely to apply to this type of organization, thereby increasing the candidate pool. Branding can decrease recruiting costs (answer A), create a positive work environment (answer C), and help employee retention (answer D); however, these are internal successes. The branding must be geared toward increasing the candidate pool for it to be helpful in talent acquisition. The branding should always have an outward focus on attracting qualified applicants.

26. B: The manager will be unable to tell if the program is effective if he or she has no baseline for the project. Once the leadership program is implemented, good statistical evidence can show if the leadership program is producing successful leaders. Contrary to answer A, the manager cannot measure effectiveness until a baseline is established and the program started, so this is not an immediate benefit. This is also true with answer C. The necessity of the program can only be determined after there are some statistics produced. Just because the manager is requesting these numbers (answer D), there is no guarantee this will increase participation in the program.

27. A: Management should explain why there is a need for the new program and point out why the program will help improve the company. Doing this will make the employees buy into the new program, which will increase its chances of success. Answers B, C, and D are all things that should be done by management prior to making the decision to implement a new program. Should any of these evaluations show deficiencies in the training, a different program should be used.

28. A: An organization trying to plan for the future should employ organizational-level training since this kind of training is designed to indicate the specific needs of the organization. Task-level training (answer B) only identifies the need for training in certain job categories, not the entire organization. Individual-level training (answer C) is meant to increase a single employee's KSAs. Though this can help the organization through increased KSAs, it is not an organization-wide plan. Career planning (answer D) is not a training plan; it is a process that helps employee development and growth in the organization.

29. B: An employee-employer relationship existed between both parties. Although the friend of the manager was not on the official company payroll, he is still considered an employee. This being the case, the company is liable for providing the employee protection through workers' compensation. Answer C is incorrect because job completion does not determine whether an employee-employer relationship exists. Answer D is also incorrect, since only employees are covered under workers' compensation. Just because someone happens to get injured while at the site does not mean he or she can file a workers' compensation claim.

30. B: Students enrolled in technical schools earn certificates and degrees in specialized skills, like welding. Since these workers are trained prior to graduating, the companies hiring them can provide limited training and insert them quickly into the workforce. Social media job posts (answer A), employee referrals (answer C), and unemployment agencies (answer D) may garner many applicants, but the hiring manager is dependent upon the applicants' honesty regarding their skills and experience. The technical school will be able to provide documented training and certificates for the applicants.

31. A: New supervisors should know how to resolve and handle conflicts among their subordinates. Conflict resolution is a leadership skill, unlike the other three answers, which are management skills. Managerial accounting (answer B), budgeting (answer C), and employment law (answer D) are all skills that are commonly taught in business education courses.

32. B: Assimilation is a process that helps an employee take in and understand what the organization wants and expects from their employees. Cohesion (answer A) would come later in the employee life cycle once the new employee feels he or she has become part of a team. Onboarding (answer C) and orientation (answer D) are administrative functions that take place during the employment process. These are important functions, but they do not help make the employee value and buy in to the culture of the organization.

33. D: Employers with 50 or more full-time employees must file documentation with the Internal Revenue Service describing whether they provide health coverage for their employees and/or what type of coverage is provided.

34. B: Since health plans influence different business strategies, such as recruitment, finance, and operations, the final decision should be made by upper management. HR (answer A) should not be solely responsible, since health plans can affect the finances of the company. Employees or employee committees (answer C) may be apt to choose a health plan that is good for the employees but not good for the company. The finance department (answer D) may only be focused on the monetary effect of the health plan and not how it affects other aspects, such as employee satisfaction, recruitment, or retention.

35. C: Job bidding is a process that allows current employees to express interest in jobs prior to them being advertised externally or internally. This process is beneficial for current employees who are interested in transferring departments or desire to be promoted. Answer A is incorrect because vendors bidding on projects is not an HR function. Vendor bidding is a function of the procurement department. Internal job announcements (answer B) would take place after the job bidding process. This generally occurs if no employees show interest in the position. Ranking job applicants (answer D) would take place after the job bidding process, once there is a pool of interested employees.

36. B: The first step in developing a training a program should be to analyze what type of training is needed. Answer A is incorrect because the training needs should be analyzed before developing the program. Answer C, evaluation, takes place last in the training program, as results will be studied to learn if the program is effective. Identifying performance gaps, answer D, is a process in the analyzing phase; therefore, it is not seen as a standalone phase of standard training program development.

37. B: HR's role in conflict resolution is to support and advise. Professionals in the HR field understand the legalities and best practices when dealing with conflict resolution, but they should not take a direct role in its application, contrary to answer A. This should be a task for management. Managers can terminate employees as a final decision in a conflict situation, contrary to what answer C suggests. HR can advise on the best way to handle the termination but does not have to be involved in carrying it out. Any level of management can handle conflict resolution, not just upper management, so answer D is incorrect. Upper management can ask HR for advice if they wish.

38. D: Employee total rewards fall under an organization's compensation strategy, not workforce planning. All other answers are methods of workforce planning. Organizations must forecast what talent they will need before planning for future operations (answer A). A lack of available talent can cripple an organization's plans for growth. The organization should establish an effective retention policy to avoid loss of knowledge, skills, and abilities (answer B). The loss of trained and talented employees to other organizations can disrupt the internal talent pipeline. Employee evaluations (answer C) can help identify current employees for future leadership or technical positions.

39. A: Current laws allow individuals to contribute a fixed amount of their pre-tax income each year. Monetary gains made within these accounts are tax-free. Roth IRAs (answer B) are taxed after income, which may not be as financially beneficial to someone who is self-employed. 401(k) (answer C) and 457(b) (answer D) retirement plans are offered by public and private employers.

40. C: Formal complaint forms will ensure the complaint is documented and addressed. Using this technique, no complaint can be neglected. Complaints should not be handled by direct supervisors (answer A), since they may be the topic of the complaint. This procedure may also cause employees to shy away from the complaint process. Complaint or suggestion boxes (answer B) may be used by employees for random complaints or comical behavior. The anonymous nature of the suggestion box is not productive in addressing specific complaints. Scheduled meetings (answer D) may cause official complaints to become backlogged and slow to be addressed. Having a set time to address complaints is not conducive to quick and efficient solutions when dealing with employee complaints.

41. B: HR should tell the employee that HSAs are designed to help employees with medical expenses. Although employees can withdraw money from the account for any reason (answer A), there are tax penalties if employees use the money for non-healthcare expenses, contrary to answer D. Unlike what answer C suggests, HSAs are not designed to be used as savings accounts, since there is a tax penalty when used out of purpose.

42. B: To know what should be taught in the program, the company should assess what kinds of knowledge, skills, and abilities currently exist within management. Until an assessment is performed, there is no way to identify candidates who can teach the program (answer A) or research the cost of the program (answer C), since both are dependent on the assessment. The ROI of the program (answer D) can only be determined after the program is implemented.

43. A: The total rewards philosophy is based on keeping current employees that have adequate knowledge, skills, and abilities. Having employees with adequate KSAs allows the company to plan for future growth. Although a good total rewards program can attract more applicants (answer B), increase employee morale (answer C), and establish a talent pipeline (answer D), these are not as important as an organization having employees with necessary KSAs. KSAs take time and money to develop and are critical to an organization's future.

44. C: The tracking of time off by payroll or HR professionals can be a tedious process. An unlimited time off policy would reduce that burden and help save on administrative costs. Answer A would not be correct, since increased time off could be detrimental to workflow scheduling. Answer B is also incorrect because there will always need to be a method for tracking employees' time. This is the only way to ensure they are working and being paid appropriately. Better work-life balance for employees (answer D) could lead to higher productivity, but it is not an immediate advantage for the employer.

45. C: The Electronic Communications Privacy Act stipulates that an employer may monitor an employee's communications under certain conditions. This could include monitoring both the employee's email and phone. Employees give up certain privacy rights when they work for an employer, and it is important for employers to explain to new employees what privacies will be restricted prior to hiring. The act only covers monitoring while an employee is engaged in a work activity. The Equal Pay Act of 1963 (answer B) is a labor act that addresses pay disparities between genders and forbids the practice. It contains nothing about workplace communications monitoring. The Civil Rights Act of 1964 (answer A) prohibits discrimination on the basis of race, color, religion, sex, or national origin, and it does not address workplace communication. Finally, the U.S. Constitution's Fourth Amendment (answer D) protects citizens from unlawful searches and seizures by the government and contains nothing about employee/employer rights.

46. C: Job-specific tasks would generally not be included in a basic orientation program. These programs are designed to acclimate new employees to the company. Job tasks are taught once employees begin work. Company policies (answer A) and industry-specific regulations (answer B) are common topics covered in an employee orientation. Recently, organizations have begun implementing team building training (answer D) during employee orientation. This is especially typical in larger organizations with numerous new hires at one time.

47. D: A hybrid approach depending on the level of applicant interaction would be best. It would be appropriate to call applicants that were interviewed, since they met with company personnel. For applicants who did not get an interview, an email stating they were not chosen is sufficient. Applicants should always be notified of their application status, contrary to answer C. This will allow applicants to search for other employment immediately. Having applicants come back to tell them they were not selected (answer A) is unreasonable and a waste of time for both the company and the applicants. Mailing denial letters (answer B) would incur postage costs and should be avoided. Any costs in this process would be detrimental to the HR budget.

48. B: A work-life balance program should be geared towards making employees more productive and dedicated to producing good work. This will lead to higher profits and less downtime for the organization if implemented properly. The other three answers, decreasing sick days used (answer A), decreasing accidents (answer C), and allowing managers to focus less on personnel issues and more on strategy (answer D), would be benefits of the program as well, but an employer should primarily use the program for employee well-being.

49. A: Corporate restructuring can eliminate redundancies and change processes within an organization to increase production. Restructuring could help the plant be productive while remaining part of the organization. Closing the plant as answer B suggests would not be advisable until a formal restructuring is attempted. If restructuring fails, this may be a viable option. Selling the plant (answer C) would allow the competition to add to their assets. This could possibly lead to increased competition and, therefore, lower profits. Retooling (answer D) would cost thousands of dollars in equipment and labor costs. This would not be a wise solution for the short-term goal of increasing profits.

50. C: Allowing employees to purchase company stock is a way for them to gain financial interests in the company and its performance. Executive benefits (answer B), such as supplemental retirement plans, are normally offered to high-ranking employees who are responsible for important decision making. Fringe benefits (answer A), such as tuition reimbursement, are offered to employees to supplement their pay and provide incentives for being with the organization. Intrinsic benefits (answer D), such as self-fulfillment, are positive feelings experienced by the employee when working.

51. D: Different population groups may have different average scores on aptitude tests. This may be seen as discriminatory; therefore, they are not valid tests. Personality tests (answer A) and drug screenings (answer B) are based on scientific methods that can be used in determining candidate fit. Face-to-face interviews (answer D) are the most common pre-employment tests. Although this method is not scientific in nature, valuable information about a candidate can be gained by employing commonly used interview methods.

52. A: Formative evaluations gather information before training is designed. This ensures that the new training includes the necessary information to benefit both employees and the company. Both trainer (answer D) and trainee (answer B) evaluations take place after training is complete. A summative evaluation (answer C) determines the effectiveness of the training after it is over, not prior to it beginning.

53. B: The company needs to develop and use an appropriate leave or PTO (paid time off) policy. Doing this will help retain employees by improving their work-life balance. Remote options (answer A) in production jobs will not work, since employees have to be present to produce goods. Hiring more workers (answer C) and slowing production (answer D) are both options the company would want to avoid. Both of these have the potential of causing higher costs to the company, thereby lessening profitability.

54. B: A mentor is someone who focuses on guiding an employee to achieve success. All other functions listed should be handled by others. Monitoring an employee's performance (answer A) is a function of the employee's direct supervisor, not a mentor. The training or HR departments should be responsible for training employees (answer C) and developing employee skills (answer D).

55. B: An onboarding program begins the process of knowledge development for new or current employees. Onboarding is a program that provides the employee with information and strategies on how to be effective. Although successful onboarding programs have been shown to increase retention rates (answer A), as well as provide management with an early look at an employee's talent (answer C), the primary focus is developing knowledge. Providing information about policies and practices (answer D) is part of growing the employee's knowledge, but the onboarding program should focus on a much broader scope of knowledge development.

56. B: The effectiveness of an employee training method can be measured by comparing pre- and post-training levels of production. Answer D would not be correct, since market factors or unforeseen overhead expenses could affect overall profitability. Surveying workers (answer C) and trainers/managers (answer A) is too subjective to be effective. Individuals within both groups may have different opinions, which would not provide a reliable measurement.

57. C: Successful onboarding programs will lead to higher quality and better productivity in an organization. Established quality metrics can measure if these programs are contributing to higher productivity. Employee feedback (answer B) and supervisor feedback (answer C) can be too subjective in nature to be used as measures of success. Retention rates (answer D) cannot be directly related to the success of an onboarding program, since there are many other factors within the organization that will influence these numbers.

58. A: Having new employees acknowledge that they understand and will abide by company policies will reinforce positive employee behavior. Positive employee behavior can be key to overall employee success. Drug testing (answer C) and checking references (answer B) are both activities HR would conduct prior to hiring an applicant, not during onboarding. It is not a reasonable practice to try to identify future supervisors (answer D) during onboarding. The onboarding process should be focused on training and introducing the employee to the organization.

59. D: Salting is a method used by unions to help in the organizing process. The employee selected for the salting position is hired to gain support for the union by persuading employees to unionize. Inside organizing (answer A) occurs when existing employees attempt to form a union. Leafletting (answer B) is a common union practice where the organization distributes pamphlets about why the employees should unionize. This is done by the union in hopes of gaining support from current employees. Picketing (answer C) is conducted by the union in situations of strikes or lockouts. Picketing is not seen prior to a union's organization at a facility.

60. C: Health savings accounts would be classified as health benefits. HSAs are offered to employees to supplement high deductible health plans but are not considered fringe benefits. Options A, B, and D are all considered fringe benefits. Housing assistance (answer A) is offered by organizations to help new employees find lodging when onboarding with the company. This benefit is helpful to the new employee and beneficial to an organization's recruitment strategy. Gym memberships (answer B) can improve employee wellness and help lower health premiums for organizations. Tuition assistance (answer C) can help both employees and the organization. Employees are given the chance to earn a better education, while the company benefits by gaining better trained personnel.

61. B: Interns are college students studying for either high-performing scientific or management roles. A successful internship program will allow management to identify potential candidates for future management positions while the interns are working with the organization. External job postings (answer B) bring in applicants from outside of the organization. Because of this, management has no sure way of knowing if the applicants will be a good fit for the position. Internal job postings (answer D) allow employees an opportunity to grow within the company; however, they may need to be trained in management philosophy. This will incur training costs, which can lessen the organization's profits. Promoting based on seniority (answer A) is not a wise practice, since the senior employee may not have a desire to manage. This course of action could lead to lower productivity or morale.

62. B: The employee should be reprimanded for violating the policy that led to the injury, and then she should be retrained. The retraining should cover the forklift operation policies. Contrary to answer A, the injury described here does not meet the requirements of an OSHA-recordable injury, since it did not require hospitalization or x-rays. Moving the employee to another department (answer C) would be a failure of management to correct negative employee behaviors. The employee could be terminated for violating policy (answer D); however, it would be wise to use progressive discipline. Should the employee continue violating policy after the initial reprimand, termination may be an appropriate action.

63. C: Fees to staffing companies are not recruitment costs. These costs would fall under payroll and compensation, as staffing is not a recruitment function. Traveling to job fairs, conferences, and other events is common in recruiting (answer A). In today's business world, it is necessary for successful organizations to recruit via online resources (answer B). This allows candidates to learn about the company and quickly search open positions. Many organizations offer commissions to recruiters who are successful in bringing in candidates (answer D).

64. B: Having new employees read and acknowledge company policies should take place during their first day of training. Only employees should have access to company policies. An interviewee (answer A) would not fit this category, since they have not been hired. The employee should understand the policies prior to going on shift, unlike answer C suggests. An employee should know the company's policies before beginning work. Since probationary periods last for months or even years, it would not be wise for the policies to be presented after the probationary period like answer D argues.

65. C: Because the employee is part of a union, the supervisor must offer and allow the employee to have a union representative present during the meeting. This practice is known as an employee's Weingarten Right. Should the company violate these rights, the National Labor Review Board can issue fines and other civil penalties. The supervisor could have notified HR of the intent to reprimand (answer A), but there still would have been a need for a union representative's presence. Since sleeping on the job was defined as a "gross violation," the employee needed more than just verbal counseling, making answer B incorrect. These types of violations are serious and could cause safety hazards to other employees; therefore, there needed to be a written reprimand at the bare minimum. Terminating the employee on the spot (answer D) would not have been advisable. Since the employee is in the union, there are rules for terminations that are agreed upon in the labor contract.

66. B: The company should allow legal unionization activities. Any attempt by the management to interfere with these activities is forbidden by the National Labor Relations Act (NLRA), meaning answers C and D would be violations of the NLRA. It is also illegal to terminate employees that engage in unionization activities, meaning option A is inappropriate as well.

67. B: It would be advisable to have all employees sign a non-disclosure agreement (NDA) stating they will not give out confidential company information. This agreement is a legal document that can protect the company from information leaks. Lawsuits can be brought against employees who violate the NDA. A company-wide email warning employees not to leak information (answer A) could be effective, but a written agreement, such as an NDA, carries consequences for forbidden actions.

68. B: The OSH Act of 1970 established OSHA as an independent federal agency tasked with protecting workers' rights to a hazard-free workplace. The Fair Labor Standards Act (answer A) established minimum wage limits and overtime pay. The Civil Rights Act (answer C) prohibited employment decisions based on race or gender. The National Labor Relations Act (answer D) created legal protection for workers desiring to unionize.

69. A: A hostile work environment is one in which employees are subject to unwelcome conduct. This conduct can be verbal or physical in nature. Investigation of hostile work environment complaints are handled by the EEOC. Quid pro quo (answer B) is a Latin term meaning "this for that." Since the male supervisor has not asked for anything, this situation would not apply. Sexual harassment (answer C) occurs when one employee makes unwanted sexual advances towards another employee or touches another employee without his or her consent. The jokes in this scenario are not directed at a certain individual; therefore, this would not be the appropriate answer. Lastly, the company should have a company ethics violation policy (answer D) forbidding hostile work environment situations; however, it is unknown if the company in question has adopted such a policy.

70. B: The ADA protects workers from discrimination based on physical or mental disabilities. Bipolar disorder, a mental health condition, would classify as a mental disability according to the ADA.

71. A: Having an effective career management program can ensure that the business continues to function when market conditions or business needs change. Although higher production levels (answer C), return on investment (answer D), and employee retention (answer B) can be influenced by career management and planning, these outcomes are dependent upon other business functions being used in unison to achieve better results.

72. A: The EEOC investigates complaints against employers concerning employee discrimination. Answer B is incorrect, as OSHA's responsibilities include establishing safety regulations and investigating accidents that occur in the workplace. The NLRB (answer C) was created to enforce labor laws concerning unions and collective bargaining. The Social Security Administration (answer D) primarily deals with retirement and disability benefits.

73. C: Severance packages are designed to help workers who are being laid off due to workforce reductions. Severance pay is not required by law, but many companies offer these packages as a gesture of goodwill to affected employees. Severance packages should not be used to appease employees threatening lawsuits like answer A suggests. Doing this can potentially make the organization appear guilty of the alleged offense. Unlike what answer B argues, retiring workers should not be given severance packages. Retirement packages in the form of company-sponsored IRAs or 401(k)s should be used to pay retirees. Contrary to answer D, severance pay should not be given to any employee refusing an alternative employment position in lieu of a layoff. The employee must accept the position if it is a "reasonable" alternative.

74. D: A business can request that an OSHA compliance warrant be obtained prior to an inspection. OSHA cannot enter without permission, nor can they arrest the manager as answers A and C suggest. Answer B is incorrect because OSHA is authorized to perform random inspections; however, consent must be given by the business's management.

75. C: The incident should be formally documented. Documentation of negative employee behavior can protect the organization during future legal proceedings or depositions. Although an organization could, in many cases, terminate the employee for being late (answer D), it would be advisable to use documentation tools because it is the employee's first offense. Negative employee behavior should not be ignored (answer B). This will lead to a breakdown of discipline and reduced production. Warning the employee verbally (answer A) is not wise, since it is not a formal procedure. All disciplinary actions should be formal in nature.

76. B: The employee's direct supervisor should perform the appraisal. This manager will have the most information and recommendations on how the employee can improve. The company owner (answer C) and HR representative (answer A) will be focused on business functions apart from appraisals. They also may not be familiar with the employee, since they do not directly supervise the employee. Mid-level managers (answer D) may know the employee being appraised, but they do not directly supervise the employee and may not be able to provide recommendations on improvements.

77. A: Exit interviews led by the HR staff would be the best way of learning about reasons for turnover. Employees already leaving the company will be more apt to give honest opinions about their reasons for leaving. Periodic HR–employee meetings (answer D) are not efficient for the company, and current employees may not be honest about their current feelings about their jobs. Anonymous surveys (answer B) may lead to general "griping" about the company instead of truthful answers about compensation. Salary and wage surveys (answer B) can be used to determine if current compensation rates are low for the region; however, these studies can be expensive and may not provide company-specific information.

78. A: Forecasting the cost of labor would be a strategic function generally handled by the HR department. Job costing (answer B) is an analysis of the profitability of certain projects. Accounting (answer D) and financing (answer C) functions generally involve analyzing and storing financial information.

79. A: Conducting a job analysis helps management learn how a job will progress for a prospective leader as he or she gains the KSAs needed for success. Once identified, the skill sets and competencies of potential employees can be reviewed and a plan can be put in place for their possible succession to higher positions. Business goals (answer B) should be developed early in the organization's creation. Succession planning should be built around these already-established goals. Selecting employees for promotions (answer C) is not wise until the specific job has been analyzed. The organization should select employees for succession based on the KSAs that the job requires. Performance evaluations (answer D) help indicate whether an employee performs well in his or her current position. It should not be used solely to identify an employee's potential for new positions where a different set of skills are needed.

80. A: A learning management system would save time and money by instituting e-learning at the company. Although the initial setup of the LMS may be expensive, the LMS would eventually allow the company to lessen the number of staff normally needed to train employees. These payroll savings would achieve the company's goal. Combining the HR and L&D departments (answer B) would cause an additional workload for current employees. This increased workload may lead to employee dissatisfaction, which would cause excessive turnover. Outsourcing the training (answer C) would not save money, since contracted personnel tend to be expensive to use over long periods of time. Having managers administer training (answer D) would be detrimental to the company, since these managers should be focusing on production, efficiency, and quality—not training.

81. A: Increasing overtime opportunities may be good for employee compensation, but it will not increase employee engagement. Employee engagement should be based on employees' intrinsic values and not monetary gains. Implementing employee feedback programs (answer B), work-life balance programs (answer C), and stay interviews (answer D) works to make employees feel valued and heard by the organization. These feelings will encourage the employees to engage and interact with management to make the organization a better and more enjoyable place to work.

82. C: Employees should be trained on company policies during their onboarding with the organization. A supervisor training program should focus on general business skills, such as financial analysis (Answer A), as well as leadership and management practices, such as progressive discipline (answer D). It should also cover communication skills (answer B).

83. B: Since the manager already knows the company's policies, procedures, and practices, virtual training would be appropriate to train the manager on the essentials of the new position. Instructor-led training (answer A) is more appropriate for entry-level employees, since they have no knowledge of the company's practices or even the job for which they have been chosen.

Shadowing (answer C) should be used when there is a newly promoted manager that needs to see management techniques being performed. External classes (answer D) would be appropriate for employees wishing to gain education to potentially be promoted or to move to a technical position. This type of delivery may also be geared towards employees wishing to learn management skills in order to be promoted.

84. D: Pay grades are primarily for establishing a defined compensation range. This allows the company to properly budget and plan their compensation strategy. Pay grades should not be used solely for budgeting, like answer A suggests, or compliance with compensation regulations, like answer B suggests. These reasons are administrative only, and the pay grade system should be based on business strategy. Contrary to answer C, pay grades should never be used as justification to pay some employees more or less than others. This is an unethical practice that should be avoided.

85. A: Any advertising done by management in response to union organization must be conducted off-site. The company cannot disseminate any information to employees in the mill dissuading them from unionizing. Television and radio commercials speaking against unionization are commonly used by company management. The other three answers are actions forbidden by the National Labor Relations Act. Company management cannot threaten current workers about unionizing nor prohibit new hires from joining the union.

86. A: Employee recognition programs will help the company financially by improving employee morale. Higher morale leads to greater productivity, less turnover, and better product quality. A properly run program may incur added payroll costs (answer B), but the company will be able to cover those costs from the added profits gained from the rewards of the recognition plan. Unlike answer C suggests, there is no guarantee that employee recognition programs will contribute to a company's growth. The company should use a program that is directly geared toward the organization's longer-term goals for it to be effective in this way. Employee recognition plans will inevitably cause resentment among some workers (answer D); however, management can limit this side effect by striving to ensure fairness and consistency in the program.

87. B: Internal recruiting would be best in this situation because the candidate would be familiar with the company and the industry. There would be little need to train the candidate in the ways of the organization. Also, the candidate would already be comfortable and proficient with the organization's strategies. Social media and job boards (answer A) would be beneficial for hiring experienced professionals, but a significant training cost would be incurred. Third-party recruiters (answer C) would take the burden of locating candidates off the staff; however, these types of companies charge considerable fees for their services. Advertising in industry periodicals (answer D) could be effective, but the candidate pool would be limited to subscribers. This method would not be wise if the organization wants a diverse pool of applicants.

88. B: Salary surveys ask competitors to provide information on what they pay their employees. This is a common HR practice that facilitates industry-wide transparency regarding pay scales. Only regional companies should be surveyed because different locations will pay more or less based on the cost of living in the area. Unlike what answer A suggests, HR should not use the BLS's information on salaries, since the salaries provided are based on the whole country, not certain regions. Asking engineers if they are being paid fairly (answer C) is too subjective. Answers can be vastly different among the employees, which will not aid in making the final determination. Turnover rates (answer D) would not be a good way to determine if the salaries are competitive because turnover is not always a result of salary dissatisfaction.

89. B: Current economic conditions must be regarded by HR professionals. These conditions should influence compensation decisions so that overall company profitability is not negatively affected. Current economic conditions may influence how much or how little employees receive in cost-of-living adjustments (answer A). They may also influence whether benefits should be reduced (answer C). However, both cost-of-living adjustments and the reduction of benefits should be factors in the overall compensation strategy. Management should evaluate the compensation strategy prior to any of these decisions being made. Answer D is incorrect since the compensation structure should be based on overall market conditions.

90. B: The accuser should always be interviewed first. This allows the HR manager to hear the accusations firsthand from the person making the complaint. Valuable information only known by the accuser can be gleaned from this meeting. Identifying witnesses and taking statements (answer A) should be done after the accuser is interviewed. These testimonies can either corroborate or invalidate a claim. Suspending the accused prior to an investigation (answer C) is unfair to the accused and may cause legal liabilities for the organization. Information leading to a suspension should always be gathered prior to this action. Assigning the parties to different departments immediately (answer D) is unwarranted without cause. Doing so may cause distress among all of the parties in the claim.

How to Overcome Test Anxiety

Just the thought of taking a test is enough to make most people a little nervous. A test is an important event that can have a long-term impact on your future, so it's important to take it seriously and it's natural to feel anxious about performing well. But just because anxiety is normal, that doesn't mean that it's helpful in test taking, or that you should simply accept it as part of your life. Anxiety can have a variety of effects. These effects can be mild, like making you feel slightly nervous, or severe, like blocking your ability to focus or remember even a simple detail.

If you experience test anxiety—whether severe or mild—it's important to know how to beat it. To discover this, first you need to understand what causes test anxiety.

Causes of Test Anxiety

While we often think of anxiety as an uncontrollable emotional state, it can actually be caused by simple, practical things. One of the most common causes of test anxiety is that a person does not feel adequately prepared for their test. This feeling can be the result of many different issues such as poor study habits or lack of organization, but the most common culprit is time management. Starting to study too late, failing to organize your study time to cover all of the material, or being distracted while you study will mean that you're not well prepared for the test. This may lead to cramming the night before, which will cause you to be physically and mentally exhausted for the test. Poor time management also contributes to feelings of stress, fear, and hopelessness as you realize you are not well prepared but don't know what to do about it.

Other times, test anxiety is not related to your preparation for the test but comes from unresolved fear. This may be a past failure on a test, or poor performance on tests in general. It may come from comparing yourself to others who seem to be performing better or from the stress of living up to expectations. Anxiety may be driven by fears of the future—how failure on this test would affect your educational and career goals. These fears are often completely irrational, but they can still negatively impact your test performance.

Elements of Test Anxiety

As mentioned earlier, test anxiety is considered to be an emotional state, but it has physical and mental components as well. Sometimes you may not even realize that you are suffering from test anxiety until you notice the physical symptoms. These can include trembling hands, rapid heartbeat, sweating, nausea, and tense muscles. Extreme anxiety may lead to fainting or vomiting. Obviously, any of these symptoms can have a negative impact on testing. It is important to recognize them as soon as they begin to occur so that you can address the problem before it damages your performance.

The mental components of test anxiety include trouble focusing and inability to remember learned information. During a test, your mind is on high alert, which can help you recall information and stay focused for an extended period of time. However, anxiety interferes with your mind's natural processes, causing you to blank out, even on the questions you know well. The strain of testing during anxiety makes it difficult to stay focused, especially on a test that may take several hours. Extreme anxiety can take a huge mental toll, making it difficult not only to recall test information but even to understand the test questions or pull your thoughts together.

Effects of Test Anxiety

Test anxiety is like a disease—if left untreated, it will get progressively worse. Anxiety leads to poor performance, and this reinforces the feelings of fear and failure, which in turn lead to poor performances on subsequent tests. It can grow from a mild nervousness to a crippling condition. If allowed to progress, test anxiety can have a big impact on your schooling, and consequently on your future.

Test anxiety can spread to other parts of your life. Anxiety on tests can become anxiety in any stressful situation, and blanking on a test can turn into panicking in a job situation. But fortunately, you don't have to let anxiety rule your testing and determine your grades. There are a number of relatively simple steps you can take to move past anxiety and function normally on a test and in the rest of life.

Physical Steps for Beating Test Anxiety

While test anxiety is a serious problem, the good news is that it can be overcome. It doesn't have to control your ability to think and remember information. While it may take time, you can begin taking steps today to beat anxiety.

Just as your first hint that you may be struggling with anxiety comes from the physical symptoms, the first step to treating it is also physical. Rest is crucial for having a clear, strong mind. If you are tired, it is much easier to give in to anxiety. But if you establish good sleep habits, your body and mind will be ready to perform optimally, without the strain of exhaustion. Additionally, sleeping well helps you to retain information better, so you're more likely to recall the answers when you see the test questions.

Getting good sleep means more than going to bed on time. It's important to allow your brain time to relax. Take study breaks from time to time so it doesn't get overworked, and don't study right before bed. Take time to rest your mind before trying to rest your body, or you may find it difficult to fall asleep.

Along with sleep, other aspects of physical health are important in preparing for a test. Good nutrition is vital for good brain function. Sugary foods and drinks may give a burst of energy but this burst is followed by a crash, both physically and emotionally. Instead, fuel your body with protein and vitamin-rich foods.

Also, drink plenty of water. Dehydration can lead to headaches and exhaustion, especially if your brain is already under stress from the rigors of the test. Particularly if your test is a long one, drink water during the breaks. And if possible, take an energy-boosting snack to eat between sections.

Along with sleep and diet, a third important part of physical health is exercise. Maintaining a steady workout schedule is helpful, but even taking 5-minute study breaks to walk can help get your blood pumping faster and clear your head. Exercise also releases endorphins, which contribute to a positive feeling and can help combat test anxiety.

When you nurture your physical health, you are also contributing to your mental health. If your body is healthy, your mind is much more likely to be healthy as well. So take time to rest, nourish your body with healthy food and water, and get moving as much as possible. Taking these physical steps will make you stronger and more able to take the mental steps necessary to overcome test anxiety.

Mental Steps for Beating Test Anxiety

Working on the mental side of test anxiety can be more challenging, but as with the physical side, there are clear steps you can take to overcome it. As mentioned earlier, test anxiety often stems from lack of preparation, so the obvious solution is to prepare for the test. Effective studying may be the most important weapon you have for beating test anxiety, but you can and should employ several other mental tools to combat fear.

First, boost your confidence by reminding yourself of past success—tests or projects that you aced. If you're putting as much effort into preparing for this test as you did for those, there's no reason you should expect to fail here. Work hard to prepare; then trust your preparation.

Second, surround yourself with encouraging people. It can be helpful to find a study group, but be sure that the people you're around will encourage a positive attitude. If you spend time with others who are anxious or cynical, this will only contribute to your own anxiety. Look for others who are motivated to study hard from a desire to succeed, not from a fear of failure.

Third, reward yourself. A test is physically and mentally tiring, even without anxiety, and it can be helpful to have something to look forward to. Plan an activity following the test, regardless of the outcome, such as going to a movie or getting ice cream.

When you are taking the test, if you find yourself beginning to feel anxious, remind yourself that you know the material. Visualize successfully completing the test. Then take a few deep, relaxing breaths and return to it. Work through the questions carefully but with confidence, knowing that you are capable of succeeding.

Developing a healthy mental approach to test taking will also aid in other areas of life. Test anxiety affects more than just the actual test—it can be damaging to your mental health and even contribute to depression. It's important to beat test anxiety before it becomes a problem for more than testing.

Study Strategy

Being prepared for the test is necessary to combat anxiety, but what does being prepared look like? You may study for hours on end and still not feel prepared. What you need is a strategy for test prep. The next few pages outline our recommended steps to help you plan out and conquer the challenge of preparation.

STEP 1: SCOPE OUT THE TEST

Learn everything you can about the format (multiple choice, essay, etc.) and what will be on the test. Gather any study materials, course outlines, or sample exams that may be available. Not only will this help you to prepare, but knowing what to expect can help to alleviate test anxiety.

STEP 2: MAP OUT THE MATERIAL

Look through the textbook or study guide and make note of how many chapters or sections it has. Then divide these over the time you have. For example, if a book has 15 chapters and you have five days to study, you need to cover three chapters each day. Even better, if you have the time, leave an extra day at the end for overall review after you have gone through the material in depth.

If time is limited, you may need to prioritize the material. Look through it and make note of which sections you think you already have a good grasp on, and which need review. While you are studying, skim quickly through the familiar sections and take more time on the challenging parts.

Write out your plan so you don't get lost as you go. Having a written plan also helps you feel more in control of the study, so anxiety is less likely to arise from feeling overwhelmed at the amount to cover.

STEP 3: GATHER YOUR TOOLS

Decide what study method works best for you. Do you prefer to highlight in the book as you study and then go back over the highlighted portions? Or do you type out notes of the important information? Or is it helpful to make flashcards that you can carry with you? Assemble the pens, index cards, highlighters, post-it notes, and any other materials you may need so you won't be distracted by getting up to find things while you study.

If you're having a hard time retaining the information or organizing your notes, experiment with different methods. For example, try color-coding by subject with colored pens, highlighters, or post-it notes. If you learn better by hearing, try recording yourself reading your notes so you can listen while in the car, working out, or simply sitting at your desk. Ask a friend to quiz you from your flashcards, or try teaching someone the material to solidify it in your mind.

STEP 4: CREATE YOUR ENVIRONMENT

It's important to avoid distractions while you study. This includes both the obvious distractions like visitors and the subtle distractions like an uncomfortable chair (or a too-comfortable couch that makes you want to fall asleep). Set up the best study environment possible: good lighting and a comfortable work area. If background music helps you focus, you may want to turn it on, but otherwise keep the room quiet. If you are using a computer to take notes, be sure you don't have any other windows open, especially applications like social media, games, or anything else that could distract you. Silence your phone and turn off notifications. Be sure to keep water close by so you stay hydrated while you study (but avoid unhealthy drinks and snacks).

Also, take into account the best time of day to study. Are you freshest first thing in the morning? Try to set aside some time then to work through the material. Is your mind clearer in the afternoon or evening? Schedule your study session then. Another method is to study at the same time of day that you will take the test, so that your brain gets used to working on the material at that time and will be ready to focus at test time.

STEP 5: STUDY!

Once you have done all the study preparation, it's time to settle into the actual studying. Sit down, take a few moments to settle your mind so you can focus, and begin to follow your study plan. Don't give in to distractions or let yourself procrastinate. This is your time to prepare so you'll be ready to fearlessly approach the test. Make the most of the time and stay focused.

Of course, you don't want to burn out. If you study too long you may find that you're not retaining the information very well. Take regular study breaks. For example, taking five minutes out of every hour to walk briskly, breathing deeply and swinging your arms, can help your mind stay fresh.

As you get to the end of each chapter or section, it's a good idea to do a quick review. Remind yourself of what you learned and work on any difficult parts. When you feel that you've mastered the material, move on to the next part. At the end of your study session, briefly skim through your notes again.

But while review is helpful, cramming last minute is NOT. If at all possible, work ahead so that you won't need to fit all your study into the last day. Cramming overloads your brain with more information than it can process and retain, and your tired mind may struggle to recall even previously learned information when it is overwhelmed with last-minute study. Also, the urgent nature of cramming and the stress placed on your brain contribute to anxiety. You'll be more likely to go to the test feeling unprepared and having trouble thinking clearly.

So don't cram, and don't stay up late before the test, even just to review your notes at a leisurely pace. Your brain needs rest more than it needs to go over the information again. In fact, plan to finish your studies by noon or early afternoon the day before the test. Give your brain the rest of the day to relax or focus on other things, and get a good night's sleep. Then you will be fresh for the test and better able to recall what you've studied.

STEP 6: TAKE A PRACTICE TEST

Many courses offer sample tests, either online or in the study materials. This is an excellent resource to check whether you have mastered the material, as well as to prepare for the test format and environment.

Check the test format ahead of time: the number of questions, the type (multiple choice, free response, etc.), and the time limit. Then create a plan for working through them. For example, if you have 30 minutes to take a 60-question test, your limit is 30 seconds per question. Spend less time on the questions you know well so that you can take more time on the difficult ones.

If you have time to take several practice tests, take the first one open book, with no time limit. Work through the questions at your own pace and make sure you fully understand them. Gradually work up to taking a test under test conditions: sit at a desk with all study materials put away and set a timer. Pace yourself to make sure you finish the test with time to spare and go back to check your answers if you have time.

After each test, check your answers. On the questions you missed, be sure you understand why you missed them. Did you misread the question (tests can use tricky wording)? Did you forget the information? Or was it something you hadn't learned? Go back and study any shaky areas that the practice tests reveal.

Taking these tests not only helps with your grade, but also aids in combating test anxiety. If you're already used to the test conditions, you're less likely to worry about it, and working through tests until you're scoring well gives you a confidence boost. Go through the practice tests until you feel comfortable, and then you can go into the test knowing that you're ready for it.

Test Tips

On test day, you should be confident, knowing that you've prepared well and are ready to answer the questions. But aside from preparation, there are several test day strategies you can employ to maximize your performance.

First, as stated before, get a good night's sleep the night before the test (and for several nights before that, if possible). Go into the test with a fresh, alert mind rather than staying up late to study.

Try not to change too much about your normal routine on the day of the test. It's important to eat a nutritious breakfast, but if you normally don't eat breakfast at all, consider eating just a protein bar. If you're a coffee drinker, go ahead and have your normal coffee. Just make sure you time it so that the caffeine doesn't wear off right in the middle of your test. Avoid sugary beverages, and drink enough water to stay hydrated but not so much that you need a restroom break 10 minutes into the test. If your test isn't first thing in the morning, consider going for a walk or doing a light workout before the test to get your blood flowing.

Allow yourself enough time to get ready, and leave for the test with plenty of time to spare so you won't have the anxiety of scrambling to arrive in time. Another reason to be early is to select a good seat. It's helpful to sit away from doors and windows, which can be distracting. Find a good seat, get out your supplies, and settle your mind before the test begins.

When the test begins, start by going over the instructions carefully, even if you already know what to expect. Make sure you avoid any careless mistakes by following the directions.

Then begin working through the questions, pacing yourself as you've practiced. If you're not sure on an answer, don't spend too much time on it, and don't let it shake your confidence. Either skip it and come back later, or eliminate as many wrong answers as possible and guess among the remaining ones. Don't dwell on these questions as you continue—put them out of your mind and focus on what lies ahead.

Be sure to read all of the answer choices, even if you're sure the first one is the right answer. Sometimes you'll find a better one if you keep reading. But don't second-guess yourself if you do immediately know the answer. Your gut instinct is usually right. Don't let test anxiety rob you of the information you know.

If you have time at the end of the test (and if the test format allows), go back and review your answers. Be cautious about changing any, since your first instinct tends to be correct, but make sure you didn't misread any of the questions or accidentally mark the wrong answer choice. Look over any you skipped and make an educated guess.

At the end, leave the test feeling confident. You've done your best, so don't waste time worrying about your performance or wishing you could change anything. Instead, celebrate the successful completion of this test. And finally, use this test to learn how to deal with anxiety even better next time.

> **Review Video: Test Anxiety**
> Visit mometrix.com/academy and enter code: 100340

Important Qualification

Not all anxiety is created equal. If your test anxiety is causing major issues in your life beyond the classroom or testing center, or if you are experiencing troubling physical symptoms related to your anxiety, it may be a sign of a serious physiological or psychological condition. If this sounds like your situation, we strongly encourage you to seek professional help.

Additional Bonus Material

Due to our efforts to try to keep this book to a manageable length, we've created a link that will give you access to all of your additional bonus material:

mometrix.com/bonus948/aphr

Made in the USA
Monee, IL
06 November 2024

69485647R00164